Ethics of Procreation
and the
Defense of Human Life

Ethics of Procreation and the Defense of Human Life

Contraception, Artificial Fertilization, and Abortion

Martin Rhonheimer

Edited by William F. Murphy Jr.

The Catholic University of America Press
Washington, D.C.

Library of Congress Cataloging-in-Publication Data
Rhonheimer, Martin, 1950–
Ethics of procreation and the defense of human life : contraception,
artificial fertilization, and abortion / Martin Rhonheimer ;
edited by William F. Murphy Jr.
p. cm.
Includes bibliographical references and index.
ISBN 978-0-8132-1722-2 (pbk. : alk. paper)
1. Human reproductive technology—Religious aspects—Catholic
Church.   2. Abortion—Religious aspects—Catholic Church.
3. Contraception—Religious aspects—Catholic Church.   I. Title.
RG133.5.R56 2010
179.7′6—dc22
2009038932

Contents

Acknowledgments

Chapter 1 was originally published in *The National Catholic Bioethics Quarterly* 9, no. 3 (Fall 2009) and is reprinted by permission. An earlier and less-developed form of chapters 2 and 3 originally appeared as "Contraception, Sexual Behavior and Natural Law" in the *Linacre Quarterly* (1988). This original material was stylistically revised and integrated with material that had been later written by the author and originally published in German. This new material was translated by Joseph T. Papa, as were the essays that now appear as chapters 4, 5, and 6. Chapter 4 was originally published in the *Josephinum Journal of Theology* 14, no. 2 (August 2009) and is reprinted with permission. Chapter 7, which originally appeared in the *American Journal of Jurisprudence,* was translated by Paolo Carozza and is reprinted by permission. Acknowledgments regarding some of the additional texts are included in the author's introduction. Some of the translation and editing expenses for this volume were generously funded by the Cardinal Pio Laghi Chair of the Pontifical College Josephinum.

Editor's Preface

The present volume brings together, for English language readers, a collection of essays in which the Swiss philosopher Martin Rhonheimer addresses some of the most difficult and contested questions regarding the ethics of procreation. As indicated by the subtitle, the questions addressed range from that of contraception—and special cases related to it— to those of artificial fertilization and abortion. His treatment of the long-disputed question of contraception is unique and compelling, and few English-language scholars have shown familiarity with it. The present availability of it in extended form, following the fortieth anniversary of *Humanae Vitae,* therefore offers a valuable resource for those theologians and philosophers who still hope to move beyond the stalemate that has developed especially around this question, but extending more broadly. Such readers will also find this volume particularly helpful in considering related questions such as the use of contraceptives under threat of rape. Readers will also find that Rhonheimer's reading of Thomistic virtue ethics from the "perspective of the acting person" sheds surprising new light on the questions of artificial fertilization and abortion.

Moralists who want to rethink these and other difficult questions, while taking into account the lively ongoing debates regarding the retrieval of Thomistic moral theory in light of *Veritatis Splendor,* will be particularly interested in the present volume because of Rhonheimer's central role in these theoretical debates. They will therefore want to read the present volume in conjunction with the others that are available, or are becoming so, in English. These include his somewhat exploratory *Natural Law and Practical Reason: A Thomist View of Moral Autonomy,*[1] which was published in the year 2000, and the recently published *The Perspective of the Acting Person: Essays in the Renewal of Thomistic Moral Philosophy,*[2] which includes many of his most important essays in moral theory, along with an introduction that outlines his broader body of work while locating it in light of alternative readings of Aquinas. Complementary works also include his applied work *Vital Conflicts in Medical Ethics: A Virtue Approach to Craniotomy and Tubal Pregnancies,* published by the Catholic University of America Press in 2009, and his systematic ethical treatise *The Perspective of Morality: Philosophical Foundations of Thomistic Ethics,* forthcoming from CUA Press.[3] It is my hope that readers will find the present volume a valuable contribution to the literature and that it will facilitate greater consensus on the particular questions it addresses and regarding moral theory in general.

I would like to offer special thanks to Martin Rhonheimer for his collaboration in this and other projects, to Dr. Joseph T. Papa for his careful work in translating and copyediting much of the present text, and to Damian X. Lenshek for his editorial assistance with several aspects of the project. Particular thanks are due to the staff of the Catholic University of America Press, especially James Kruggel and Beth Benevides, for their skilled facilitation of this project.

William F. Murphy Jr.
Pontifical College Josephinum

1. New York: Fordham University Press, 2000, Translated by Gerald Malsbary.

2. Washington: The Catholic University of America Press, 2008, edited with an introduction by William F. Murphy Jr. The reader is referred to this introduction for an overview of Rhonheimer's major works in ethical theory.

3. Also in preparation is another volume of Rhonheimer's essays that I am editing, which is tentatively entitled *The Common Good of Constitutional Democracy: Essays in Political Philosophy and on Catholic Social Teaching.* Yet to be translated is his *Praktische Vernunft und Vernünftigkeit der Praxis: Handlungstheorie bei Thomas von Aquin in ihrer Entstehung aus dem Problemkontext der aristotelischen Ethik* (Berlin: Akademie Verlag, 1994), which might be rendered in English *Practical Reason and the Rationality of Praxis: Thomistic Action Theory in the Context of its Origin in Aristotelian Ethics.*

Introduction

Human Life

Between Protection and Threats

Never before in the course of history has such great importance been given to the protection of human life (and with such protection being realized in so broad and effective a manner) as in the modern liberal-democratic societies in which a large part of humanity lives. Notwithstanding wars, manifold forms of violence and criminality, and small- and large-scale catastrophes brought about by technology, the individual today possesses a degree of security, guaranteed by the state, that was never experienced in earlier historical epochs. Nevertheless, paradoxical as it may seem, this same contemporary civilization—guarantor of an almost complete security against every possible risk to life—has created structures that lead to new threats against life and human dignity, even as these structures are frequently praised as progress.

Threats to life are certainly as old as humanity itself. Such threats have taken a variety of forms that clearly and indisputably merit condemnation (wars, murders, torture, exploitation of labor in ways threatening and harmful to life, etc.). As such, the ethical characterization of these actions has rarely raised questions of a fundamental nature, which is not to say that they are easily eliminated from the life of society. Other forms of threat against life have traditionally been similarly (or in even greater measure) stigmatized, yet in contemporary society they seem to receive a growing tolerance, if not even acceptance in principle. This is true above all regarding the practice of abortion—the killing of the fruit of the maternal womb—and regarding euthanasia.

These threats to human life, increasingly tolerated and accepted, are at the same time less and less considered to be precisely *threats*. Certainly, the majority of people in today's world would rule out abortion and euthanasia as behavioral possibilities for themselves. A great number of thoughtful people, however, are disposed to tolerate such behavior in others and to reject, as discriminatory and intolerant, a general proscription of such behavior by the society and the state.

Thus, an entirely new situation has arisen. "Tolerance" is no longer the tolerating of a practice concerning the evil of which there exists more-or-less common agreement, though the perpetrator is left in peace so as to not jeopardize higher values; rather, tolerance becomes in a certain sense the acceptance of modes of behavior that one would never consider for oneself, but that are to be allowed for others as legitimate alternatives for action. It is clear that such "tolerance"—which in reality is much more than simple tolerance—cannot fail to have significant consequences in juridical systems, as well as in people's thoughts and sensibilities, and thus with respect to the socio-psychological bases of entire societies, given that such an attitude is ultimately not tolerance, but recognition.

Some of these problems are discussed in the following essays, collected here in a single volume; in particular, the essay concerning abortion and the protection of life in the constitutional democratic state addresses the just-mentioned question. The overall theme of the book, however, is essentially broader, even if it does limit itself to questions concerning the beginning of life. The book will address not only of modes of behavior that threaten life directly and per se, but also behaviors that threaten life only very indirectly: the artificial production of human life in a test tube, and contraception. It may surprise the reader that artificial fertilization might have something to do with threats to life; indeed, it would seem to be just the opposite. Don't such procedures create new life where it wasn't before, and indeed where there was no possibility of life? And isn't it true that life is here neither threatened nor destroyed? When one becomes aware, however, of the fact that it is often couples who are no longer able to have children because of an earlier abortion who resort to artificial fertilization, and when one learns as well of the widespread practice in this context of the destruction of fetuses and of the number of "extra" embryos that are not implanted, he can begin to readily see the connection between artificial fertilization and threats to life.

The essay in this volume that deals precisely with in vitro fertilization will not, however, depart from this question; it will rather shed light so to speak on a deeper level of the problem: the link between the "domination" of man over the beginning of life and over its end. If artificial fertilization is seen not simply as a "therapeutic" technique for overcoming infertility, but as a specific form of domination over the beginning of human life—and where indeed this underlying attitude is more important than the technical aspects of the procedure—then the connection with domination over the end of life becomes increasingly clear, whether in the fetal state, in conditions of chronic illness, or in cases of painful or incurable disease.

Contraception is a different case, however, and one that would seem to have nothing to do with this issue. Indeed, to address contraception in this context of threats to human life such as abortion runs the risk of asserting something that has always resulted in strong objections, including when such assertions have been made regarding the Catholic Church's teaching. I refer to an unjustifiable way of linking contraception and abortion, which undermines the condemnation of abortion by, for example, implicating in acts of deliberate abortion those couples who use contraception for serious reasons.

In the encyclical *Evangelium Vitae* the magisterium of the Catholic Church has effectively cut the ground from under this objection that the Church confusedly associates contraception too closely with abortion by making clear that contraception and abortion are two different violations of the moral law. Only the latter is properly to be considered a violation of the commandment "Thou shalt not kill" and of the virtue of justice, while the problematical nature of contraception pertains to the virtue of chastity. Nevertheless, *Evangelium Vitae* asserts concerning both of these modes of behavior that "despite their differences of nature and moral gravity, contraception and abortion are often closely connected, as fruits of the same tree."[1]

1. John Paul II, *Evangelium Vitae*, 13. Cf. also my analysis: *Contraccezione, mentalità contraccettiva e cultura dell'aborto: valutazioni e connessioni*, in Pontifical Academy for Life,

The analysis undertaken on this theme will attempt to clarify these "connections." The key word here will be "responsibility," or more precisely "procreative responsibility," not only with respect to the procreation (or not) of human life, but with respect to one's own sexual behavior, that is. the bodily dimension of human love as an integral component of its fully personal meaning. The practice of contraception is presented here as actions pertaining to one's sexual behavior that intentionally separate sexual acts from procreative responsibility. It will thus become clear that the separation of the two meanings of human sexuality ("love" and "responsibility for life") effected by contraception encourages a mentality that can ultimately view the violent destruction of an unwanted new life almost as an "alternative form" of contraception. A contraceptive measure that either fails or is applied "too late" thus leads to a killing, and as such is intimately connected with the widely diffused "abortion mentality."

In fact, responsibility for life begins where human life begins, in the intimate bodily union between man and woman. If bodily love—sexuality—becomes structurally an event in which the dimension of responsibility toward the generation of new life no longer plays any role (because one's sexual behavior has been consciously and voluntarily deprived of this dimension through contraception), then the attitude toward life and its coming into being must necessarily change as well. A life that is no longer considered to issue essentially from the loving union of man and woman, but is rather the collateral and "planned" product of a sexuality that itself no longer has an intrinsic connection with the transmission of life, may—one could then say—be legitimately produced in other ways as well. At the same time, a new human life would seem to possess no unconditional right to exist if, due to contraceptive failure, it comes about unexpectedly and contrary to the wish of the parents. Abortion thus becomes contraception *ex post,* or "after the event," and the circle is closed between an undesired baby that is aborted and a baby generated in a test tube. Both are fruit of the same "culture of death," which is thus named not so much because it kills, but because in a certain way man exalts himself as judge and lord over life and death.

Commento Interdisciplinare alla "Evanglium vitae," ed. R. Lucas and E. Sgreccia, 435–52 (Vatican City: Libreria Editrice Vaticana, 1997).

These thoughts provide the general theme of the following essays and the common thread connecting them. The initial essay illustrates how the retrieval of Thomistic ethics employed in the present defense of human life is properly understood as consistent with the directions encouraged by John Paul II in his encyclicals *Veritatis Splendor* and *Evangelium Vitae*. The long treatment of contraception as an ethical problem in part 1, under the subheading, "Sexuality and Responsibility"[2] provides our way of approach, so to speak, to the whole discussion. Central to the argument of these chapters is the elaboration of the concept of a moral virtue, called here "procreative responsibility" and understood as the integrating element of conjugal chastity, as a human perfection, in which man's bodily-spiritual unity is shown in an exemplary way. Indeed, every question that in some way or another has to do with the understanding of human life is tied up with the understanding of human sexuality. The questions addressed in this opening part are also relevant for the themes of in vitro fertilization and abortion, though these latter themes each contain completely new, specific, and unique problems.

Concluding the treatment of the ethics of procreation is the brief fourth chapter, which attempts to address the concrete question of the use of contraceptives in the case of a foreseeable rape.[3] The fifth chapter, on reproductive technology,"[4] shows, as mentioned above, domination over human life from what might be called a "positive," that is a "pro-

2. Original version: *Sexualität und Verantwortung. Empfängnisverhütung als ethisches Problem, Studi IMABE* no. 3 (Vienna: IMABE, 1995). A lecture given in English, entitled "Contraception, Sexual Behavior, and Natural Law: Philosophical Foundation of the Norm of 'Humanae vitae,'" at the 2nd International Congress of Moral Theology at Rome is based on this text. It was published in *"Humanae vitae": 20 anni dopo. Atti del II Congresso Internazionale di Teologia Morale*, Rome, November 9–12, 1988, (Milan: Edizioni Ares, 1989), 73–113; and in *Linacre Quarterly* 56, no. 2 (1989): 20–57.

3. This article's first publication was entitled "Minaccia di stupro e prevenzione: un'eccezione?" in *La Scuola Cattolica* 123 (1995): 75–90. It was later published in English as "The Use of Contraceptives under Threat of Rape: An Exception?" in *Josephinum Journal of Theology* 14, no. 2 (August 2007): 168–81. Cf. *The Catechism of the Catholic Church*, no. 2370; *Veritatis Splendor*, no. 80.

4. Originally published as "Die Instrumentalisierung des menschlichen Lebens. Ethische Erwägungen zur In-Vitro-Fertilisierung," in *Fortpflangzunsmedizin und Lebensschutz*, ed. F. Bydlinski and T. Mayer-Maly (Innsbruck-Vienna: Tyrolia-Verlag, 1992), 41–64. In a slightly shorter form, the text can also be found as part of the essay: "Zur Begründung sittlicher Normen aus der Natur. Grundsätzliche Erwägungen und Exemplifizierung am Beispiel der I.v.F.," in *Der Mensch als Mitte und Maßstab der Medizin* (*Medizin und Ethik*, vol. 1), ed. J. Bonelli, 49–94 (Vienna: Springer, 1992).

ductive," point of view. Conception and life itself become means for fulfilling the desire and happiness of those who "produce a child" by these methods. Human life is thus no longer a reality that is excluded, even if not completely, from human intervention, and that can therefore claim an *unconditional* respect. In the context of reproductive technologies, respect for human life rather becomes a changeable function of the desire of third parties. Reproductive technologies thus represent that facet of "dominion over life" whose other face is precisely the killing of an *undesired* life in the mother's womb.

The sixth and seventh chapters consider the theme of abortion. Chapter 6, "Human Fetuses, Persons and the Right to Abortion: Toward an Absolute Power of the Born?"[5] attempts a systematic refutation of an extremely "consequentialistic" position that is more and more widely held, and likewise extremely dangerous: the utilitarianism of an "ethics of interest" espoused by such thinkers as, for example, P. Singer, M. Tooley, M. Anne Warren, B. Steinbock, and H. Kuhse; the argumentation has been advanced in German principally by the legal philosopher Norbert Hoerster. At the core of this systematic argumentation, which my essay attempts to refute, is the distinction between "man" and "person." The article considers the essential categories necessary to demonstrate that human embryos and fetuses are worthy of an absolute recognition as persons, and therefore possess a corresponding right to life.[6]

The seventh and final chapter treats of the right to life of the unborn from the points of view of political or legal philosophy, and that of the State.[7] It was written on the occasion of John Paul II's encyclical *Evangelium Vitae*, which appeared in 1995. Here we are no longer dealing

5. Original version: *Absolute Herrschaft der Geborenen? Anatomie und Kritik der Argumentation von Norbert Hoersters "Abtreibung im säkularen Staat,"* Studi IMABE, no. 4 (Vienna: IMABE, 1995).

6. Cf. here also R. Spaemann, *Personen—Versuche über den Unterschied zwischen "etwas" und "jemand"* (Stuttgart: Klett-Cotta, 1996), in English as *Person: The Difference between Someone and Something* (Oxford: Oxford University Press, 2006).

7. The chapter was originally published under the title Diritti fondamentali, legge morale e difesa legale della vita nello Stato costituzionale democratico. L'approccio costituzionalistico all'enciclica "Evangelium vitae," in Annales Theologici 9 (1995) 271–334. A Spanish translation exists in the volume Derecho a la vida y estado moderno. A proposito de la Evangelium vitae (Madrid: Rialp, 1998). It was published in English as "Fundamental Rights, Moral Law, and the Legal Defense of Life in a Constitutional Democracy: A Constitutionalist Approach to the Encyclical *Evangelium Vitae*," in the *American Journal of Jurisprudence* 43 (1998), 135–83.

with a question only of morality or of the personal conduct of one's life, but of the legitimacy and limits of an intervention by the state to efficaciously protect unborn life. More precisely, it responds to the question of the protection of life and the need for a corresponding and coherent political-juridical-ethical argumentation in the context of the modern democratic constitutional state, which has its own distinctive criteria for handling questions concerning the relation between civil law and morality.[8]

The question is a highly complex one. Our treatment begins with fundamental considerations concerning the relation between the moral plane and the juridical-political plane.[9] It continues through a consideration of the role of civil law in the course of history, the relevant doctrine in the encyclical *Evangelium Vitae*, and a paradigmatic treatment of the rendering of judicial judgments (at the level of the respective constitutional courts) in the United States and Germany. It proceeds further through a presentation of the most significant argumentative strategies for denying a protective function of the state with respect to the unborn. Finally it presents, in connection with *Evangelium Vitae*, an argument demonstrating why state protection of the unborn must be considered an urgent demand of the common good.

This completes the summary of the themes considered in this volume. The reader may wonder about the absence of treatments of current themes such as genetic technology. Certainly, one encounters in such technologies questions of responsibility with respect to the transmission of human life and its protection. Procedures such as experimentation on living human embryos, interventions on the genetic code for eugenic purposes, and even human cloning would seem to raise fewer fundamental questions than the practices treated here, however, perhaps pre-

8. The encyclical *Evangelium Vitae*, no. 71, 3, offers perhaps the interpretive key for this, when it says: "Certainly the purpose of civil law is different and more limited in scope than that of the moral law."

9. On this theme cf. also M. Rhonheimer, "Perché una filosofia politica? Elementi storici per una risposta," *Acta philosophica* 1, no. 2 (1992): 233–63. Other related questions can also be found, in a more systematic treatment, in M. Rhonheimer, "Lo stato costituzionale democratico e il bene comune," in *Ripensare lo spazio politico: quale democrazia?* ed. E. Morandi and R. Panattoni, in *Contratto, Rivista di filosofia tomista e contemporanea* 7 (1997): 57–122. These two essays are forthcoming in English in a collection of my works edited by William F. Murphy Jr., and tentatively entitled *The Common Good of Constitutional Democracy: Essays in Political Philosophy and on Catholic Social Teaching.*

cisely because of their clear unacceptability. Contraception, the production of human life in a test tube, and abortion, on the other hand, even where they cannot be said to be generally accepted, seem to most people to be admissible at least in certain cases. Precisely for this reason the systematic analysis of the ethical dimension of these modes of behavior seems to be particularly important.

Moreover, it is worth mentioning that the increasingly wider acceptance of the practices discussed here hints at the possibility of addressing these questions without being concerned about having an immediate practical effect. Contraception, reproductive medicine, and abortion are more or less recognized realities in advanced societies. This is no reason, however, to cease to be concerned with their respective ethical problems. On the contrary! The pathology of a society in which these modes of behavior are accepted can perhaps be correctly understood only if corresponding parameters for judgment are provided by the ethical perspective. In fact moral philosophy—ethics, morality—addresses itself to man and to his happiness.[10]

Immoral action can lead to enjoyment and pleasure, but it does not promote happiness. And the pathologies of today's society—with all of its undeniable blessings and movement toward progress—are precisely pathologies of man defrauded of his happiness, seeking enjoyment and pleasure but unable to find a happiness that is authentic and enduring.

A word on contraception. Like none of the other practices discussed here, contraception is widely accepted and practiced in many forms. Personally, I assume that most people are convinced that in contraception they do something completely normal, unproblematic, and even reasonable. What is written here in no way intends—and I want to say this explicitly—to denigrate those who practice contraception, considering them in some way as "potential murderers" of unborn children. My thoughts concerning this latter argument are explicitly articulated in the course of the book.

Some may nevertheless be troubled by the fact that contraception and

10. See R. Spaemann, *Glück und Wohlwollen—Versuch über Ethik* (Stuttgart: Klett-Cotta, 1989); M. Rhonheimer, *La prospettiva della morale. Fondamenti dell'etica filosofica* (Rome: Armando, 1994). The latter is forthcoming in English as *The Perspective of Morality: Philosophical Bases of Thomistic Virtue Ethics* (Washington, D.C.: The Catholic University of America Press, 2009).

abortion are here often considered together; the predication of certain connections, however, between these two erroneous types of behavior in no way implies the intention to impute the same degree of gravity to both. Abortion is the killing of an innocent living human being, that is, of a human individual with eternal value. Contraception, on the other hand, is an erroneous means for arriving at an end which in itself may be exceedingly correct, and even morally demanded, and for which there also exist morally just means for reaching: the avoidance of the coming into being of a new living human being. I view attempts to consider contraception as the potential killing of a living human being, simply on the basis of its motivation and intentionality, to be misleading; the reader will find my precise reasons for this in what follows.

This completes my introductory comments on the contents of the book. The author hopes that it will serve to clarify some of the issues that led John Paul II in *Evangelium Vitae* to speak of a "culture of death," which is to be opposed by a "new culture of human life." The "culture of death," one may say, is characterized by a new—and highly dangerous—link between protection of life and threats to life. On the one hand priority is given in our modern societies, as never before, to the protection of the physical integrity of the person, to his health, and to the support of people with handicaps of every sort. On the other hand these same societies, with their comprehensive social security nets and public health entities, increasingly tend to exclude any "disturbing elements," or those that are too burdensome, from the system—and this, to be frank, on the basis of clearly identifiable interests that discriminate against certain groups of people.

In fact, there can be no other explanation why the killing of the unborn is supported as a *procedure* of social insurance and health entities, while on the other hand the public tendency is rather to reduce abortion procedures on the handicapped. Thus, public health authorities establish discriminatory structures in the interest of the already born, those with financial means, the healthy, and so on. The fact that the elderly—who are increasingly a burden on health systems because of advances in medical technology, increased average age, and the increasing disproportion between earners and pensioners—are less exposed to the dangers of this discriminatory dynamic is due above all to the still-effective mechanism of democracy based on majority rule: the elderly are in fact more and more the majority in developed nations. This could eventually lead, however, to an "insurrection of the young" when they, as the working population, feel themselves held hostage to the interests of a generation of elderly—a generation, by the way, that continues to bear responsibility for the demographic disequilibrium *between* the generations.

The creation of a "new culture of human life" called for in the encyclical *Evangelium Vitae* must nevertheless take place on a variety of levels, with the political-juridical level being only one aspect. Laws, however, "play a very important and sometimes decisive role in influencing patterns of thought and behavior."[11] In a society shaped with reference to individual rights, laws and court decisions are expressed in the public space through a "language of responsibility," and possess therefore an expressive function shaping the popular mentality.[12]

Ultimately, then, the creation of a culture of life must occur in the place where life comes into being and receives its earliest development: in the heart of the family. *Evangelium Vitae* points this out clearly. The family is the place where consciences are formed, and where charity, readiness to serve, and those virtues that lead to the acceptance of human life in all its states and conditions, as both a gift and a task, must be experienced and learned. In this way the family becomes a focal point of the interest and the protection of all.

I would like to express particular thanks to Professor Bill Murphy of the Pontifical College Josephinum for proposing this collection, for conceiving its form, for securing translation of the various components, and for integrating the originally published English text of part 1 with later expansions of it, and for his execution of the entire process.

Besides those journals mentioned in the acknowledgments, thanks are due also to Tyrolia Publishers of Innsbruck, to the Institute of Medical and Bioethical Anthropology (IMABE) of Vienna, and to the magazines *Annales Theologici* of the Pontifical University of the Holy Cross in Rome and *La Scuola Cattolica* of the Archbishop's Seminary of Milan, for their friendly permission to reprint the present essays or for translation rights.

11. *Evangelium Vitae*, 90, 3.
12. M. A. Glendon, *Rights Talk: The Impoverishment of Political Discourse* (New York: Free Press, 1991), 101ff.

Additional thanks are due to Joseph T. Papa for translating several chapters and for creating the initial bibliography and final index, to Paolo Carozza for translating the eighth chapter, to Damian Lenshek for creating the initial index, to the *National Catholic Bioethics Quarterly* and the *American Journal of Jurisprudence* for reprint permissions, and to the staff of the Catholic University of America Press.

May the present volume serve to make the works collected here accessible to a wider public.

Ethics of Procreation
and the
Defense of Human Life

1

Natural Law and the Thomistic Roots of John Paul II's Ethics of Human Life

No previous pope dealt with the theme of natural law, in his own magisterium, as extensively as did John Paul II, inserting it with great clarity in the context of the relationships of an anthropology that coherently understands man as a creature made in the image of God. In particular, the encyclical *Veritatis Splendor* appeared as a *novum,* in that it did not address a specific theme in Catholic morality, or propose as its theme Catholic morality as such, but dealt with Catholic moral theology as it is taught as an ecclesiastical discipline by theological faculties. In this context, the encyclical does not refer to the natural law only to establish concrete doctrines in the moral sphere—in particular in the sphere that may be called "ethics of human life"—but it addresses the very *definition, essence,* and *characteristics* of the natural law. This, again, is a *novum,* even if John Paul II took a cue from another encyclical, written a century earlier, which had already produced a definition of the natural law: the encyclical *Libertas Praestantissimum* of Leo XIII, the teaching of which is completely marked by St. Thomas Aquinas, and yet this encyclical had left little trace on the way ecclesiastical doctrine since then has dealt with "natural law" as the basis of moral action. This changed with *Veritatis Splendor:* the Thomistically inspired teaching of Leo XIII has been brought to fruition in all its richness and significance.

At first sight it could seem trivial to say that the teaching of the Church on the natural moral law would have an intrinsic link with its doctrine on questions regarding the ethics of life (abortion, euthanasia, stem-cell research). What seems much less trivial, however, is the precise way in which the Church applies the natural law to establish the respective norms. How do things stand in this regard in the teaching of John Paul II? In what follows, we will examine this question. It will not, however, be possible to respond in a completely neutral way, that is, without reference to the previous understanding that I, as the author of the present article, bring to these questions. The arguments that I will propose in what follows claim, of course, to be a faithful representation of the teaching of John Paul II; nevertheless, it is impossible to expound this teaching without at the same time inserting it in a wider and more systematic context, and therefore to a certain extent also offering an interpretation. I say this explicitly, for the sake of intellectual honesty. Even if I will seek to stay as close to the texts as possible, it would be inappropriate to claim that my exposition is the only valid way they can be understood. In what follows, therefore, I will refer to some of my publications on the topic, which I assume not only will be helpful for advancing my argument in this setting, but also will clarify the moral philosophical principles on which I base my reading of the texts of John Paul II.[1]

Allow me, however, to first offer a brief anecdote. In November 1988, on the occasion of an audience granted by John Paul II to the members of the Congress of Moral Theology for the twentieth anniversary of the encyclical *Humanae Vitae,* I met the pope personally—having given a paper, I was in the first row at the audience as he went down the line from speaker to speaker—and when John Paul II read my name card, he said in a loud voice in Italian before all those gathered: "Ah, Rhonheimer... the natural law! I am reading, and I will continue to read." In fact, some

1. Especially my *Natur als Grundlage der Moral. Die personale Struktur des Naturgesetzes bei Thomas von Aquin: Eine Auseinandersetzung mit autonomer und teleologischer Ethik* (Innsbruck-Vienna: Tyrolia-Verlag, 1987); translated in various languages; English translation: *Natural Law and Practical Reason: A Thomist View of Moral Autonomy* (New York: Fordham University Press, 2000). A sort of recapitulation, with further clarifications, can be found in my article "The Cognitive Structure of the Natural Law and the Truth of Subjectivity," *Thomist* 67, no. 1 (2003): 1–44; reprinted as chapter 7 in my *The Perspective of the Acting Person: Essays in the Renewal of Thomistic Moral Philosophy,* ed. with an introduction by William F. Murphy Jr. (Washington D.C.: The Catholic University of America Press, 2008).

months earlier someone had given the Holy Father my above-mentioned book *Natur als Grundlage der Moral,* on the natural law in St. Thomas Aquinas. I will leave it to historians to decide whether my book in some way influenced the encyclical *Veritatis Splendor,* the content of which I also had the occasion to discuss with John Paul II, together with a group of other specialists on the theme, at a luncheon at the Apostolic Palace. Frankly, the encyclical did not seem entirely foreign to me when I read it for the first time. Still today I think that my vision of the natural law drawn from Thomas Aquinas is at least a valid reading of the relative doctrine of this encyclical, and I will thus occasionally refer to this vision in what follows.

The Natural Law according to the Encyclical Letter *Veritatis Splendor*

The Natural Law: A Law of Reason

In its teaching on the natural law, *Veritatis Splendor* (*VS*) takes its inspiration entirely from the thought of Thomas Aquinas. The natural law is not understood—as in the tradition of the Stoa—as the *logos* intrinsic to the cosmos, an eternal law, immanent to nature itself and simultaneously deduced from it, but rather as an active participation of the rational creature in the ordering function of the divine reason. The theory on natural law of *VS* is based on the thesis of the autonomy of man and on the active role of reason in distinguishing between good and evil (*VS*, nos. 12, 40, 42, 44). The natural moral law "has its origin in God and always finds its source in him" (ibid.), but at the same time it is also "a properly human law" since, according to Aquinas, "it is nothing other than the light of intelligence infused in us by God, whereby we understand what must be done and what must be avoided. God gave this light and this law to man in creation" (ibid.).[2] I call this Aquinas's "core doctrine" of natural law,[3] although to point out the core or focal meaning of natural law is not yet to provide a complete Thomistic account of it. Such an account includes other aspects that will be briefly discussed

---

2. The Thomistic citation is taken from the work: Thomas Aquinas, *In duo praecepta caritatis et in decem legis praecepta exposition,* Prologus I in *Opuscula Theologica,* vol. II (Turin: Marietti, 1975). The original text reads: "lex naturae . . . nihil aliud est nisi lumen intellectus insitum nobis a Deo, per quod cognoscimus quid agendum et quid vitandum. Hoc lumen et hanc legem dedit Deus homini in creatione."

3. See my *The Perspective of the Acting Person,* 288–92.

below. They mainly refer to what I have extensively shown to be what I called the *passive participation* of all creatures, also of human persons, in eternal law, mainly expressed in the natural inclinations of all beings.[4] The main challenge of any natural law theory as a properly moral theory is precisely to show how a complex of principles of the practical intellect—which are what Aquinas calls the precepts of the natural law—are founded *not only ontologically but also epistemologically (or cognitively) in the natural inclinations on the basis of which we then also speak of the primary and secondary precepts of the natural law.*[5]

The core teaching of John Paul II on the natural moral law is, therefore, strictly linked with the theory that holds man to be created in the image of God as a free and rational being, who bears within himself—through the divine creation—the light of reason, by which he is capable of distinguishing between good and evil. It is precisely this capacity of discernment—and in a derived sense the successive distinctions between what must be done and what must not be done, as well as the precept of human reason to pursue the good and avoid evil—that constitutes a natural law. This law is called "natural," as the encyclical points out, "not because it refers to the nature of irrational beings but because the reason that promulgates it is proper to human nature" (*VS*, n. 42), given that it is reason—the reason of the human person—that formulates this law and commands accordingly. This reason is precisely part of human *nature*, and thus we are dealing with a *natural* law (as opposed to the divine law of the New and Old Covenants, which is based on revelation, or human law, expressed through the positive juridical order).[6]

4. See *Natural Law and Practical Reason*, 66–68 and 246–51; e.g., page 67: "all existing things are already 'measured' and 'ruled' in their existence by the creative reason of God. This passive participation in the *lex aeterna* is expressed in 'the inclinations to the proper operations and ends' (*inclination in proprios actos et fines*) of each species (see I-II, q. 91, a. 2). All creatures—including man—possess this passive *impressio* of the eternal law in their very being, expressing itself in their natural inclinations to specific actions and goals."

5. I addressed this very question in several of my publications, especially in my article "The Cognitive Structure of the Natural Law and the Truth of Subjectivity," reprinted as chapter 7 in my *The Perspective of the Acting Person*.

6. *VS* closely follows Thomistic terminology. It is important to understand why the natural law is a *natural* law and not a divine law: not because it does not come from God, but because it pertains to creation. It is part of nature, of human nature. Like all nature it clearly has its origin in God, but precisely as a law it is something that belongs to nature—that is, to natural human reason—*lex naturalis,* and in precisely this sense it is not a divine law (*lex divina*). In fact, it is not formulated and promulgated by God, but by human reason. This will become clearer below.

The natural law is therefore a law that is intrinsic to man as a rational creature. It is a direct expression of God's care for man, who is a person and therefore is not guided "'from without,' through the laws of physical nature, but 'from within,' through reason, which, by its natural knowledge of God's eternal law, is consequently able to show man the right direction to take in his free actions" (VS, n. 43). In this way, following Thomas Aquinas, man becomes a participant of Divine Providence itself. The natural law—natural moral knowledge in the sphere of good and evil, which man fills out with his own reason, given to him by God—is itself a constitutive element of the divine government of the world.[7]

In this context VS refers back to the earlier teaching of Leo XIII, which expressed precisely these relationships. This long-ignored doctrine, expressed in the encyclical *Libertas Praestantissimum*,[8] is not an expression of a late neo-scholastic concept of a natural moral law as a natural order set before man, from which the moral subject can simply "read" the norms of the natural law. Leo XIII conceived the natural law rather as the ordering act of human reason itself in the sphere of good and evil. The natural law, according to the citation of Leo XIII's text in VS n. 44 "is written and engraved in the heart of each and every man" (and is thus not simply an "objective natural order," or a law in the sense of conformity to the laws of nature). The "seat" of the natural law is the heart of man, at the center of his person as an image of God. It is so, continues Leo XIII, "since it (the natural law) is none other than *human reason itself* which commands us to do good and counsels us not to sin" (emphasis mine).

This mode of expression leaves no doubt about the fact that for Leo XIII the natural moral law is not simply a natural order recognized by reason, but rather reason itself, to the extent that it allows one to naturally distinguish between good and evil, and imposes on man the obligation of doing good and avoiding evil. This capacity of discernment of the human subject, and thus the cognitive character of the natu-

---

7. Cf. Thomas Aquinas. *Summa contra Gentiles* II, ch. 113; *Summa theologiae* I-II, q.91, a.2.

8. An indication of this ignoring of Leo's exposition on natural law is that it is cited only marginally, without paying any attention to it, in the exposition of the various conceptions of natural law in the systematic and fundamental work by Joseph Fuchs in the 1950s on the doctrine of natural law. Apparently the author did not know what to make of Leo XIII's definition of natural law. Cf. J. Fuchs, *Lex Naturae. Zur Theologie des Naturrechts* (Düsseldorf: Patmos, 1955); on this see *Natural Law and Practical Reason*, 8–15.

ral law, is strongly emphasized in *VS* (see especially nos. 12, 40, 42, 44). One must not forget, however, the basis on which reason possesses the capacity to distinguish good and evil, at the same time authorizing it for this task and conferring on it moral and legislative force. This is so, explains Leo XIII as cited in *VS*, because the human reason that appears as the natural moral law is "the voice and the interpreter of some higher reason"—the reason and wisdom of God—"to which our spirit and our freedom must be subject" (no. 44). The autonomy that is shown by the interior possession of the natural law and by the capacity to exercise it "from within," based on reason's own capacity of discernment, that is, of choosing good and avoiding evil, is an autonomy subject to God, indeed regulated by him. For this reason, as *VS* says, again citing Leo XIII who also here follows Thomas Aquinas, "the natural law is itself the *eternal law*, implanted in beings endowed with reason, *and inclining them towards their right action and end*; it is none other than the eternal reason of the Creator and Ruler of the universe" (no. 44). It is precisely in this sense that the natural law is clearly a "law of God." But the decisive point is that it is recognized *as a law* precisely through the action of human reason, and not by means of some other source (such as, e.g., revelation). The natural law is therefore the eternal law, but this latter is not accessible to man except by revelation.[9] The eternal law is made manifest to man precisely in the natural law, that is, through the moral-normative knowledge proper to him.

Precisely for this reason *VS* had emphasized earlier that, regarding this knowledge of good and evil, man "does not originally possess such 'knowledge' as something properly his own, but only participates in it by the light of natural reason and of Divine Revelation,[10] which manifest to him the requirements and the promptings of eternal wisdom" (*VS*, n. 41). Man's autonomy is therefore in reality a "participated theonomy" (ibid.), a theonomy that is autonomy through human reason, and pre-

---

9. St. Thomas says of this with categorical clarity: "licet lex aeterna sit nobis ignota secundum quod est in mente divina; innotescit tamen nobis aliquiter vel per rationem naturalem, quae ab ea derivatur ut propria eius imago; vel per aliqualem revelationem superadditam." ("Although the eternal law is unknown to us according as it is in the Divine Mind: nevertheless, it becomes known to us somewhat, either by natural reason which is derived therefrom as its proper image; or by some sort of additional revelation": Thomas Aquinas, *Summa theologiae* I-II, q.19, a.4, ad 3).

10. This latter clearly does not belong to the natural law.

cisely for this reason is not a "creative" reason, that is, having as its own a decisional power in the formation of moral norms. Rather, man "finds" something, which had already been thought in the divine wisdom and is made known to man through natural reason.[11]

Reason and Nature: The Body-Soul Unity of Human Nature

Certainly, many questions remain unanswered from what has been said thus far. Is it really possible to reduce the natural law to "reason" in this way? A human being is not only spirit and reason, but also matter in a physical and biological sense. He is constituted bodily, a living being endowed with thought: not pure *ratio*, but *animal rationale*. Indeed, the definition of natural law elaborated to this point could lead one to think that the corporeal dimension of man is left to the decisional power of human freedom, and does not contain in itself any normativity. One could thus object that moral reasoning must align itself precisely to "nature," understood as corporeity, and to the laws and teleological structures inscribed in it. The question that is therefore asked in *VS*, n. 48, is about "the place of the human body in questions of natural law."

In this context John Paul II emphasizes above all the decisively important anthropology that asserts the essential union of body and soul: the "rational soul is *per se et essentialiter* the form of [the] body," man is "*corpore et anima unus*" (*VS*, n. 48). According to this anthropology, as it was elaborated by Thomas Aquinas, in the case of man body and spirit do not constitute two different natures, but precisely one nature. Perhaps we are not always aware of the implications of this assertion. This lack of awareness is seen, in my opinion, in the still widespread bad habit of not only distinguishing between "nature" (in the sense of corporeality) and "reason" (as pure will) or between freedom and nature, but opposing the one to the other in an almost Cartesian sense. In man, however, nature and reason, or corporeality and rationality, together form *a single*

---

11. Russell Hittinger in his book *The First Grace. Rediscovering the Natural Law in a Post-Christian World* (Wilmington, Del.: ISI Books, 2003) offers the hypothesis that *VS* took the term "participated theonomy" from my above-cited book *Natur als Grundlage der Moral* (Natural law and practical reason). Though I did use the expression in that work, I want to point out that the expression was inspired by a source, to which I made explicit reference, and that is: J. De Finance, "Autonomie et théonomie," in *L'agire morale*, ed. M. Zalba, Atti del Congresso Internazionale Roma-Napoli (April 17–24, 1974) su "Tommaso d'Aquino nel suo settimo centenario," vol. 5, 239–60 (Naples: Edizioni Domenicane Italiane, 1974).

nature, and thus a substantial unity of being. This means that human reason cannot even be thought of without corporeality. Conversely, nor can corporeality, without reason, be affirmed as morally relevant and normative: the biological *Physis* of man is never of itself "human nature." As such, it can be known and held to be ethically relevant only within the horizon of the spiritual acts of the human person.

The consequences of this fact are significant. *VS* expresses these in the statement: "The person, including the body, is completely entrusted to himself, and it is in the unity of body and soul that the person is the subject of his own moral acts" (ibid.). The person is subject in both dimensions, which form a single nature: in his corporeality and in his rationality, or in his capacity to aspire to something based on reason, which means *to will* (the will is in fact the *appetitus in ratione*). This also means that there can be no rationally relevant knowledge that does not take into account the corporal constitution of man. The normative role and the power of human reason, as these are shown in the natural law, are at the same time inserted in man's corporeity and in the structure of his sensory aspirations. As "natural" reason, human reason is always also dependent on the fact of its link to the body. [12]

What does this mean, concretely and practically? What does it mean for the establishment of moral norms? It means that a reason that would prescind from "nature" as the corporeity of the human person would be suspended in the void from the cognitive point of view. Human cor-

---

12. This was in fact one of the main "messages" of my *Natural Law and Practical Reason.* In his article "Natural Law and Natural Inclinations: Rhonheimer, Pinckaers, McAleer," *Thomist* 70 (2006): 155–201, Matthew Levering has analyzed my view on the relationship between natural inclinations and the practical reason; though obviously trying to give a fair account of my thought, in this analysis he mistakenly attributes to me the position I have precisely argued *against* in *Natural Law and Practical Reason.* Among other things, Levering asserts that according to me, human reason "humanizes" the natural inclinations and serves to "freely" order the natural inclinations "to the ends that befit the human person," which "transcends nature" (174). Such a view is not mine. Ironically, it corresponds to that famously held by Karl Rahner and those who were then influenced by him, a view to which I oppose. To argue against *this* view was precisely the main aim of my book, originally published in 1987. Levering's misreading perhaps springs from not sufficiently distinguishing ontological and epistemological questions. See for this my "The Moral Significance of Pre-Rational Nature In Aquinas: A Reply to Jean Porter (and Stanley Hauerwas)," *American Journal of Jurisprudence* 48 (2003): 253–80 (reprinted as chapter 6 of my *The Perspective of the Acting Person*), which Levering cites, but perhaps has not sufficiently taken into consideration. (Levering has later republished his article from "The Thomist" as Chapter 3 of his book *Biblical Natural Law. A Thecoentric and Teleological Approach,* Oxford University Press, Oxford 2008.)

poreity expresses goods and values, which for reason—in the so-called natural inclinations—become the point of departure according to nature, even if these in turn display their true moral dimension only once they are inserted into the horizon of reason. Thus the sexual instinct, the attractive force between the two sexes that serves reproduction and the preservation of the species, is given by nature to human corporeity, and is therefore received by reason naturally—and thus spontaneously and necessarily—as a human good. Nevertheless, only within the intellectual horizon of reason does this good reveal its truly human—personal— character, as love and communion between two persons, who in the reciprocal gift of themselves fulfill the task of the transmission of life. Note that I have implied that the moral relevance of the sexual inclination is grasped by reason not simply in the inclination but in the flowering of marital chastity, of which the inclination is the seed.

Nature and reason, body and spirit, nature and freedom, must not, therefore, be opposed to one another in a dualistic sense (cf. *VS*, n. 50). The human person, as has been said, is a unity, a unity that includes precisely body and spirit, reason and nature, nature and freedom. This unity forms itself one complex but indivisible unity or nature: the nature of the human person. But it can still be asked what this means for reason, that is, for the moral law, which, as we have seen, is precisely *the light of reason* that distinguishes good from evil.

The question of whether "nature" or "reason" is the actual moral norm is not further addressed by John Paul II, at least not in *VS*, and is thus not answered. In fact, it is a question that cannot be reasonably addressed in an encyclical, being more appropriate to an ethical-philosophical dissertation or a treatise of fundamental morality, things that cannot be presented as a task of the teaching of the Church's magisterium. It would be interesting, however, to know what the then-professor Karol Wojtyla might have thought on this question, and if such an opinion might help in the correct understanding of his teaching on the law of nature, which he so vigorously expounded once he became pope.

In fact John Paul II, when he taught at the University of Lublin, expressed himself clearly on this question. Even if clear conclusions cannot be drawn concerning the meaning of the encyclical *VS* on the basis of these statements—this would be problematic from a strictly methodological point of view—it could nevertheless be interesting and enlightening to know what John Paul II thought about this question during the years when he was still a professor of philosophy.

The Normative Character of Reason

The text that I will refer to is a lecture held at the Faculty of Philosophy of the University of Lublin in the year 1956–57. The title of the lecture was "Norm and Happiness."[13] Here Wojtyla, departing from a Thomistic perspective, arrives at the following conclusion: "[R]eason, which according to its nature grasps in a concept the essence of the good, gives to man the power to govern his own being." This would mean that reason becomes *regula moralitatis* precisely when it "guides individual actions, when it carries out its practical and normative function" (284).

It is interesting to note how in this context Wojtyla refers to the classic work of L. Léhu,[14] written against P. Elter and Odon Lottin, in which he demonstrates that according to St. Thomas it is not the "rational nature" or the "substantial form" of man, but reason, that is the measure of morality. It seems to me extremely significant that John Paul II would study and make use of Léhu, all the more because neo-thomistic moral theology, which characterized moral teaching during the first six decades of the twentieth century, was influenced less by Léhu's position than by that of Elter and Lottin.

In a perfectly correct way and from a Thomistic perspective, Léhu showed, in opposition to those authors, that the norm that is nearest to human action is not nature—or "rational human nature" or the *forma substantialis* of man's being—but reason. It is obvious, in turn, that human reason itself and its normative role find their basis in human nature or in the *forma substantialis*[15] of the human being. Wojtyla summarizes this as follows: "The participation of nature cannot be denied, because nature is the foundation of the intellect and therefore of knowledge, and *eo ipso* the foundation of the norm, and consequently it can be defined as '*regula fundamentalis.*' The true and proper norm, however, is represented by the intellect, which must not be confused with

13. The text was published in German in Johannes Paul II, *Lubliner Vorlesungen* (Stuttgart: Seewald Verlag, 1980), 255–414. The original Polish title is: *Norma i szczęście*. The German translation is by Danka Spranger.

14. L. Léhu, *La raison, règle de la moralità d'après Saint Thomas* (Paris: J. Gabalda et Fils, 1930).

15. Cf. Thomas Aquinas. *Summa theologiae* I-II, q.18, a.5.

nature" (285). The intellect "dominates nature," and is not pure necessity, as is nature. The intellect, or reason, is open to the multiple, and thus is not a rule in the sense of pure and simple "nature," but in the sense of a behavioral norm. It is, as Léhu correctly said, the rule and norm of human action, the *dictamen rationis practicae* (286).

This notwithstanding, neither Léhu, nor Wojtyla twenty-five years later, set nature and reason in mutual contrast, because this *dictamen* of reason is correct—and therefore *recta ratio*—only when it "agrees with nature" (287). By this they seem to have fallen into a loop. Nonetheless, reference is made to the natural inclinations, or as Wojtyla says, to "the natural finality of the human being": the practical intellect understands these ends innately, thus in a direct, intuitive way, and is "improved" by moral virtue, being led in this way to its moral perfection in prudence. At the same time, thus informed by the natural inclinations, the practical intellect can, and this is the key point, "continually provide prudence with the first and general principles as its foundation, which permit the formulation of more concrete judgments in all their detail. These judgments, in turn, become commands, which guide action." While the *dictamina* of practical reason, the concrete and direct guides of action, are judgments of the intellect, the already mentioned "first general practical principles," which are anchored in the natural inclinations of the being, constitute precisely that which Aquinas calls *lex naturalis*, natural law (even if Wojtyla does not use this term in this passage). The natural law is the entire complex of those first practical principles, which confer to prudence the fundamental orientation in the sphere of the good, which formulates the goals of the single moral virtues and only through the work of the moral virtues therefore also acquires its ultimate perfection.

I consider this perspective, as it was developed by John Paul II at the time when he was a philosophy professor at Lublin in reference to the classic work—too often forgotten—of Léhu, to be basically correct, and expressed with a Thomistic character and tone.[16] It is surprising to see,

16. When in preparing the study *Natur als Grundlage der Moral* I came across Léhu's book; it was an important discovery for me, and one that had a decisive influence on my reading of St. Thomas. Léhu in fact offers an interpretation of the doctrine of St. Thomas in which Thomas's statements on reason as the measure and rule of morality, on the moral object, prudence, and the *recta ratio*, as well as the doctrine on natural law, are seen in a

as we have mentioned, that this perspective does not correspond at all to the neo-thomistic perspective that at the time was the most widely held in discourse on the natural moral law. For such thinkers, the natural law was seen—precisely in a Stoic sense—as a "law of nature," in the sense of a rule intrinsic to nature, which must be "read" and "applied" by human beings. This frequently led, however, to argumentative difficulties, and precisely in the areas of bioethics and sexual ethics—it is enough to think of the contraception question, which was too often argued referring to the "biological structures" of human nature, rather than placing the theme, as was done later in the encyclical *Humanae Vitae,* in the context of the virtue of chastity (i.e., nos. 21–22) and of intentionality (i.e., the intentional definition in no. 14, using the Latin *intendat*), and not in the purely biological openness of the sexual act to the transmission of human life.[17]

In any case, I believe that we can recognize without difficulty in John Paul II and in the doctrine set forth in the encyclical *Veritatis Splendor* the philosophy professor of 1956. As he already did in his lectures, he sees man as a person created in the image of God, who in virtue of the power of his intellect (which is a participation in the intellect and in the guiding wisdom of God), orients his actions toward his own true good. It is a reason anchored in the being of the human person, having in particular its point of departure in the natural aspirations of this being. Through these natural inclinations and *in* them he thus understands the human good so as to make of these inclinations (yet in the horizon of reason, that is, in the context of the entirety of the human being) the point of departure, the rule, or what is more, the law—precisely a natural law—of human action.

The Foundation in Reason of Ethical Argumentation
in the Sphere of Natural Law

The question that thus presents itself regards the repercussions that might follow from such a concept of natural law for the formulation and foundation of moral norms, especially in the area of the ethics of human life. Before addressing this problem, however, it is necessary to clarify an

---

systematic and coherent unity. I do not remember, however, whether I came across Léhu as a result of reading Wojtyla's Lublin lectures.

17. See chapters 2 and 3 of this volume.

even more basic question: what does it actually mean to establish moral norms on the basis of natural law? The criticism of arbitrariness is often raised against just this type of argumentation, since often what is asserted as "natural," and consequently "good," is simply what corresponds to one's own values and convictions, which obviously one had already possessed. Recourse to "nature" would thus serve only an after-the-fact legitimation of subjective and essentially arbitrary evaluations,[18] giving them an appearance of objectivity. The history of ethics has in fact always known new references to "nature," which risk giving an impression like that of Tertullian, who declared shaving one's beard or wearing colored clothing (because it does not match the natural color of sheeps' wool) to be unnatural, and thus morally prohibited. On more serious questions, until not long ago the question of organ transplants suggested the opinion that they were unnatural and therefore morally unacceptable, a position that has clearly been surpassed by today's moral theology. Similarly, in the area of social doctrine, worker participation was initially seen as incompatible with natural law, whereas not long afterward it was declared to be a natural right. Conversely, there were moral theologians shortly before *Humanae Vitae* who held that methods of hormonal control in the regulation of conception were not at all unnatural, given that nature acted similarly: moral reservations were thus thought to be unnecessary. Some, citing the natural occurrence of spontaneous abortions, went so far as to justify abortion, understanding it as a simple imitation of nature and thus something "natural," and morally licit in some cases.

Recourse to nature, therefore, also has its dangers and is sometimes treacherous. The problem is located basically in the fact that "nature in ethical argumentation can never appear solely as 'nature.'" As Léhu had already established, we do not come to know the natural law through human nature, but we do come to know human nature (fully) through the natural law. According to St. Thomas, the nature or essence of things, in itself, is unknown to us. We recognize it by means of the virtues (recall that for Thomas the inclinations are the seeds of the virtues) and the act of being in question.[19] Human nature manifests itself in the natural

18. See for example the critical article of G. Zagrebelsky, "Le false risposte del diritto naturale," *La Repubblica* 80, no. 4 (2007): 1–23.

19. Thomas Aquinas, *De veritate*, 10, 1. "Quia vero rerum essentiae sunt nobis ignotae,

inclinations, as understood by reason as a human good. Consequently, to be relevant ethically, "nature" always has need of a further recourse to reason. Nature must in some way be shown as a necessary presupposition—according to Thomas, as a *praesuppositio*—of the *ordo rationis* that is built on it; that nature is such a presupposition, and why it is so can, in turn, be shown only by reason.[20] This is so because the "human nature" to which one wants to have recourse goes beyond "nature" in the strict sense, since it also includes in itself the spiritual dimension of man, his rationality, and his freedom. In man, these latter are also, even if in a different way, "nature." They do not belong to an externally visible nature, but they do constitute a "nature," which is (once again) accessible only through the self-consciousness of the subject's intellectual acts (in fact spiritual acts—acts of reason and will—cannot be perceived from the outside, but are accessible only to the introspection of the subject who performs these acts; only by means of reflexive self-consciousness can we thus know "human nature").

Therefore only reason, and not "nature pure and simple," allows it to be shown that "nature"—as corporeity—is morally relevant and normative, and in what way. And it is precisely here that we locate the function of the natural law. Precisely for this reason we are dealing with a law, and therefore with a natural rule, because, like every law, it pertains to reason and, as Thomas says, is "constituted" by reason as *dictamen rationis* at the level of the most fundamental and general practical principles. The "true meaning of the natural law," underscores John Paul II in *Veritatis Splendor,* "refers to man's proper and primordial nature, the 'nature of the human person,' which is *the person himself in the unity of soul and body,* in the unity of his spiritual and biological inclinations and of all the other specific characteristics necessary for the pursuit of his end" (*VS,* n. 50).

virtutes autem earum innotescunt nobis per actus . . . ." Cf. on this M. Rhonheimer, *La prospettiva della morale. Fondamenti dell'etica filosofica,* 2nd expanded ed. (Rome: Armando, 2006), 161–66 (in English as *The Perspective of Morality: Philosophical Foundations of Thomistic Virtue Ethics* [Washington, D.C.: The Catholic University of America Press, forthcoming]), and "Sulla fondazione di norme morali a partire dalla natura," *Rivista di filosofia Neo-Scolastica* 89 (1997): 515–35.

20. See e.g., II-II, q.154, a.12. I analyzed this passage extensively in *Natur als Grundlage der Moral,* 111–125 (= *Natural Law and Practical Reason,* 94–109). See also "The Moral Significance of Pre-Rational Nature in Aquinas" (reprinted as chapter 6 in *Perspective of the Acting Person*).

Nature is revealed as *human* nature only and exclusively insofar as it is the object of reason—thus in its intelligibility. Thus also the natural inclinations are "natural law" only insofar as they are a *bonum rationis*, therefore as "regulated" by reason.[21] Ethical arguments that have recourse to nature must consequently have a rational character, demonstrating why and in what sense here "nature"—understood as a collection of natural facts, or as a biological structure, and so on—would be relevant in a normative and moral sense. For example: a woman's natural cycle as such, that is, as a biological fact, is not yet morally relevant. It would be mistaken, for example, to maintain the following argument: given that sexuality is by nature oriented toward reproduction, it would be immoral to have sexual relations in naturally infertile periods. It would be similarly mistaken to define as morally just the use of the natural periods of infertility to regulate conception, simply because it is natural in this biological sense. Both cases are in need of argumentation based on reason. In the first case it is precisely reason that shows that here "nature" is not morally relevant: even if sexuality is preordained to reproduction, in the conjugal context of personal love it is characterized by a further dimension, which in the light of moral reasoning provides a justification of sexual activity also in infertile periods. In the second case, on the other hand, the opportunity to respect the natural cycles offered by the practice of periodic continence does not result only from the simple fact that it is "natural," but because it corresponds to the essence of the human person as a free and responsible being, who becomes conscious of his responsibility—conjugal, parental, procreative responsibility—precisely according to "human nature," taking into account, that is, the body-spirit unity of man.[22]

21. Thomas Aquinas, *Summa theologiae*, I-II, q.94, a.2, ad 2: "All the inclinations of any parts whatsoever of human nature, e.g. of the concupiscible and irascible parts, in so far as they are ruled by reason, belong to the natural law . . . ."

22. John Paul II sought to clarify these relationships in his 1984 catechesis on *Humanae Vitae*. Nevertheless, the recourse to nature and the use of the concept "natural law" in this catechesis, which precedes *Veritatis Splendor* by almost ten years, is anything but univocal; rather, it oscillates between "nature" and "reason" or "virtue." One gets the impression that in 1984, John Paul II still had difficulty putting the two together. From the four catecheses of August 8, 22, and 29 and September 5, it is clear that John Paul II did not argue on the basis of a direct and simple recourse to nature (see John Paul II, *The Theology of the Body: Human Love in the Divine Plan* [Boston: Pauline Books and Media, 1997], 395–403). Even if he gives the impression of seeing the woman's natural cycle as a "natural law" that imposes a submission to this regulation, and thus seeing in it a moral norm, an attentive examination

The recourse to nature in ethical argumentation, therefore, is in reality more complex than it often seems. A second element, however, must also be considered. As we have seen, the concept of natural law, as expounded by John Paul II in *VS*, is not reducible to the notion of a "natural order" or of a legality given according to nature; in a wider sense, again inspired by Thomas Aquinas, natural law belongs rather to the practical reason of the acting subject, who in his reason participates in the eternal reason of the Creator, and in this way orders his action to the good. This is why St. Thomas calls the *lex naturalis* a "*partecipatio legis aeternae in rationali creatura.*"[23] The natural law is a participation in the eternal law, because the light of divine reason is reflected in human reason itself. This also explains Thomas's continual recourse to a citation from Psalm 4 (according to the Latin translation of the old Vulgate) where the psalmist says, "*The light of your face, Lord, has been impressed upon us*" so that we might recognize the good,[24] "as though he wanted to say that the light of natural reason, with which we distinguish good from evil—which is the task of the natural law—is none other than an impression in us of the divine light."[25]

Now, if the natural law that formulates the maxims and fundamental principles—in the form of the commandments (or prohibitions) of the natural law—is "a work of reason,"[26] not understood as a creative reason,

---

shows that the argument is more complex. In fact, the moral-normative importance of the "natural rhythms" is shown once they are set in relation to an anthropology of the moral virtues, and in particular of the virtue of chastity, which in turn has as a presupposition the concept of the person as a free and rational creature who is master of his own actions. The decisive argument for explaining the difference between ethically illicit contraception and morally unexceptionable periodic abstinence is found, as John Paul II explains, in the context of the free choice of one's behavior (as was already emphasized in *Humanae Vitae*, n. 16). Only based on this presupposition can the cycles of fertility, and thus "nature," become recognizable with respect to their moral relevance. More clear and consistent, and focused on the essential point, is John Paul II's argumentation some years later in his greeting of January 10, 1992, to the participants in a course of formation for teachers of natural methods (available at: http://www.vatican.va/holy_father/john_paul_ii/speeches/1992/january/documents/hf_jp-ii_spe_19920110_metodi-naturali_it.html).

23. *Summa theologiae* I-II, q.91, a.2.

24. Ibid., I-II, 91, 2; "Multi dicunt, Quis ostendit nobis bona? . . . Signatum est super nos lumen vultus tui. Domine." Cf. also *VS* 42.

25. Ibid., cited in *VS*, n. 42: "quasi lumen rationis naturalis, quo discernimus quid sit bonum et malum, quod pertinet ad naturalem legem, nihil aliud sit quam impressio divini luminis in nobis."

26. Ibid., I-II, 94, 1: "lex naturalis est aliquid per rationem constitutum; sicut etiam propositio est quoddam opus rationis."

but as a created reason which participates in the eternal and creating reason of God, then this means that the moral "species" of actions, which we can identify as morally good or evil according to their object, are also in some way dictated by reason. St. Thomas, in fact, defines the moral "*species*" of an action, and thus also its so-called "moral object," as a *forma a ratione concepta*.[27] The objects of action, which determine actions in their "species," are not preexisting "things of nature," entities or elements already found in nature,[28] but something in the formation of which reason takes part in an essential and constitutive way. The moral "*species*" and the objects of human action are configurable, therefore, only in the light of natural reason, not only in the obvious sense, that is, that human reason is capable of recognizing them, but in the sense that in the recognition of nature pure and simple there is a "more," or that which St. Thomas calls the *bonum rationis:* the objects of actions become a good of reason and recognizable by reason (as an evil, by contrast, opposes reason).[29] This does not mean that these objects must be thought of as a free construction of reason; rather they are the knowledge of structures, which are already prefigured in the divine intellect and come to be recognized in the natural inclinations precisely through the light of natural reason.

Without wanting, in this context, to further investigate some implications of this Thomistic doctrine, we nevertheless want to ask whether it had repercussions in *Veritatis Splendor,* and specifically in the place where the encyclical speaks of the object of human action (especially *VS*, n. 78). I would argue that it did. Indeed, from the outset *VS* treats the question from a perspective that refers continually to the conception of natural law just articulated. The decisive passage in *VS*, n. 78, begins with the following words: "The morality of the human act depends primarily and fundamentally on the object rationally chosen by the deliberate will" (*deliberata voluntate rationaliter electo*). The object is thus defined from the outset as a matter of reason. To understand this, according to *VS*, we must put ourselves "in the perspective of the acting person," meaning that the objects of human actions must be distinguished with respect to their species (as

27. Ibid. I-II, 18, 10: "sicut species rerum naturalium constituuntur ex naturalibus formis, ita species moralium actuum constituuntur ex formis prout sunt a ratione conceptae."

28. I should note that some scholars, such as Lawrence Dewan, O.P., and Stephen L. Brock, disagree with this claim, but the present context does not allow for a detailed response to their helpful contributions to the discussion.

29. For the Thomistic doctrine on the *bonum rationis* cf. Léhu, *La raison.*

"good" and "evil," "just" or "unjust," or more specifically as "homicide," "giving alms," "lying," or "gratitude"), and not understood as "a process or an event of the purely physical order." The object of an action, rather, is the "proximate end [*finis proximus*] of a deliberate decision" ("decision" is the word used in the official English translation on the Vatican's Web site; yet the Latin text says "*electio*," that is, "choice," though on the Vatican's Web site there is an amusing typo because it says "*delectio*").

The object is thus described as a type of "end";[30] as we will see, it is precisely the end of the *election,* or choice. It is something intentional. It refers to that fundamental proximate end (*finis proximus*) that regards in the first place the elective will, entirely independent of other objectives for which the action has been chosen (and which are traditionally called *finis operantis*).[31] The *finis proximus* is that which decides what, prescinding from other intentions, is done. Even if in the manuals the "object" is generally distinguished from the "end," "proposal," or "intention," in a certain sense the object itself, precisely as the *finis proximus* of a free choice, is also an "end" that the one who acts pursues, and therefore a *finis operantis*.[32] Nevertheless, the object is not, so to speak, freely at our disposal, because if in fact someone (with full consciousness of the meaning of his action) fires a gun aiming at a person's heart, we have, independently of other intentions—therefore purely from the point of view of the object—an act of homicide. The question is not as simple as that, however, because we always distinguish killing as mur-

<hr/>

30. This also was already clearly seen by Léonard Léhu; "l'objet est la fin de l'acte" (*La raison,* 49); Thomas Aquinas, *Summa theologiae* I-II, q.73, a.3m "Obiecta autem actuum sunt fines eorum."

31. With this the formulation in *VS,* n. 80, also becomes comprehensible, viz., that some actions are "intrinsically evil" (*intrinsece malum*) "always and per se, in other words, on account of their very object, and quite apart from the ulterior intentions of the one acting and the circumstances." These "ulterior intentions" indicate that the object itself is an "intention," something foreseen by the elective will guided by reason, that which one "aims at," i.e., precisely the *finis proximus* of the action.

32. Servais Pinckaers called attention to this now many years ago, in his pioneering study: "Le rôle de la fin dans l'action morale selon Saint Thomas," in *Le renouveau de la morale* (Tornai: Casterman, 1964), 114–43; orig. published in *Revue des Sciences philosophiques et théologique* 45 (1961): 393–421). I personally owe much regarding my understanding of Thomas to the perspective that Pinckaers develops in this treatise, even if on some points I would have some reservations and would make some changes; see on this M. Rhonheimer, "The Perspective of the Acting Person and the Nature of Practical Reason: The 'Object of the Human Act' in Thomistic Anthropology of Action," *Nova et Vetera* (English ed.) 2, no. 2 (2004): 461–516, note 29; reprinted as chapter 8 in my book *The Perspective of the Acting Person.*

der from killing to carry out the death penalty, killing in war, and killing in (private) self-defense. All of these actions are, at least according
to the traditional teaching, "different" according to their object. Only
reason can distinguish this difference, however, and only in the perspective of reason—the "perspective of the acting person," according to *VS*,
n. 78—can such acts be recognized as homicide, murder, or something
specifically different with respect to their objects.[33]

The fact that the morally relevant object of a human action is an
object of reason, and only as such is the object of the will and of its *finis
proximus*, also makes it possible that between the principles of practical
reason, from which derive the precepts (or the prohibitions) of the natural law, there is a recognizable and unequivocal connection. All of the
goods that reason naturally comprehends as human goods in the natural inclinations of the human subject, and that take form in relation to
the principles of practical reason and the precepts of the natural law[34]—
for the most general principles, this occurs with natural spontaneity—
are precisely objects of reason and ends of the will, a *voluntas ut natura,*
which at this higher level establishes the fundamental rationality, and
thus the morality, of human aspirations. It is precisely this, then, that is
concretized and "specified" in relation to specific types of action (which
are seen in themselves as good or evil), which can be defined according to the specific object: "friendship," "abortion," "euthanasia," "theft,"
"lying," "sodomy." (It is actually easier to define erroneous behaviors
than good ones, given that the latter are less delimited; thus most of the
commandments of the Decalogue are negative commandments, indicating prohibited, morally evil actions. An action considered from the
perspective of a good object—for example, to give alms—does not yet
say anything about whether the action that is actually performed is a
good one, given that, despite the good object, the further intentions—
and with these the entire action—can be evil. If the action is already

---

33. For Thomas, exactly this is the case, for example, with adultery: the difference between sexual relations in a legitimate marriage and in adultery is not in the "nature" (of the
sexual act), but in the definition of the sexual partner as "my wife" or "my husband." This
distinction is, for Thomas, one of reason, see Thomas Aquinas, *De malo,* q. 2, a. 4: "conoscere mulierem suam et conoscere mulierem non suam, sunt actus habentes obiecta differentia
secundum aliquid ad rationem pertinens; nam suum et non suum determinantur secundum
regulam rationis."

34. Thomas Aquinas, *Summa theologiae* I-II, q.94, a.2.

made evil by its object, however, further good intentions can not change the fact that the entire action is to be judged evil.)

With this we can finally turn to the question of the way in which this doctrine on the natural law, as expounded in *VS*, is applied with respect to the ethics of human life, and especially concerning the three great themes that John Paul II addressed in the encyclical *Evangelium Vitae*: the direct killing of an innocent person, abortion, and euthanasia. It should already be clear that we must not look so much on the side of pure and simple "nature" as on the side of the will guided by reason. The question regarding the contradiction of the mentioned actions with the natural law in effect becomes the following: why does a certain action, as a *finis proximus*, as an immediate end of the choosing will guided by reason, contradict the natural law and therefore also the fundamental human good? This question was responded to by John Paul II in the encyclical *Evangelium Vitae* (*EV*).

The Natural Law and Ethical Argumentation in the Area of the Ethics of Human Life

It will not be difficult to identify this response, given that we are now ready to focus our attention on the essential formulations. Above all, it seems important that we correctly understand the formulations by which the respective ways of acting are precisely described, and in this way defined in their ethical content. We will begin with the action that the Church condemns as "homicide" or "murder," that is, the prohibition of killing.[35]

The Foundation on Natural Law of the Absolute Prohibition of Killing According to *Evangelium Vitae*

The doctrine on the sacredness and inviolability of human life, as expounded in *EV*, is certainly basic from the perspective of the theology of

---

35. I have written on this argument more thoroughly and systematically in my *Vital Conflicts in Medical Ethics: A Virtue Approach to Craniotomy and Tubal Pregnancies* (Washington, D.C.: The Catholic University of America Press, 2009), especially 138–44. This work was originally written in 2000, for the Congregation for the Doctrine of the Faith, and was published at their explicit request as M. Rhonheimer, *Abtreibung und Lebensschutz. Tötungsverbot und Recht auf Leben in der politischen und medizinischen Ethik* (Paderborn: Schöningh, 2003).

creation, and yet from an ethical-practical point of view it is insufficient for precisely distinguishing murder from other forms of killing that may be legitimate. Human beings are not "sacred cows" that cannot be killed even when another person becomes an immanent threat to their lives, as in the case of legitimate defense or, collectively, in a just defensive war. Given that there seem to be cases in which the killing of persons on the part of other persons is legitimate—which has never been denied by the Church, indeed the opposite is true—the "sacredness" and "inviolability" of human life cannot be the sole and final factors in the justification of the prohibition of killing, that is, the prohibition of homicide or of murder.

The question is also put in these terms in *EV*. Recourse to the sacredness of human life alone, in which the image of God is present, does not yet provide a justification of the absolute norm of the prohibition of killing. The reference to the sacredness of human life is more useful for establishing that in every actual violation of the prohibition of killing—where this truly occurs—we are dealing with "a particularly serious sin," because "only God is the master of life" (*EV*, n. 55). With this, however, it is not yet said *when* a transgression takes place. The decisive word for the foundation of the prohibition of killing on natural law is in fact said in *EV*, n. 57. It begins with a restriction to *innocent* people. Already, the category of "innocent" alludes to the fact that we are dealing with an object of reason. Guilt and innocence are not found in nature; rather they pertain to the nature of free action and of social relations understood as juridical relations, which in their turn are not natural facts or circumstances, but goods of reason. The distinction between legitimate and illegitimate killing is in fact a distinction of reason.

Decisive at this point, however, is the formulation of the true and proper prohibition of killing (*EV*, n. 57): "the deliberate decision [the official Latin texts says: *deliberatum consilium*] to deprive an innocent human being of his life is always morally evil and can never be licit either as an end in itself or as a means to a good end." Why is this formulation so important? Because it describes illicit killing as a "deliberate decision" (or "choice"), and therefore as a conscious decision or choice to make the death of a (innocent) person the *means* or (more improbably) even the *final objective* of an action. It should be emphasized that *EV* does not speak of "direct killing," but of "killing as a means." This is worth noting, since in this way the ambiguity of the term "indirect killing," used by moral theologians—a term that the magisterium has never used, nor is it used in *EV*—is avoided. Better than the expression "indirect killing," therefore, would be "killing that is not chosen as a *means*," as this expression is used in *EV*.[36]

The addition of the term "innocent" is important for excluding the case of the death penalty. Even if the Church increasingly rejects the death penalty, it nevertheless sees its execution, from the point of view of the object, as a different action, which could be justified in some circumstances (or could be in the past). But in the case of legitimate defense it is no longer necessary to add the term "innocent," given that it is never licit to choose the death of the aggressor (even if it is an "unjust aggressor") as a means, that is, to intend to kill him.[37] It is licit only to accept his death as a consequence of an action of self-defense that attempts to block the act of aggression.

The ethical substance of the prohibition of killing resides precisely in the fact that it is a violation of the principle of equality, and essentially of the Golden Rule, one of the first principles of the natural law in the sphere of justice ("Do not do to others what you would not want done to you!"). It is not the mere physical "destruction" of a life that constitutes the substance of the prohibition of killing, but the violation of equality, a fundamental relationship between human beings. The "right to life"— understood not so much as a civil right or as a general human right, but in the sense of a fundamental right that derives from the being of the person and from the natural inclination to the basic good of self-preservation inscribed in it—this right to life is violated precisely when one chooses the death of his equal as a means (and thus has the intention to kill) to reach some end, even a praiseworthy one (and obviously, also—despite its being both improbable and virtually a non-issue, except

36. "Indirect" is not the same thing as "not direct." "Not direct" is the negation of a category; "indirect" is a separate category, although a very equivocal one. It is better therefore to use "not direct," not as a synonym of "indirect" but in the sense of "not chosen as a means or an end." A more in-depth explanation of this can be found in my study, cited above: Rhonheimer, *Vital Conflicts in Medical Ethics, 147–48.*

37. Thomas Aquinas, *Summa theologiae* I-II, q.64, a.7: "it is not permitted that a man will the death of another man, to defend himself" (*illicitum est quod homo intendat killing hominem ut seipsum defendat*). See Rhonheimer, *Güterabwägung,* 174–78. On this also see Rhonheimer, "Sins against Justice," in *The Ethics of Aquinas,* ed. Stephen J. Pope (Washington, D.C.: Georgetown University Press, 2002), 287–303.

in pathological cases—when one chooses the death of another as an end).

EV, n. 57, continues: "As far as the right to life is concerned, every innocent human being is absolutely equal to all others. This equality is the basis of all authentic social relationships which, to be truly such, can only be founded on truth and justice, recognizing and protecting every man and woman as a person and not as an object to be used." Basic equality thus is the basis of the Golden Rule and the foundation of social life. Unjust killing always means to arrogate to oneself discretional power over the life of an equal, to use him for other ends, to the point of issuing judgments on the slight value of the life of another person or arriving at such circumstances that a good can be attained only through the act of killing. Moreover, unjust killing makes life together in society impossible, because the destruction of equality between people in turn undermines the foundations of relationships of justice. Every form of unjust killing, that is, every killing that comes under the absolute prohibition of killing, is therefore to be morally rejected.

These are not mere tautological word games or empty formulas. Rather, we touch here the very foundations of morality, and have entered the realm of first principles and of the moral commandments, precisely as they have been formulated by the natural law. To violate these commandments would mean to destroy moral knowledge, ethical reasoning, entirely, removing it from its moorings through grave internal incoherencies, throwing open the doors to moral arbitrariness and ultimately to the justification of human injustice. This is also the direction indicated by *EV*: it does not offer a purely theological argumentation (as, e.g., "a person is not authorized to dispose of human life, which is created by God and sacred"), but an argumentation that shows precisely at the level of natural law—therefore of the fundamental moral consciousness of the practical reason of the acting subject—that killing is unjust and morally unjustifiable when it violates, in a fundamental sense, the principle of justice, which in turn is based on the principle of equality. This is also expressed, incidentally, by the word "innocent": in the case of a guilty person, that is, one declared guilty of a serious crime in a legitimate trial, condemned to death, and executed according to the law, this person's "right to life" is not violated and thus there is no violation of the principle of equality (indeed, as *EV* emphasizes, equality is reestablished through such an action). From the theological point of view, capital punishment could be defined as immoral only if there were a positive divine commandment forbidding such an act. If anything, the opposite is the case. This does mean that capital punishment is in principle morally licit. It is immoral when it is unnecessary for attaining the end of reestablishing justice, and in this way protecting the foundations of social life—which means that today it is almost never justifiable (as in *EV*, n. 56). With respect to killing in war, on the other hand, it must be pointed out that in this case also it is not licit to choose the death of the aggressor as a means or even as an objective. The acts done in war, even those that by their nature aim at killing, must not be chosen *with the intention of killing,* but only to the end of blocking the aggression and of rendering the aggressor inoffensive (even when this means killing him). International humanitarian law considers the killing of the enemy outside of combat to be a war crime—homicide. Enemies who are no longer capable of fighting must be spared, and given medical care to the extent possible. Even in war, the death of the enemy must be neither a means nor an end; it therefore also falls under the prohibition of killing formulated in *EV*, n. 57. (To see the aggressor in the case of war as "guilty" and thus exempt from the prohibition of killing is unconvincing, given that, though the aggression may be unjust, the individual soldier in general does not bear the guilt, even if it is licit to fight him as part of an enemy combat unit; in any case, this case differs slightly from that of a guilty person who is condemned to death for a crime in a trial. Killing in legitimate defense is similar to the case of war, but here the fact is added that the killing, in a true and proper sense, occurs *praeter intentionem.*)

It seems to me that these are the essentials concerning the foundation of the absolute prohibition of killing in natural law. Although there is not space in this setting for the corresponding analyses and arguments to be expounded in detail, John Paul II nevertheless offers, in *EV,* the points of departure for these analyses and explanations, as I have attempted to show.

An Application: The Absolute Prohibition of Abortion

In *EV* John Paul II speaks of the absolute prohibition of abortion, which derives directly from the general prohibition of killing, and is a simple application of it. Nevertheless, an additional difficulty presents itself here, that of whether the unborn child is actually an "equal"—which means a human person—and with this, if his killing can actually violate equality and justice, especially if urgent reasons and the safeguarding of higher goods would have a bearing on the decision to end his life.

It is clear that an unborn child would fall a priori under the category of "innocent." Even when he represents a danger to the mother's life, not only is he not an "unjust aggressor," but he is not an aggressor at all, since he does no action that could represent an aggression: an embryo or a fetus performs no "human acts" (in the classical sense of *actus humanus*). In certain cases his existence in the mother's womb could constitute a danger to the life or health of the mother, but this is certainly not an aggression. One cannot, for example, define highly contagious people as aggressors and do away with them, even if they do constitute a grave threat to others; such a threat does not make them aggressors. Moreover, it is morally illicit—at least, as mentioned above, if one follows St. Thomas—to intend to kill an aggressor to save one's own life. One can only oppose the aggression, even if this could have mortal consequences. In any case, none of this is applicable to a fetus whose presence in the womb constitutes a threat to the life of the mother (and is even less applicable if a pregnancy or the birth of a baby results in other disadvantages thought to be serious).

If it is presumed that human embryos and fetuses are persons and therefore "equals," then with abortion the right of equality that is at the foundation of the right to life, and with it justice, are entirely trampled upon; in this case we have pure discrimination against the unborn on the part of those already born. For the latter, such discrimination poses absolutely no risk, given that it is based on a simple difference of power. Moreover, one who is born could never find himself in the situation of an unborn child (in a way even clearer than the fact that juridical discrimination against blacks poses no risk for whites, given that those doing the discriminating run no risk of finding themselves in the group being discriminated against).[38]

Thus *EV,* n. 62, condemns abortion as "the deliberate killing of an innocent human being," employing the same argumentation used for the

---

38. See on this my argumentation in M. Rhonheimer, "Fundamental Rights, Moral Law, and the Legal Defense of Life in a Constitutional Democracy: A Constitutionalist Approach to the Encyclical Evangelium Vitae," *American Journal of Jurisprudence* 43 (1998): 135–83, which is reprinted as chapter 7 of the present volume.

general prohibition of killing. The question remains, however, whether the unborn are in fact "persons," that is, human beings with the same moral status as those who have been born (e.g., a newborn or a three-year-old child). This is actually not a moral question—or a question of natural law—but one of facts. Obviously, facts are very important for morality. In this case, however, the fact that the unborn are human persons adds nothing to the argumentation underlying the moral norm—the prohibition of killing—but only to its *application* or its *extent*.

I must admit that, in my opinion, *EV* lacks courage on this question, speaking only with hesitation of the unborn as *persons* (see *EV*, n. 60). As I have said, this does not invalidate the argument that underlies the prohibition of killing as such. Nor does it weaken the theological foundation of the prohibition of abortion, which is based on divine revelation, the sacred Scriptures, and the Christian Tradition. *EV* also mentions the projective nature of human life from the genetic perspective, beginning at the moment of fertilization and with the corresponding continuity and necessity in its development. Attention is rightly called to the fact that "the presence of a spiritual soul cannot be ascertained by empirical data." Nevertheless, it gives the impression that strict arguments do not exist that are apt for demonstrating the personal character of embryos and fetuses, but only "indications" in this regard. Their being a person is established rather by the rhetorical question: "Could a human individual not be a human person?"[39]

This is the question that remains to be clarified. The response is truly close at hand, even if *EV* does not clearly express it. It is a response of a metaphysical or ontological nature, and is based simply on the fact that an individual that has in itself the potential, the capacity, to develop the typical characteristics of a person (and which characteristics pertain to the nature of the person) must already be a person. *Only persons can develop the qualities of a person, drawing these qualities from themselves,* even though these characteristics, at a particular stage of development, are possessed only potentially, as predispositions. Precisely because they possess in potential the properties of persons, human embryos and fetuses are themselves persons. They are not, for example, "*potential* per-

39. In reference to the 1987 Instruction *Donum Vitae* by the Congregation for the Doctrine of the Faith. The 2008 Instruction *Dignitas Personae* by the same Congregation, however, is much clearer on this subject.

sons"; their "being a person" is *actual*: they are, therefore, according to their nature, human persons. "Being a person" is not a property; rather, it defines the "nature" of a being. Individuals that according to their nature are persons will develop the corresponding properties over time, precisely by the fact that they are, by their nature, persons. Therefore, as has been said, they are absolutely not "potential persons"; not *being* a person, but the *properties* of the person, are possessed only in potential—and this precisely because they are persons.

Human embryos and fetuses possess, therefore, already *in actu,* the first and most essential property of the person: the intrinsic capacity to develop all of the other properties of the person. (Even though newborns and small children do not yet possess all of the properties of [adult] persons, they are not because of this less persons than adults are. Being a person is not a collection of properties, but a *nature,* according to which one possesses or develops such characteristics).

These are fundamental ontological truths, which are also at the basis of our everyday moral judgments. Just because it is not possible to see the "being a person" of fetuses, or because the properties typical of persons have not yet been formed in them (though we know with certainty that they possess the potential for these), one cannot deny their being a person. Likewise, it is not a problem, as *EV* says, that the soul cannot be observed by experimentation—since neither can the souls of adults be seen by experiments! It is the qualities of persons, rather, that are observable, which derive from this soul and are caused by it. Human embryos and fetuses, for their part, possess the capacity, based on their genetic program, to necessarily develop these properties *on the basis of their very nature,* and they will in fact develop them if they are not killed first: they therefore possess the capacity to develop and show the properties typical of the person. One does not need to be able to observe the soul to understand this fact. Indeed, the opposite is true: a being that possesses the capacity to develop properties that essentially presuppose a soul—and therefore the properties of a person—already possesses a soul! The soul is the substantial form and the principle of life, which confers on matter a specific actuality. A being that according to its nature is a person and develops personal (spiritual) properties, must consequently possess a corresponding soul—the soul of a human *person*—from the beginning of its development. From this we can, through metaphysical argumentation and even on the basis of observation and scientific verification, deduce the existence of a spiritual soul in individual unborn humans, to the point of arriving at the following statement: every individual that belongs to the species *Homo sapiens* is a person.

For this reason, based on the argumentation expounded in *EV*, one can also justify on the basis of natural law the necessity of applying the absolute prohibition of killing also to the unborn, in every stage of development beginning with conception. For the cited reasons, an unborn human individual possesses *at least one* right: the right not to be killed, or better, the *right to live*. To terminate his life would be to prevent him from developing according to what he is: a human person. For this reason every abortion is *unjust* in the most basic sense, and thus morally inadmissible.

Euthanasia and the General Prohibition of Killing

The final case to be addressed in this setting is the prohibition of euthanasia. On this theme we encounter problems analogous to those above. From a moral perspective, an action or an omission that provokes the death of a dying person, *in a purely physical-causal way,* cannot yet be generally qualified as illicit. In the argument against euthanasia, the relationship between the natural law as a commandment (prohibition) of the practical reason and the rational determination of the moral object as a *finis proximus*—and thus of its intentional character—stands out very clearly.

This becomes evident in the definition of euthanasia proposed by *EV*, n. 65 (for the cases of the act of killing in general and of abortion, the simple description of the action is less difficult): "Euthanasia in the strict sense is understood to be an action or omission which of itself and by intention causes death, with the purpose of eliminating all suffering." Referring to the 1980 Declaration on Euthanasia *Iura et bona* of the Congregation for the Doctrine of the Faith, the two key elements are again highlighted: the "purpose of the will" and "the mode of proceeding." Insufficient, therefore, is a simple action (or failure to act) that "by its nature" provokes death (this would be the "mode of proceeding"), but also necessary is "the deliberate will to bring about death," a consideration that applies in cases of both action and omission. Legitimate (so-called passive) euthanasia is not characterized therefore by the fact that it must involve a "simple omission"—such as the interruption of artificial respiration, or refraining from nourishing as opposed to poisoning—but is indicated by an act or an interruption perpetrated *without the intention of killing*. The moral object of the action called morally inadmissible "euthanasia," on the other hand, can be indicated if the death of the patient is intended as the *finis proximus* of the action or the omission, thus including the fundamental intentional relation of the concrete act or omission with the physical consequence of death. (Also, the omissions spoken of are not simply non-actions—as the absence of a practical choice—but are based on a conscious choice, precisely the choice not to do something).

This said, euthanasia can now be referred to the general prohibition of killing. It is an act of killing precisely because it includes the intention of killing—the death is chosen as a means for shortening suffering—but not simply because it provokes death in a purely physical or biological sense. A passive or legitimate "euthanasia," which would be a doing or an omission of something—here also, both are possible—can be the physical cause of death, without however there being present a homicidal intention; the death in this case is chosen neither as a means nor as an end. What is done, or what is omitted, is not done or omitted for the end of killing, but because the judgment has been reached that the prolongation of life is no longer reasonable. To distinguish these two—killing and the non-prolongation of life—further criteria are needed. The most widely known of these is the distinction between ordinary and extraordinary means of prolonging life. Despite the fact that gray areas can exist—things are not always clear—this criterion is apt for identifying those cases in which it can be claimed that nature has already decided, and one is dealing only with not prolonging further the final struggle with death. In this case we are not dealing with killing, but with ceasing to slow, or even to stop, the process of death by artificial means: it is a matter here of letting someone die.

Conclusion

I believe that the three examples addressed in the encyclical *Evangelium Vitae* show how the magisterium of John Paul II, through his teaching on natural law, has presented a coherent doctrine on the determination of the moral object of an action, and the application of this doctrine in the area of the question of the prohibition of killing. This doctrine reflects throughout the characteristics of man understood as a free being endowed with reason, created in the image of God—and, in the sense articulated above, autonomous—who, based on the light of reason and dominion over his own acts, realizes his "being man," perfecting himself according to the moral virtues. Thanks to the light of reason, received from God, as St. Thomas says, at the moment of our creation, the natural law is formed, which finds expression in a series of first and universal principles of action (commandments and prohibitions) through which we can orient our action to the true human good. These principles at the same time constitute, as natural law, the foundation of human coexistence in society.

PART I

Sexuality and Responsibility

Contraception as an
Ethical Problem

Prologue

Contraception and Virtue

Since 1968 the public debate about *Humanae Vitae* has been
undermined by the erroneous and confusing assertion that the
encyclical specifically rejects *artificial* birth control, considering this to be an illicit interference with nature.[1] Yet in *Humanae Vitae* there is no such teaching. The encyclical actually unfolds what had been briefly stated by Vatican II in *Gaudium et
Spes* (no. 51): that "the question of harmonizing conjugal love
with the responsible transmission of life ... must be determined by objective standards" that are "based on the nature
of the human person and his acts" and "preserve the full sense
of mutual self-giving and human procreation in the context of
true love." This, the text concludes, "cannot be achieved unless
the virtue of conjugal chastity is sincerely practiced."

Unfortunately, right from the start dissenting theologians
interpreted the encyclical's teaching in the light of the naturalistic and legalistic patterns in which they had been educated
before Vatican II, based on a misreading of the Thomistic tradition. Imbued with the logic of a naturalistic understanding
of natural law, and at the same time trying to escape from its
shortcomings, they now said that interference with nature by

1. This prologue was originally written in 2004 as a brief and readily accessible account of the present approach to explaining the teaching of *Humanae
vitae* regarding the morality of contraception. It is included here to indicate the
basic lines of the account that will be developed at length in the first part of the
present volume.

"artificial" methods was not necessarily immoral, provided it was done for the good of the person. In an attempt to convince the pope, the (rejected) majority report of the papal commission, which was instituted to study the problem, asserted, for example, that contraception was similar to capital punishment: causing a physical evil to achieve a higher moral good.

Yet the teaching of *Humanae Vitae* on responsible parenthood wisely emphasizes conjugal love and the virtue of chastity and not the "natural" as opposed to the "artificial." Because of its complexity and delicate nature, it is a teaching that is not easy to summarize and convey. Admittedly, the encyclical's text seems sometimes confusing and lacking in clarity, partly because it brings together different approaches to the problem. Yet, an encyclical is not meant to be a systematic treatise of moral theology, but an authoritative teaching of Catholic doctrine. What is that doctrine?

Some people have found it very difficult to understand *Humanae Vitae* because of what they consider a contradiction in its text: at one point the encyclical asserts that "each and every marriage act must remain open to the transmission of life"; but elsewhere the same document declares conjugal intercourse to be lawful for expressing marital love even if foreseen to be infecund, provided this is "for causes independent of the will of the husband and wife" (no. 11). What does this "openness" mean and why is it so important?

The obscurity comes in part from the English translation. The official Latin text does not speak about "openness" but says that each and every marriage act has to be "per se orientated (*per se destinatus*) toward the transmission of life." In other words, the required "openness" of each marital act to procreation is not a property of marital acts insofar as they are physical acts, but considered as *intentional* actions, that is, insofar as they are the object of a choosing will. Such intentional openness means that every marital act must always be chosen and carried out as an act that embodies the spouses' commitment to responsibly serving the task of transmitting life. This intentional openness rules out an intentional act against the transmission of life, but it does not rule out marital acts that cannot be physically generative independent from one's intentions (e.g., for natural reasons).

Humanae Vitae grounds this teaching on the principle that both the unitive and the procreative meanings of human sexuality are constitutive for each other and must therefore be considered as inseparable: only in their connection do they form a *conjugal* act of love. Human life springs from conjugal love, and conjugal love is characteristically shaped by the task of transmitting human life. Yet, the inseparability principle is not sufficient to understand why contraception is evil whereas limiting marital acts to unfertile periods, when reason dictates one ought not to conceive, is good. This is the crucial question that must be answered.

What is contraception? *Humanae Vitae* no. 14 describes it by declaring that "excluded is every action which, either in anticipation of the conjugal act, or in its accomplishment, or in the development of its natural consequences, propose, whether as an end or as a means, to render procreation impossible." The moral norm prohibiting contraception thus refers to a choice—the contraceptive choice—that is the choice of an act that prevents freely consented performances of sexual intercourse, which are foreseen to have procreative consequences, from having these consequences, and that is a choice made just for this reason. The moral evil of contraception resides precisely in the choice of this type of act, not in the fact of subsequent infertility.

The contraceptive choice is essentially an alternative to abstaining from the sexual act that might have procreative consequences. The contraceptive act is chosen precisely to avoid the need of such acts of refraining from sexual intercourse. Thus, the morality of contraception is not properly framed as a question of artificially interfering with nature, but rather as one regarding how spouses intelligently and virtuously relate to their own bodies, to the body of their partner, and generally to sexuality and its natural dynamics of desire, pleasure, and procreation.

As, in fact, *Humanae Vitae* no. 16 points out, the reason why contraception is wrong appears in the light of the reasons for which periodic continence is good. By abstaining periodically for reasons of responsibility, spouses carry out their sexual acts responsibly, according to reason and virtue, and consistent with their nature as bodily constituted persons, growing in the virtuous integration of their fertility as they do so. The bodily and sexual dimensions of conjugal love are therefore properly recognized as integral to the acting person. Marital love, responsibly lived, thus speaks what John Paul II calls the "language of the body." In this way, the natural inclination of sexuality is shaped by the

spiritual logic of personal love and mutual self-giving. This is the virtue of chastity, part of the cardinal virtue of temperance, which enables us to follow our sensual drives in accordance with reason and true love.

As Thomas Aquinas says, vices must be understood in the light of the virtue to which they are opposed. Because of the contraceptive choice and act underlying it, "contracepted" sex is structurally vicious—though in different degrees, depending on circumstances—because contraception has purposely rendered needless a specific sexual and bodily behavior of virtuous self-control informed by procreative responsibility. When it is intentionally shaped by a contraceptive choice, conjugal sexuality is no longer an act that embodies mutual love of two persons who are responsibly engaged in the task of transmitting human life; in reality it is sex deprived of its specifically marital meaning.

In contrast, by a couple's adopting periodic continence, both acts of responsibly and periodically abstaining and acts of marital intercourse during knowingly unfertile times fully share in this life-giving meaning of sexuality. The unitive meaning of marital sexual acts is enriched by the awareness of being jointly engaged in the task of responsibly transmitting human life. This enrichment, of course, may also imply a burden, cause considerable hardship, and demand sacrifice. But all this will be, or ought to be, an additional source for the deepening and maturation of conjugal love; and it is quite consistent with a Christian life ordered to sanctity and rejecting minimalism.

Periodic continence is not simply another method, "natural" instead of "artificial." In contrast to contraception, it is not a method at all (although the means to gain knowledge about the cycle are); rather, it is a virtuous lifestyle in which the spouses are continuously engaged as a community of persons at the service of the responsible transmission of life. Animals fulfill the task of transmitting new life guided by instinct; they cannot be unchaste. Human persons fulfill this task guided by reason and through responsible self-control of their sensual drives and bodily acts, in a common, shared experience of love. This, again, is the virtue of conjugal chastity.

The body and with it sexuality is not—as Karl Rahner has confusingly written—a "sub-personal" sphere of the human being that can be "treated" or "manipulated" like a thing; rather it is the human subject itself and an intrinsically constitutive part of the human person. *Huma-*

nae Vitae puts forward a non-dualistic anthropology that sees marital love as essentially sexual and human sexuality as essentially marital and personal. Because it implies at least a choice against modifying one's own sexual behavior for reasons of procreative responsibility and thus denies the behavioral unity of body and spirit, contraception ultimately contradicts the nature of human sexual acts *as acts of a person* who is constituted bodily.

Although contracepted intercourse can be subjectively perceived as an expression of true love, it is objectively distorted by an underlying dynamic that is self-gratifying and isolating and therefore deficient in contributing to marital unity. Moreover, this self-gratifying dynamic, as *Humanae Vitae* clearly points out in no. 17, is corrosive of marital love. Unlike naturally given infertility, contraception deliberately deprives sexuality of its basic self-transcending meaning—of its proper "task." By eschewing the need of common renouncement and self-denial, contraception not only circumvents the cultivation of those virtues that make one capable of spousal self-giving, but despoils conjugal sex of what is arguably its most unitive and enriching feature. Paradoxically, thus, contraception must be rejected precisely to safeguard the unitive purpose of conjugal sex.

Admittedly, marital acts rendered sterile through contraception can still be to some extent psychologically unitive. The degree to which contraception will undermine the unitive capacity of conjugal sex depends on many factors. It will be more corrosive for the capacity of expressing and nourishing conjugal unity when it is part of a selfish or materialistic life-project that intends to avoid completely or reduce the burdens of raising children; and it will be less grave, but still morally disordered, if chosen as a last resort in real hard cases that do not include such a selfish or small-minded life plan.

Chastity, of course, is not the highest virtue, and there are other factors that can be corrosive for conjugal love. But chastity is indispensable for human persons to achieve emotional maturity and to be able to really give themselves to another person in true and faithful love. Those who desire sex at low cost will tend to be less willing to pay the high price of enduring love and lifelong faithfulness.

In an ethical outlook centered on the virtues, the question is not "How far can I go so as not to violate the law and still remain a respectable person?" but "In which direction do I have to go so as to attain the goal of human and Christian fulfillment that virtue proposes and the universal call to holiness demands?" In this perspective of virtue and holiness, everything that is intrinsically opposed to this goal can be understood as a moral evil. Contraception is intrinsically evil because it is essentially opposed to conjugal chastity and its requirement of a parentally responsible and virtuous bodily-sexual behavior. It is therefore opposed to the human good, natural law, and the sanctity to which we are called.

The moral law both natural and divinely revealed is not simply a set of prescriptions or rules not to be violated, but the expression of the human good that consists in the virtues, and the guideline to practice these virtues and to attain holiness. Marriage and conjugal love involve the common journey of two persons toward this goal. What is most important in a journey is to take the right path and to follow it with every single step. This is why an acceptance of the procreative task of marriage *in general* is not sufficient; rather "each and every marriage act must remain open to the transmission of life." And this, as *Gaudium et Spes* has clearly asserted, "cannot be achieved unless the virtue of conjugal chastity is sincerely practiced."

The general acceptance of contraception has led to the widespread disconnection between sexuality and procreation. This view of sex as not intrinsically procreative promotes a lack of responsibility toward the undesired procreative consequences of one's sexual behavior; it thus generates a mentality that easily tolerates abortion, and ultimately promotes it as a positive good. Without caring for the rights of the unborn, this mentality sees abortion as a means of undoing the undesired generative consequences of one's sexual behavior. In turn, disconnecting sex from procreation has also led to the acceptability of procreation without sex: the transmission of human life not by an act of love but by biological engineering and productive calculus.

In reality, the bond between human sexuality and procreation is nothing else than the bond between conjugal love and the transmission of human life. When this inseparable unity between love and life is no longer firmly present in the collective conscience of a civilization, the basis for the respect due to every human being is severely undermined, and Christians will fail in their task of fostering the "culture of life" that is part of the "civilization of love."

2

The Post-conciliar State
of the Question on Contraception

The Encyclical, Relevant Case, Arguments, and
Description of Contraception

Introductory Remarks toward Understanding
the Encyclical *Humanae Vitae*

Contraception and "Natural Law"

The encyclical *Humanae Vitae* teaches that contraception violates natural law. "Natural law," however, is a rational standard for dividing actions into morally "good" and "bad" ways of behaving—a standard springing from man's natural reason. Ultimately—as the Church itself teaches in the encyclical *Veritatis Splendor* (nos. 12, 38–44)—the natural law is none other than the light of our intellect, by means of which we distinguish good and evil. The "natural law" as a "moral law" is not therefore "something" that would be the "object" of rational human knowledge (as, e.g., a "law of nature"). The natural law is rather what reason itself knows, that is, its practical judgments regarding good and evil, by means of which we responsibly carry out our free actions. As such, the natural law is a standard that derives from the human being's natural reason. This law is called "natural" because reason is part of human *nature*. This natural reason formulates—entirely independently of faith and revelation and in this sense "autonomously"—the fundamental demands of morality and humanity, demands that derive from the human being's humanity itself. For this reason, the analyses of the moral exigencies based on natural law pertain in the first place to philosophical ethics.

In order to show that contraception is the wrong thing to do for everybody, I think, the *basic* argument will therefore be one on the philosophical level. Yet, the aim of the encyclical *Humanae Vitae* was to teach authoritatively the Church's doctrine about true responsible parenthood, but not to substantiate it with a thorough, rational argument. This task is properly left to a further philosophical-ethical, and natural law, analysis. To provide such an analysis and therefore to offer a proper natural-law argument against contraception, understood as a particular type of human action, is the aim of this first part of the present book.

Someone might nevertheless object that there *is* rational and philosophically relevant argumentation contained in the encyclical itself. Admittedly, *Humanae Vitae* not only pronounces some ethically relevant anthropological principles but also includes arguments that obviously are aimed at justifying these principles, and it draws concrete moral conclusions from them. The fundamental contention of the encyclical is that contraception violates natural law. That is, it goes against the basic demands of morally good action, which also correspond to the dignity and good of the person—and *for this very reason* it contradicts God's will and his loving design for man. But does *Humanae Vitae* provide an answer to the question of why contraception violates natural law?

Surprisingly, most criticism of the encyclical was based on the assumption that its very wording actually did provide such an answer, and that this answer was simply derived from a naturalistic and "biological" understanding of natural law. According to these critics, *Humanae Vitae* teaches that the biological patterns inherent in the human generative faculty must never be acted against but must be respected unconditionally. "This," a well-known critic has asserted, "is undoubtedly the philosophy underpinning the argumentation of the whole encyclical. It goes so far as to declare biological laws as absolutely binding on the conscience of man."[1] A commentary published immediately after the encyclical ap-

1. See B. Häring: "The Inseparability of the Unitive-Procreative Functions of the Marital Act," in *Contraception: Authority and Dissent*, ed. C. Curran (New York: Herder and Herder, 1969), 180. Cf. as well the editor's contribution in this volume: C. Curran, "Natural Law and

peared says further: "The encyclical's teaching seems to stand simply on the basis of the physiological data of the conjugal act."[2]

Interpreting *Humanae Vitae* in this way, its critics had an easy job of rejecting its doctrine. But a careful look at the encyclical's text will give evidence that it never identifies "natural biological laws" with natural law in the *moral* sense, which would mean subordinating human good and moral action simply to such "natural laws."[3] For example, when no. 10 speaks of the biological forces of man's procreative faculty, *Humanae Vitae* there mentions only the first and basic requirement of responsible parenthood: the requirement of knowing what is going on with one's body, and of knowing that the physiological laws of this body and its sexual drives belong to the Self of human personhood. But other exigencies of responsible parenthood are added immediately: the requirement of exerting dominion by reason and will over one's "innate drives and emotions"; the requirement of either "prudently and generously" deciding "to have a large family" or, "for serious reasons and with due respect to the moral law," choosing "to have no more children for the time being or even for an indeterminate period"; finally the requirement of integration of all these aspects into the "objective moral order instituted by God—the order of which a right conscience is the true interpreter." Up to this point obviously nothing has been determined about *what* the requirements of this "objective moral order" concretely are.

In no. 11 the encyclical mentions the "laws of nature and the incidence of fertility," which, as a sign of God's wisdom, grant a certain

---

Contemporary Moral Theology," 159: "The encyclical on the regulation of birth employs a natural law methodology which tends to identify the moral action with the physical and biological structure of the act."

2. L. M. Weber, "Excurs über *Humanae vitae*," in *Lexikon für Theologie und Kirche*, vol. 14 (added vol. 3), (Freiburg-Basel-Vienna: Herder Verlag, 1968; reprinted 1986), 608.

3. Cf. the corresponding criticism in L. Oeing-Hanhoff, "Der Mensch: Natur oder Geschichte," in *Naturgesetz und christliche Ethik. Zur wissenschaftlichen Diskussion nach Humanae Vitae,* ed. F. Henrich (Munich: Kosel-Verlag, 1970), 13–47. Unfortunately the author works with incredible superficiality. He begins, for example (p. 17), a (as he says) "brief outline of the argumentation of the encyclical" with the following statement: it bases its argument on the fact that "man arrives at his true happiness, which is to say to a good, fulfilled life, including moral fulfillment, only to the extent to which he follows the laws inscribed by God in his nature. By these laws are intended especially 'biological laws,' e.g., the infertility given by nature according to its biological laws before ovular maturation. Because with the method of the choice of time—and only with this method—the biological laws inscribed by God in the nature of the woman are observed, this way of regulating conception is morally legitimate."

spacing of births. Yet, *Humanae Vitae* does not contend thereby that these "laws" are instituting a *moral* order; that is, that they are "natural law" in the *moral* sense. One must assume that the encyclical's critics have understood the (moral) natural law in this manner, and therefore *interpret* the encyclical in conformity with this preconception.[4]

In fact—it is clear from the context—the existence of biological rhythms of fertility is mentioned at this place for another reason, namely to draw a fundamental conceptual distinction: The distinction between *voluntarily induced* infertility and *naturally given* infertility; while the first poses a moral problem (i.e., precisely the point that the encyclical treats), the second does not. *Humanae Vitae* obviously wants to teach at this point that the conjugal act performed in naturally (non-voluntary) sterile periods is perfectly licit: "These acts, by which husband and wife are united in chaste intimacy, and by means of which human life is transmitted . . . do not cease to be lawful if, *for causes independent of the will of husband and wife,* they are foreseen to be infertile" (emphasis mine). Further, it intends to teach that non-intentional (naturally given) sterility of the procreative faculty does not deprive sexual intercourse of its intrinsic value and dignity as expression of marital love. Finally, it teaches that the spacing of births resulting from fertility cycles may be considered as a sign of the Creator's wisdom. Notwithstanding that, absolutely no reason is intended to be given here for settling the question *why* voluntarily induced sterility is illicit. At this point the encyclical pronounces nothing but its fundamental teaching that each conjugal act must remain *"per se" open* to procreation ("ut quilibet matrimonii usus ad vitam humanam procreandam *per se destinatus* permaneat"). Understood in its context, this text means: a conjugal act must not be *impeded voluntarily* from having those procreative consequences that would result from its naturally given (physiological) conditions (according to which procreation is not always possible). Thus, the encyclical wants to show that "openness to procreation" is not a physical, but an *intentional,* category.[5] But it has not yet pronounced *why* this openness is a moral requirement.

4. I discussed in detail, and criticized, both a similar understanding on the part of neo-scholasticism and some efforts to overcome it in *Natur als Grundlage der Moral.*

5. For the general difference between acts of intercourse considered as *intentional actions* and considered *physically* see: G. E. M. Anscombe: *You Can Have Sex without Children: Christianity and the New Offer,* in *The Collected Philosophical Papers of G. E. M. Anscombe,* vol. 3: *Ethics, Religion and Politics* (Oxford: Basil Blackwell, 1981), 82–96, especially 86–87.

For this reason it is important to note the fact that the encyclical, with its requirement of a "per se ordering to procreation," is clearly making an affirmation concerning the "conjugal act"—that is, a freely chosen human act, proceeding from the will—and not an affirmation concerning the biological act of the procreative faculty.[6] On this basis, the following criticism would seem to be particularly inaccurate:[7] that the doctrine concerning the "*per se* ordering" to procreation would contradict the truth that "in fact, viewed according to its biological laws, the concrete act could be directed either to 'procreation' or to 'non-procreation.'" In other words, at the biological level, concrete acts of intercourse are either procreative or not. To deduce from this fact that one cannot require of the conjugal act a *continual* or essential (*per se*) openness to procreation would truly be a "biologistic" argument, because effectively one would be equating the term "act" in the expressions "conjugal act" and "act of physical copulation" (as a natural event). *Humanae Vitae*, however, makes no statement at this point concerning the biological event; rather, it makes an assertion concerning the *human action* "conjugal act," and speaks of the requirement of openness to procreation on the part of the *will* of one who completes this act. The perspective of *Humanae Vitae* seems to be anything but that of the critic cited here.[8]

The perspective of the encyclical is in effect consistent with the Second Vatican Council's pastoral constitution *Gaudium et spes,* where in no. 49 it says of nuptial love and of its actuation in the conjugal act: "This love is uniquely expressed and perfected through the appropriate enterprise of matrimony. The actions within marriage by which the couple are united intimately and chastely are noble and worthy ones. Expressed in a manner which is truly human, these actions promote that mutual self-giving by which spouses enrich each other with a joyful and a ready will."

6. The expression rendered "conjugal act," in the original text of the encyclical is *usus matrimonii,* which is clearly not simply the physiological act.

7. F. Böckle, "*Humanae vitae* und die philosophische Anthropologie Karol Wojtylas. Zur päpstlichen Lehrposition zur künstlichen Befrüchtung und ihrer Begründung," in *Herder Korrespondenz* 43 no. 8 (Freiburg: Herder, 1989): 376. The term "fertilization" (*Befrüchtung*) in the subtitle of the publication is certainly an oversight; it should rather be "contraception."

8. The same erroneous interpretation is also the basis of Noonan's argument. Cf. J. T. Noonan, "Natural Law, The Teaching of the Church and the Regulation of the Rhythm of Human Fecundity." The article, which originally appeared in the *American Journal of Jurisprudence,* can be found as an appendix in the second edition of J. T. Noonan, *Contraception: A History of Its Treatment by the Catholic Theologians and Canonists* (Cambridge, Mass.: Harvard University Press, 1965, 2nd ed. 1986), 535–54; especially 550.

This means that the conjugal act is, in conformity with its essence, an act of love, expressing a particular type of love: marital love. It is not simply a "means" of the transmission of life, and for this reason it preserves its meaning and intimate dignity even when that transmission is not possible. At the same time, however, *Humanae Vitae* teaches that this character of the conjugal act being an "act of love" is only the case when the act retains an intentional openness to the procreation of human life. In fact, the love that it expresses is a love characterized precisely by this openness. Compare *Gaudium et Spes,* n. 50: "Marriage and conjugal love are by their nature ordained toward the begetting and educating of children." The intentional openness (i.e., "to be *per se* ordered to") of the conjugal act cannot, however, be destroyed by an infertility that is independent of the will, but only by a voluntarily induced infertility. Therefore the decisive point is this: the encyclical wants to hold firmly that this openness is a *condition* for the conjugal act to be an *act of love.*

The Inseparability Principle

Only in the subsequent no. 12 does the encyclical address its underlying argumentation ("That teaching, often set forth by the Magisterium, is founded upon"), namely, that this doctrine is based on the inseparable connection, established by God, of the two fundamental meanings of the conjugal act: "union of love" and "transmission of life."[9] At this point, *Humanae Vitae* teaches four things. First, it teaches that human sexuality has two fundamental meanings: the meaning of loving union of the spouses ("unitive meaning") and the meaning of transmission of human life ("procreative meaning"). Second, it teaches that according to the design of the Creator these two meanings are inseparably connected. Third, it insists that man on his own initiative may not break this connection. And fourth, the encyclical affirms that by contraception the connection of these two meanings in fact *is* broken.

The first, second, and third ones—which jointly form what I shall call the *Inseparability Principle*—must first be rightly understood so as to deal correctly with the last question. The widespread criticism of

9. This statement refers to the significant contents of the marital sexual act, and not to the so-called ends of marriage. We will see below that these two concepts deal with different questions.

Humanae Vitae does not contest the fact that, in the conjugal act, love and "service of the transmission of human life" are mutually connected. Rather, the criticism was, and still is, a denial of the claim that contraception in fact *does* break the connection of these two meanings while periodic continence does not. Critics thereby contend that the connection of these two meanings need not be maintained *in each single conjugal act* as long as conjugal love *as a whole* remains ordered to procreation and hence to the task of transmitting life. By this denial and contention, they answer in the affirmative a question explicitly brought up by the encyclical itself (no. 3). "Could it not be admitted . . . that procreative finality applies to the totality of married life rather than to each single act?" Critics give their affirmative answer to this question by opposing what *Humanae Vitae* explicitly teaches in no. 14. The claim was, to put it more clearly, that as long as contraception is adopted in the context of a marital life that is open *in its totality* to its procreative meaning, not opposing that meaning—that is, as long as contraception serves only as a means for responsibly limiting or planning offspring without excluding offspring *on principle*—there would be no breaking of the connection of the two meanings of the conjugal act. (Frankly, this is a dubious use of the so-called Totality Principle.) Moreover, critics contend that intentional openness to procreation would thereby be fully maintained; to refer to the Inseparability Principle in order to show the wrongness of contraception, critics contend, would be mere question begging.

The Misleading Discussion Concerning "Artificial" Contraception

By faithfully following the misleading notion that it forbade contraception because it is artificial, critics of the encyclical's teaching thought, and still think, that periodic continence is only another *method* of contraception: the one being a "natural method" and the other an "artificial method." This concentration on the alternative "natural" or "artificial" method has been a fatally misleading move; it has led many to miss the very point at issue and to overlook the crux of the problem. Misled in this way, they were induced to promote an interpretation according to which *Humanae Vitae* condemns contraception because of its *artificial* character, because of its shortcoming with respect to naturally given structure of human sexuality. Unfortunately, this is often the opinion of those who seek to defend *Humanae Vitae*'s doctrine, as well.[10] It is worth noting that J. T. Noonan, offering a plausible, although incorrect, interpretation of the encyclical, did recognize that its condemnation of contraception had nothing to do with the latter's artificiality.[11]

The discussion—which in my opinion should be completely abandoned—concerning "artificial contraception," or rather of a supposed ecclesiastical condemnation of *artificial* contraception, unfortunately removes the focus from the real problem, which is not the *artificiality* of contraception, but rather the effort to *prevent and impede* conception. Furthermore, this way of speaking suggests the idea that the alternative of "periodic continence" is also a form of contraception—and therefore a "natural method"—whereas in reality periodic continence is not a form of impeding conception. We will consider below the true nature of the two alternatives and the profound moral significance of their diversity. They consist, on the one hand, in "avoiding the procreative consequences of sexual acts *that have been performed*," and on the other in "avoiding the procreative consequences of sexual acts by means of the *abstention from such acts*." In any case, let us note that the encyclical itself never employs the term "artificial" in its formulation of the norm concerning contraception (n. 14): "Similarly excluded is every action which, either in anticipation of the conjugal act, or in its accomplishment, or in the development of its natural consequences, proposes, whether as an end or as a means, to render procreation impossible."

This addresses, for example, the so-called coitus interruptus. And as we will see below, there *are* artificial (physically) contraceptive interventions that have nothing to do with the type of behavior just described, and that therefore do not fall under the norm proposed by *Humanae Vitae*. The norm, as such, has nothing to do with the *artificiality* of an intervention. One must not be misled, therefore, by the expression "in the devel-

10. In my book *Natural Law and Practical Reason*, I begin from the question of why "artificial" contraception is wrong. The first step in the analysis conducted there was not to oppose "artificiality" to "naturalness," but to look at that which issues from voluntary self-control (cf. p. 109). The consequence of this distinction was then the idea that the problem is with contraception itself, not with its artificiality.

11. Cf. Noonan, *Contraception*, 551: "The encyclical does use the term 'artifice' to refer to certain contraceptive means, but it does not rest its condemnation on the artificial character of contraceptives, nor does it rest its condemnation on the fact that contraception involves human intervention in a natural process." We will return briefly to Noonan's interpretation below.

opment of its natural consequences," because the decisive words here are "every action which . . . proposes . . . to render procreation impossible."[12] We will need to return to this in what follows.

The notion that *Humanae Vitae* is interested in the preservation of the "natural" element rather than artificial intervention is also often inferred from *Humanae Vitae* no. 16, where it says: "In reality, there are essential differences between the two cases; in the former, the married couple make legitimate use of a natural disposition; in the latter, they impede the development of natural processes." More often than not, this passage is cited only up to this point; the text, however, continues on, and by ignoring the continuation its meaning is falsified.[13] We will return to this passage below.

In the first place, therefore, it is necessary to ask: are there arguments in the encyclical *Humanae Vitae* that would oppose the mentioned false interpretation, according to which the encyclical would be at heart concerned with the respect of "nature," and its defense against artificial interventions, contrary to nature?

In my opinion, *Humanae Vitae* did not intend to show *why* contraception violates the Inseparability Principle; it only affirmed that it does. Likewise, the encyclical did not intend to provide a philosophical (ethical) reason why contraception violates natural law; it sought only to affirm that it does. Nor does it explicitly refer to any definite concept of natural law. It applies, in the light of revelation (holy Scripture and Tradition), its perennial, prophetical teaching on the matter to new developments in the field of contraceptive devices without putting forward a properly philosophical argument.[14]

12. The formulation of *Humanae Vitae* takes up in a slightly modified form that of Pius XII in his discourse of October 29, 1951. In fact, the contemporary reception of this text centered precisely on the words "unfolding in its natural effects"; cf. Noonan, *Contraception*, 467–68. Among the moral theologians who rejected contraception for this reason, Noonan cites in the German context Josef Fuchs and Bernhard Häring. This was certainly—based on the formulation of "Casti Connubii"—an understandable emphasis, although nevertheless mistaken. The only thing worth commenting on today is that, for its critics, this antiquated viewpoint is also insinuated in the teaching of *Humanae Vitae*.

13. Cf., e.g., L. Bertsch, "Akzente der kirchlichen Ehelehre con Pius XI bis Johannes Paul II. überlegungen aus der Sicht eines Pastoraltheologen," in *Der umstrittene Naturbegriff*, ed. F. Böckle (Düsseldorf: Patmos Verlag, 1987), 128.

14. How deeply the encyclical's teaching is in harmony with the Church's doctrinal tradition has been brilliantly shown by G. E. M. Anscombe: *Contraception and Chastity* (London: Catholic Truth Society, 1975).

However, there clearly exists a fundamental, philosophically *relevant* perspective underlying the encyclical's teaching, a perspective that also reflects an important doctrinal development: *This perspective is not to defend the demand of respecting natural patterns inherent in the biological or physiological constitution of man and his generative acts, but to stress what has been called the "intentionalness of the thing one is doing" by contracepting, an intentionalness that relates to the nature of the virtue of chastity and to its specific requirements within the context of procreative responsibility.*[15] Here, procreative responsibility means responsibility with respect to the procreative consequences of sexual acts; that is, the responsibility of being parents. This, I think, is the key to a proper understanding of the encyclical, which, in my opinion, leads to what is probably the only way to explain why contraception violates natural law, which is none other than an explanation based on the structure of the moral virtues.

Methodological Specifications: The Perspective of Single Acts and the "Relevant Case"

Contraception as a Principled Refusal of Assuming Parental Responsibility

Before I continue, I have to settle a fundamental methodological question. When *Humanae Vitae* talks about the procreative meaning of marital love, it explicitly refers not only to marital life in its totality, but, as was already mentioned, to *each single conjugal act.* Thus, the perspective of *Humanae Vitae* consists in providing a moral judgment about a specific type of *action,* that is, about the concrete performance of *human acts.*

In the first place, therefore, it is necessary to precisely identify the mode of behavior that is being evaluated. In order to *identify* the act under question, a most important restriction has to be effected for methodological reasons. "Contraceptive behavior" is or can involve a complex structure in which several aspects must be distinguished. The most typical and widespread case of contraceptive behavior consists in an overall attitude of excluding procreative finality from marital love, either in part

---

15. Quoted material in ibid., 17.

(based on *a certain number* of children desired, or for *a certain period of time*) or totally. In this case, which is the one of primary pastoral concern, contraceptive behavior has its root on the level of life plans and overall intentions involved in marital commitment. This life plan consists in wanting—mostly as a result of *other* preference—to exclude, in part or totally, the possible restrictions and burdens expected from or imposed by pregnancy and the rearing of children.

This is not a case of "responsible parenthood," but rather of "deficient parenthood," because something pertaining to the essence of parenthood itself is partly or totally rejected. Much more, they are acts of restricting or even suppressing altogether the procreative meaning of marital love, which is intrinsically a love at the service of the transmission of life. They are intentional acts of disconnecting in part or totally the unitive meaning of sexual behavior from its procreative function; spouses, in this case, simply close their mind at least partially to the task of generously transmitting human life. For such acts of partially or completely excluding procreation from marriage, however, the use of contraceptive techniques is not the only way, even if nowadays it may be the most commonly used; periodic continence can also serve for such a project, and still does so in some cases. The moral failure of this project, however, does not consist essentially in the contraceptive behavior itself, but already in the overall intention with which either contraception or periodic continence is adopted. One must not, therefore, make the mistake of identifying contraception exclusively with this attitude ("contraceptive behavior," selfishness, hedonism, presumption, arbitrariness, etc.). Similarly, one must not make the mistake of presupposing that it not be possible, in principle, to choose contraceptive behavior *independently* of such attitudes. For example, it is possible to choose contraceptive behavior with the same attitude according to which periodic continence could be *legitimately* practiced. This must be recognized for methodological reasons, but also simply because in effect the question, "contraception, yes or no?" does not present itself only in the just-described context of attitudes contrary to the generous service of human life. It also arises in situations for which opponents of contraception would judge the practice of periodic continence as not only morally unassailable, but even required.

For this reason it seems to me incorrect to speak of periodic continence practiced with a "contraceptive mentality." This, and in general the too hasty condemnation of a "contraceptive mentality," presupposes in fact that contraception, considered *in itself* and therefore in its essence, is already that which periodic continence could become only on the basis of an *ulterior* morally unacceptable intention, yet to be added (e.g., anti-life). Such a manner of speaking risks obfuscating the basic intention that is crucial to a proper description of the contraceptive act.

My argumentation, rather, will show that a further intention, which could render periodic continence morally inadmissible, is not identical to the basic intentionality that characterizes contraception intrinsically, that is, on the level of the chosen object. For this reason neither can one, without risking great confusion, characterize in principle the fundamental anti-procreative attitude described above as a "contraceptive mentality." Indeed, using this terminology, one would presuppose a response to the question of why contraception is wrong, without having yet posed the question in a proper way. Both in the analysis of periodic continence and in that of contraception, we must—as a minimum—distinguish the following two questions: "First: is the *sort* of act we contemplate doing something that it's all right to do? Second: are our further or surrounding intentions all right? . . . Contraceptive intercourse fails on the first count."[16]

The Contraceptive Choice in the Context of Responsible Parenthood

To identify the act of contraception in its "purity"—*for analytical reasons*—we should therefore consider another case, which is the one about which the encyclical *Humanae Vitae* is primarily concerned. This is the proper case of responsible parenthood: the case of spouses who are plainly open to their parental vocation but for serious reasons, in which they detect God's will, they conclude that *they ought* not to have any more children, at least for the time being. *Humanae Vitae* has perfectly sketched this situation when it states (no. 16): "It cannot be denied that in each case married couples, for acceptable reasons, are both perfectly clear in their intention to avoid children and mean to make sure that none will be born." According to the encyclical's teaching, periodical

16. See ibid., 18.

continence would be perfectly licit in this case; contraception, however, would not. In this case, one and the same upright intention leads to a different choice of actions. The intention here *is not* to disconnect marital love from its procreative meaning in favor of other preferences that do not derive from parental responsibility. On the contrary, the insight of the spouses—"We should not have another child" or "She (I) should not become pregnant"—which is based on serious and justified reasons, is an insight plainly embedded in the parental and procreative meaning of marital love. Common to our two cases, those couples who reject their parental vocation and those who seek to carry it out according to God's will, is the *intention of avoiding conception* (as long as present circumstances continue), but only the latter is integrated into the very context of procreative responsibility.

After forming this common intention, however, the choice of conduct—that is, the means chosen for the sake of avoiding conception—will be different. The contraceptive choice involves a volition to act in a way that *prevents* sexual intercourse from being fertile; it is a choice to *prevent* conception where it is foreseen to occur. The choice of periodic continence, on the other hand, does not involve the volition of preventing naturally fertile acts from being fertile; instead it *avoids* conception by *abstaining* from those acts that are foreseen to bring it about. Why is the former choice wrong, while the latter is not? That exactly, and only that, is the question that has to be answered. All the other possible reasons that are additionally provided to show that contraception involves moral disorder—if they don't want to ultimately miss the mark—actually presuppose having resolved this basic problem.Some Known Arguments against Contraception

It seems to be useful to address, up front, several arguments that intend to defend the doctrine of *Humanae Vitae*. The analysis of these arguments will help to clarify further the point at issue.

The Naturalistic, or "Perverted-Faculty," Argument

The most traditional of these arguments is the "perverted-faculty" argument: contraception impedes the unfolding of an event whose structure is given by nature. Since nature is created by God, the perversion of the natural procreative event is immoral. In particular, this immorality lies in impeding the natural unfolding of the procreative act.

This argument—on the basis of the misunderstandings regarding natural law and action theory—was held by many of those who, some years later, rejected the Church's teaching as it was pronounced in *Humanae Vitae*. It is both amazing and sad to see how most critics of *Humanae Vitae* once held this kind of naturalistic theory. In the late fifties and early sixties, some of them began to consider that the "pill" does "not violate the integrity of naturally given structures," since it simply brings about "artificially" what nature often does spontaneously; nothing is mutilated in the generative faculty, and there is no vitiation in the performance of the procreative act. According to this understanding, the pill—in contrast to other contraceptive methods—would therefore not be "against nature" in any way.[17]

Others, abandoning this rather "naturalistic" way of moral thinking, stopped speaking about the "integrity of the generative faculty" and fully subscribed to the licitness of contraceptive practices, though without giving up a rather crudely "physicalist" or "biologistic" view of sexuality. The problem was now simply considered as analogous to any other medical intervention in human physiology.[18] When critics finally read *Humanae Vitae* they obviously did not understand that the encyclical's view was quite different.

Backed up by the mass media, various critics persistently spread the reproach—though without really proving it on the grounds of the wording of *Humanae Vitae*[19]—that the perspective underlying the encyclical's teaching was just this biologistic concept of morally binding natural patterns, which as they rightly emphasized, the majority of moral theologians had already abandoned.

17. For a brief analysis of this evolution, see J. M. Finnis: "*Humanae Vitae*: Its Background and Aftermath," *International Review of Natural Family Planning* 4 (1980): 141–53. A more detailed analysis can be found in Noonan, *Contraception*, 460–533.

18. This has been nicely pointed out by T. G. Belmans, *Le sens objectif de l'agir humain. Pour relire la morale conjugale de Saint Thomas* (Vatican City: Libreria Editrice Vaticana, 1980), 327–411. For "physicalism" in actual Moral Theology see also my *Natur als Grundlage der Moral*. B. Häring, in "The Inseparability of the Unitive-Procreative Functions," for example (183), simply equates the natural patterns involved in sexuality with "biological functions," which he thinks "may be interfered with and even destroyed if it is necessary for the well being of the *person*." According to him, this would be a merely medical problem. Häring regards the contraceptive pill as something that "preserves the ovule which, here and now, is not needed because procreation would be irresponsible" (185).

19. Except by quoting sentences (or fragments thereof) taken out of their context, of which C. Curran, *Contraception*, 160, provides a typical example.

I would like to think that there is no longer any need to explicitly refute the naturalistic, or perverted-faculty, argument, or similar arguments grounded in the need to respect natural patterns (in the physiological sense).[20] It is still worth recalling what Germain Grisez, one of *Humanae Vitae's* most ardent defenders, wrote many years ago about the naturalistic argument. The following quotation makes clear how an author who today defends the encyclical's teaching was, at that time, already well ahead of subsequent critics in his rejection of "biologistic" thinking:

"The naturally given structure of the sexual act"—that is a phrase one often encounters in discussions of contraception. The contention here is that there is no such thing, if we are talking about the *human act*; for human acts have their structure from intelligence. Just insofar as an action is considered according to its naturally given structure, it is to that extent not considered as a *human act*—i.e., as a moral act—but rather as a physiological process or as instinctive behavior. Action with a given structure and acts structured by intelligence differ as totally as nature differs from morality. Nature has an order which reason can consider but cannot make and cannot alter. Morality has an order which reason institutes by guiding the acts of the will.[21]

I fully subscribe to this criticism, while adding that to act against nature does not automatically imply *moral fault*. This *could* be the case, but it has always to be shown why a violation of natural patterns is *morally wrong* and therefore a violation of the moral order established by reason: *agere contra naturam* (to *act* against nature) is not equivalent to *peccare contra naturam* (to *sin* against nature). A reason must always be given as to *why* a violation of nature—that is, of the course of the body's natural processes—does or does not have moral relevance; that is, it must always be shown how a violation of nature has to be qualified from a moral point of view.[22]

Why is contraceptive sexual intercourse not simply like rendering "a

20. In the original version of this essay, I was able to write, from a somewhat European perspective, that no serious moralist holds—at least expressly—such an argument, even if critics of *Humanae Vitae* continue to be convinced that this is what the encyclical really teaches and moreover that it is the only way its doctrine can be justified. However, it seems that such thought is still influential in the English-speaking world.

21. G. Grisez, "New Formulation of a Natural-Law Argument against Contraception," *Thomist* 30, no. 4 (1966): 343.

22. See my *Natur als Grundlage der Moral*, 108–09; see also *Natural Law and Practical Reason*, 94–95.

man's eating non-nutritive for a day or two," or like installing "a substitute for lung-breathing by some reversible operation (with a view to underwater exploration, say)" or like chewing sugarless gum for the pleasure of chewing, excluding nutrition as the "natural goal" of chewing?[23]

Thus, an argument against contraception based upon the naturally given structure of the sexual act does not resolve anything. Provided that one does not want to maintain that the naturally given imposes *in all cases* the moral obligation of not altering it, which would plainly lead to absurd consequences, such arguments against contraception simply beg the question. In effect, they presuppose that, in this case, respect of nature has already been demonstrated to be a moral command. It does not help to additionally cite the fact that contraception is not an intervention that affects the health or survival of the organism, a type of intervention on the natural organic structure that *is* legitimate, because it is effectively "in conformity with nature," since bodily health is in itself in conformity with nature. This vision is obviously valid. Recall that we have assumed, however, that the avoidance of conception in certain determined circumstances is for the good not only of the body, but of the entire person, matrimonial communion, and family. In this case, prima facie, it is hard to understand why this good would not also justify medical intervention, since it is not considered problematic but even required to bring about a good that is in itself less valuable than that at stake in questions of contraception, such as the health of the *body*, or the preservation of physical existence.[24] For this reason, further argumentation is necessary.

Every argument that tries to defend naturally given structures from being altered by human intervention needs a *further* argument, which precisely must not be based on the very "naturalness" of natural patterns, but which needs to be an additional *ethical* argument showing the *moral relevance* of natural patterns.[25]

23. This latter example is given by G. Grisez, *The Way of the Lord Jesus*, vol. 1, *Christian Moral Principles* (Chicago: Franciscan Herald Press, 1983), 105; the former by G. E. M. Anscombe, *Sex without Children*. 87.

24. B. Häring, "The Inseparability of the Unitive-Procreative Functions," 181, uses precisely this argument. It cannot be set aside too quickly, however, because in the first place it must be clear that not only individual bodily organs are ordered to the health of the entire organism, but similarly the health of the body is ordered to the good of the entire person. The body is in reality an integral component of the entire person.

25. An author like G. Martelet (see his article "Morale conjugale et vie chrétienne,"

A second argument, based on the metaphysics of creation, is the one I will call the "creationist" argument. It seeks to provide just such an ethical argument for the inviolability of naturally given structures. It runs as follows: In procreation man is a cooperator with God, who in every act of generation immediately creates the human soul. Through contraception man overrides God's right as a Creator, contradicts his creative will, and claims for himself to be the master over human life.

This argument obviously applies to anti-procreative overall intentions, because these aim at withdrawing marital love from its procreative meaning, which is its meaning as cooperation with God's creative love. Foreclosing the procreative meaning of marital love means overriding God's creative designs over man and falsifying one's own situation as a mere cooperator with God. As we can see, this argument attempts to overcome the insufficiency of the naturalistic way of thinking, by emphasizing the following. The process given by nature is in fact not exclusively a natural process: God is also directly involved. Whoever *in the case of human procreation*—only in reference to this does the argument claim to be valid—does not respect what is given by nature, not only goes "against nature," but also goes against God inasmuch as God is co-involved in the creation of a new human being, and indeed it is God himself who determines to create.

It is necessary to ask whether it is possible to *substantiate* that contraception is contradictory to the divine creative will. In truth, it seems as though those who hold such an argument believe the simple referral to the dependence of human procreation on a divine creative act is in itself sufficient for such a substantiation.

Let us suppose that in every procreative act God really does directly create the human soul. The procreative act, or rather the duty of transmitting human life, is therefore a direct cooperation with the divine cre-

---

Nouvelle revue théologique 87 [1965]: 245–66) has indeed pointed out the moral relevance of sexuality. Therefore, his argument against contraception has not to be subsumed under the perverted-faculty argument. The anthropological arguments that I will use later are not very different from Martelet's. But, as I have remarked above, Martelet's argument failed by omitting to show why and how his anthropology becomes relevant for judging *single human actions*. He neither worked with the concept of moral virtue, nor did he engage in action analysis. So, as it seems to me, he missed the point. Also man's eating, which aims at nutrition, is *morally* relevant (because self-preservation of the individual is so). The problem is how this relevance will affect the judgment about single performances of nutritive acts.

ative action (by this, it is not yet clear what relevance this fact has for the moral judgment concerning the action). This cooperation presupposed, the metaphysics-of-creation argument in fact applies to an attitude directly orientated against the procreative meaning of sexuality. This attitude separates conjugal love from its procreative meaning and intends to deprive it of its meaning as a cooperation with the divine creative love. To close oneself in this way to the procreative content of matrimonial love is to oppose the divine creative plan of collaboration with God.

Yet, for such an argument it is not necessary to refer to an immediate act of creation by God, who intervenes directly. It would be more than sufficient to refer to the connection between the procreative act and the consequent genesis of a human person as a *creaturely reality,* that is, within the creaturely context established by the divine creative work. Contraception is also an intervention in this context, but it does not consist in "impeding" God, so to speak, from intervening creatively *in* the procreative act.[26]

But as I say, periodic continence also could be used to oppose oneself to the divine creative plan. Or perhaps the difference simply lies in the fact that in one case one intervenes actively, whereas in the other the couple limits themselves to marital relations only during those times when God *could not* in fact create anything, nor does he want to—after all, hasn't God himself disposed nature in such a way that there are times of infertility? In this way the creationist argument would end by saying that the choice to reserve intercourse to times of infertility is admissible, because here man entrusts himself to a possibility disposed by God the

26. This, however, seems to be the thought of J. Seifert, "Der sittliche Unterschied zwischen natürlicher Empfägnisverhütung und künstlicher Empfägnisverhütung," in *Elternschaft und Menschenwürde,* ed. E. Wenisch (Vallendar: Patris-Verlag, 1984). Cf. 213: "To perform an act, in connection with which God creates a spiritual and immortal soul, but intervening so as to eliminate the creative action of God, intentionally and actively, destroying in the act the same bond which joins it with the infinite depths of the divine creative love, is a terrible hubris, a rebellion against God." One senses a certain forcing of the argument, inasmuch as it supposes a fertile procreative act in which one prevents God from intervening creationally. This is illogical, because with contraception it is not God's creative activity that is impeded (i.e., it is no more than a potentially creative act at stake), but rather the link between the procreative act and fertility has been removed; what is done is no longer a procreative act, and therefore neither is it an act "in connection with which God creates a spiritual and immortal soul." The relevant question is solely whether it is legitimate to sever this link. For addressing this question, the argument adopted here seems to be circular. Only after addressing this question, however, does it seem possible to show why contraception is an "illegitimate" impediment of the divine creative action, while abstinence is legitimate.

Creator, thus comporting himself in a way in conformity with his status as a creature. There is nothing objectionable in this interpretation. All that it presents, however, is an argument for the admissibility of periodic continence. But the problem is exactly the opposite: has the creationist argument yet demonstrated that contraception is a fault that goes against one's position as a creature? No. The consideration that periodic continence is an ordered act does not yet demonstrate that contraception is disordered.

The creationist argument, to be adequate, must also demonstrate this second aspect. This would lead, however, to serious difficulties. Consider the case we began with, which presupposes the spouses' insight that they *"ought* not to have another child at present" or "we are *obligated* to avoid a conception at this time" (for serious reasons of parental responsibility). Suppose also that this "ought not" is a judgment of conscience that the spouses—supposing they take conscience seriously—will interpret as God's will. According to the teaching of the Second Vatican Council's pastoral constitution *Gaudium et Spes* (no. 50), not only are the spouses cooperators with God's creative and loving will, but they also are *"interpreters* of God's love." Hence, their task is to cooperate with God's creative love, precisely by interpreting what this love requires of them; it is their responsibility to judge in conscience whether God wants the coming-to-be of a new human being under the present circumstances of their conjugal life. This equates to judging whether God, *at present,* wants to make use of their loving union to create a new human being. Our case supposes that the spouses have rightly come to the conclusion that God, at present, does not want them to have another child; this conclusion fully involves the consciousness of being both *cooperators* with God and *interpreters* of his creative love.

We will now try to develop a line of argument leading to a judgment regarding the concrete behavior of the spouses in this crucial test case. Indeed, if the creationist argument is capable of addressing this question, it must be clear and incisive in doing so. Otherwise it would be irrelevant for judgments of conscience and therefore also irrelevant morally.

Now if procreation were the only meaning of the conjugal act, those spouses who judge they should not conceive should abstain completely from sexual intercourse. But they know that procreation is not the only meaning inherent in sexuality, so it may be appropriate for them to engage in sexual intercourse to express their mutual love, even if God wants them to avoid pregnancy for the time being, or even altogether. "If we contracept," they might argue, "we will not necessarily deprive sexual intercourse from its *cooperative meaning* [here they might be thinking of a revisionist notion of "totality"], but only from its *procreative efficacy*." "And this," they might assert, "we are allowed to do according to God's will, for we know that he wants us to avoid pregnancy." In other words, knowing that mutual love is one of the inherent meanings of sexual intercourse, and judging that God does not want them to conceive at this time, they conclude that contraception is the morally correct way to meet the demands of conjugal love and God's will. Referring at this point to the cooperative aspect of procreation to refute them would beg the question by presupposing what has yet to be demonstrated; it is simply not sufficient, because one has not yet proven why depriving intercourse from its procreative efficiency *is not an appropriate means for cooperating with God's will of avoiding conception*; that is, why it is not an appropriate *interpretation* of how to cooperate with God's creative love. To show this, one should provide reasons for the wrongness and unjustifiability of the contraceptive *act* and only *then,* based on such reasons, would it be possible to derive its implications for cooperation with God's creative love.

Someone might object that God's creative intervention is "automatically" involved in every act of sexual intercourse, which by its natural condition is fertile and therefore a procreative act. Consequently man has no right to render it infertile; for this would be equal to setting limits to God's creative power, impeding what only he has a right to dispose of. Man would usurp the place of God.

To this I would answer as follows. Even if the acts of procreation are, by their very *object* and therefore by their essence, acts of cooperation with the Creator, and therefore something like "God's property," it would not be evident that rendering them infertile by such a means of "procreative responsibility" would override God's rights. This injustice could be demonstrated only by assuming that, through the conjugal act, *God wants to* create a new human being even in the case of spouses whom at *present he wants to avoid conception*. This assumption, however, is clearly self-contradictory, for it implies that God's creative will is inconsistent. Or else it implies that in executing his creative will, God is confined by secondary causes (like the body's fertility rhythms). In the end, to show that man is always bound to act within the limits of these rhythms would require that one begin from the argument that God is bound in the same way, which is obviously absurd. One should, in the case we are considering, at least be able to give arguments for this. That is, one should be able to give arguments that show why interventions upon natural structures are not permitted for the good of the whole person, of marital communion, of the family, and even for the fulfillment of the will of God (while the same interventions carried out for the purpose of bodily health are not considered to be morally problematic, even when they cause infertility, as a foreseen but not directly willed collateral consequence). Yet, an instinctive intuition arises here: we are dealing with two completely different things; but what is the underlying reason for this difference?

Provided that God both presently wants spouses to avoid conception and fully approves the unitive meaning of intercourse, it seems much more plausible to suppose that he does not require that *single conjugal acts* keep their actual meaning of cooperation with a divine act of *creation*. Whether this supposition is actually sound is precisely the point at issue. It can be reasonably argued for, however, on the grounds that spouses *know* two things: first, that God, presently and *in their* very case, *does not* want to create a new human life through *their* bodily acts; second, that the procreative meaning is not the only meaning of the conjugal act. The only way of saving, at this point, the creationist argument would be by assuming that what God wants spouses to do is conditioned by natural patterns; but this is plainly absurd, or at least it will lead back to the naturalistic, or perverted-faculty, argument.

At this point, the creationist argument will "bite back" as an effective argument *in favor of* contraception. In particular, the contraceptive choice could be justified precisely on the grounds of "cooperation with the Creator," which requires the agent to interpret responsibly his will. In fact, it is not possible—independent of revelation—*on the basis of* a consciousness of the "will of God," to deduce what we must do; rather, we can only, based on an understanding of what we must do, *work back* to the idea that this now is the will of God as recognized by us in the judgment of conscience. But what *must* we do? This is the first question.

So it might be asserted that, in the present case, the cooperative meaning of procreation demands—for serious and legitimate reasons pertaining to responsible parenthood—an act that prevents intercourse from having procreative consequences. Thus, one could assume, without any peril of inconsistency, that cooperation with God's will demands *now* that we alter a natural pattern for the very sake of fulfilling God's will. The question at issue is whether *this* is a morally sustainable conclusion, and therefore whether this is a *correct* judgment concerning what the couple must do (and therefore of the will of God). The moralist who wants to refute *this* contention without merely resorting to the perverted-faculty argument should give a *further* reason, which must not be drawn from the cooperative meaning of procreation.

To sum up: contracepting spouses will concede that by contraception they *withdraw* sexual intercourse from being involved in a divine act of creation; but this, they will argue, is done according to God's will. Therefore, what has to be proven is *why,* in order to fulfill God's will of avoiding conception, it is illicit to *prevent* conception on the level of secondary causality and thereby to *withdraw* the conjugal act from involvement in the creative act of the primary cause.

So the very crux of the problem—namely, why acts that prevent sexual acts from being fertile are not appropriate means for responsibly cooperating with God—remains far from being resolved because the creationist argument obviously needs a *complement,* which addresses it. Nobody denies that man has no right to override the Creator's prerogatives; the crucial question to be answered, however, is the following: *Why* is the Creator's right overridden by contraception? This can be answered only by showing why contraception in itself is a wrong means for fulfilling procreative responsibility and thereby cooperating with God's creative will. In other words, *only on the basis* of showing that contraception is morally wrong *can we then deduce* that it also goes against God's will.

The creationist argument only manifests the real gravity of contraception as an offense to God, but it depends upon a preceding analysis that shows the intrinsic immorality of this practice and its contradiction to the demands of the human good. Moreover, the creationist argument points out the real gravity of contraception pursued in the context of the overall intent to withdraw marital love completely from the procreative context. Unfortunately, proponents of this argument often assume from the outset that this overall intention is in every case the reason for a contraceptive choice, which leads to a failure to understand the relevant case addressed by *Humanae Vitae*. Indeed, we are allowed to argue that spouses have no *right* to this overall rejection of procreation within a marriage, because the task of procreation and the bodily acts that render it possible are not at man's disposal; they are but realities through which man cooperates with the Creator. Prescinding entirely from the biblical basis of this teaching (something with which the philosopher does not concern himself), this corresponds also to the fact that human life is not "made" by men, but "given" by God *through* the bodily act of conjugal love. And this diffusion of his divine creative love is, *in principle,* precisely that with which God wants married people to cooperate. Hence, this is different from the case in which spouses have reasons of procreative responsibility to suppose that God *at present* does not want to make use of *their* marital intercourse to spread the gift of life. Thus, as an argument that refers to "God's rights" *within* the context of "responsible parenthood," the creationist argument seems to fall short of resolving the problem at issue. It overlooks the need for a moral analysis on the level of the human act that would make out the "good for man," according to Aquinas's famous dictum: *Non enim Deus a nobis offenditur nisi ex eo quod contra nostrum bonum agimus.*[27]

The "Contralife-Will" Argument

A further argument is that which I call the "contralife-will" argument after its Anglo-Saxon authors.[28] It intends to show that the contra-

27. "For we do not offend God except by doing something contrary to our own good," *Summa contra Gentiles* III, 122. In this volume, all of Aquinas's works are cited according to the Marietti edition (Turin); the only exception is the *Commentary on the Sentences,* which is cited according to the edition used in the *Index Thomisticus: S. Thomae Aquinatis Opera Omnia,* vol. 1, ed. Roberto Busa (Stuttgart–Bad Cannstatt: Frommann-Holzboog, 1980). The translation here is that of Vernon J. Bourke from Thomas Aquinas, *Summa contra Gentiles: Book Three Providence,* Part II, trans. Vernon J. Bourke (Notre Dame: University of Notre Dame Press, 1956, paperback 1975), 143.

28. I refer to the presentation of this argument, published by its authors in common: G. Grisez, J. Boyle, J. Finnis, W. E. May: "Every Marital Act Ought to Be Open to New Life: Toward a Clearer Understanding," published in *The Thomist* 52, no. 3 (1988): 365–476, and (in an Italian version) in *Anthropotes* 4, no. 1 (1988). I wish to thank Germain Grisez for having sent me the manuscript before its publication. I was pleased to see that this last version of the argument takes into consideration some objections I had occasion to raise in common

ceptive act involves a "contralife will," somewhat similar to a homicidal will, an intention oriented against the life of a person. Clearly, contraception is not homicide; but according to this argument the killing of a person means that the will of one who acts thusly is oriented against the existence of a person. Analogously, in the contraceptive act, the will of the agent is said to be oriented against the existence (the coming into being) of a human life. The contralife-will argument holds that such an intention must necessarily also be malicious, because it is evil to orient one's will directly against a fundamental human good (such as "life"). In fact, this "will oriented against life" is understood not as one that merely includes "bad intentions" or "ill will," but as a will in direct opposition to the fundamental human good of "life."[29]

It should be understood that the analogy with homicide—according to the argument's authors—does not mean that contraception is something similar (analogous) to the killing of a person; the analogy refers, rather, only and exclusively to the relative *relation* between the physical execution of the action and the willing involved in it. Just as the physical act of killing (for example, to shoot someone) involves a will oriented against life, making this a particular type of human action that is judged to be morally evil, so too the physical act of contraception (for example, the employment of a means to block ovulation), involves a will oriented against the coming into being of a person, a will that explains why such an action is morally evil. And precisely insofar as—and only insofar as—contraception involves such a will oriented against "life," does it possess a similarity to homicide.[30] This argument, which in its exposition is very sophisticated, needs to be further examined, I think. It is based on a theoretical-practical analysis that is extremely ingenious and precise. If

---

discussions about the subject. Here is also the place to thank both Germain Grisez and John Finnis for raising some very useful objections to my own argument and having helped me thereby to introduce some important refinements.

29. See "Every Marital Act," 371: "Since contraception must be defined by its intention that a prospective new life not begin, every contraceptive act is necessarily contralife. Those who choose such an act often also intend some further good—for example, not to procreate irresponsibly with bad consequences for already existing persons. But in choosing contraception as a means to this further good, they necessarily reject a new life. They imagine that a new person will come to be if that is not prevented, they want that possible person not to be, and they effectively will that he or she never be. That will is a contralilfe will. Therefore, each and every contraceptive act is necessarily contralife."

30. "Insofar as contraception is contralife, it is similar to deliberate homicide" (ibid., 372).

the argument is removed from this context, however, it becomes falsified and even scandalous, because contraception could then be seen as analogous to homicide or even to murder. It is not possible for us here to enter into the details of the argument (the complexity of which—despite its exactness—casts doubt on entire argument); it is nevertheless clear that the authors do not and could not mean that contraception is a type of murder.

I think this contralife-will argument contains some essential errors. The most important is its basic and decisive presupposition that the contraceptive act—considered *in itself* as an intentional act—does not refer in its essence to the fulfillment of sexual acts but rather (with respect to its intentionality) *only and exclusively* to impeding the beginning of a human person, which would be immoral.[31] (In other words, this argument presumes that contraception is a question of justice, not chastity.)

The question is simply whether this basic supposition that contraception is not intrinsically related to sexual acts is correct. If it is, then the issue would be to justify the analogy (not identity) of intention with a voluntary act of killing. Certainly, the aim of killing, considered in itself, is against the life of a person. Therefore, if such an analogy does exist, then there would truly be a relationship between the physical event and the will contained in it.[32] Nevertheless, there seem to me to be a number of objections to this.

Let me offer only a few, insufficient, remarks. What the argument claims, I think, would be true only if children came into being spontaneously; in this case, adopting a device that impedes this would then intentionally be nothing but "impeding the beginning of a person's life." But babies come into being as a consequence of a human (sexual) act. Taking, for example, an ovulation-inhibiting pill does not, in itself, impede babies from coming into being; it only impedes ovulation. You

---

31. Cf. ibid., 369–71.

32. It is also not particularly clear how such a will oriented against the life of a person who does not yet exist should be valued morally. Even if there is an intentional analogy, it is not yet clear whether there is also an analogy in the moral valuation of situation. For the authors of the contralife argument, this analogy is supplied by means of a moral evaluation based on their theory of practical reason, with the difference between an already existing person and an only possibly existing person being secondary, and the "fundamental good of human life," thought of in rather abstract terms, taking the primary place. Cf. G. Grisez, J. Boyle, J. Finnis, "Practical Principles, Moral Truth and Ultimate Ends," in *American Journal of Jurisprudence* 32 (1987): 99–151.

cannot rationally take it with the intention to impede the beginning of a baby's life, unless you simultaneously choose to engage in sexual intercourse, and precisely *for this reason* you choose to prevent intercourse from causing a baby's life by inhibiting ovulation. It seems, therefore, impossible to describe a contraceptive intentionality *independent* of the will to carry out a sexual act that in turn is the *cause* of the beginning of a new human life. This, however, would contradict the basic assumption of the contralife argument, according to which contraception, considered in itself, has nothing to do with the carrying out of sexual acts, but is rather directed essentially and exclusively against the coming into being of a new human life.

Therefore, it seems to me that contraception seeks only and precisely *to prevent sexual intercourse from causing* the beginning of a person's life. From this it also follows that, insofar as the *intentional* relation to "the beginning of new life" is concerned, the volition involved in a contraceptive choice does not differ from the volition necessarily involved also in a choice to *refrain* from intercourse: *in both cases* one chooses "not to cause the initiation of new life" (and precisely to not cause it by means of *sexual acts,* not sexual acts in the sense of intercourse itself, but in the sense of acts pertaining to the virtue of chastity). So, it does not seem that the difference between contraception and periodic continence is due to their different intentional relation toward "the beginning of a person's life." It is due, rather, to their different intentionalness with regard to *sexual activity* and its being a possible *cause* of the initiation of new life. Contraception and periodic continence are therefore primarily and essentially two different modes of sexual behavior (that is, pertaining to chastity) and not two different ways of relating intentionally to the life of a person.[33]

33. If one considers the intentional orientation against "the bringing about of the beginning of a new human life" to be "contralife," then continence as well must be considered a "contralife act." The authors of the "anti-life" argument therefore expressly say that "not want to cause the baby" is not a "contralife will" (*"Every Marital Act,"* 405). This is obviously correct. To claim that a contraceptive act is essentially "contralife," the authors are therefore constrained to assert that it must be described as intentionally independent of the choice to carry out sexual acts that could cause the birth of a new human being. Described thus, the contraceptive intentionality would be: "Those who make this choice do not want the baby" (ibid.). It is precisely this that I contest.

Finally there is the anthropological argument, based precisely on the doctrine of the inseparable connection of the two meanings of the marital act. That is, it presents the indissoluble link between the unitive and procreative meanings of the conjugal act as *in itself* an argument against contraception. This doctrine, I think, is basic as a starting point and as the indispensable anthropological background for any argument against contraception. It does not seem to me sufficient, however, for also arguing that in each *single act* of contraceptive intercourse this connection is denied in a way that is essentially different from periodic continence. One might still object that periodic continence, the intentional limiting of sexual intercourse to infertile periods, is simply *another* "method"—although not "artificial," but "natural"—of disconnecting sexual intercourse from its procreative meaning. To simply state that contraception, on the other hand, involves positively "doing" something that "impedes" conception is not sufficient; it would simply beg the question, or perhaps imply the perverted-faculty argument. Why, in fact, should an "active intervention" of itself constitute a morally relevant factor? Rather, it has to be shown why actively *preventing* intercourse from causing conception violates the Inseparability Principle, while *abstaining* from causing conception does not. I intend to provide an argument for exactly this purpose.

Descriptions of the Relevant Case and the Contraceptive Choice

Contraception as an Intentional Human Action

In the subsequent analyses, I will concentrate on the problem of the contraceptive choice itself as a determinate sort of human act, one that deliberately employs a contraceptive measure. This analysis applies to the above-mentioned relevant case, which involves the following descriptive elements:

1. The spouses' *morally upright intention* to avoid pregnancy.

2. The fact that *periodic continence is therefore a licit alternative.*

3. The at least implicit *choice not to adopt periodic continence,* which is the refusal to abstain from those acts that are foreseen to have procreative consequences.

4. *Instead of choosing periodic continence,* the choice to adopt means that *prevent* possibly procreative consequences of all sexual intercourse performed in any moment. This means can be the "pill," as well as other chemical, mechanical, or surgical techniques such as condoms, IUDs, or sterilization, but also "natural" means such as *coitus interruptus* (the interruption and onanistic conclusion of intercourse). On this level of argument about distinctively human acts, these means involve the same kind of act.

We are thus analyzing contraception as a type of *human act.* For the present purpose I will suggest the following description (descriptive definition) of the choice of this human act: *A contraceptive choice is the choice of an act that prevents freely consented performances of sexual intercourse, which are foreseen to have procreative consequences, from having these consequences, and that is a choice made just for this reason.* It seems to me that this is a complete description of the contraceptive choice, and it does not matter whether it refers to contraception within or without marriage. It involves:

1. to intend to engage in sexual intercourse;
2. to foresee that this possibly may cause the initiation of new life;
3. to choose a performance that prevents this consequence; and
4. to choose this precisely for the sake of preventing this procreative consequence.

As I have already remarked, this description also applies to onanism by coitus interruptus because this behavior intentionally prevents the actual engagement in sexual intercourse from having its procreative consequences. On the other hand, it obviously applies to surgical sterilization, which embodies a strong intentionality against procreation. In some way it even covers abortion, insofar as abortion is intended as part of a contraceptive policy. In other words, it covers abortion insofar as it is *previously anticipated* for undoing the foreseen procreative consequences of sexual intercourse. In this case abortion involves both the contraceptive choice and the choice of killing an already existing human being.

Notice that the description of contraception that I adopt is absolutely independent of what is happening on the physical level. In order to resolve the problem at issue, it makes no difference whether one considers the case of preventing a performed sexual intercourse from being fertile by taking the pill, or the case of interrupting intercourse so as to consummate it in an onanistic way. Of course, there are differences of *other* kinds; but they are not relevant in the present context. The suggested description also disregards the differentiation between "doing" and "refraining from doing," because coitus interruptus is a kind of "refraining" and because, moreover, this description obviously *does not* apply to adopting contraceptives to prevent possible procreative consequences of foreseen rape, for this person does not choose to engage in sexual intercourse or to prevent a possible consequence of her own sexual behavior. The same holds for an athlete who, for example, during the time of the Olympic Games takes a preparation that blocks ovulation, so as to avoid menstruation. Thus, what I have called the "ethical context"—and therefore the *object* of the action—is completely different.[34] It does apply, on the other hand—although even here there would need to be further specification—to forced sexual intercourse between spouses, because marriage involves commitment to engage in the conjugal act.[35]

By adopting this description, which brings into clear relief the theoretical-practical substance of the human action "contraception," we will be able to point out that the reason why contraception is wrong is not simply because it violates naturally given structures of the generative faculty or other "natural" laws. This description helps us to account for the fact that not every act of intentionally preventing conception (such as periodic continence) implies such inference with natural processes, and that other acts—such as taking a ovulation-inhibiting pill under fear of rape, or to avoid menstruation in a sporting event—do interrupt natural processes but are not the human act forbidden by *Humanae Vitae* in our relevant case.

Many erroneous judgments are based simply on an insufficient definition of the *human action* "contraception," or rather on a definition

34. See my *Natur als Grundlage der Moral*, 367–74, in English as *Natural Law and Practical Reason*, 475–84.

35. This is certainly not to say that forced intercourse within marriage is morally justifiable. This problem needs a special treatment, although here is not the place to address it. I will say this, however: in cases where a woman is regularly "raped" by her husband (who, for example, is an alcoholic), the only truly human solution would be separation, at least temporarily (not divorce), and certainly not anti-conceptive measures. Contraception, in fact, would only worsen the woman's situation morally! In such cases, one must offer real help, rather than "solutions" that only further degrade the woman, making her all the more simply an object for the man. Solutions valid for all cases we cannot offer, however, at least here.

on the purely medical-technical level. Regarding contraception in *this* merely physical sense, however, no moral judgment can be made, but at most a judgment concerning technical effectiveness. As such, there are "better" and "worse" contraceptive methods, with respect to their effectiveness, side-effects, and so on. To make a moral judgment, we must describe "contraception" as a mode of action issuing from free will (as an *actus humanus*). Only in this way does it become clear that not every action that is "contraceptive" medically—such as blocking ovulation—is also the human action of "contraception." Rather, from the point of view of the *moral object,* there could be completely different actions: on the one hand, what we have defined as "contraception," and on the other the action of "self-defense from the procreative consequences of a physical aggression," or "maintaining physical fitness."

This definition also accords exactly with the formulation of the norm adopted in n. 14 of *Humanae Vitae*. We cite it again: "Similarly excluded is every action which, either in anticipation of the conjugal act, or in its accomplishment, or in the development of its natural consequences, proposes (*intendat*), whether as an end or as a means, to render procreation impossible." Note that we find here a limitation to the "conjugal act." Even if the norm is applicable in a similar way to sexual relations outside marriage, this mention of the conjugal act implies that we are dealing with a norm directed at freely chosen sexual relations. Secondly, the formulation of the norm speaks of *an intention,* which is part of the description of the action (and therefore of its object): "to render procreation impossible," whether as a means intended in view of another end, or as an end willed in itself. In our case we are interested only in the first: the intention to impede the transmission of human life chosen as a *means* of reaching the legitimate end of "avoiding a conception." This description does not regard either the case of rape or that of the athlete: in the first there is in fact no choice to carry out sexual acts (indeed just the opposite choice), even though the end here is precisely to "impede procreation"; in the second case, there is no intention to prevent procreation, at the level either of a means or of an end. The only thing that the act "intends" is to impede menstruation or the resulting damage to one's sporting outfit.

The norm formulated in *Humanae Vitae* refers, therefore, to a specific kind of human action voluntarily performed, and *not* to the factual physical event "contraception." The formulation adopted in the encyclical does not speak at all of an intention directed against the "natural repercussions" of sexual acts, rather of an intention oriented toward "the impediment of the transmission of life." Consequently, those "contraceptive" physical acts that—notwithstanding their "artificiality"—are not directed toward the regulation of the procreative consequences of freely chosen sexual relations and do not intend to impede the transmission of life do not in any way fall under the norm formulated in *Humanae Vitae*. And the recurring expression "in the development of its natural consequences" is here completely without relevance. Rather, it refers to a state of affairs relevant for the description of that action *to which* the norm refers; but it is not itself an integral component of the norm itself, much less of its foundation.[36]

On the Structure of the Following Argument

In the next chapter, I shall develop my argument in the following steps:

1. An initial exposition of the anthropological meaning of the Inseparability Principle; this will lead to the definition of the *object* of sexual intercourse. *This is the cornerstone of my argument.*

2. A clarification of what "procreative responsibility" as derived from the Inseparability Principle means within the context of an ethical theory that is based on the concept of moral virtue. *This step renders anthropological insights applicable to concrete human actions.*

3. The analysis of the difference between contraceptive intercourse and intercourse in the context of a practice of periodic abstinence as two radically different forms of sexual behavior, containing the proof of the objective disconnection of the two meanings of the conjugal act as resulting from contraception. *This piece of action analysis forms the very core of my argument.*

4. The exposition of some intrinsic implications of contraception, mainly disintegration of sexuality and its consequences for marital love.

36. On the relation between "intentional actions," "descriptions of action," and "moral norms" see my *The Perspective of Morality: Philosophical Bases of Thomistic Virtue Ethics* (Washington, D.C.: The Catholic University of America Press, forthcoming), originally published in German as *Die Perspektive der Moral. Philosophische Grundlagen der Tugendethik* (Berlin: Akademie Verlag, 2001).

This shows that contraception in fact contradicts the good of persons, because the separation of the (inseparably linked) meanings destroys the unitive significance of marital sexuality. *This shows the gravity of the moral disorder implied in contraception.*

5. Finally, I shall point out *why by this argument contraception has been shown to violate natural law.*

I would like to draw attention to the importance of the *methodological order* implied in the following way of proceeding. Equally, I wish to stress that I shall *not derive* an argument against contraception from the Inseparability Principle, but rather *prove* the very *truth* of this principle on the level of single performances of actions. The anthropology implied in the Inseparability Principle is nothing but the starting point of the argument and its cornerstone; the proper core of the argument, however, will be contained in the third step: the analysis of the morally relevant *difference* between periodic continence and contraceptive behavior.

Do allow me just one supplementary remark. I shall not speak of "natural family planning" (NFP), or even use the term, for three reasons. In the first place, because "natural" is a rather misleading term in this context, in the sense that it insinuates, although incidentally, a difference with "artificial." Therefore, instead of NFP, I will speak only of "periodic continence" and "procreative responsibility." Second, periodic continence does not necessarily mean a "planning" of the family, but it refers in the first place to a form of behavior by means of which, for serious reasons of procreative responsibility, the conception of offspring can be avoided. Third, in the treatment of NFP the accent is placed on certain *methods* by which one determines with greater security the times of fertility and infertility. What is essential to periodic continence vis-à-vis contraception is not, however, something "methodological." If one speaks, therefore, of NFP as an alternative to contraception, the emphasis is put on something that already leads away from what is essential.

3

Toward an Adequate Argument in Support
of *Humanae Vitae*

The Necessary Integration of Anthropology, Action
Theory, Virtue, and Natural Law

The Meaning of the Inseparability Principle,
or the "Object" of the Marital Act

The Anthropology of Corporeal-Spiritual Unity
and the Human Person

Like all basic principles, the Inseparability Principle must be
"shown" rather than demonstrated. It is an anthropological
principle expressing the fundamental unity of human persons
as compound beings of body and spirit. In his consciousness,
the acting person spontaneously possesses at least implicit
awareness of this complex unity. A human person experiences
the body, and the body's acts, as "his" or "her" body and "his"
or "her" acts that belong to one's personal "Self." Metaphysical
anthropology will, in a systematic way, elucidate this experience, coming to the following results. Man is essentially a
bodily being, and as such he belongs to the genus of animals.
At the same time man is also spirit. He is, as Aristotle says, a
organized organic body animated by a spiritual soul; according to the terminology of the scholastics, which in part refers
back to Aristotle, he is *animal rationale*: a living being endowed with reason. The spiritual soul is the substantial form

of a body, which therefore is a *substantial unity*. Consequently, man's corporeality is fully integrated into the structure of spiritual life; it is "informed" (essentially actuated and determined) by spiritual life, becoming itself the *subject* or "carrier" of spiritual acts.

So the acting human subject is always a body-spirit *unity*: Human acts are not *either* spiritual *or* bodily acts; nor are they acts of a spiritual substance that makes use of the body as its "instrument." Human acts are always, although in different ways, acts of body *and* spirit *cooperating*. Human acts are therefore, even in the case of properly inner acts of intelligence and will, always acts of a *body*, though of a *spiritually informed body*. Likewise human acts are, even in the case of properly bodily acts, always acts of a *spirit*, although of a *bodily bound* spirit, that is, of a spirit that by its own nature is the substantial form of a body. Thus, there is only *one* "suppositum" (real, existing individual thing), whose nature (or "essence") includes body and spirit and which we call the *human person*. Thus, Thomas Aquinas says that the *soul separated* (after death) from the body can no longer be called a "person"; it is rather the soul of one who at one time was a "human person": a concrete individual bodily-spiritual "human being."[1]

This differs entirely from the christological—hypostatic—union of two natures in one person; man therefore is not a "incarnated spirit." Nor is he "spirit in the world" (K. Rahner), or "reason in nature" (W. Korff), because he does not belong to the genus of spirits, but rather to that of *animals*. For this reason it is erroneous to equate the "personal" element in man simply with his spiritual element, so as to then oppose this to an understanding of "nature" as the corporeal element as a "sub-personal structure," or as merely "thingly" and "beneath man."[2] Man indeed is a

---

1. Cf. *Summa theologiae* I, q.29, a.1, ad 5. Also on this see W. Kluxen, "Anima separata und Personsein bei *Thomas von Aquin*," in *Thomas von Aquino. Interpretation und Rezeption*, ed. P. Eckert (Mainz: Matthias-Grünewald, 1974), 96–116.

2. Cf. e.g., among many: K. Rahner, "Das 'Gebot' der Liebe unter den anderen Geboten," in *Schriften zur Theologie*, vol. 5 (Einsiedeln-Zürich-Cologne: Benziger, 1962), 513; F. Böckle, "'Humanae vitae' und die philosophische Anthropologie Karol Wojtylas. Zur päpstlichen Lehrposition zur künstlichen Befrüchtung und ihrer Begründung," in *Herder Korrespondenz* 43, no. 8 (Freiburg: Herder, 1989): 376; L. Bertsch, *Akzente der kirchlichen Ehelehre con Pius XI bis Johannes Paul II. überlegungen aus der Sicht eines Pastoraltheologen*, in *Der umstrittene Naturbegriff*, ed. F. Böckle (Düsseldorf: Patmos Verlag, 1987), 122; H. Rotter, "Tendenzen in der heutigen Moraltheologie," in *Stimmen der Zeit* 4 (1970) 265–66; A. Auer, *Die Autonomie des Sittlichen nach Thomas von Aquin*, in *Christlich glauben und handeln*, ed. K. Demmer and B. Schüller (Düsseldorf: Patmos, 1977), 31–32.

person *because of* his spirituality (without the spirit there would be no person); but the human person is the *entire* man, because he is an essential subsistent bodily-spiritual unity, a *substance*. Alternatively, what we might call the "spiritualistic" concept of the human person falsifies the interior unity of the person and tends toward understanding the body as the instrument and "material" of the spirit, of the person's freedom, or of the spiritual subject. Therefore, it could not but seem equivocal when "norms of sexual behavior" are understood to refer merely to "*thingly* mechanism*.*" In this case, they are taken as not yet "true moral norms [which are] expressions of the structure of the person," because they are seen to refer only to the "structure of things," which are said to be "*beneath man.*" According to the spiritualistic anthropology, moreover, "[m]an may change them, subdue them, to whatever extent he can; he is their master, not their servant: ultimately, the only structure of the person which adequately expresses him is the fundamental capacity to love."[3] While we certainly agree with the last phrase, we cannot agree with the penultimate: man is neither the master nor the servant of his "nature" and bodiliness; rather he *is* precisely this bodily nature and he *is* a body. And, inasmuch as that nature and bodiliness are always an integral part of the language of human love, they find, as we have said, their adequate fulfillment as the structure of the person only through the fundamental capacity for spiritual *love*.

The full, essential integration of love and its acts into the life of the spirit—that which specifies man as a being joined to the material world—includes also the integration of the body in the structure of spiritual *love,* a love that is based on free will and reason, and whose specific act is the free gift of self. This love therefore also implies *dilectio*: voluntary choice of, and dedication to, another person.

---

3. Rahner, "Das 'Gebot' der Liebe," 507 and 513–14. Similarly, Rotter, "Tendenzen in der heutigen Moraltheologie," 264, calls the structure of corporeity an integral part of the sub-personal "laws of nature." This "sub-personal nature bears traits that are expressly inhuman. It must therefore be cultivated, or manipulated, by man." For this reason it may also "not be a moral obligation to simply respect such laws. Man must rather seek by means of medicine, regulation of births and political activity to neutralize them. Man's dignity therefore requires a cultivation, in the sense of the humanization of nature." The author plays with the idea that, in the past, inhuman "ordering factors" such as war and high mortality "prevented even worse catastrophes, such as the diminishing of hereditary patrimonies, overpopulation, poverty and hunger." For him, therefore, regulation of births would have a function analogous, but human, to the "humanization of nature," in the sense of the latter's "cultivation."

Because of this fundamental substantial unity of body and spirit, human love is not only a spiritual reality, but also a corporal one (a truth that is also relevant to our love of God).[4] The spiritual human soul also speaks the "language of the body," which is proper to it because this spirit is, *by its very nature,* the substantial form (the soul) of the body.[5] The body has to be considered as "subject," and not as "object" or "means" of spiritual love: *The human body fully belongs to the subjectivity of the acting person.* It is part of the human "I." This "I" is not only the spirit; the body also constitutes the human "I." The "I" (as spiritual soul) does not find itself "facing" the body, rather it *is* this body. This is why one finds in Thomas Aquinas the pregnant phrase: *Anima mea non est ego:* "My soul is not identical with my 'I.'"[6]

The Essential Unity of Procreation and Love

On the other hand, there is a simple fact based upon the bodily constitution of man: propagation of the human species takes place through bodily acts of procreation. Human procreation, therefore, is a *basic human good* (and not only a good on the physiological level in the sense of a mere "natural" outcome of a biological process). Procreation is a basic human good to the same extent as is human life: the outcome of the procreative process is not simply a "living body," but a living *human person.*[7] Because of the substantial unity of man, moreover, this act of procreation cannot be disconnected from the spiritual dimension of the soul: the corporal act of procreation necessarily acquires a spiritual dimension; the act of human procreation *is* essentially a spiritual act as well. Being integrated in human nature, it is also spiritual love; it is *dilectio* in the sense of rational and voluntary loving, and is therefore marked by the seal of free mutual self-giving of two human persons. Indeed, the act of conjugal love is not simply an act of the procreative faculty or of the body, but rather that of a person, and therefore a human

4. Cf. on this my annotation on virginity and celibacy in *Natur als Grundlage der Moral,* 127–28; in English, see *Natural Law and Practical Reason.*

5. "Spirit" and "soul," however, are not simply equivalent; the human soul is also the principal form of all the other vital functions of man; it is, nevertheless, essentially a spiritual soul.

6. *Commentario all Prima lettera ai Corinti, 15, lect. 2.*

7. Cf. also M. Rhonheimer, "Sozialphilosophie und Familie. Gedanken zur humanen Grundfunktion der Familie," in *Familie—Herausforderung der Zukunft,* ed. B. Schnyder (Freiburg: Freiburger University Press, 1982), 113–40; and M. Rhonheimer, *Familie und Selbstverwirklichung* (Cologne: Verlag Wissenschaft und Politik, 1979).

act that is carried out voluntarily. Neither is the marital act a simple "material mechanism," in which the structure of spiritual love is not an intimate component, as part of a human action.[8] Rather, a human act of procreation, on the basis of the essential integration of all bodily acts in the nature of the human person, is itself already and essentially an act of spiritual love. Of course, it could also be carried out contrary to the logic of love. According to its nature, however, it is an act of personal, and therefore also spiritual, love; it is truly the act of a human person.

If the marital act were not such a unity of body and spirit, it would involve a deep dichotomy—and principle of disintegration—within the structure of the person. This would imply a kind of dualistic anthropology, not one that opposes the body, but one that understands it precisely as "subpersonal," as that which must be *made* human, that is, elevated to the human level.[9] Thus, *Humanae Vitae* no. 10 rightly points out that the biological laws of the generative faculty are not merely a "biological" fact that man meets while experiencing his bodily drives; *rather they are human goods belonging to the human person,* an integral part of man's personal subjectivity.[10]

For the same reason, this spiritual act (love between male and female and its expression in the "language of the body") is bound to the conditions of the body itself, because, as we have seen, the body is *subject,* "carrier," of spiritual acts. In every act of procreation, spiritual soul and body are thus *mutually correlated* and *cooperating;* they are—strictly analogous to the matter-form composition on the ontological level—*cooperating principles in the act itself;* they are two cooperating prin-

8. As Rahner seemed to intend; cf. "Das 'Gebot' der Liebe," 507.

9. Although the footnote reference in *Humanae Vitae,* no. 10, to *Summa theologiae* I–II, q.94, a.2, is sometimes misunderstood as implying a dualism between body and person, it should instead be understood as I have just explained. This dualistic interpretation seems to have been held in the theological working paper of the "majority group" of the famous Pontifical Commission on Population, Family, and Births. See for this G. Grisez, "Dualism and the New Morality," in *L'Agire Morale* (*Atti del Congresso Internazionale: Tommaso d'Aquino nel suo settimo centenario,* vol. 5, ed. M. Zalba (Naples: Editions of the Italian Dominicans, 1975), 323–30. See also my previously cited *Natural Law and Practical Reason* (originally *Natur als Grundlage der Moral*) for a more detailed examination of spiritualism and anthropological dualism underlying some influential schools of post-conciliar moral theology (mostly those influenced by Karl Rahner).

10. Whereas the majority group of the mentioned Pontifical Commission wrote: "foecunditas biologica in sfaeram humanam assumi debet" (biological fecundity must be assumed into the human sphere), a statement that Grisez, in his above-cited article, rightly reproaches for implying anthropological dualism. See his "Dualism and the New Morality," 328.

ciples which will yield in each case *one single* human act. So, through the spiritual, the body acquires a new dimension; and through the body the spirit acquires a new dimension as well.

From this, several consequences follow. In the case of man, sexual acts are more than simple sexual copulation ordered to procreation; they are *essentially* acts of the free, mutual, self-giving of two loving persons. On the other hand, acts of marital love, which consist in reciprocal self-giving, are in their bodily dimension always acts of "this" body, which entails that they have a procreative meaning. No one can deny *this* procreative meaning without rejecting a constitutive property of the body, although by emphasizing this fact, one is not asserting that every act of sexual copulation is, or should be, procreatively *effectual*.

Based upon this analysis, we are now equipped with the elements required to understand precisely the two meanings of the conjugal act, as well as the principle of their intrinsic connection:

1. To be fully human, *procreation presupposes spiritual love:* the act of mutual self-giving. Human procreation has its place within the context of spiritual love, which is the context of a community of persons, and not instinct; it is informed by the "logic" of this love as the body is informed by spiritual life. And this is the case, even though man possesses instincts and impulses. That "function" which in animals pertains to instinct, in the case of man pertains precisely to spiritual love, formed by reason, which carries out its acts in freedom. Acts of human procreation are therefore destined to receive their form from this love, and precisely in the measure to which the body is formed by the life of the spirit. Procreation withdrawn from this context would no longer be fully *human* procreation. Nor would it be merely animal, because it would lack a specific completeness proper to the procreative acts of animals: the sufficient guidance of the impulses on the part of instinct. If human-personal subjectivity were understood in a purely spiritual way, the biological structures of procreation inscribed in the human person would be interpretable as a simple instrument that the "spiritual subject" "uses" for his desired ends. The boundary with procreative technology would in that case be fluid.[11]

11. See chapter 5 of the present volume, which was originally published in a shorter version as "Zur Begründung sittlicher Normen aus der Natur. Grundsätzliche Erwägungen

2. By the same token we may affirm the following. *Love between male and female,* insofar as it tends, *by its very nature,* toward consummation in bodily union—that is, insofar as it springs from the *naturalis inclinatio ad coniunctionem maris et feminae,* from sexual inclination—*possesses a procreative dimension,* because it is love between two bodily-constituted spiritual beings. In other words, the loving bodily union of male and female is, by its own nature, "service to transmission of life." Of course, there exist different forms of love between persons, and different possible forms of love between human beings of different sexes. For example, we find mere fellowship, camaraderie, friendship, the love between brother and sister, and that between parents and children. However, the loving attraction between male and female, which springs from the sexual inclination and tends toward bodily union in sexual acts, is—taking into account the body-spirit unity of man—*specified by* this very tendency. This implies that love between man and woman is specified by the naturally given condition of the body to be "procreative love," which has a "function," or better: a task.

Therefore, the "inseparable connection" of the two meanings signifies their *reciprocal inclusive correlation.* The bodily reality of procreation receives its fully human specification from spiritual love; the spiritual love of the married persons receives its specification as a determinate *sort* of love from the procreative function of the body.

Thus, for a correct and exhaustive understanding of the Inseparability Principle, it is decisive to recognize that these two meanings are neither merely "added" to each other, nor merely conjoined or accumulated "functions" of which each has its full intelligibility *independently* from the other. Rather, each receives its full intelligibility as a *human* reality—its fully *human* meaning—precisely *from the other.* Procreation considered independently from spiritual love *is no longer the same thing.* And spiritual love tending to the bodily union between male and female, when considered apart from its procreative meaning, *is no longer the same thing.* This precisely is what follows from man's substantial body-spirit unity.

---

und Exemplifizierung am Beispiel der I.v.F."; it was then published in the fuller form as "Die Instrumentalisierung des menschlichen Lebens. Ethische Erwägungen zur In-Vitro-Fertilisierung," in *Fortpflanzungsmedizin und Lebensschutz,* ed. F. Bydlinski and T. Maly, Pubblicazioni del Centro di Ricerca Internazionale per le Questioni di fondo delle Scienze, Salzburg, Nuova Collana, vol. 55 (Salzburg, Innsbruck-Vienna: Tyrolia Verlag, 1992), 41–64.

If we consider things in this perspective of the substantial unity of body and spirit, then the reason why these two meanings are inseparably connected becomes obvious: by separating them we would *alter* both the meaning of human procreation *and* the meaning of marital loving union. Both meanings are not extrinsically, but *intrinsically* connected: *The very connection constitutes the specifically human content of both meanings.* And, the horizon within which this link is understood is the corporeal-spiritual composition of the human person.

A Further Specification: The Distinction between "Function" and "Meaning"

Let us further specify a point that is somewhat implicit in the foregoing exposition: *Humanae Vitae* no. 12 speaks about the inseparable connection of two *meanings* (*significatio*), and not of two *functions* of the marital act. Only a *fertile* sexual act can have a "procreative *function*"; an *infertile* act, by definition, will never have a procreative "function," but it may have a procreative *meaning* if it is intentionally open to procreation. "Procreative function" depends on actual fertility, which in a determinate moment may or may not be biologically given.[12] Thus, to speak about "inseparability" of procreative and unitive "functions" would not make much sense; for only a few sexual acts are actually "fertile" and therefore have—from the physiological point of view—a procreative "function."[13]

12. The failure to distinguish between these two aspects is, it seems to me, one of the central errors of J. T. Noonan, "Natural Law, The Teaching of the Church and the Regulation of the Rhythm of Human Fecundity," 550. See also the excellent response of J. Boyle, "Human Action, Natural Rhythms and Contraception: A Response to Noonan," *American Journal of Jurisprudence* 26 (1981): 32-46. Noonan rightly sees that *Humanae Vitae* does not condemn contraception because of its artificial character or because it disturbs the natural process (551); but he then asserts that the condemnation is based on the will, implied in contraception, to destroy the connection between the conjugal act and the natural rhythms of fertility, a connection that is constitutive and "symbolic" for conjugal love. Noonan gives his assent to *HV*'s teaching interpreted in this way, and then goes on to justify "exceptions" (on the basis, among other things, of reflections on the structure of the cycles of fertility). Noonan's interpretation of *HV*, however, is inadequate, as Boyle shows in his response. In fact, Noonan focuses entirely on the question of fertility cycles. Boyle ("Human Action, Natural Rhythms and Contraception," 39) is fully justified in his reproof: "Biological rhythms are relevant for the employment of the norm which forbids contraception, but their moral relevance presupposes the norm."

13. The misunderstanding and confusion between "function" and "meaning" is obvious in B. Häring, "The Inseparability of the Unitive-Procreative Functions of the Marital Act," 178

"Inseparability," however, means that this "cannot" be done, where "cannot" means it is "not *permitted*." If this were all that *Humanae Vitae* (*HV*) said on the matter, then reference to a "double function" of the conjugal act would be completely irrelevant, because it would not demonstrate how that which in effect *can* be done is nevertheless not licit to do.[14] Obviously, the procreative "*function*" *can* be entirely suppressed or separated from the love-expressing "function of the marital act. The Inseparability Principle, as stated by *HV*, does not simply state that one is "not allowed" to separate these functions. Instead, it says that one *cannot* do so without destroying the very *meaning* of the marital act. The encyclical in fact refers not to "functions," but to "meanings" of the conjugal act, and it claims that one cannot separate these two meanings without destroying *both*, and therefore its *entire* meaning as an act of conjugal love. As it says in n. 12: "By safeguarding both these essential aspects, the unitive and the procreative, the conjugal act preserves in its fullness the sense of true mutual love and its ordination towards man's most high calling to parenthood."

Therefore, the emphasis on the inseparability principle seems to be not because it formulates a norm ("it is not permitted"), but rather that it provides the *reason for* the norm. This is evident from the phrase introducing the paragraph: "That teaching . . . is founded upon." And the reason states: the preservation of *both* the meanings is dependent precisely on their being linked (as has been shown in the preceding section). The point is that *HV* speaks about an *anthropological* inseparability of the two meanings, which are not two functions but two *aspects* of the one and indivisible *essence* of the marital act; therefore *HV* refers also to the two meanings as "essential aspects" or "essential qualities" (*utraque eius essentialis ratio*) of the marital act. In reality, both meanings form

---

(already this title expresses the misunderstanding): "The expression 'open to the transmission of life' has much less meaning now. The marital act during pregnancy is acknowledged as being 'open to new life', and so is the conjugal act in the infecund periods despite the fact that scientific calculation might practically eliminate the probability of any transmission of life. It is unfortunate that Pope Paul uses the same phrase in referring to the 'constant doctrine' of the Church when historically the expression originated at a time when scientific theories on infecund periods were unknown." Häring still thinks in biological patterns instead of adopting an intentional (moral) viewpoint.

14. Based on such reasoning, L. M. Weber, "Exkurs über *Humanae vitae*," 608, necessarily arrives at the conclusion: "Why this link is indissoluble, and why man may not intervene precisely here to guide things, is not said."

together *one single, but complex, unity of meaning,* which is a true expression of man's substantial and therefore essential unity of body and spirit.[15]

Only on these grounds, I think, it is possible to fully render justice to what HV affirms in no. 11: that *every* marital act must be open to procreation, and must have a procreative meaning, which is *inseparably* connected with the unitive meaning. This analysis is valid also for those acts that, by nature, are biologically infertile and therefore have no procreative "function." Such human acts, which in themselves (*in se*) and by their essence (*per se*) are ordered to the "generation of human life," contain a procreative significance. The intentional aspect—the will of the spouses—is therefore decisive, and in this sense HV speaks of a necessary "openness" of conjugal acts with respect to the "generation of human life." A lack of this intentional openness would result in the destruction of both the procreative and unitive meanings of the conjugal act, which is to say its content of love. Both are therefore *inseparably* linked, the one to the other.[16]

It is only in this light that we can grasp the true meaning of *HV,* which *articulates the necessary conditions such that matrimonial sexuality can be an expression of true love.* In fact, regarding the question of contraception—about which we are not yet ready to express a judgment—one does not treat so much the "transmission of life" itself, as the defense of matrimonial sexuality as the true expression of personal, con-

15. Of course, without a basic, naturally given procreative "function" of sexuality no sexual act could bear a procreative "meaning." But, even if "meaning" has its roots in a "function," as the intentional content of a human act it possesses a certain independence from the actual fertility of the act. This follows from integration of the "natural" into the higher order of the spirit.

16. Let me again quote Häring, "The Inseparability of the Unitive-Procreative Functions of the Marital Act," 188: "It is not easy to explain the relationship of the procreative to the unitive good in the marriage of proven sterile partners. Their marriage can fulfill the unitive meaning while it cannot truly and really fulfill a procreative role." Again, the same misunderstanding, overlooking meaning for the sake of function seems to be at work. But afterward, surprisingly, Häring affirms: "However, I think the combined functions are not totally excluded in such marriages, in which the partners truly consider each other as spouses, and love each other in a way *that would keep them open for the parental vocation were such within the range of possibility.* One who sincerely loves his spouse as spouse would not refuse to have him or her as parent of his or her child *if the choice were given*" (the emphasis is mine). This is surprising, because it is entirely correct; Häring here focuses the problem in a clearly intentional way. If he had treated the problem of contraception in the same way, he would have been able to understand the encyclical's teaching.

jugal *love*. Thus, *HV* is entirely on the same plane as *Gaudium et Spes,* and there is no reason to claim that "*HV* would not correspond to the need according to which a moral norm is not to be judged with respect to natural ends, but rather according to the *bonum humanum*."[17] In fact, the encyclical's teaching is just the opposite; even those who reject it should at least take note of its true intention and theme.

The Inseparability Principle, therefore, is not simply a reformulation of a negative precept, but the very (anthropological) *rationale* that provides the reason *why* one *cannot* separate one meaning from the other without destroying the whole. And because one *must not* destroy conjugal love (a point on which everyone agrees), this explains why *it is illicit* to effect such a separation. Philosophically speaking, we may thereby *conclude* that such a separation would be contrary to God's will and that, therefore, one *may not* realize it. With this, however, we are still far from a demonstration that contraception in fact realizes a separation of these two meanings, whereas periodic continence does not. It is important that we proceed one step at a time.

The "Object" of the Conjugal Act

From the Inseparability Principle derives the identification of the *object* of the marital act of sexual intercourse. The object of a *human act* (which is an act conceived as proceeding from a deliberate will) is its *act-specifying* content. These so-called moral objects are the objects of the rationally guided will's choices to do something.[18] Thus, objects of human acts are neither the naturally given goals of inclinations (that is, natural ends) nor "things" for which we are acting or aiming. Instead, they are, as Aquinas says, "*formae a ratione conceptae*."[19] Or using words

17. Oeing-Hanhoff, "Der Mensch: Natur oder Geschichte," 34. It is also said here—incorrectly—that the encyclical does not base itself "in its rational argumentation on the question of whether a good, reasonable life of the partners and that of humanity are damaged by the artificial regulation of births—in fact it neither wrongs nor damages anyone—rather, on the already mentioned presupposition, ultimately derived from the Stoa, that the criteria of morality must be the following of physical natural laws."

18. This has also been well-demonstrated by W. E. May, *Moral Absolutes, Catholic Tradition, Current Trends, and the Truth,* 41–42.

19. See I–II, q.18, a.10, where Aquinas properly says: "Species moralium actuum constituuntur ex formis, prout sunt a ratione conceptae." But the *species* is formed by the object of an act (which includes also the goal of the intention, which as well is a specifying object). For a detailed interpretation of this doctrine see my previously cited *Natural Law and Practical Reason,* 90–93, 410–51; originally published as *Natur als Grundlage der Moral,* 91–98; 318–74.

of a contemporary author: "We must always remember that an object is not what what is aimed at *is*; the description *under which* it is aimed at is that under which it is *called* the object."[20] This somewhat complicated formulation means something very simple. If, for example, person A robs a horse from person B, the object of this action is not "the horse which, according to the law, belongs to B." In other words, the moral object is not merely the object at which A aims, with respect to "what it is in itself"—that is, simply the horse. Rather, it is this horse, to the extent that it enters into a description that also tells us what A *desires or chooses* when he takes the horse from B. In other words, the object of the moral act is what A does in an intentional sense: rob the horse from B to take it as his own. The object of the action, "to steal a horse," is therefore: "To rob a horse which, in conformity with the law, is possessed by another" (or: "to take it for oneself"). For this reason, such descriptions according to which actions are chosen (their "object") are the *intentional content of these actions*, which content in fact can only be the object of reason; they are "formae a *ratione conceptae*." "Object" refers therefore to that which one does when one here and now does something *with an intention*. Such descriptions under which actions are chosen are meant to be the *intentional contents of these actions*; they refer to *what* one is doing when one does "this" on *purpose*.[21] Precisely in this intentional manner we earlier described and defined the objective structure of the action "contraception" as a specific type of intentional action.

As we have seen, the human act of procreation essentially is an act

---

Compare with this the rather naturalistic and biological intent of defining the object of the marital act made by the "earlier" Josef Fuchs in his "Biologie und Ehemoral," *Gregorianum* 2 (1962): 225–53.

20. Anscombe: *Intention*, 2nd ed., 1963 (Oxford: Basil Blackwell, 1979), 66, 35.

21. Cf. Anscombe: *Contraception and Chastity*, 17. There is an ambiguity in the term "intention." "Intention" always signifies to relate to something by one's will; where there is an act of the will, there is an intention informed by practical reason. Human acts are chosen and, therefore, referred to with an act of deliberate (rationally guided) willing. Thus, "objects" of human acts have to be described in terms of intentions. See also Anscombe: You Can Have Sex without Children, 86: "We always need to distinguish the intention *embodied in* an action from the further intention *with* which the action is done; I am here concerned only with the former. Whatever ulterior intentions you may or may not have, the question first arises: what intention is inherent in the action you are actually performing? It is one thing to have or not have certain further intentions, another to modify the intentional action you in fact perform. What concerns us is the question: what are you here and now doing on purpose—whatever your ulterior aims?" What one is "here and now doing on purpose," and this means: what one is intentionally doing, this precisely is called the *object* of the act.

of loving bodily union. Its unitive meaning is not just "one" mean-ing and the openness to procreation "another." It would be nonsense to say that *sometimes* spouses perform intercourse to express mutual love and *sometimes* to procreate a new human life, or that *sometimes* they "do both things" together. What they deliberately choose (that is, the description under which their doing is chosen) is always one and the same: to give themselves with their whole spiritual, affective, emo-tional, and sexual being to loving union (which, of course, *physically* is copulation; surely, however, "to copulate" is not the description under which normal couples *choose* or even desire physical copulation; hence, it is not to be called the "*object* of sexual intercourse"). They give them-selves to loving union whether procreation is actually intended or not. The reason for this is as follows. *Every* act of intercourse—even if the intention to procreate is the direct and explicit reason for actually en-gaging in intercourse—is by its very nature an act of the *loving* union of bodily-spiritual persons; procreation is effectuated precisely by lov-ing, mutual self-giving of the spouses in the totality of their body-spirit-unity. Therefore, every procreative act actually *is* expressing loving union; human life arises from this love between a man and a woman. In the rather extreme case that sexual intercourse were performed without *any* mutual affection (exclusively for the sake of "making a baby," say), the act would be profoundly vitiated. When sexual intercourse, on the other hand, is performed in knowingly infertile periods, the nature of the act is again the same: loving union, mutual self-giving of the spouses. If, for physiological reasons, procreation were not possible—and were even permanently foreseen as such—the objective meaning of the spouses' action would not be affected by this. The reason is that what they *inten-tionally* do (what they "choose") is to engage in an act of loving bodily union, which by its very nature serves procreation. The act they perform is a generative sort of act;[22] even if it does not have a procreative *function* (because of its being infertile) it nevertheless maintains its procreative *meaning*. If this act—for natural reasons beyond intention—cannot have procreative efficiency, this does not alter what one *intentionally* does (what one chooses) as long as one did not *do* (choose) anything for the end of *preventing* procreation. Human acts are specified by the object of one's will, and not by facts of nature that fall outside the reach of human

22. For this I refer again to Anscombe: *You Can Have Sex without Children*, 85.

choices. As has been already emphasized above, the two meanings of the marital act are two inseparable aspects of *one* object.[23]

Consequently, an act of loving union that is knowingly infertile may be *objectively* procreative, when it is considered as an intentional action—a human action of that type (*species*) which, on the basis of its essence (*per se*) is ordered to the generation of human life. Therefore, the "object" of the conjugal act is neither "procreation" nor "expressing mutual love." We should rather define it as something like "loving bodily union" or "mutual self-giving in the totality of one's bodily-spiritual being." In so doing, however, we must take into account that "loving bodily union" of the spouses has to be understood as "consummation of marital love," which obviously *includes* both the intentional openness to procreation (because of the very nature of the body as well as of the sexual character of marriage) and cooperation with God's creative love (because of procreation's involvement in God's creative love).[24] We must, above all, provide an adequate definition of *marital love*; then we will be able to understand correctly the object of marital intercourse as precisely the *consummation* of this love. Thus, conjugal acts would be altered in their *objective* meaning—in their very meaning as acts of "loving union"—by intentionally excluding their openness to procreation.

Two brief comments would be appropriate here. In the first place, it must be emphasized that, by this discussion, we are not ignoring the possibility of sexual relations *outside* of marriage. The decisive point, however, is that sexuality possesses essentially a marital (or "spousal") meaning—and this *properly* and *exclusively* in the case of human beings. Marital union is therefore not only a "possibility" of performing sexual

23. Precisely this was overlooked in Josef Fuchs's previously cited article "Biologie und Ehemoral." He considered the marital act as having two objects, or *fines operis*, a primary and a secondary one. It may seem paradoxical, but Fuchs was not able to conceive the objective unity of the marital act because he considered "objects," and especially the "procreative meaning," as a kind of "natural function," and not as the content of intentional actions. As an example of "biologism," this article is still illuminating.

24. T. G. Belmans comes to a very similar result in his *Le sens objectif de l'agir humain*, 425. Here the object of the conjugal act is defined as follows: "l'union sexuelle entre conjoints, ouverte quant à son sens vécu, à la transmission de la vie." The German edition of Belmans's very accurate study, *Der objektive Sinn menschlichen Handelns: Die authentische Ehemoral des heiligen Thomas von Aquin* (Vallendar: Patris Verlag, 1984), puts it even better at p. 478: "die geschlechtliche Hingabe an den Ehegatten" ("sexual self-giving to the spouse"), "die inbezug auf ihren erlebnismässigen Sinngehalt für eine mögliche Weitergabe des Lebens offengehalten wird" (what, more simply, could be expressed as "intentionally open to procreation").

intercourse between man and woman; the true nature of sexuality—considered as a human and personal reality in the full sense—consists precisely in its *matrimonial* meaning: the reciprocal self-giving of two human persons of different sexes, without reserve and permanently. *The marital bond is the truth of human sexuality,* the specifically human-personal perfection of the sexual impulse. The human phenomenon "marriage" arises therefore precisely from the sexual impulse—indeed, "marriage" *is* essentially sexuality, or rather sexuality in its full anthropological truth, in its *specifically human form* as an impulse of *persons,* that is, of bodies (or of "living bodily beings") animated by spirit, a form in which the impulse and the bodily acts that issue from it are precisely "love," that is, the reciprocal gift of self of two persons permanently and without reserve. Sexual relations outside of marriage are in no way a fulfillment of *this kind* of love, and therefore contradict the *objective* meaning—the truth—of human sexual acts.

In the second place, the traditional doctrine of the "two ends of marriage" (*fines matrimonii*) does not refer to exactly the same thing as the "two meanings of the conjugal act"—a distinction that is often missed. The *finis secundarius,* that is, the secondary end of marriage (the *mutuum adiutorium,* mutual help in life), does not, as such, have anything to do with the conjugal act, the unitive meaning of which obviously is not identical with "mutual help in life." This "secondary end" refers rather to marriage as a special type of *social reality,* which in conformity with traditional doctrine, is a communion of man and woman specified primarily (fundamentally) by the task of the transmission of human life. The so-called primary end of marriage is therefore that end which *specifically distinguishes* the conjugal communion from other social bodies. The "conjugal act," however, is obviously not the same thing as "conjugal communion"; the conjugal act is rather the ultimate and most intimate fulfillment (*consummatio*) precisely of that love *from which springs* the conjugal commuion; or rather, the fulfillment of that love by means of which two persons bind themselves to one another to form a communion of life, a communion of persons who, on the basis of their corporeal-sexual identity, are at the service of the transmission of human life.

With this, however, we are not saying that the relationship of love between the spouses is characterized or justified "primarily" by the end of the transmission of life and "secondarily" by their mutual assistance and help in life. If things were such, one would then have to conclude that each spouse loves the other "primarily" only for the love of the children that issue from the marriage, and "secondarily" because of the help in life that the other offers; one ends in reality with loving only one's children, or the other as a "help in life"; the marriage partner would be simply a "means" of reaching these ends, and would be loved only for the love of something else. Clearly, this would be absurd.

Love between spouses is rather—as with every authentic human love—love for a concrete person, which also means, in a certain sense, love for a person *for himself*. If human beings do not love one another in this manner, they simply do *not love*—this is true, although in different degrees, for *every kind* of interpersonal love. The discussion concerning the two ends of marriage necessarily presupposes this, and at the same time includes it. In this sense also the "purpose" or "end" of love for a person is the person himself, and nothing else. And in the case of marriage, bodily-sexual union is precisely the ultimate fulfillment and expression of this love.

The discussion of the "ends of marriage" refers, then, to something different: it refers to the fact that from this love between persons who give themselves to one another without reserve arises a new human life, and that this is the primary fruit of this love, which *specifically distingushes it from all other types of interpersonal love*. Only secondarily is it proper of this marital love that it also bears the "fruit" of reciprocal help in life, something that in fact could also be characteristic of other types of communion of human life. But the "service of the transmission of life" is *specific* to the marital bond between man and woman, and therefore it is also called its primary end. The reason for this priority is that only in marriage, and by means of it—that is, in the environment of a communion of personal love—can the natural end of the "transmission of life" be reached in a manner worthy of man (this exclusivity would be difficult to affirm concerning the "secondary end" of marriage). The "ends" of marriage are therefore, so to speak, the functions given by nature in the realm of (1) the preservation of the human species and (2) the preservation of human communal life. Love, however, is neither an end or a function; rather, it is a way of assuming "ends" and "functions" consistent with human dignity.

Love could not be an "end" of marriage; it is rather its foundation and content, a content that is, nonetheless, characterized by a natural end in a specific way: at the service of life.[25] In effect, man is a "structured, ordered unity of reason, personhood, functionality and nature."[26]

From this we can conclude that to speak of the *object* of the conjugal act is, from a *conceptual* point of view, something completely different than to speak of the ends of marriage. In the "object" of the conjugal act, the aspect of "loving union" (its unitive content) is the *fundamental* aspect (and not at all secondary), *and as such it implies the procreative meaning* (which, in its own turn, is neither primary nor secondary, but rather inseparably linked with the former). Precisely *this,* which is the essentially and intrinsically procreative meaning of the love between man and woman, is then the reason for which procreation can be, and must be, the end that principally specifies the conjugal communion. This marital communion possesses this procreative purpose in the measure to which, as a "conjugal communion," it is a communion of persons who love one another and are inclined to bodily union (because it is a sexually characterized love). By this we can conclude that the traditional discussion of the "two ends of marriage" and that of the "two meanings of the conjugal act" belong to two *different* (even if closely connected) sets of questions.[27]

In the 1930s, an influential theologian, Herbert Doms—originally a zoology student—attempted to develop a more personalistic doctrine on marriage,[28] precisely to oppose a doctrine that was generally held at that time, and that Doms himself understood in an overly biologistic way. According to this doctrine, procreation was considered the "primary

25. See also, concerning this, my previous reflections in "Sozialphilosophie und Familie," and *Familie und Selbstverwirklichung.*

26. W. Kluxen, "Menschliche Natur und Ethos," *Münchener Theologische Zeitschrift* 23 (1972): 17.

27. They therefore express dimensions that are not mutually exclusive, but rather complementary. Today, discussions of questions of marriage law often seem to take too little account of this; they fail to recognize the distinct but complementary nature of these doctrines when they more or less replace the doctrine of the inseparable link between the two (equally legitimate) "meanings of the conjugal act" with that of the two (hierarchically ordered) "ends of marriage."

28. H. Doms, *Vom Sinn und Zweck der Ehe* (Breslau: Ostdeutsche Verlag, 1935), published in English as *The Meaning of Marriage,* trans. George Sayer (London: Sheed and Ward, 1939). See also Noonan, *Contraception,* 496–500.

end," or *finis operis,* of the conjugal act.[29] Because Doms—as many after him—failed to see why this doctrine was equivocal, he arrived unfortunately at false supposition that "loving union" must be considered the primary end of marriage (and of sexuality in general), whereas in reality "loving union" is the fundamental aspect of the *object of the conjugal act.* In my opinion, contemporary moral theology still suffers from the consequences of this misunderstanding and the confusion it caused.[30]

Insufficiency of Referral to the Principle of Inseparability

With this determination of the "object" of the conjugal act, the meaning of the Inseparability Principle should be clear. What have I shown up to this point? I have shown that the intentional foreclosing of the procreative dimension of loving bodily union alters *objectively* the very nature of this union into a kind of "love" that is at odds with the anthropological truth of man: it contradicts the substantial unity of body and spirit. In the context of our case, however, this is not a sufficient proof for the contention that contraception *does* in fact involve such a foreclosing. So, I wish to emphasize the following: *I have not yet proven that contraception is wrong.*

The reason for this is that our case is based on the presupposition that avoiding pregnancy is rightly demanded by procreative responsibility; that spouses *ought to* avoid conception here and now. On this supposition someone could rightly ask the following question: "Why in order to meet this requirement while maintaining fully the procreative meaning of marital love *in its totality,* should one not be allowed to uncouple sexuality's procreative efficiency from its unitive function *at least on the level of single performances of marital acts* (that is, 'sometimes,' 'occasionally,'

---

29. G. Martelet—certainly one of the most influential co-redactors of *Humanae Vitae* and one of the most resolute defenders of its doctrine—in his article cited above, "Moral conjugale et vie chrétienne," approved and made his own this same criticism of Doms (cf. 247–48) that I have just summarized. Martelet rejects the notion of "procreation" as the *finis operis* of the conjugal act, that is, as its true and proper "object." He says instead that the conjugal act, based on its essence, is before all else an act of love—a specific kind of act of love—and, also essentially, the source of new human life. The entire encyclical is characterized by this perspective, namely that the marital sexual act is in its essence an act of love, but an act that is also characterized by the fact that this love is a love that is in the service of the transmission of human life.

30. Cf. for example the well-known comment of B. Häring on *Gaudium et Spes,* n. 47–52, in *Lexikon für Theologie und Kirche,* 2nd ed., vol. 14 (supplementary vol. 3) (Freiburg: Herder Verlag, 1986), 423–46.

or 'temporarily')?" Contraceptive intercourse then would be supposed to receive its procreative meaning from the overall intention with which marital life is lived in its totality. "Why not," one could ask, "adopt contraception, given that we are bound to avoid pregnancy precisely for reasons of procreative responsibility?" "Why not prevent sexual intercourse that is foreseen to have procreative consequences from having these consequences?" "Why should the suppression of the procreative *function of single sexual acts* necessarily suppress also their procreative *meaning, provided that* contraception is chosen on the grounds of the very intention of *responsibly* serving the transmission of life?" "Why is this basic intention not sufficient for respecting the inseparable connection of the two meanings required by the 'truth of man'?" "Why is this unity required to be maintained also on the level of single performances of conjugal acts?" And finally: "Why is periodic continence—abstaining from those acts that are foreseen to have procreative consequences— the only behavior that is an upright, and therefore morally permissible, way to live the virtue of procreative responsibility under given circumstances? Is this claim not a piece of subtle hair-splitting, is this not mere sophistry, the only point of which could be seen in the rather abstract demand of respecting the biological patterns inherent in human nature, a demand which, in the given situation, can hardly be made intelligible as a *moral* requirement?"

Such questions actually show that appealing to the Inseparability Principle *alone* does not yet resolve the problem of contraception. Precisely at this point, critics of the encyclical have employed the so-called principle of totality (*Ganzheitsprinzip*). R. McInerny has shown that such a use is not valid here.[31] Actions that, as intentional single acts, are immoral with respect to their object cannot be justified by means of the totality of the development of a life; for example, individual lies cannot be justified based on a life dedicated, in its totality, to truthfulness— they remain lies. Instead, individual actions determine and shape the development of a person's life as a whole: the life of one who here and now lies is, in its totality, less dedicated to the truth than that of one who always speaks the truth. The effectiveness of this response, however, presupposes that it *first* be shown that the action in question is, as a *single*

31. Cf. R. McInerny, "*Humanae vitae* and the Principle of Totality," in *Why Humanae Vitae Was Right: A Reader*, ed. Janet Smith (San Francisco: Ignatius Press, 1993).

action, immoral on the basis of its object. Only then can the argument we have just cited be put to use.

In the case of contraception, the simple reference to the principle of inseparability *by itself* is in fact not capable of responding to this fundamental question. We need a *further* argument to substantiate that contraceptive acts *do* indeed violate this principle *in every case.* That is, we need an argument that shows the Inseparability Principle is indeed valid on the level of *single performances of actions* as well as on the level of overall intentions. Therefore, additional action analysis is required. I shall have to show why contraception and periodic abstinence are two very different kinds of human behavior and why the former is not compatible with procreative responsibility while the latter is. This is equivalent to showing that contraception is incompatible with the *objective* meaning of single performances of the conjugal act. Without so doing, it could not be proven that the Inseparability Principle is a principle valid for judging *each single performance of the conjugal act.* To reject contraception requires that we establish such a principle, because otherwise resorting to it would be simply question begging. To establish that the Inseparability Principle is indeed valid for judging single conjugal acts, I will have first to say a few words about "procreative responsibility." I wish to emphasize that *only at this point* we are entering into the proper perspective of natural law, and also that of the moral virtues.

Procreative ResponsibilityProcreative Responsibility as an Integral Part of the Virtue of Chastity

Procreation in the realm of animals is steered by instinctive drives. According to the famous dictum of the roman lawyer Ulpian, "the natural inclination to the conjunction of male and female" is something "that nature has taught all animals," including man. Yet, with St. Thomas Aquinas we have to add that nature did not teach all animals to follow this inclination under the guidance of reason and will; that is, to pursue it *responsibly.*[32] Non-rational animals follow their instincts, and so they fulfill the will of the Creator. But man—the "rational animal"—can ful-

32. About Ulpian and Aquinas see the article by William E. May "The Meaning and Nature of the Natural Law in Thomas Aquinas," *American Journal of Jurisprudence* 22 (1977): 168–89, and the references given there.

fill this will only as a responsible agent, as the master of his own actions, as a "interpreter of God's will," participating in the Creator's providence by his own acts of intelligent understanding. Precisely this *active, intelligent* participation in divine providence, or the ordination (brought about by human acts under the guidance of rational intelligence) toward what is good for man, is what properly is called "natural (moral) law" (*lex naturalis*). Man has to judge regarding what is right or appropriate to do or to omit. By simply following his instincts he could not fulfill the will of his Creator.

Humanae Vitae (no. 10) says the following about "procreative responsibility" or "responsible parenthood":

- One must know and observe the specific functions of the biological processes involved in procreation and that they belong to the human person;
- one must exert dominion by reason and will over one's "innate drives and emotions";
- one must judge responsibly one's own physical, economic, psychological, and social conditions in order to decide about either enlarging the family or not having any more children, either for the time being or even for an indeterminate period; finally,
- "Responsible parenthood also implies, above all, a more profound relationship to the objective moral order." In their consciences, spouses ought to integrate the means into the right moral order, taking into account their duties toward God, themselves, their family and human society.

This description of responsible parenthood also provides a precise characterization of the virtue of chastity. Chastity means not simply continence, but mastery of one's sexual drives so as to integrate them into the order of personal love. Chastity—as with every virtue—is aimed at love, service, and responsibility, not only toward one's spouse, but also toward the human community. That is why, according to Thomas Aquinas, chastity is not contradicted by what he calls an only "apparent incontinence," proceeding from that "passion of the sensitive appetite [that is] good in so far as it is regulated by reason."[33] Indeed, normally

---

33. See Aquinas's *Summa theologiae* II–II, q.156, a.2. As for all translations from the *Summa theologiae*, unless otherwise noted, this one is from that of the English Dominicans (Westminster: Christian Classics, 1981).

sexual intercourse is elicited by spontaneous sensual desire. That conjugal acts be "according to reason" does not require engagement in them on the grounds of rational deliberation (aiming at procreation or at rendering the marriage debt). This would be quite an unrealistic view; however, this is not to say that the oft-criticized "fulfillment of the marriage debt" couldn't be done by one of the partners out of a genuine motive of charity, faithfulness, and goodwill, since to do something simply for such love of another is indeed an act of love. Fortunately, we need not subscribe to Benjamin Franklin's grimly utilitarian and puritan view, "Rarely use venery but for health and offspring." Conjugal love has its own spontaneity that follows from sexual inclination and the drives proper to it, which is quite different from "acting purely for pleasure." What is required is *habitual* or *virtual* integration of this desire into the order of reason that is also the order of human love.

Besides the very important and often neglected fact that responsible parenthood may also lead the spouses to decide to *enlarge* their family, procreative responsibility basically means the morally upright and virtuous integration of sexual drives into the dominion of reason and will. It means following sexual inclination reasonably and, therefore, responsibly performing sexual acts as *human acts* guided by reason-informed will. Thus, procreative responsibility means sexual behavior fully integrated in the requirements of spiritual life, a specific kind of *virtuous self-control*.

Procreative Responsibility, Chastity, and the Virtue of Temperance

Procreative responsibility as part of the virtue of chastity is not compatible with just *any* kind of integration. Because procreative responsibility is part of the virtue of chastity, and chastity implies the virtue (habitual perfection) of a capacity of sense appetite and desire, this integration is such that it also brings to perfection this capacity of desiring, in correspondence with the anthropological truth of man as a bodily-spirit unity. The body and its sexual drives are not "nature" in the sense of nature which "surrounds" us, or in which we merely live, "find ourselves," or are "acting on." The body's sexual drives do not belong to such an object-world of nature, but to a nature that *contributes to the constitution* of our own substantial being and, therefore, *belongs* to our own *subjectivity*. We are not spirits simply "placed in the environment of a body." We do not "have" a body, but we *are* bodies. Sexual drives of the body are called to be informed by spiritual life and, on the other hand, to be themselves *subject* of this spiritual life. This entails that acts of procreative responsibility do not consist in just *any kind* of rational and voluntary "controlling," "guiding," or even "suppressing" sexual drives. Sexuality is not a mere *object* of procreative responsibility, but must become its subject: man's substantial unity requires that sexual behavior, the sexual acts themselves, be informed by the requirements of responsibility.

This applies generally to the moral virtue of *temperance,* to which chastity belongs: the virtue of temperance means tempering, modifying the very sensual appetites according to reason. This means neither "suppressing" them nor rendering them "harmless," but "impressing in them the seal of reason"[34] and its requirements, so as to enable sensual appetites *themselves* to pursue what is according to reason and responsibility.[35] Referring to Aristotle, Thomas Aquinas says that the sensual desires are "by nature oriented to obey reason." "As such, the capacity of concupiscent desire, as well as the irascible capacity, can be *subjects* of human virtue. In the degree to which they participate in reason, they are a *principle of human action*."[36] The decisive issue in the virtues of temperance and of fortitude consists precisely in the following: they make sensual concupiscence into a *principle of action* in conformity with reason, that is, a cause that moves action and governs it, in such a way that the demands of reasonableness inform the action precisely *by means of* the sensual impulses. This amounts to the same as the already cited *integration* of these impulses into the context of human action, in accord with its fundamental anthropological truth (the bodily-spiritual unity of man). This obviously does not concern those bodily functions that are not "by nature oriented to obey reason," such as the heartbeat, blood circulation, the functioning of the liver, digestion, and the like.

34. See Thomas Aquinas: "Virtus appetitivae partis nihil est aliud quam quaedam dispositio sive forma sigillata et impressa in vi appetitiva a ratione" (*De Virtutibus in communi,* a.9).

35. See, e.g., *Summa theologiae* I–II, q.56, a.4, where Aquinas explains that the sensual appetites are "natae rationi obedire," so as to conclude: "Et sic irascibilis vel concupiscibilis potest esse *subiectum* virtutis humanae: *sic enim est principium humani actus,* inquantum participat rationem."

36. *Summa theologiae* I–II, q.56, a.4.

These can never be principles of action because they are simply organic bodily functions; at most, they can be the object of action, as in a medical intervention. Of course, sexuality includes such purely organic functions. But *the sexual drive* itself is much more than such a function; it is a human desire subject to the dominion of reason and will, a desire that has as its object what we call a *human good,* pursued by an agent in his free action.

Moral virtue never consists in acts of repelling or suppressing sensual inclinations and their proper goods or goals. Such acts can be necessary as a part of the inner struggle by which a virtue is acquired or its possession preserved; indeed, "through continence man becomes recollected and brought back to the unity from which he was alienated, dispersing himself in the many."[37] Nevertheless, to conceive virtue itself in this way would be a rather spiritualistic conception, implying anthropological dualism. Acts of temperance—and therefore acts of chastity and procreative responsibility—will always be acts whose subject is in some way the sensual appetite itself, modified in accordance with reason. They will be *acts of sexual behavior,* and not merely acts of a behavior that has sexual organs as its object, acting upon them by means of some measure (analogous to the intervention of a doctor). This means that sexual acts engage not only reason but the *whole* human person, including his bodily dimension that is striving for those goods that, according to dictates of practical reason, the will pursues. Thus, acts of procreative responsibility will be acts in which the body has the function of a *principle* of actions.

The elaboration of this concept of procreative responsibility as an integral part of the virtue of chastity is the pivotal move toward a differentiation of contraceptive sexual behavior and sexual behavior in the context of periodic continence. This concept of procreative responsibility as a moral virtue corresponds fully to the Inseparability Principle, but it enables us to bring this principle down to the level of single performances of sexual acts, to the level of concrete sexual behavior.

To show the validity of the Inseparability Principle, not only on the level of the guiding intentions underlying marital love in its totality but also on the level of single conjugal acts, we need to understand two com-

37. Augustine, *Confessions* X, 29.

plex points. First, that "procreative responsibility" is not simply responsible behavior *in relation to* sexuality, but rather a specific, responsible sexual behavior in which our sexuality itself is a *subject* and therefore a operative *principle* of procreative responsibility. Second, that "openness to procreation"—as a part of the objective content of the conjugal act—means "procreative responsibility." For virtues are shaped by and aim at concrete performances of *acts* and their corresponding choices; and single acts and their corresponding choices are morally specified by their intentional contents, which spring from the virtues to which they belong. This will become clearer when we proceed in the argument, analyzing now the difference between contraceptive intercourse and intercourse in the context of periodic continence *precisely as two different kinds of sexual behavior.* With this, we are arriving at the core of the argument as it will be treated in the following section, which offers an analysis of the difference between contraceptive sexual behavior and periodic continence.

Contraceptive Sexual Behavior and Periodic Continence

It is therefore only this third step that contains the argument against contraception, properly speaking. To identify the wrongness of the contraceptive choice, we have to start, however, by considering the practice of periodic continence. This, I think, is a necessary methodological requirement. In themselves, "failures" or evils of any kind have no intelligibility; for they have a "privative" character—they are the absence of a due good; that is, they are a deficiency. To discover the lack, therefore, we must in the first place know the good the absence of which constitutes the evil. *Moral failures, evils, or vices are intelligible only in light of the goods or virtues they oppose.*[38] Therefore, we have to consider first what spouses really *do* (and, therefore, choose) when they are responsibly practicing periodic continence.

38. This is the method adopted by Aquinas; see the Prologue to II–II: "peccatum, cuius etiam cognitio dependet ex cognitione oppositae virtutis" (sin, knowledge about which depends on knowledge of the opposing virtue). And: "est autem eadem materia circa quam virtus recte operatur et vitia opposita a rectitudine recedunt" (it is the same matter about which virtue rightly operates from which the opposing vice recedes). So, the method consists in "totam materiam moralem ad considerationem virtutum reducere" (the entire subject matter of morals being thus condensed under a consideration of the virtues). The original translation from the Latin was by the author.

Spouses adopt the practice of periodic continence guided by a reason to avoid pregnancy, which induces them to refrain from sexual intercourse at appropriate times. They know that there are some periods in which intercourse is likely to lead to pregnancy, and others in which it is not; and perhaps, with the help of an appropriate "method," they are able to discern which is the case. But they equally know that the conjugal act is perfectly licit even if it is performed only for the reason of expressing mutual love. They will therefore *abstain* from intercourse during knowingly fertile periods; and they will have intercourse only in periods that are foreseen to be infertile. Notice: the "method" (if ever adopted) in itself does not serve to avoid conception, nor does it prevent it. The "method" only provides some *knowledge* about fertility rhythms. What *regulates* conception is the act of abstaining from knowingly fertile intercourse. Independent from acts of continence, so-called natural methods do not regulate anything. Thus, to speak comparatively about so-called natural methods and artificial (contraceptive) methods is entirely misleading; they are both "methods," but with entirely different immediate aims, functions, and outcomes. In the case of natural methods, the method itself is not essential; it only helps periodic continence to attain its purpose. Therefore, we are not dealing with a (natural) method of avoiding conception, much less a (natural) method of *contraception.* In the case of contraception, as we will see, the method is simply the whole; it is what essentially and sufficiently regulates conception by simply rendering sexual acts infertile.

It is important to emphasize that the given description of periodic continence includes not just one, but *two different,* although closely related, acts of "sexual behavior," in the sense of pertaining to the ethical context of the virtue of chastity. *Both* the performance of engaging in intercourse *and* the performance of continence—the voluntary act of *refraining* from intercourse—are authentic acts of *sexual behavior.* Moreover, the act of refraining is an action proceeding from a common decision of the spouses; both are engaged in abstaining from an action that is foreseen to effect conception, which they both wish to avoid. They realize their intention to avoid this conception by avoiding the performance of the act that would lead to it. This act of avoiding *is* a bodily act of procreative responsibility. It is not simply an "omission" in the sense of "not doing something," something purely "negative"; rather it is an act of willing renouncement to engage here and now in sexual intercourse and, thus, a *determinate kind of voluntary bodily action,* to say a *deliberate human act of sexual behavior.*

Moreover, this act of refraining from intercourse is a real *conjugal* act; it is obviously not one of sexual intercourse itself, but it is a conjugal act of renouncement. In such an act of restraint, the two meanings of marital love are present; it is an act with a fully procreative meaning, in the sense that it is performed for reasons of the virtue of procreative responsibility. *It actually is, by its very intentional content—and thus objectively—a bodily act of procreative responsibility.* By abstaining from possibly fertile intercourse, spouses relate virtuously to sexual acts, to themselves, and to each other as a possible cause of new life. This respecting of their sexual activity as such a cause—and provided that they feel obliged not to beget a baby—is precisely the reason why they abstain from intercourse. By acting together in their restraint, the spouses moreover act as two persons "united in one flesh": their behavior proceeds from procreatively responsible marital love and serves this love. Therefore, such acts of procreatively responsible continence have a proper *marital* and even *parental* meaning; they are loving acts of bodily constituted persons, who by mutually and commonly renouncing intercourse respond responsibly to the exigencies of their marital and parental vocation. *In another way than intercourse itself, such acts of responsibly abstaining from it are true expressions of both the procreative and the unitive meaning of sexuality, inseparably connected.*[39]

The problems, burdens, and difficulties possibly involved in a practice of periodic continence, to which its critics so often refer, have to be considered as the burdens and difficulties involved in faithfully carrying out marital commitment and *not—as* critics usually do— as something interfering with marital love. These burdens and difficulties may be overcome precisely by the fact that continence *is* an act of marital love in itself. The very nature of responsible abstinence includes the dynamic principle for overcoming these difficulties: this principle is precisely "marital love," which must be continually deepened,

39. Cf. the well-argued article by J. Bajda: "Verantwortete Elternschaft und Antikonzeption," in *Elternschaft und Menschenwürde,* ed. E. Wenisch (Vallendar: Patris Verlag, 1984) 243–60.

in this case through renunciation *for the sake of love* and responsibility.

By responsibly abstaining from intercourse, spouses only abstain from a determinate *kind* of bodily expression of mutual love; *but they obviously do not thereby abstain altogether from marital love and reciprocal self-giving.* This common task of overcoming possible difficulties involved in practicing periodic continence will be a proper component and a fruitful touchstone of marital love. Within the context of the "logic" proper to periodic continence, what may seem like a burden changes into a source of maturing in love and increasing in mutual self-giving. Only in light of an already deeply implanted contraceptive mentality may such practice of periodic continence appear unreasonable.

Sexual intercourse is, actually, not the only way to express marital love, even in a bodily manner, and it is not the only way of mutual self-giving. Leaving aside other expressions of affection, acts of continence will also be such acts if they are informed by responsible love. This is what is commonly overlooked. Equally, one often overlooks that sexual desire is not frustrated or spoiled by the fact of not being satisfied; just the contrary is the case. Responsibly abstaining from sexual intercourse does not involve forcing oneself to "stoic insensibility," shelving sexuality from marital life or even denying it. By the very act of responsibly refraining from its satisfaction, sexual desire is both *affirmed and integrated* into the "logic" of personal love. In this way, it is affirmed as a *human good to be pursued responsibly,* and as a source of increased unity between the spouses. At the same time, it is also true that periodic continence is not the only means by which this integration can come about; it ordinarily comes about by means of the consciousness that a new life could begin as the result of sexual acts, and the intentional openness to this fact. In the case we are discussing, however, continence itself is the temporary condition for the preservation of the procreative significance of sexual acts, and therefore for the integration of sexuality into the larger context of personal love.

On the other hand, sexual intercourse performed in this context of periodic abstinence during knowingly infertile periods is not only an act of loving union, but also an act that fully conserves its procreative meaning, because it is intentionally, and therefore "objectively," embedded in the structure of procreative responsibility. The point I wish to make here is that *these spouses live this responsibility by the means of*

*their bodily love, by sexual behavior, modifying this behavior for reasons
of responsibility.* So sexuality, including its procreative dimension, is
fully integrated into procreatively responsible behavior, into the life of
the spirit: this operative integration is nothing other than the virtue of
chastity as described above (see section on procreative responsibility,
chastity, and the virtue of temperance).

It seems, therefore, that chastity is bound to the condition that sexual intercourse never be intentionally prevented from bearing procreative
consequences; this, as it seems, is just what *HV* calls the "*per se* openness
to procreation." But notice: this is only a *previous condition* and not the
rationale of the virtue of chastity. It is a condition made out *as a* condition precisely through providing a *further* argument that finally reveals
its being such a condition. Respect of the natural rhythms of fertility is
neither a norm nor the basis for a norm, but it becomes perceivable as
a moral demand—as J. Boyle rightly argues against J. T. Noonan—only
in the light of the moral norm, which latter cannot be deduced from the
"naturalness" of fertility rhythms.[40]

Contraceptive Sexual Behavior

Let me now consider *contraceptive behavior.* Contraception signifies that, to avoid conception, sexual behavior need not be modified. Of
course *something* in the behavior must be modified: there is required a
certain discipline, from one of the spouses at least in taking the pill, say,
according to medical prescriptions (but this is incidental, as the cases of
sterilization and IUDs show). In any event, sexuality, precisely the sensual appetite or drive, need not be modified (which, of course, is equally
the point of onanistic orgasm achieved by coitus interruptus).

Thus, while the former couple, by performing the bodily act of responsible continence chose to *avoid* those acts that were foreseen to have
procreative consequences, contraception means to choose an act that
impedes possible procreative consequences of sexual intercourse. Thus
on the level of performed sexual acts, spouses do not modify anything;
what they do is *prevent* these acts from being fertile so as to render needless the responsible modification of sexual behavior. Unlike continence,
this act of preventing sexual behavior from possibly procreative conse-

40. Cf. Boyle, "Human Action, Natural Rhythms, and Contraception," 39.

How is limiting intercourse to infertile times being *per se* open to procreation?

because of abstinence during fertile times?
seems contradictory

quences is not in itself a *sexual act*; it is exclusively a "method," which *relates to* sexual acts only by preventing their procreative consequences.

This clearly shows that the contraceptive act is problematic not because of its "unnatural" character, understood in the sense of "artificially" obstructing the natural process of ovulation or fecundation, which, as it is obvious, does not happen in the case of coitus interruptus. Rather, in this case—which is different from other types of artificial interventions (for example, medical ones)—the unnaturalness or artificiality is problematic only because the *mode of behavior* connected with it is morally wrong. Contraception is problematic precisely because of the fact *that it renders needless a specific sexual behavior informed by procreative responsibility; it also involves a choice against virtuous self-control by continence.*

The act of procreative responsibility in the case of contraception is a pure act of deliberate will, which treats sexuality and the body as its *object* (equal to a diseased liver, heart, or digestive apparatus). Consequently, sexual behavior itself is withdrawn from being informed by responsibility regarding its being a cause of new life; in addition, it is withdrawn from its being called to be *subject and principle* of this act of responsibility and of procreatively responsible marital love. Procreative responsibility of the sexual act itself is eliminated and denied. Sexual acts are impeded from being a cause of new life, and the acting person is no longer acting as such a cause. Mostly in the case of sterilization, there is no longer need for even *thinking* about procreative responsibility. The procreative dimension of marital love is entirely "turned off," and precisely at the level of its bodily expression. All that remains—leaving aside the intention in our case, in itself licit, of avoiding a conception for responsible reasons—is the claim of expressing marital love by these acts; but this love has altered its meaning by the very exclusion of its procreative meaning. These acts *cannot* be an expression of *conjugal* love, because conjugal love is that between two persons who are joined in a communion of life at the service of the transmission of human life.[41] So,

41. One could certainly deny this meaning of marriage; to argue against such a denial, however, is not the purpose of the present argument. The critics of *Humanae Vitae* in fact do not want to deny this either. Cf., e.g., Böckle, "'Humanae vitae' und die philosophische Anthropologie Karol Wojtylas," 375 (regarding "Familiaris consortio"): "It is incontestable that 'the fundamental task of the family is to be at the service of life,' as with the statement that bodily and/or spiritual fecundity are the "fruit and sign of conjugal love' (n. 28)."

the connection of the two meanings of marital intercourse has *objective-ly* been broken precisely on the level of *intentional actions,* on the level of the concrete sexual behavior that one has deliberately chosen, and that is: on the level of single acts of contraceptive intercourse.

Let me sum up: contraception renders sexual acts to be acts without any procreative consequences. Acts whose foreseen procreative consequences have intentionally been prevented can no longer be carried out as "generative acts," and therefore can no longer be procreatively responsible acts;[42] precisely for reasons of procreative responsibility, they no longer require the domination of reason and will, which are the principles of human acts. So, sexual acts lose *objectively* their character of *human acts* of the species "procreative responsibility," while acts of periodic continence and of intercourse in this context fully maintain this character.[43]

Thus, insofar as the contraceptive choice involves intentionally reject-ing procreative responsibility for one's sexual behavior, it also involves an anti-procreative volition. But it is specifically a peculiarity of man that he should integrate his sexual inclination and the acts deriving from it into the structures of responsibility and, thereby, into the life of the spirit. Contraception thus destroys the proper way in which human sexuality is meant to be a part of responsible human behavior: instead of rising to the requirement of responsibly caring about what essentially is a cause of transmitting new life, spouses who contracept adopt a device that with-draws their sexual acts—*and therefore themselves*—from being such a cause of that regarding which responsible behavior is required. This is a fundamental attack both on the integrity of the human person as a body-spirit unity, and on marital love, which expresses this unity.

42. Notice that this does not apply to the case of naturally given sterility, for this condition does not imply a *choice* of rendering needless the modification of sexual behavior. So the *intentional* relation to naturally given and voluntarily produced sterility is different. It is precisely this intentional relation that specifies and shapes further actions. Of course, in-fertility by nature or disease may also be abused—as with periodic continence. But this does not depend on the intentional structure of the mode of action itself, but on further intentions with which one does what one does.

43. The argument of G. E. M. Anscombe (in the two essays we have cited so far) is based exclusively on the demonstration that contraceptive sexual intercourse as an intentional ac-tion is no longer an act with a procreative meaning (it is no longer an "act of the procreative type"); she does not, however, seem to provide a convincing argument to show why this fact in itself makes the act morally wrong. A note on this lacuna is found in J. Teichmann, "Inten-tion and Sex," in *Intention and Intentionality. Essays in Honour of G. E. M. Anscombe,* ed. J. Diamond and J. Teichmann (Brighton: Harvester Press, 1979), 147–61.

Contraceptive intercourse *is not* an expression of *marital* love, properly speaking. *In itself* (disregarding the marital context)—in its objective intentional structure—its point does not differ from that of other forms of sexual activity that characterize non-marital sexual relations, such as "petting" (mutual stimulation to the point of orgasm) or sodomy (oral or anal sex). In fact, in contraceptive sexual relations, only the purely exterior mode of physiological behavior has anything in common with a procreative act; in reality, however, this behavior is functionally equivalent to and replaceable by *any* other physiological mode of sexual stimulation. Understand, this state of things in itself does not yet include a moral judgment on this type of sexual behavior. Rather, it merely notes—with respect to the structure of *intentional* action at the level of the "object"—that there is simply no clear reason to distinguish contraceptive sexual relations from *any* other form of reciprocal sexual stimulation and satisfaction, supposing that these other forms are also understood (subjectively) as expressions of mutual love. At the same time, if one wanted to affirm that these other forms are in fact objectively possible forms of expression of mutual love, it would then be difficult to see anything wrong with homosexual intercourse, presupposing of course that the "partners" claim a relationship of personal love.[44]

The aim of the present argument has been accomplished, however, with the demonstration that intentionally contraceptive sexual intercourse is not a human action of the type "generative act," and can therefore be grouped with other forms of mutual sexual stimulation. In fact no one—providing he has an elementary knowledge of human procreation—would claim that "petting" or oral or anal sex would be expressions of the link of the unitive and procreative meanings of human sexuality. One, however, who wants to claim that there is a difference between these other forms of sexual activation and (vaginal) contraceptive intercourse must be aware of what he is saying: he would be claiming in fact that the purely physical structure of the act would constitute the decisive difference. This would be a completely naturalistic argument, unless of course one wishes to consider the differences of the type discussed in erotic manuals.

44. Anscombe made this point repeatedly in texts such as *Contraception and Chastity* and *Sex without Children*.

What I have shown up to this point is that the contraceptive choice properly *excludes* a basic disposition of modifying one's sexual behavior for reasons of procreative responsibility. Thus, contraceptive intercourse is an act withdrawn from the logic of the procreative task; *intentionally* it is not "open" anymore to procreation (and this means: it is *objectively* no longer open). This is the case neither in acts of periodic continence nor in sexual intercourse during infertile times. Consequently, as far as procreation is concerned, both of these latter kinds of behavior have a very different intentional structure from contraceptive acts. Contraception is indeed *contralife* in the sense that it involves the negation of sexual behavior as an integral part of responsibility in regard to the task of transmitting human life.

This may be less obvious in the very special, but theoretically possible, case in which contraception is chosen exclusively for reasons of adopting a *safer* way of avoiding pregnancy (a notion that typically comes from information that ignores the fact that the "most reliable" methods, probably including the IUD, are all simultaneously abortive, meaning that they can prevent implantation after a conception has occurred). Nevertheless, in this case one would also choose against continence, the modification of one's sexual behavior, though not with the intention of avoiding the possible "burden" of continence but for the reason of aiming at security. But *objectively*, on the level of the sexual behavior one freely, and therefore intentionally, chooses to engage in, continence, and thus responsible modification of sexual behavior, are equally excluded.

It may, of course, be the case that one does not make such reflections, that one does what everyone else does or what a trusted doctor recommends, or even that there be such a scant knowledge of the need of integrating one's corporeity into a context of responsible behavior that it is not possible to speak of a real *choice* against the requirement of responsibly modifying one's sexual behavior. Even good (further) intentions, however, do not justify wrong means. Whether an action that in itself actually does have a proper moral content and relevance (and that therefore is not *indifferens ex specie*) is a good means for carrying out a determinate purpose has to be settled independently from such further intentions, however good and justified they may be.

This view seems to be confirmed by what the Second Vatican Council's pastoral constitution *Gaudium et Spes* has established as a basic moral criterion for responsible parenthood:

[W]hen there is a question of harmonizing conjugal love with the responsible transmission of life, the moral aspect of any procedure does not depend solely on sincere intentions or on an evaluation of motives. It must be determined by *objective standards*. These, *based on the nature of the human person and his or her acts,* preserve the full sense of mutual self-giving and human procreation in the context of true love. Such a goal cannot be achieved unless the virtue of conjugal chastity is sincerely practiced. (No. 51)

It would not seem an exaggeration to say that everything we have said to this point is confirmed, and even summarized, by the criteria offered here. We can also recognize the importance of an often overlooked passage in *HV,* in the final paragraph of its no. 16: periodic abstinence and contraception, the encyclical affirms, are two radically different kinds of behavior. At a first glance, the substantiation of this claim looks rather deceiving and odd: "In the former, the married couple make legitimate use of a natural disposition; in the latter, they impede the development of natural processes."

These words have become the *locus classicus* demonstrating the "naturalistic" perspective of *HV.* Again, it seems that the reason given for the wrongness of contraception is its unnatural character, its lack of respect of naturally given patterns. However, according to the encyclical's literal wording this is not yet a moral judgment, but only the *description* of two types of action about which a moral judgment has to be given. The rationale for this moral judgment (and therefore the rationale of the decisive intentional content of the described action) is provided only in the following two sentences (which are rarely cited): the reason why it is licit to restrict oneself to performing intercourse only during infertile periods, the encyclical says, is that in this case, during fertile periods, spouses perform acts of *abstaining* from intercourse. Let us cite the text (the emphasis is mine):

In reality, there are essential differences between the two cases; in the former, the married couple make legitimate use of a natural disposition; in the latter, they impede the development of natural processes. It cannot be denied that in each case married couples, for acceptable reasons, are both perfectly

clear in their intention to avoid children and mean to make sure that none will be born. But it is equally true *that it is exclusively in the former case that husband and wife are ready to abstain* [*se...abstinere valiant*] *from intercourse during the fertile period* as often as for reasonable motives the birth of another child is not desirable, while making use of it during infertile periods to manifest their affection and to safeguard their mutual fidelity. *By so doing, they give proof of a truly and integrally honest love.*

The morally relevant difference between the two behaviors is therefore— according to this passage—not in the fact that the choice of infertile periods, as opposed to contraception, is in accordance with the biological rhythms given by nature (given of course that the mode of behavior could be exteriorly described in this way). The morally relevant difference, and consequently the moral judgment, between the two behaviors is solely in the fact that "only in the former case are they able to renounce the use of marriage in the fecund periods" (*se . . . abstinere valeant*). This "readiness to abstain from intercourse" is equal to an at least implicit choice of modifying one's sexual behavior for reasons of procreative responsibility; it refers to a fundamental and decisive disposition. So *HV* seems to assume the following: for discovering what is wrong with contraception one must not concentrate on the question, "What's wrong with obstructing the procreative process in having its natural course?" The question that has to be asked rather is, "What is wrong with procreative responsibility carried out by rendering modification of one's sexual behavior needless and even useless?" Or, put in another way, "What is wrong with a choice for avoiding pregnancy that *excludes* the choice of modifying one's bodily behavior?" For that, precisely, is the point of contraception. In the light of these sorts of questions only, the attempt to interfere with natural processes by preventing conception manifests itself as a *moral* problem. Unless one realizes that contraception opposes the requirements of virtuously carrying out procreative responsibility in accordance with the bodily-spiritual constitution of the human person, one will not be able to substantiate why the act of preventing conception implies moral fault.[45]

---

45. Another point that causes misunderstandings is *HV* 17, the last paragraph, where it speaks of a limit "to the possibility of man's domination over his own body." It adds: "Such limits cannot be determined otherwise than by the respect due to the integrity of the human organism and its functions." This passage, however, must be read in its context: it is not the basis of the norm, but presupposes the norm as already established, noting possible

This moral fault then consists in withdrawing the body from the context of responsibility, treating it as a mere "object to be responsibly regulated," instead of integrating it into the structure of human action and respecting it as part of the "responsibly acting subject," that is, as a *principle* of human acts and in itself as a principle of responsibility. With such acts, the inner truths of the human person as a substantial unity of body and spirit and the body-spirit-unity of marital love are attacked, in their very integrity, by a specific sort of behavior, by concrete performances of single acts: contraceptive intercourse regarded as an intentional action is *another sort* of sexual act than sexual intercourse in the context of periodic continence.

As I have shown, this intent to withdraw sexuality from the context of procreative responsibility is equivalent to acting against the virtue of chastity, which ensures the virtuous self-control of sexual acts. This, at it seems to me, is the fundamental perspective underlying the teaching of *Humanae Vitae*, which is already announced in the final paragraph of its no. 2 and finally settled in no. 21:

The honest practice of regulation of birth demands first of all that husband and wife acquire and possess solid convictions concerning the true values of life and of the family, and that they tend towards securing perfect self-mastery. To dominate instinct by means of one's reason and free will undoubtedly requires ascetical practices, so that the affective manifestations of conjugal life may observe the correct order, in particular with regard to the observance of periodic continence. Yet this discipline which is proper to the purity of married couples, far from harming conjugal love, rather confers on it a higher human value, etc.

In his catechesis on *HV*, John Paul II called this doctrine concerning chastity

---

consequences of not observing it. The sentence cited above already presupposes that contraception is an illicit manipulation, so as to now say: if the Church were to nevertheless declare it admissible, no one could then prevent the governments of states from "applying to the solution of the problems of the community those means acknowledged to be licit for married couples in the solution of a family problem." The argument is here addressing the danger of arbitrary measures that damage the "respect" due the body, whether on the part of private persons (e.g., doctors), or by public authorities. This is not dealing, however, with the question or whether contraception is immoral; as such, the text of *HV* adds: "according to the principles recalled earlier."

the true reason in terms of which Paul VI's teaching defines the ethically up-right regulation of births and *responsible fatherhood and motherhood*. Al-though the "'periodic" character of continence is in this case applied to the so-called "natural rhythms" (*HV* 16), still, *continence* itself is a definite and permanent moral attitude, *it is a virtue,* and thus, the whole line of conduct guided by it becomes virtuous.[46]

In this light, the following also becomes understandable, which rela-tivizes the terminology regarding "methods," referring to *HV* 2 and 21:

This extension of the sphere of the means of "domination . . . of the forces of nature" threatens the human person for whom the method of "self-mastery" is and remains specific. It—that is self-mastery—corresponds in fact to the fundamental constitution of the person: it is indeed a "natural" method. The [resort] to "artificial means," by contrast, *breaks* the constitutive dimension of the person, deprives man of the subjectivity proper to him, and turns him into *an object of manipulation.*[47]

At first sight it is not immediately clear why John Paul here speaks of "manipulation" of the person. This is understood only when one takes account of the fact that the human body *is itself* already a "person," and from this fact flow the consequences resulting from the anthropological context we have described above, and from the structure of the moral virtues. From this perspective, contraception becomes recognizable as a "manipulative measure, and as a manipulation of the *person.*"[48]

Intrinsic Implications of Contraception

Disintegration of Sexuality and of Marital Love

Our way of demonstrating the wrongness of contraception has been through an explanation of the need to assume responsibility with respect to the procreative consequences of one's sexual acts. We have

46. John Paul II, *Man and Woman He Created Them: A Theology of the Body* (Boston: Pauline Books and Media, 2006), 635, (General Audience of August 29, 1984). The pope also added that this doctrine concerning chastity is "*not* merely a question of a certain 'technique,' but of *ethics* in the strict sense of the term as the morality of a certain behavior."

47. John Paul II, *Man and Woman He Created Them,* 631 (General Audience of August 22, 1984).

48. F. Böckle ("*Humanae vitae*" und die philosophische Anthropologie Karol Wojtylas," 377) in his critique of the concept of "manipulation" has unfortunately not taken this funda-mental text into account, nor the entire perspective behind it. Böckle refers to previous writ-

dealt precisely with the type of responsibility that is proper to the acting subject, whose personhood is constituted as a *substantial unity* of body and spirit. The way of arguing adopted so far to substantiate this claim may seem rather abstract and complicated. But once its leading insight has been grasped, I think it turns out to be a very straightforward argument, with strong intuitive appeal. If one explains to contracepting people what they are doing when they contracept, precisely by making them aware of what they *would* do *instead* if they practiced periodic continence, then they are enabled to immediately grasp what they are *failing* to do by adopting contraception. To explain vices, one has to talk about the virtues to which they are opposed. Many people have an intuitive awareness that something is wrong with contraception: an often unconscious feeling of shame about this behavior is manifest in a reluctance to speak about it. This reflects the "silent presence" in human conscience of the demands of natural law, whose voice is never completely silenced. And this demand of natural law in human conscience is precisely the insight into the requirements of the virtue of chastity, connected with the consciousness of one's dignity as a bodily constituted person.

There are some other aspects deriving from this analysis, which will finally show what really is at stake and how profound is the moral disorder involved in contraception. For example, one might say (despite all the preceding analysis), "Is it all that bad? Things seem to go just as well anyway!" One could say that periodic continence is a "best-case scenario," practiced perhaps in extreme cases or by particular people (perhaps for pious reasons), without it being a moral obligation. To show the extent to which the separation of sexual behavior from the context of responsibility threatens the good of persons, of marriage, and of the family—in short, *marital love*—one must add what follows. A moral norm that does not refer to the *preservation of the human good* would indeed not be a *moral* norm. In effect, moral norms express only what is truly good for man.

Humanae Vitae lists a great number of goods that result from periodic continence, practiced responsibly and for valid reasons.

---

ings of the then professor of ethics Wojtyla, rather than making use of magisterial texts of Pope John Paul II. The texts cited above were not taken into consideration by Böckle.

[Such discipline] demands continual effort yet, thanks to its beneficent influence, husband and wife fully develop their personalities, being enriched with spiritual values. Such discipline bestows upon family life fruits of serenity and peace, and facilitates the solution of other problems; it favors attention for one's partner, helps both parties to drive out selfishness, the enemy of true love; and deepens their sense of responsibility. By its means, parents acquire the capacity of having a deeper and more efficacious influence in the education of their offspring; little children and youths grow up with a just appraisal of human values, and in the serene and harmonious development of their spiritual and sensitive faculties. (*HV* 21)

All of these are endangered, if not completely lost, by contraception. Indeed, these goods might even begin to be experienced subjectively as evils, because of the effort and sacrifice required to attain them. The state of marriage in contemporary society (especially the incapacity of the young to form marriages, and the increase of separation and divorce) reflects in fact a situation *opposite* to one marked by the above goods, which derive from responsible love and the corresponding "self-discipline" of the spouses.

Against this background, and in light of our analysis, we consider the possible causes of this breakdown. As we have seen, the act of abstaining from intercourse within periodic continence is an act *common* to both spouses, who are united as two persons in one flesh and live a common vocation to serving responsibly the transmission of human life. Yet, a contracepting couple undermines also this affective kind of communion in the realm of bodily communication. Contraception does not need common agreement, at least not to carry out the behavior itself, and very often it is adopted against the will of one of the spouses, or on the basis of a decision independent from the other. Theoretically this could happen also with periodic continence, which could also be practiced in an illegitimate way, but this is not the question under discussion. But even if contracepting spouses *do* agree, *this agreement has no bodily expression*; sexual behavior remains untouched from this common policy. Once contraception is chosen, the care for procreative responsibility no longer informs bodily behavior. To the extent that there continues to be responsibility, such as for maintaining the effectiveness of the contraceptive measure chosen, this weighs disproportionately on the woman. Contraception need no longer be the content of further dialogue and common decisions as long as contraceptive behavior is not abandoned. The dimension of procreative responsibility vanishes from conjugal life, the bodily dimension of which comes to be concentrated in sex as a means for expressing "love" deprived from its procreative meaning.

This may engender very different consequences, and which of them will be brought about and in what degree they may occur depends on contingent factors extrinsic to contraception itself. In any event, with the adoption of contraception, something objectively decisive has changed: there is now a principle of disintegration of marital love at work. This principle of disintegration consists in the peculiarity of sensual appetite, which by its *own* nature is directed only to actual satisfaction and self-gratification. In the case of animals, this natural reference to self of the sexual drive is effectively compensated for by a perfect guidance of instinct, guaranteeing sufficient offspring. But this is not the case for man. Indeed, modern anthropology makes clear that, of itself, the sexual drive alone does not produce a bond among a man and a woman—its natural dynamic is merely self-satisfaction.

The instinct toward self-preservation, for example, aspires by nature only to "my" preservation, not toward the preservation of other human beings. For this reason man develops, based on both reason and desire guided by reason, the *habitus* of justice (goodwill, interest in others, etc.). The sexual instinct, in turn, is directed by nature toward the preservation of the human species, that is, toward the existence of individuals who are "other," but not toward the good of the sexual partner. Indeed, the sexual impulse itself is not capable of distinguishing the good of the species, something that is possible only by the reason. The accomplishment of this goal (of preservation of the species) is assured by the fact that the acts in question are accompanied by an intense experience of libido; if this were not the case, humanity would have long since been extinct; at the same time, there would be no notion that the sexual act has anything to do with love.

Even if we speak of the sexual act as an act that gives expression to and nourishes personal love, we can nevertheless not forget that, as a natural structure, it is the satisfaction of an *impulse,* associated with an intense libido. Copulation is not simply a gesture of tenderness, as is giving a kiss. A kiss does not issue from an impulse, nor does it have any "function" given by nature (even if intended, in certain contexts, as a sublimated impulse or as an act with sexual significance, and it is also a spontaneous act; the sublimation itself does not issue from an impulse). "To give a kiss" is wholly an expressive act. This, and other similar demonstrations of tenderness and affection, *are* exactly that, and only that, which they *express*. Judas's traitorous kiss was something entirely different than the kisses with which the repentant woman kissed Jesus' feet. Kisses between lovers and spouses, in their turn, are expressions of other specific intentions and affections. The sexual act, however, is not simply that which it *intends* to express on the basis of the human will; it is the fulfillment, the reaching of its aim by an impulse, an impulse that in itself, independent of other expressive contents and of the human will, possesses its own dynamism and a function given by nature. The playing out of the impulse possesses its own dynamism, completely independent of what one may wish to express with it: and this is a sensual dynamism, which *in itself* (*in se* and *per se*) has nothing to do with personal love, even if it aims, as *integrated* in the context of the bodily-spiritually constituted person, toward the realization of a human good, that is, the beginning of a new human life.[49]

Nevertheless, human sexuality is not guided by instinct. Man, in distinction from animals, is particularly poor in instincts—rather, he possesses reason and free will. This "personal" level issues from what we have called "spiritual love" between persons. The "logic" of spiritual love and the "logic" of sensual appetite are very different; sexuality needs to be operatively integrated into the "logic of the spirit"; only then, without damaging its character as an impulse, it becomes a specific human and bodily expression of spiritual love, and only then—including its libidinous component—will it promote community of persons.[50]

---

49. For this reason the acts that issue from the sexual impulse are not understandable primarily as expressive actions (*Ausdruckshandlungen*), but in the first place "efficacious actions" (*Wirkhandlungen*). On this distinction see R. Ginters, *Die Ausdruckshandlung. Eine Untersuchung ihrer sittlichen Bedeutsamkeit* (Düsseldorf: Patmos Verlag, 1976), 36–37. Precisely as a specific type of efficacious action, sexual acts are capable of acquiring expressive qualities, which derive entirely (and specifically) from the personal relationship of love between the spouses. At the same time, Ginters seems to be accurate in including sexual acts among the expressive acts (cf. ibid., 98). In general terms, this very instructive study seems to suffer from an excessive amplification of the category "expressive action" (which includes, for him, even martyrdom), which ends by leading to the consequentialist, reductionist model of action that Ginters employs. We cannot discuss this problem further here, however.

50. If I talk about "operative integration" I do not talk about "ontological integration."

We have shown that in contraceptive sexuality the activation of the sexual impulse becomes "de-functionalized" in the sense that the "orientation to the generation of human life" is no longer present. This, however, does not change the impulse; its dynamism and its libidinous function remain intact. Therefore—and this is decisive—the impulse remains a natural fact, but no longer possesses (with contraception) any function given by nature independent of the human will, and therefore no prior given meaning. The impulse, which is an integral part of personal subjectivity, of the "I", becomes a purely natural event, whose only experienced positive content is pleasure. We may call this "disintegrated sexuality."[51] The sexual act—if one does not want to consider the enjoyment of pleasure as its only meaningful purpose—must then be considered as a purely "expressive action," such as a kiss, as a gesture of love that claims to *be* only what it intends to *express*. But, as an expressive action it is inadequate, simply because it is linked to the impulse. Understood *exclusively* as an expressive action, it is a self-delusion, because expressive acts are characterized by having functional equivalents. The expressive quality of these other acts can also be conveyed by other modes of expression, especially linguistic.[52] The link between the sexual act and the impulse does not permit this, however, given that the impulse is only "interested in" its satisfaction, which does not allow "substitution" by another means. A sexual act is by nature always something more than an expressive act—the actuation of an impulse, and sensuality. And, because of its natural functionality and the related sensuality, disintegrated sexuality cannot be simply "functionalized" by the human will for use in merely expressive actions. Rather, it necessarily distinguishes itself from such expressive intentions, because as an impulse it possesses its own dynamism, which is prior to and independent of every such expressive intention.

Disintegration of sexuality, however, brought about by contraception introduces in marital love a kind of "sensual heteronomy": besides its self-gratifying character, sensual appetite *in itself* has no continuance in

---

I do not wish to say that sexuality requires to be "humanized." Sexuality *is* human by its very ontological status (because of the substantial unity of body and spirit). "Operative integration" means to take into account this ontological status while *acting*.

51. On the concept of disintegrated sexuality from a purely sociological point of view, cf. the still-valid study by H. Schelsky, *Soziologie der Sexualität. Über die Beziehung zwischen Geschlecht, Moral und Gesellschaft* (Hamburg: Rowohlt 1955), 72 ff.

52. Cf. Ginters, *Die Ausdruckshandlung*, 40.

time; it tends to decrease in the same measure as it is gratified. Thus, if a person, deeply loved at one moment, has become an object of sexual desire, then—speaking only of the logic of this desire—he or she is in turn experienced as worthless in the same measure as sexual desire is satisfied. Moreover, *on its own* sensual pleasure does not establish communion, but rather isolation and loneliness. For it is not self-transcendent to another person, but rather self-centered. By his *subjective experience* of sensual pleasure alone, the person is not able to distinguish this experience from real personal love, the expression of which it should be. An act of disintegrated sexuality is therefore well capable, on the basis of its source, of directing itself toward the other as a *person*; but, in the experience of the satisfaction of this desire, the relation to the *person* of the other disappears. Sensual appetite, moreover, can never strive for the "good of the other," but only for "its own good"; it is, by its own nature, *not able* to increase "love of friendship." So, *disintegrated* (or isolated) sexuality—that is, sexuality considered in itself, as the actuation of an impulse—is not a principle of union of two persons. To say it in a clearer way: it tends to create a *fictitious* union by transforming spouses into *accomplices* of a mutual satisfaction of the impulses, where each with the other's help does something in relation to him- and herself.[53]

I am certainly aware that this characterization of contraceptive intercourse runs a risk: the usual risk of being misunderstood. I am not saying that the intention *with which* spouses who contracept engage in intercourse is directed exclusively to the satisfaction of impulses; rather, I presume the opposite. The disintegration of sexuality that follows from contraception does not have to do with that intention; one can assume that the spouses truly love one another and want to carry out an act to express this reciprocal love. The use of contraception alone does not, at this stage, change the fact that the personal love between the two partners moves them toward bodily union, and finds its fulfillment in that union. The judgment expressed above, rather—as has been our focus throughout—refers to the mode of action itself. And our proposal is that, despite every good intention, such spouses *cannot* express such conjugal

53. See for this J. Finnis, "Personal Integrity, Sexual Morality and Responsible Parenthood," *Anthropos* (now *Anthropotes*) 1 (1985): 43–55. For a more thorough analysis see K. Wojtyla: *Love and Responsibility,* trans. H. T. Willetts, rev. ed. (San Francisco: Ignatius Press, 1993), part 3.

love, simply because it is impossible to give expression to personal love by means of acts of the sexual impulse *as such*. There is an abyss between the level of personal love and that of the bodily action of the sexual act. For this reason, sexuality as a disintegrated impulse tends to develop *its own* dynamism, that of sexual concupiscence, which is opposed to personal love as the gift of oneself to the other.[54]

This fictitious character of contraceptive intercourse is not basically different from the one implied in onanism by coitus interruptus. And even if the immediate context is different, it has a striking similarity with solitary sex.

What is lacking is precisely "the task" or "mission" of sexuality, which works as a principle of transcending and "elevating" mere sensuality, integrating it in the life of the spirit.[55] There exists a problematic gap between spiritual love as mutual self-giving of two persons to each other and the claim to express and to nourish this love by acts of sexual pleasure and satisfaction, which by their *own* nature tend only to self-gratification. This satisfaction and this pleasure involved in bodily love are very good and entirely human things, and in marriage they constitute the *affective fulfillment* of the love between two persons. But they need to be integrated into the structure of spiritual love; and this integration is hardly possible *without* the link of a principle of spiritual love *able to inform sexuality itself,* giving it a meaning within the context of spiritual love, a direction toward the "logic of the spirit" by integrating it into the "conjugal good" (as J. Finnis says), and making it a means

54. One could object at this point that the dualism merely "is made to come back in through the window, after having left through the door," that there is assumed here a dualistic opposition between "impulse" and "spirit" (as the seat of personal love), or a dualism of a "selfish" body and an "altruistic" spirit. Nevertheless, this is not a dualistic way of thinking, because we are dealing with "impulse" only in an abstract manner. The thesis is this: the impulse as such is referred to itself; but "as such" the impulse does not exist at all! In reality, the human sexual impulse is an integral part of man's bodily-spiritual unity. The impulse manifests its specifically human dimension precisely in the context of this unity, which latter in fact can be destroyed—disintegrated—through actions. Only in this disintegration at the "operative" level is the impulse "referred to itself"—and precisely for this reason it is also no longer "human." This presupposes precisely a non-dualistic vision of the body-spirit relationship, i.e., the idea that the spirit does not "express itself" by means of the body or material, but rather it becomes a subject of human action only by means of the body and in connection with it. Without the sexual impulse there wouldn't be a love—including spiritual love—between man and woman distinct from other forms of interpersonal love.

55. Cf. R. Spaemann's "Wovon handelt die Moraltheologie? Bemerkungen eines Philosophen" *Internationale Katholische Zeitschrift* 6 (1977): 307–8.

through which personal love can be expressed in a truly adequate way. Such a spiritual principle of serving the transmission of life should belong to both spiritual love and sexuality; in fact, a meaningful action cannot be produced "ficticiously," unless one proposes a "purely" expressive act, conceived in "pure freedom," something that in fact never occurs. To do something meaningful, it must have meaning *in reality*. And this principle of reality, which produces the link between personal love and sexuality, is precisely the task of serving the transmission of human life. It is precisely the link established by the procreative task, whose requirements also inform acts of responsibly refraining from intercourse, but *not* contraceptive conjugal acts.

The awareness that it is precisely this task of serving life that establishes the love between a man and a woman as *marital* love, brings it about that sexual acts can be the *expression and affective fulfillment* of marital love and that in the enjoyment of this act the other person is loved *as a person and as a spouse,* with whom, following the sexual impulse—and indeed abandoning themselves to it—the spouses know themselves to be joined in a communion of life. This informing by the "procreative task" is found in fact, as we have seen, both in acts of responsible abstinence and in acts of intercourse that are known to be infertile (given that these latter are carried out in the context of responsibly chosen periodic continence); it is not present, however, as we have shown, in contraceptive conjugal acts. When speaking of the "ends of marriage," we said that personal love always means to love the other for him- or herself, and therefore to love them as they are. Human beings, however, are never merely "persons." Leaving aside differences in character, talents, abilities, background, and so on, they are also respectively man and woman. To love someone for him- or herself means also to love them in their masculine or feminine personhood. If someone were to say, "I don't love you for your qualities x, y, and z, but simply for yourself," the other person would respond, "You don't really love *me*; you love a fictitious, abstract being." In fact, none of us wants to be loved simply "as a person," but also for the characteristics we possess as a concrete person. The possibility of being a father or a mother is also a basic characteristic for which a man and a woman love each other, a love that is appropriately expressed in sexual acts, *provided these* acts are not deprived of their procreative significance. This does not mean that spouses mutually "instrumentalize" one another for the sake of attaining the ends of "procreation" and "help in life." It merely means that they recognize each other for what they *are*: man and woman, who love each other as such, in the concrete totality of their personal being. A man loves a woman "for herself" only when he loves her also for her capability to be a mother; and vice versa. It is precisely for this reason that in sexual acts the love between man and woman can be truly expressed: because it is a love that relates to the other as a source of human life. If this expressive quality is destroyed—which in fact happens with contraception—the logic of impulse then begins to dominate.

One could then ask, what about in the case of sterility resulting from some pathology or from old age? We can respond to this question if we recall that the procreative meaning of sexuality is not linked to actual biological-physiological fertility, but solely to the intentional orientation (*per se*) of sexual acts to the generation of new human life. The procreative meaning of a sexual act means, in effect, that its execution is that of an act of the "procreative type," and this is the case—*or can be* essentially—supposing that fertility (given by nature) has not been voluntarily eliminated. In the case of periodic continence and of acts knowingly infertile, the procreative meaning is therefore preserved. We have, of course, shown that with the practice of contraception the procreative meaning of sexual relations disappears entirely.

On the basis of the argument thus far, therefore, there is no reason to suppose that couples who have become infertile because of their age—especially when they already have children—do not carry out acts of the procreative type when they have sexual relations. They simply do what they have always done, without expecting, of course, procreative consequences of their sexual behavior. If they were still fertile, they would be open to the conception of a new child, or they would abstain periodically. In the case, when they have previously practiced contraception, however—and this is no longer necessary because of sterility due to age—then they obviously carry out their sexual acts with a contraceptive will. In this latter case, the fact that the infertility is "natural" changes nothing in the intentionality of their acts; in this case, as well, the couple continues to do what they have always done.

In the case of sterility through some pathology, once again it is necessary to look at what takes place in the will of the spouses. They could take the position, "This sterility is just as well, because now we no longer have to take contraceptive measures." It is also possible, however—and this case is worth paying attention to—that they willingly desire children; indeed, they might even look to medical intervention to overcome this inability. Their infertile acts, therefore, are characterized by the openness to having children, if it were possible. The present desire, along with the basic openness to doing something in the sexual act that has to do with the transmission of human life, and the absence of any intentional action to impede this, is in this case fully sufficient for the carrying out of acts of the procreative type. In the sexual acts of such couples, the two meanings, unitive and procreative, are both intentionally present, and therefore these acts have the expressive qualities proper to conjugal love. Again, the procreative meaning of the sexual act *does not* coincide with the physiological possibility of having children, nor does it depend on the hope that new life *might* come about from one's sexual acts. We have shown that the object of the conjugal act does not consist in "the generation of a new life," but in the gift of love to the other in the totality of one's bodily-spiritual personhood. This is not to say that an infertility independent of the will of the spouses could not in itself be problematical; it could be "abused." What is solely relevant is the relationship of the will to the infertility.

For this reason also, periodic continence should not be overvalued. It is not an end in itself or an *absolute* necessity; rather, it is necessary to guarantee the procreative value of sexual acts only when it is indispensable for responsible reasons that a conception be avoided. Indeed, periodic continence could be opportune or necessary for *other* reasons, and couples who practice contraception may also have reason to abstain every now and then; the act or habit of sexual continence, in itself, is not yet a virtue—it depends on its use. The sexual impulse is not integrated into the structure of personal love *only* by continence, but rather on the one hand by the real possibility, independent of the will of the spouses, that from it comes new human life, *or* on the other hand from responsible abstention so as to avoid new life. In both cases, the spouses relate *intentionally* to their sexual acts as a potential source of new life.

Only if sexuality and its accompanying pleasure are detached from their procreative meaning—that is, when infertility derives from the human will—are they no longer able to serve for the expression of mu-

ß. S

tual, self-giving love between man and woman. Disintegrated sexuality is something like a "time bomb"; it acquires a destructive force and operates like a principle of corrosion that gradually breaks down marital love, making its bodily expression a meaningless gesture that turns the individual affectively back on himself; at a minimum it deprives the marriage of certain qualities that specifically should belong to it, and in very many cases it isolates the spouses from one another sexually.

If, how, and in what measure these effects occur can be evaluated only in individual cases; we are not dealing with a mechanism that unfolds in a necessary way. One could indeed also imagine that contraception is often used simply because couples are not sufficiently informed of alternatives—perhaps they don't even think about it that much. Assuming that there are serious reasons for avoiding a pregnancy, the negatives of contraception could possibly be contained within certain limits, and perhaps even some of the goods associated with periodic continence experienced, as well. At the same time, it must be clear that the moral essence of a mode of action is recognizable, and a corresponding norm can be formulated, only when the action is analyzed independent of any "attenuating circumstances," that is, in itself. And in fact, it is sufficiently clear that even in the "best cases," contraception tends to break down marital love, precisely because of the link between sexual acts and impulse.[56] There exists much clinically observed empirical evidence on this provided by psychopathology.[57] *So we have to defend the procreative meaning of sexual intercourse precisely in order to defend its unitive meaning.* And we may state again: both meanings are inseparably connected and reciprocally related to each other, because the human person is a substantial unity of body and spirit.

The "Contraceptive Mentality" and the Problem of Abortion

I believe that, by this way of arguing, one can easily understand the still important difference between two couples who, *for illegitimate motives* (e.g., for convenience, independence, selfishness, material or pro-

56. Cf. also Schelsky, *Soziologie der Sexualität*, 73.

57. See the contributions in the First Part of H. Wenisch, *Elternschaft un Menschenwürde*. Because, for science, this subject seems also to be a kind of taboo, there is not sufficient research on it. Pastoral experience, however, as the author of this chapter has gathered give some additional and helpful insights in these connections.

fessional advancement), do not want to have (any more) children and for this reason avoid a conception: one by adopting contraception and the other by practicing periodic abstinence for such illegitimate reasons. The difference is that, in the latter case, the procreative dimension of sexual acts continues to be a principle that informs bodily behavior; so there is less risk of sexuality's disintegration. Their sexual acts are still related to as a possible cause of new life, which therefore must be performed responsibly in the sense that the spouses must account for the possible procreative consequences. Therefore, even if they practice periodic continence illicitly, they precisely do *not* do this with a "contraceptive mentality," which consists in the first place of depriving one's concrete sexual behavior of its characteristic of being the cause of new life. Obviously, *a fortiori* this applies to a couple who, rightly and with just reasons, practice periodic continence. If, against their intention to avoid having a baby, conception nevertheless occurs, then the child will not be an "unwanted child" in the proper sense. More or less, but surely in *some* way, they will feel *responsible* for this new life that comes into being. At least *they will feel obliged to accept it,* because they know that it is the consequence of their being a possible cause of new life and therefore *of what they did* or failed to abstain from.

Contracepting spouses, on the other hand, whose policy fails (which may happen), will not feel responsible for the new life they have begotten, *because they have chosen a line of action that intentionally excludes their being a possible cause of new life and therefore equally excludes their having to account for the procreative consequences of their sexual acts*; the new human life coming to be is frustrating their very choice of adopting contraception. This "unwanted child" contradicts not only their general intention (perhaps even legitimate) of avoiding a conception, but also their choice of sexual behavior; it becomes therefore a threatening and disturbing factor in the spouses' ongoing life.

This *contraceptive mentality,* which is truly contralife, is what generates the so-called *abortion mentality.* Where contraceptive behavior spreads, the number of abortions increase. At the same time, and this connection is purely statistical—we cannot say that one who uses contraception will sooner or later make use of abortion, or is already a potential abortionist. Nevertheless, the statistical correlation between the spread of contraception and abortion calls for an explanation.

A possible explanation could be that the contraceptive mentality consists in the intentional refusal of responsibility for the procreative consequence of one's sexual behavior. This disposition is *objectively* present in every contraceptive choice—even in the case we have been considering all along where there are serious reasons for avoiding a conception. Despite these legitimate reasons, the contraceptive behavior chosen remains a behavior that—*at the level of concrete sexual behavior*—contains the structure of the contraceptive mentality, that is, the disposition of not being ready to modify one's sexual behavior for reasons of procreative responsibility, or more generally, to avoid the procreative consequences of one's sexual behavior. This attitude *could* destroy an initial disposition that is itself legitimate. Of course, we cannot say from statistical data whether this is valid in each particular case.

What has in fact happened, however—and this explains also the statistical correlation between the spread of contraception and the increase in abortions—is something quite different. General social tolerance with respect to contraception, and indeed its being seen as progress and "sexual liberation," has led to a social mentality that is quite accepting of an absence of sexual responsibility (in the sense we have been speaking of), meaning that the contraceptive mentality has become increasingly a *fundamental disposition* and a general approach to life. The spread of contraception at a mass level is not born of the need to live "responsible paternity," but from the new, relatively easy-to-implement possibilities of having "sex without babies"—*safe sex*.

If contraception were most often practiced because couples truly have serious reasons to avoid a conception, as some contemporary moral theologians claim, then only with difficulty could the presence of an attitude leading to abortion be explained. Nevertheless, the abortive attitude is *the same*, "objectively" speaking, as *every* contraceptive choice, regardless of motives. Put otherwise, the person who is in favor of contraception, at least in the presence of serious motives to avoid a pregnancy, *promotes* that mentality which leads to the spread of the practice of abortion (even if they themselves would never consider having an abortion). This mentality is based on the choice of wanting to carry out sexual acts no longer as procreatively responsible acts, and as such to be unwilling to modify one's sexual behavior so as to avoid procreative consequences.

Finally, there is also an issue of education: what arguments can parents who practice contraception use in response to their children's demands for sexual liberality? It is more likely that they would give their child the pill or a condom for the weekend with a friend or the night's party, if the children aren't using them already. Parents who demand for themselves a sexual life "without worries" are unlikely to agonize excessively over the sexual lives of their children.

Nevertheless, the connection between contraception and abortion does not consist exactly—as many think—in the fact that contraception "leads" to abortion in the sense that in the contraceptive choice there is already present the germ of what could later grow into abortion, as a logical consequence (an attitude of "annihilating life"); this notion could be justified only with difficulty, as we have shown. To explain this link, it is not necessary therefore that we presuppose that contraception is in essence "contralife," or that it must be understood as analogous even to homicide.

Indeed, no "normal" person who procures (i.e., chooses) an abortion does so because he or she wants to kill a human being (although that is what he or she does). Nor do they do so because they want, as with contraception, to eliminate the procreative consequences of their sexual behavior, and therefore the responsibility for it. The embryo or fetus is not here considered as an existing person (even though it is), but simply as the cause of a future event: the birth of a baby, a consequence that one now wants to prevent by means of abortion, instead of by contraception (i.e., because contraception didn't work). This intentional description shows how an abortion carried out with this intentionality rejects the existence of a human being, refusing to acknowledge the existence of the new life.[58] Therefore, many abortions are carried out with the contraceptive attitude of preventing the undesired consequences of one's sexual behavior, that is, to render what has already happened "as if it hadn't." Both contraception and abortion, therefore, are joined under the concept of the "birth control," which throws a veil over the whole.

Contraception doesn't imply, therefore, an "incipient" abortive men-

58. A woman who considers an abortion in situations of conflict effectively doesn't think at all of "my baby," or "our problem," which she is unable to resolve, often because she is left on her own, or even pushed toward an abortion (by the man or by relatives). If she is helped to resolve the conflicts, she will often begin on her own to think of "her baby," to accept it, and to include him or her in her plans for the future, now hopeful and constructive.

tality; rather, the opposite is true: a certain motive for abortion is only the last stage, or the ultimate means, of implementing a contraceptive mentality. The basic problem is not that of the refusal to have children, but of wanting to have "sex" without children. That this desire leads one to prevent the birth of a child either before or after conception no longer has any importance, if one considers the situation from an *intentional* point of view.[59] For this reason abortion, *intentionally,* can become a means of contraception. This could seem paradoxical, but in fact corresponds to the reality: couples are willing to risk pregnancy without using any contraceptive means whatsoever, and if one occurs, one simply takes advantage of readily available walk-in abortion.[60] In many places, such as the United States, it is even easier and less burdensome to have an abortion than to subject oneself to contraceptive measures, which often have unpleasant side effects. Furthermore, the majority of contraceptives in use today act abortifaciently, precisely so as to reduce such side effects; one who is aware of this, and accepts it, would not hesitate to make use of surgical abortion, and would also be inclined to consider the RU 486 "morning-after pill" as medical progress.

What makes this mentality so destructively aggressive is precisely the fact that it proceeds from the contraceptive mentality, in which the issue of the killing of a human being is removed. For this very reason it may be called a *contralife* attitude.[61] One who is in favor of abortion

59. Not every type of illegitimate prevention of the procreative consequences of sexual acts necessarily derives from a "contraceptive mentality." Unmarried people who have sexual relations, but choose exclusively infertile periods, act wrongly, but for other reasons; they do not act out of a contraceptive disposition. If, in the case of an "accident," they nevertheless turn to abortion (which in fact is rare), this requires another choice. The person who is used to contraceptive sexual relations, though, in the case of a pregnancy would easily move on to abortion precisely because of the fundamental attitude shared by the two.

60. For example, in the United States, up to 1.5 million abortions have been performed annually, and between 1973 and 1989 there were 21 million. Of these, 81% involved unmarried women, 62% of whom were under 25 years of age. According to data gathered by Rhomberg, McCaffrey, Riehle,and Wiliken at the 1988 "World Conference on Love, Life and Family," fully 40% of all abortions performed in the state of California were because of "failed contraception." Cf. *"Arbeitsgemeinschaft Artikel 1 Grundgesetz": Dokumente zu Abtreibung-Embryohandel-Gentechnik-Euthanasie,* n. 6, 1988 (part 1 edited by the gynecologist Dr. Rudolf Ehmann), 13.

61. This is why, in order to explain the connection between contraception and abortion, there is no need to interpret contraception as being essentially contralife or even in analogy with "homicide." I argue just the other way round: the connection between abortion and contraception is sufficiently explained by the fact that abortion, insofar as it is promoted by spreading contraception, is characterized by a contraceptive mentality; that is, by a

out of a contraceptive mentality would not be in the least disposed to discuss whether an embryo or a fetus is a human being; he would simply dispute this—despite all evidence to the contrary—or would consider it irrelevant and ignore the issue. Rather than thinking about abortion as the killing of the unborn, such a one would focus on the possibility of a "liberating" ability to have sex without being weighed down by procreative responsibility. Contraception means, in this case, doing what you can so that what could occur doesn't; abortion, then, would be to render what has already happened as though it hadn't.[62]

As we have already mentioned, these statements do *not* refer to couples who use contraception because they have a serious reason of procreative responsibility to avoid conception—I am not claiming that these couples act out of the desire for "sexual freedom" or the like. What I have said is that such a practice, in its *objective* meaning as an intentional act, possesses that structure which, in virtue of its general social recognition as a legitimate practice, becomes the basic attitude of a general lack of sexual responsibility and unrestrained promiscuity. Those couples who practice contraception for *legitimate* reasons (i.e., when they have a good reason to not conceive a child) choose, only at the level of *means,* that is, of their concrete mode of action, a behavior that is opposed to procreative responsibility as a virtue. The contraceptive mentality that leads to abortion chooses this same (contraceptive) behavior (as the couple with legitimate reason to avoid conception) at the level of ends and of the general practice of life. The *objective* structure of the two intentionalities is, however, considered in itself, identical. What is inadmissible

mentality that excludes the responsibility for the procreative consequences of one's sexual behavior. The *basic* problem is not that people do not want to have children; the basic and first problem is that they want to have sex without children.

62. These comments obviously refer only to the "epidemic of abortion," therefore to the statement of the statistical link between the mass diffusion of contraception and the increase in the number of abortions. This is not valid, however, for the "classic" cases, e.g., when only after a pregnancy, a life-threatening danger arises for the mother. In that case, there really could be a desired baby at the outset, and only later an anguished choice (morally illicit) between the life of the baby and that of the mother. Another case is that of a baby prenatally diagnosed as handicapped, where abortion is chosen because such a life is considered not worth living, or to avoid the complications involved in raising the child. In this case the abortion is also intentionally a homicide. Aside from these, however, it is not possible to draw conclusions regarding the contraceptive mentality. Even if it has literally murderous consequences, it cannot be claimed that the contraceptive choice is in itself analogous to homicide. Contraception pertains essentially to sexual behavior as regulated by the virtue of chastity and not to the virtue of justice.

at the level of ends is inadmissible at the level of means, as well. And what at the level of means—of the concrete mode of action chosen—is considered right and permissible cannot later be rejected as immoral as a general intention and practice of life. One, therefore, who is in favor of contraception as a legitimate practice—even if only for "serious" cases—promotes with it that mentality which promotes the practice of abortion that originates from this mentality.

Finally, please note that this applies equally to extramarital sexual intercourse, or fornication. Couples who are not married have a very strong reason for avoiding the procreative consequences of their mutual love. This reason is to not cause the initiation of new life *outside* of marriage, which would be irresponsible and an injustice to the child. Thus, as far as contraception is concerned, the same principles apply to them. But periodic continence is excluded as well, since the unitive meaning of sexual intercourse is fulfilled only within the context of marital commitment; sexual intercourse is in reality, according to its essence, a *conjugal* act. *Marital commitment is nothing but the very truth of sexuality itself, and sexual intercourse is the consummation of this marital love.* Thus, mutual love of a couple not yet united in marital commitment cannot be adequately expressed in sexual intercourse. Outside of marriage, therefore, the virtue of chastity requires absolute continence; this is the only genuine way of integrating sexuality as a human good in love prior to marriage, and it is essential to enabling the couple to make a mutual gift of self in the marriage.[63]

Contraception and Natural Law

Review of the Course of the Argument

Let us sum up the results of our argument so far. Contraception is wrong because it involves a type of sexual behavior that is inconsistent with procreative responsibility; this inconsistency is due to the fact that contraceptive sexual behavior *destroys the behavioral unity of body and spirit.* Destruction of this unity implies both the withdraw of sexuality

---

63. Recent research in the United States has shown that marriages among couples who have lived together prior to marriage fail more often and earlier than "traditional" marriages. This statistical data is in complete contrast with all those theories and predictions that would claim that the opposite would occur.

from its procreative meaning and therefore the disintegration of sexuality so that it can longer be a true expression of personal love. Thus, contraceptive behavior includes features specific to other forms of disintegrated sexuality such as petting, onanism, and masturbation. Because of this partial similarity to these forms of sexual self-gratification, contraceptive intercourse is not an authentic expression of the mutual self-giving of persons, but rather a principle that undermines the communion of persons. Insofar as it is practiced within marriage, contraceptive behavior additionally opposes the union in one flesh of the two persons committed to responsibly serving the transmission of human life.

What I have set forth is a natural-law argument against contraception. It consisted, first, in an *anthropological analysis of the substantial unity* of man as a compound being of body and spirit. This analysis unpacked the meaning of the Inseparability Principle. Second and on these grounds, I have elucidated "procreative responsibility" as a *moral virtue* and a species of chastity; this enabled us to apply the Inseparability Principle to the concrete performances of single actions. Third, I have analyzed *contraceptive behavior* as essentially different from periodic continence, and as opposed to both moral virtue in general and procreative responsibility in particular. By so doing, I showed that contraceptive intercourse is indeed incompatible with the Inseparability Principle and therefore with the "truth about man." Fourth, I have shown *the intrinsic implications of contraception for marital love,* which shows the real gravity of the moral disorder involved in contraception. This argument, which stresses the personalistic features of the virtue of chastity, fully conforms, I think, to the leading perspective of *Humanae Vitae.* As we will see in the next subsection, it ultimately provides an answer to the last question I intended to address: Why and in which precise sense can contraception be called a violation of natural law?

If we consider discussions of the question of contraception in the atmosphere of post-conciliar moral theology and of the criticism of *HV,* what strikes one immediately is that the key questions seem to have been bracketed. In these authors, one finds neither anthropological reflection nor a theory of action; instead, the possible legitimacy of contraception is justified by a theory of moral judgment known as "teleological ethics," "consequentialism," or "proportionalism." According to this theory, the moral rightness of a mode of action must be judged based on the action's foreseeable consequences, which consist in bringing about *non-moral* goods or evils. For example, the infertility of sexual acts is seen as a "non-moral" or "physical" evil, which—according to such theories—is licit to cause, to the extent that the possible resulting consequences are on the whole better. The problem with this approach, which in essence was already present in the infamous majority judgment of the Pontifical Commission for Population, Family, and Births,[64] is not that one considers the consequences of human actions, but rather that in the evaluation of these consequences, the objective and intentional interior structure of human action (including *human action* considered anthropologically) is completely ignored, with only so-called exterior circumstances, situations, and effects of the action being taken into account. I cannot here enter into a detailed consideration of this theory of moral action, which has been amply studied and criticized by myself and other authors.[65] Let me simply say, in general terms, that moral theologians who favor contraception fail to speak of what the spouses *choose* and *do,* in an intentional sense, when they practice contraception. For this reason, these theologians read *HV* as condemning contraception only because it is "artificial" or "unnatural," and not because it contradicts human identity as a person constituted in a bodily-spiritual unity, therefore leading to consequences that—aside from any *other* consequences involved— contradict the human good. Given this fundamental misreading of the encyclical, building upon a highly deficient action theory, along with the continual claim that the moral norm expressed in HV *cannot* be justi-

64. Cf. on this May, *Moral Absolutes,* passim, esp. 34 ff.

65. My contributions may be found most recently in chapter 8 of *The Perspective of the Acting Person* (Washington, D.C.: The Catholic University of America Press, 2008), originally published in the English edition of *Nova et Vetera* 2, no. 2 (2004): 461–516. An earlier account can be found in *Natural Law and Practical Reason,* chapters 10–12, which was originally published in *Natur als Grundlage der Moral,* esp. 273–316; 410–14. A more systematic treatment can be found in the forthcoming *The Perspective of Morality;* cf. also "Gut und böse oder richtig und falsch—was unterscheidet das Sittliche?" in *Ethik der Leistung,* ed. H. Thomas (Herford: Busse-Seewald, 1988), 47–75, or (a slightly reworked version) "Ethik—Handeln—Sittlichkeit. Zur sittlichen Dimension menschlichen Tuns," in *Der Mensch als Mitte und Maßstab der Medizin (Medizin und Ethik,* vol. 1), ed. J. Bonelli (Vienna: Springer Verlag, 1992), 137–44; "Menschliches Handeln und seine Moralität. Zur begründung sittlicher Normen," in *Ethos und Menschenbild,* ed. K. M. Becker and J. Eberle (St. Ottilien: EOS-Verlag, 1989); "'Intrinsically Evil Acts' and the Moral Viewpoint: Clarifying a Central Teaching of *Veritatis Splendor*," *The Thomist* 58, no. 1 (1994): 1–39, and reprinted as chapter 3 in *The Perspective of the Acting Person.*

fied, it becomes clear that decisive points, which form the sole basis on which the norm *can* be justified, have simply been ignored.

Contraception as a Violation of the "Natural Law"

Now we consider our last question: Why and in what precise sense can contraception be called a violation of natural law? The response to this question has already been given: to speak of "virtue" is in fact nothing other than to speak of the "natural law." I would like to say a few words here about this identification.

What *is* natural law? Referring to Thomas Aquinas, it is, as I understand it, the order established by human reason in man's natural inclinations.[66] These inclinations are given by nature, including for example the natural inclination to the conjunction of male and female. But this natural inclination, although being *natural* and, as a created reality, a participation in the eternal law of the Creator, is not yet natural *law,* since "law" is a binding guide or rule for performing right *actions* proceeding from reason and will. Natural law, on the other hand, is the *order of practical reason* established *in* this inclination, or the ordering (*ordinatio*) of the practical reason, by means of which this ordering of human actions in view of what is good for man is brought about. A natural inclination integrated into this order of reason presupposes that practical reason has already grasped this natural inclination as a *human good* to be pursued within the order of reason.[67] The "natural law," then, is nothing other than the "natural" mode for man to order his inclinations and the cor-

---

66. For further details I refer to my *Natural Law and Practical Reason,* chapter 2, and *The Perspective of the Acting Person,* chapter 7. A summary is to be found in my "Die Konstituierung des Naturgesetzes und sittlich-normativer Objektivität durch die praktische Vernunft" in *Persona, Verità e Morale. Atti del Congresso Internazionale di Teologia Morale* (Rome, April 7–12, 1986) (Rome: Città Nuova, 1988), 859–84. See also the above-mentioned article by William E. May on "The Meaning and Nature of the Natural Law."

67. We may consider natural law either "formaliter" or "materialiter." "Formaliter" considered, natural law is *ordinatio rationis,* the (universal) prescriptive acts of natural reason by which the order of reason is established in man's inclinations. "Materialiter" considered, natural law is the natural inclinations *insofar as* they are integrated in the order of reason. Both considerations refer to the same reality; the former, however, aims at indicating the very essence of natural law; the latter stresses on its contents. As I think to have shown in my work about this subject, natural law is essentially the work of man's practical reason. Aquinas calls it, like "law" generally, an "opus rationis" (I-II, q.94, a.1) and "aliquid a ratione constitutum" (ibid.). When talking about natural law, the "reason" that is referred to is *natural reason* ("ratio naturalis").

responding actions to that which is good for him, that is, to act not on the basis of the instinctive guidance of impulse, but rather on the basis of the rational knowledge (which guides free will) of what is good for man, avoiding corresponding evils.

Note that the term "natural law" is somewhat equivocal, because it does not mean a "law *of* nature" (analogous, for example, to the laws of physics), but rather a "natural law" *of reason*. Every law is, in effect, according to its essence, an ordering *of reason* (*ordinatio rationis*). It consists, according to the classic doctrine, in the divine spirit that orders all creatures toward their ends, or also in positive human laws, which derive from reason ordered by human legislators. "Laws" can also be revealed by God (for example the Decalogue, the Mosaic law in general, and the "new law" of the Gospel). The term "natural law," then, does not meant that "nature"—in opposition to reason—forms a law of its own, but rather that in man there is a law, an "ordering of reason," which, entirely independent of positive laws both human and divine—precisely "naturally"—produces an ordination toward what is good for man. Because man is by nature a reasonable being, there exists also a law of reason, which are acts ordered by his practical reason in which man distinguishes good and evil, feeling himself bound to do the good, based on the rational understanding of what is good for man. This function of practical reason, natural in man, constitutes therefore a "natural law," not because it is simply "natural", but because it is present not in the divine spirit, but in "human nature" (which includes reason), and because it is not known by means of a positive statute, but solely in virtue of practical reason, which is part of the *nature* of man.

In our case, this order of reason is of the sexual inclination, which means the order of loving, mutual self-giving and procreative responsibility, which are inseparably connected. It is an order of reason established in the sexual drives and in the acts and modes of behavior that derive from them. Spouses who modify their sexual behavior according to the demands of procreative responsibility act according to natural law; they live the virtue of chastity because natural law makes us live the virtues. In the case of contraception the situation is quite different. Here the entire natural inclination to conjunction of male and female is withdrawn from the context of procreation and the requirement of being ordered by reason, and of being dominated by reason-informed will for responsible motives; it is therefore also withdrawn from the context of virtuous self-control.

Of course—as I have already remarked—the adoption of a contraceptive policy is also a kind of rational and voluntary dominion and "control" over sexuality. But it is not a kind of *virtuous* dominion; that is to say, it is not a dominion that conforms to the anthropological truth of the substantial unity of the body and the spirit, because it is not a sort of dominion that informs *sexual acts,* but one that only refers to procreative *consequences* of sexual acts. Therefore, in themselves, these acts no longer need to be considered as a possible cause of new life and therefore no longer need to be responsibly modified. Contraceptive dominion is instead a kind of "technical" dominion over the conjugal act as a possible cause of new life and over the human drives that lead to it. Contraceptive behavior produces a profound alienation of the personal Self from its body, because it treats the body—in a "technical" way—as a mere *object,* destroying its character of being the subject of human corporeity. So, in the originally spiritual act of mutual self-giving as effectuated in the conjugal act, contracepting spouses no longer give themselves in their totality as bodily-spiritual beings.[68] We could interpret in two different ways this act of contracepting spouses (which corresponds only remotely to a bodily act that truly expresses personal love), though neither interpretation is satisfactory. First, we could say that these spouses perform an act of spiritual love by merely *using* their bodies (each using their own body and that of the other) as something like an instrument for expressing this spiritual love. Second, we could say that these spouses perform a mere bodily act that is not informed by spiritual love and, therefore, tends to be mere gratification of the senses. The former is what contracepted sexuality *intends to be*; the latter is what it actually *tends to become.* In any case, contraception *falsifies* sexuality as a profoundly human reality, called to be a true expression of the mutual love of two persons united in one flesh.

When talking about "technical" dominion I do not want to refer to

68. This often quoted anthropological insight, enunciated, e.g., in *Familiaris Consortio,* No. 32, is, as it seems to me, not evident *by itself.* However true it may be, in a philosophical context one has to argue for it, at least if one deals with a case of true responsible parenthood. With the foregoing analysis I indeed claim to have provided such an argument, which gives plain evidence of what John Paul II affirms in *Familiaris Consortio.* Therefore, I do not agree with those who simply repeat this teaching as an *argument,* using it as it were self-evident.

the "artificial" as opposed to "natural" character of most contraceptive techniques. "Technical" behavior rather means a kind of behavior distinguished from "virtuous" behavior. The capabilities of artificial means of contraception only render easier and more tempting such technical behavior. The wrongness of technical behavior, however, does not consist in its artificiality, but rather in its fundamental amorality: in its denial of the requirements of moral virtue. In the case of contraception, this denial is—by its very objective structure—absolute and radical. Thus, it contradicts the basic requirement of human behavior guided by natural law, which calls for the establishment of a rational order *in* the natural impulses and inclinations themselves.

Contraception not only signifies acting against some determinate precept of natural law, as in the case of someone who, knowing the serious need to avoid a conception, nevertheless simply follows the dynamism of his sexual impulses; such a person would act against reason and against virtue, that is, intemperately. Contraception is also much more radical than such intemperance, since it withdraws the sexual inclination from the requirement of being informed by natural law *at all*. It eliminates, at its very root, the ordering efficiency of natural law, which includes human reason, reason-guided freedom, and freedom's responsibility. This is understood only when one considers the relationship between natural law and moral virtue: the natural law is not simply a group of rational commandments, but rather the rational structure ("law") of the moral virtues. In other words, it is the law that conforms to the order of reason, of human impulses, of inclinations, and of the actions that issue from them. Contraception, in contrast, renders *superfluous* procreative responsibility for one's sexual acts and the corresponding virtue of temperance. We can even say that it leads to a *bodily* behavior in which the "image of God" is no longer present, and therefore it is a sort of behavior inappropriate to fulfill the essential call of marital love to cooperate with God's creative, life-giving, love. I think that is what the encyclical *Humanae Vitae* wanted to teach us. The sadly obvious consequences of contraceptive behavior—some of them mentioned in no. 17 of the encyclical—may show that this teaching was truly prophetic, even if this prophetic truth will be misjudged exactly in the same measure as procreative irresponsibility spreads.

I have treated the problem of contraception from a strictly philosophical-ethical viewpoint. Therefore, I did not deal with theological and pastoral questions. In any event, pastoral care has to take its measure from the "truth about man." And moral theology should not only respect but *integrate* philosophical (anthropological and ethical) insights about man as a moral agent.[69] The practical demands that spring from this "truth about man" may be considered hard, but the alternative to respecting this truth is much harder; it is not a desirable alternative.

The Church always has taught that—in the given situation of fallen mankind—all the exigencies of natural law cannot be fulfilled except by the help of redeeming grace, which, as far as human weakness is concerned, has a healing power. Thus, the truth may be hard, but the means offered by the Church to overcome this hardship are most efficient. They permit man not only to strive for sanctity, but thereby to fully develop his very humanity. This striving always has been the seal of authentic Christian life, which is also called to defend worldly goods—such as sexuality, human love, and marriage—against their depravation by a world marked by both sin and the human weakness springing from it.

The Church's mission is not to condemn anybody, but to illumine man's conscience and to simultaneously offer God's mercy and grace, faithful to the mission of the Christ who has been sent by the Father not to judge this world, but to save it (Jn 3:17). This is often forgotten: the Church teaches a morality in which the Church itself participates as a community of faith, hope, and love. The Church is not only teacher, but above all the presence of divine mercy, forgiveness, and salvation. And this liberating presence of God is an essential part of the Christian fulfillment of parental responsibility.

It would be un-Christian to deny the difficulty of the marital and sexual morality proclaimed by the Church, and to lightly judge or even condemn people. On the other hand, the encyclical *Veritatis Splendor* emphasizes that "it would be a very serious error to conclude . . . that

---

69. That precisely this full integration of the philosophical *moralis consideratio* into the higher context of moral theology may be considered as a specific feature of Aquinas's *Secunda pars* of his *Summa theologiae* has been convincingly shown by G. Abba: *Lex et virtus: Studi sull'evoluzione della dottrina morale di san Tommaso d'Aquino.* (Rome: LAS, 1983). See also my *Natur als Grundlage der Moral*, 195, and *Natural Law and Practical Reason*.

the Church's teaching is essentially only an 'ideal' which must then be adapted, proportioned, graduated to the so-called concrete possibilities of man" (*VS* 103). As the encyclical underscores, the Church in its doctrine does not speak simply of "man," but of man *redeemed* in and through Christ. Therefore, the effort to live this teaching it is not an issue of overburdening people, or of an insensitive magisterium, but of "the *reality* of Christ's redemption. *Christ has redeemed us!* This means that he has given us the possibility of realizing the entire truth of our being" (*VS* 103).

For this reason *Veritatis Splendor* identifies the modern Pharisee as one with a new kind of "self-satisfied conscience": while the Pharisee in the Gospel (cf. Lk 18:9–14) is "under the illusion that [he] is able to observe the law without the help of grace" (*VS* 104), the modern Pharisee wants to adapt the "law"—that is, moral norms—to the capacity of man, such that he, as every Pharisee, "would seek to eliminate awareness of one's own limits and of one's own sin" (*VS* 105).

It is nevertheless Christians who, as "salt of the earth," "light of the world," and "leaven in the dough," must recognize their calling to give testimony to the reality of the redeemed person. Here the Church is defending not merely something specifically "Christian," but humanity *tout court*. And the Church *can* do this precisely because it at the same time is empowered to convey the mercy of God and the grace of Christ, in virtue of which its teaching can become the basis of a fulfilled life, the underlying reality of a development in life that is "human" in the full sense of the term.

4

The Use of Contraceptives under
Threat of Rape: An Exception?
Clarifying a Central Teaching of *Veritatis Splendor*

A Test Case for the Argumentative Structure
of *Veritatis Splendor*

In light of the tragic circumstances of the war in Bosnia-Herzegovina,[1] the question was again raised whether, in the face of a direct threat of rape, a woman could legitimately make use of contraceptive measures in a preventative way so as to avoid a possible pregnancy. There seems to be uncertainty and confusion regarding the application of Catholic doctrine on contraception in this specific case. For many, an affirmative answer to this question does not seem reconcilable with the Church's teaching that contraception is an intrinsically evil act, and therefore can never be justified.[2] Further, there is the fear that such a "justification" could open the door to any number of "exceptions," whose morality would be left to the judgment of the agent.

In fact, a precise explication of the contraceptive choice

---

1. This chapter was first published as "Minaccia di stupro e prevenzione: un'eccezione?" *La Scuola Cattolica* 123 (1995) 75–90. It was later published in English as "The Use of Contraceptives under Threat of Rape: An Exception?" *Josephinum Journal of Theology* 14, no. 2 (August 2007): 168–81.

2. Cf. *The Catechism of the Catholic Church* (Vatican City: Libreria Editrice Vaticana, 1994), no. 2370; *Veritatis splendor*, no. 80.

that the Church rejects as immoral is required to explain the moral legitimacy of the case in question, and at the same time to affirm the intrinsically disordered—and therefore evil—character of contraception. It is worth recalling that in 1961 this problem was submitted to the authoritative judgment of three prestigious moralists, who unanimously considered the use of contraceptive measures to be legitimate in this case. According to these authors, such a use of contraceptives pertains to a legitimate act of self-defense.[3] This position has been confirmed recently in an article by Giacomo Perico, written in response to the events in Bosnia-Herzegovina;[4] indeed, it can be said that this position is commonly accepted by moralists. The problem today, however, is on a different level.

Presuming that—according to the Church's magisterium—the norm that prohibits contraception is among those negative norms that are valid without exception (*semper et pro semper*), *the reasons adopted* for sustaining the licitness of the use of contraceptive measures in the case of a foreseeable threat of rape are obviously of highest importance. Indeed, it would seem that the reasons justifying the use of contraception in this case would amount to the admission of an "exception" that negates the absolute illicitness of contraception. They could even be seen as a justification of the proportionalistic method rejected by the encyclical *Veritatis Splendor*. From the point of view of fundamental moral theology, therefore, the question bears great importance.

Defending the positive judgement on the licitness of the behavior in question, I want to first show the extent to which the reasons offered by the mentioned authors are not completely acceptable. I will then present an argument that seems to me to preserve both the intrinsically evil character of contraception and the morally licit use of contraceptive measures in the case of the threat of rape. The question will be primarily one of how to correctly determine the *object* of the act that, under the

3. "Una donna domanda: come negarsi alla violenza? Morale esemplificata. Un dibattito," *Studi Cattolici* 27 (1961): 62–72; with interventions by S. E. Monsignor Pietro Palazzini, then secretary of the Sacred Congregation of the Council (pp. 62–64); Fr. Francesco Hürth, S.J., professor at the Pontifical Gregorian University (pp. 64–67); and Monsignor Ferdinando Lambruschini, professor of moral theology at the Pontifical Lateran University (pp. 68–72).

4. G. Perico, S.J., "Stupro, aborto e anticoncezionali," in *La Civiltà Cattolica* 3 (1993): 37–46. Fr. Perico's article has stimulated extensive discussion; cf. G. Valente, "La pillola e la leggitima difesa," in *30 Giorni* 7/8 (July–August 1993): 12–17.

name "contraception," is called intrinsically (i.e., *per se*) evil, independently of any *ulterior* circumstances or intentions.[5]

Some Responses Given in the Past

A close reading of the writings of the three moralists (Palazzini, Hürth, and Lambruschini) consulted on this question in 1961 shows that they tended to consider contraception above all as a type of (temporary) sterilization, and therefore as an infringement on the natural order—an order according to which the act of sexual copulation possesses a procreative quality that would be eliminated by the contraceptive act. In such a view, focused on contraception as an artificial interference with the natural processes and ends of the sexual act, it was not easy to exempt from this judgment the case under consideration, given that it also treats of the artificial suspension of a natural function.

Nevertheless, already in 1961 one of the three authors consulted, Fr. Hürth, rightly affirmed that a norm such as the one prohibiting an act of sterilization could refer only to an act of sexual copulation *freely consented to* by the woman.[6] Thus, the case in question treats of what he calls a "sterilization in an *absolute* sense" (given that physically, sterilization is brought about, in this case an anovulatory effect), but not a sterilization in a "*relative* sense," that is, of an act "which induces, as a cause, sterility in a subject who *freely and deliberately* wants or permits sexual intercourse, and who *simultaneously*, with a delibarate will, deprives her sexual act of its reproductive capacity."[7] According to his analysis, "objectively," the preventative use of a contraceptive in the case of the threat of rape would not be comparable to that sterilizing (or contraceptive) act which is morally unacceptable; objectively, in fact, we are dealing with a legitimate act of self-defense. The distinction adopted by Fr. Hürth effectively corresponds to the classical distinction according to which an act may be considered either at the "physical" level (i.e., Thomas's *genus naturae,* corresponding to Hürth's "in an absolute sense") or at the

5. Cf. *Veritatis Splendor,* no. 80.

6. P. F. Hürth, "Il premunirsi rientra nel diritto all legittima difesa," *Studi Cattolici* 27 (1961): 65.

7. Ibid.; also cf. F. Lambruschini, "È legittimo evitare le conseguenze dell'aggressione," *Studi Cattolici* 27 (1961):69 (with less explicit argumentation, but analogous on this point).

"moral" level (i.e., Thomas's *genus moris,* corresponding to Hürth's "in a relative sense"). We will speak more on this later.

Frs. Palazzini and Lambruschini, on the other hand, attempted to resolve the problem on the basis of the "principle of double effect" and the "principle of totality." As such, the principle of the psychological health of the woman and her legitimate self-defense would be simply the "proportionate reason" or "excusing cause," which would change the sterilizing act into an "indirect sterilization," or a "justified" sterilization.[8] This argument, however, which is essentially different from that of Fr. Hürth, would seem to be problematic. This is for precisely the reason that, in the case at hand, one chooses, *as a means,* the use of a contraceptive measure with the end of preventing a possible conception. It would seem, therefore, that one does exactly what the Church condemns as an intrinsically evil act. In this matter, as with others like it, the use of the principle of double effect tends to create not-insignificant ambiguities,[9] and in recent years has even contributed to the justification of the so-called proportionalist theory in some circles of Catholic moral theology.[10]

A More Recent Use of These Earlier Responses

A position recently set forth, in the above-mentioned article by Giacomo Perico, is essentially based on the argumentation put forth by Palazzini, although integrating the more personalistic vision of the Second Vatican Council. The author begins by clearly laying out the problem, indicating that "it is above all necessary to clearly identify the real and primary reason for which the moral law prohibits recourse to contraceptives in the conjugal act."[11] He then states that, the marital

---

8. As Fr. Palazzini affirmed in his contribution, "Si può e si deve proteggere l'equilibrio della persona," *Studi Cattolici* 27 (1961): 63–64.

9. Later, Cardinal Pietro Palazzini further specified his argument, along the lines of Fr. Hürth's, adding moreover that the norm taught by *Humanae Vitae* refers only to sexual intercourse freely chosen within marriage, and not to persons forced against their will (we will speak of this below). See the above-cited interview in *30 Giorni* by Valente, "La pillola," 17.

10. For example: P. Knauer, "La détermination du bien et du mal moral par le principe du double effet," *Nouvelle revue théologique* 87 (1965): 356–76; or "The Hermeneutic Function of the Principle of Double Effect," in *Readings in Moral Theology,* no. 1, ed. C. E. Curran and R. A. McCormick (New York: Paulist, 1979), 1–39.

11. Perico, "Stupro, aborto e anticoncezionali," 41.

act being by nature an "act of love," and an "act open to procreation," freely chosen, "contraception interferes with this reciprocal gift of love and in the mechanism of reproduction activated by it, as an impediment to the fusion of the germinal cells, resulting in non-conception. It is precisely in this voluntary exclusion of conception, to which the act of love between the spouses could lead by its nature, that the moral disorder of contraception consists."[12]

This approach, however, leads to the problem of being unable to identify an argument whereby the author could show that contraception is illicit also in cases where the spouses—for legitimate reasons of paternal and maternal procreative responsibility—know themselves to be *obligated* to avoid a new conception. Indeed, this is the case that must be primarily considered, not that in which the spouses' intention is to arbitrarily exclude procreation from their marriage. How could one explain, then, in a case of authentic procreative responsibility, the moral difference between contraception and periodic continence? The author does so simply by referring to the natural-physiological structure of the act.[13] As such, he began his discourse, as we have seen, by saying that the conjugal act is *by its nature* an "act of love"; he now adds that the conjugal act *by its structure and nature* is an "act open to procreation," where the "nature" of the act refers to physiological fertility or infertility. At this point there seems to reappear, as a Deus ex machina, precisely that "naturalistic" (or "biologistic") argumentation that the author had initially sought to overcome through personalistic language. In any case, his reasoning cannot be considered conclusive.

For Fr. Perico, then, it is easy to resolve the case of a foreseeable rape on the basis of the principles he has set forth, but he pays a very high price in doing so. Obviously, a sexual act perpetrated by a rapist is not an act of love, but merely an assault. The author rightly affirms "the profound difference between the two behaviors, at the moral level, is clear";[14] he recognizes the fact that we are dealing with two different behaviors, in which there is a difference from the point of view of the object of the act.

Later, however, he uses a formulation that recalls the vocabulary of proportionalism, as well as that of situational ethics. He claims:

12. Ibid.
13. Ibid., 41 (fourth paragraph).
14. Ibid., 42.

In this concrete situation, it becomes morally licit that the [the woman], so as to avoid a possible pregnancy, make use of the only means available, i.e., of contraception. As such, that act of intercourse, extorted by violence, is rendered sterile, only because she intends to safeguard values which are of maximum importance for her future from a psychological-affective point of view.[15]

This formulation contains, in my judgment, the serious defect of not recognizing the difference between:

1. "contraception" as a human act that can be qualified morally; and

2. the act "to take a contraceptive measure," considered as a "physical act," as a technical, anovulatory procedure rendering conception impossible, that is, an act described at the physiological level.

According to whether one uses the word "contraception" in the first or the second sense, the term "means" also acquires a significantly different meaning. In the second case, "means" signifies only the technical, physiological, "pharmaceutical" dimension of an act (in the same sense that, e.g., aspirin is a "means" used against a headache).[16] In the first case, however, "means" would be an act freely chosen for a purpose, that is, a *praxis* by which one intends to arrive at an ulterior end. For example, "taking an aspirin" could be a practice or act of "getting rid of a headache," with the ulterior end, perhaps, of being able to sleep. The question then is: presupposing that contraception is intrinsically evil, why is it licit "in this concrete situation" to choose it as a *means* for a good end? What is the meaning of "contraception" in the case we are considering? Is it a *praxis,* as in the first sense, or a simple "means," as in the second sense?

Fr. Perico arrives, necessarily, at the affirmation that "contraception" is a physical procedure—a means in the second sense—which in this case would be proportioned to "safeguarding a value of highest importance." As such, we would be dealing with an act of self-defense. With this argumentation, however, contraception would *always* be considered

15. Ibid. Fr. Perico relies in this context also on the authority of Fr. Ivan Fucek, interviewed by L. Brunelli, "La pillola congolese," in *Il Sabato,* March 13, 1993, 32–33.

16. Where we use the term "means" in its moral, practical sense, Thomas uses the Aristotelian phrase "ea quae sunt ad finem," which signifies, freely translated, "what is done for the sake of an end." These means, thus, are properly *actions,* done for the sake of attaining a goal.

licit in cases where one "intends to safeguard values of highest importance." This is certainly not the result for which the author was aiming. I think that he rather wanted to show why contraception, in the case in question, is an act that is different from the point of view of its *moral object*. I do not think he wanted to show, however, that it is, in itself, only a choice at the "physical" (pre-moral) level, to then be justified according to the values at stake according to the intention of the agent.

Fr. Perico's article, therefore, does not make clear whether the act of taking a contraceptive in the case of the threat of rape would be

(a) a contraceptive act, chosen with the end of legitimate self-defense, although in a specific situation that renders the choice "proportionate," making it licit as an exception (the object of the act would be contraception, and the ulterior end, self-defense); or

(b) objectively an act of self-defense, and *not* the choice of a contraceptive act (the object of the act would be to "protect oneself from the undesirable consequences of another's assault on one's body," which is objectively a different kind of act than "contraception").

Obviously, only solution (b) is compatible with the teaching that contraception is an intrinsically evil act (supposing that one wishes to maintain the licitness of taking contraceptive measures in the case of the threat of rape). Fr. Perico's article, though it is certainly well-intended and at times can even give the impression that it favors option (b), seems to me to be in fact oriented toward option (a); this also seems confirmed by the way in which it refers to the opinion of the three moralists consulted in 1961.

A Note on the Proportionalist Solution

The resolution of this question cannot, therefore, consist in asking the question whether the behavior in question, judged *in principle* to be objectively dishonest, could nevertheless be later "justified" in a specific case. It would rather be necessary to examine whether that which the Church condemns as "contraception," on the one hand, and the preventative use of contraceptive means in the case of the threat of rape, on the other, are not in reality two *objectively* different types of human acts, which are therefore subject to different moral norms. Responding to this question, one would also clarify what is meant by "the object of a human act," in the way that this term seems to be used by the Church's magisterium.

Before proceeding, however, I want to insert a brief comment. For adherents of the proportionalist or consequentialist theories (it is not necessary to distinguish between these here), the case would be resolved, more or less, in the following manner. Having as a point of departure the type of argument just presented (in Fr. Perico's article), they would say that the solution given is neither coherent nor sincere. The proportionalist, in fact, would say that it makes no sense to speak of an act that is evil based on its object, and then, by means of rather complicated reasoning, attempting to justify an exception. The proportionalist would simply begin with the idea that the contraceptive act "as such"— that is, in the second sense of a procedure considered at the technical-physiological level—cannot yet be qualified morally. It would be necessary, he would claim, to *also* take into consideration the circumstances and the intentions of the agent, referring to the realization of other goods or to the prevention of other evils. Only with reference to *all* of these elements could one arrive, in each specific case, at the object of the act.[17] This methodology, it seems, is in essence similar to the one just presented, with one significant difference: it universalizes the method, and in this sense it is more coherent.[18]

On the basis of this methodology, however, it would no longer be possible to formulate a universal norm prohibiting the choice of a concrete

17. Cf., e.g., J. Fuchs S.J., "Der Absolutheitscharakter sittlicher Handlungsnormen," in *Testimonium veritatis: Philosophische und theologische Studien zu kirchlichen Fragen der Gegenwart*, ed. H. Wolter, Frankfurter theologische Studien, vol. 7, (Frankfurt: Josef Knecht, 1971), 211–40; esp. 231 ff. The author later confirmed this position in a commentary on the encyclical *Veritatis Splendor:* J. Fuchs, "Das Problem Todsünde," *Stimmen der Zeit* 119 (1994): 7–86; esp. 83. See also my extensive criticism, "Intentional Actions and the Meaning of Object: A Reply to Richard McCormick," *Thomist* 59 no. 2 (1995): 279–311, which was written as a response to McCormick's "Some Early Reactions to *Veritatis splendor,*" *Theological Studies* 55 (1994): 481–506. My reply was reprinted in *Veritatis Splendor and the Renewal of Moral Theology*, ed. J. A. Di Noia and Romanus Cessario (Princeton: Scepter Publishers; Huntington: Our Sunday Visitor; Chicago: Midwest Theological Forum, 1999), 241–68; and also as chapter 4 of *The Perspective of the Acting Person: Essays in the Renewal of Thomistic Moral Philosophy*, ed. with introduction by William F. Murphy Jr., (Washington, D.C.: The Catholic University of America Press, 2008)

18. In this sense one understands how the proportionalists continue to affirm that they, in essence, merely make use of a traditional method, applying it, however, in a universal, and thus coherent, way.

behavior, given that—according to the requirements of the methodology—all of the possible circumstances could not be taken into consideration at the moment of the formulation of the norm. The norm could only contain a more-or-less formal prohibition: "Never have recourse to contraception without a proportional reason." Such a norm obviously does not conform to the Church's teaching.

To clarify our problem it will therefore be indispensable at first to show, in detail, precisely that in which consists the "contraceptive choice" rejected by the Church, and why such a choice and the associated behavior are to be considered morally disordered. To this end, the encyclical *Humanae Vitae* provides a formulation of the norm prohibiting contraception, a formulation that will allow us to respond to this question in a clear and technically unambiguous way.

The Contraceptive Choice According to the Encyclical *Humanae Vitae*

On the one hand, sterilization is presented in the encyclical *Humanae Vitae* only as a particular case of a more generic choice; that is, the contraceptive choice. Compared to earlier accounts, it is no longer presented in the opposite manner, as if contraception (hormonal or mechanical procedures) were a particular case of sterilization and therefore of mutilation. On the other hand, the teaching on contraception is situated, in a clearer and more explicit way, within the context of conjugal love, which, according to the teaching of Vatican II, is considered the intimate union and mutual self-giving of two persons.[19] The council presents conjugal love as that of free subjects who are responsible for the transmission of human life and who, in their bodily and spiritual union, cooperate by means of their love with the love of the Creator. As such, the discussion is no longer centered on a simple respect for natural processes and ends, but rather on the conjugal union—the loving union of two persons—as the responsible subject of the transmission of life.

Paul VI, faithful to the teaching of his predecessors, meant to defend this conjugal love when he affirmed that every matrimonial act, in order to remain an expression of that loving mutual donation of the spouses,

---

19. Cf. Vatican Council II, *Pastoral Constitution Gaudium et Spes,* nos. 48–49.

"must remain open to the transmission of life."[20] Later on, Paul VI's encyclical *rejects* as a means of responsible parenthood "every action which, either in anticipation of the conjugal act, or in its accomplishment, or in the development of its natural consequences, proposes [*intendat*], whether as an end or as a means, to render procreation impossible."[21]

The norm, as it is set out in *Humanae Vitae* (and in essence as it had already been presented in the encyclical *Casti Connubii* of Pius XI), explicitly refers to conjugal acts; these latter obviously imply a fundamental mutual right to sexual relations with the other spouse and a respective consent of both. From this, it can easily be deduced that the applicability of the norm presupposes—in the agent to whom it refers and consequently in his actions—a *twofold* purpose or free choice: (1) that of having sexual intercourse with another person; and (2) the purpose or intention—at the level both of means and of ends—to prevent that such freely chosen sexual intercourse would have procreative consequences.

We would, in fact, call "contraception" a type of human action animated by this twofold intentionality. It is not, therefore, only and simply and act that prevents the causing of the conception of a new life; it is *rather an action that prevents that one's freely consented-to sexual acts would become the cause of a conception.* The human act "contraception," therefore, is an act that is part of one's own sexual behavior, and indeed is a constitutive element of sexual behavior. It is an act that, presupposing the necessity and/or the will to avoid causing a new conception, essentially and objectively—and despite wanting to avoid causing a new conception—pursues the end of carrying out sexual relations that otherwise could be fertile.[22]

It seems that it is precisely here that we find the nucleus of the moral disorder present in contraceptive choice. Whether it be carried out by

---

20. *Humanae Vitae*, no. 11.

21. *Humanae Vitae*, no. 14. As previously noted, the Latin text of the encyclical uses the verb *intendere*: "id tamquam finem obtinendum aut viam adhibendam intendat, ut procreatio impediatur."

22. As discussed in the previous chapter, I try, following Thomas's methodology, to explain moral disorders by their opposition to a determinate virtue, here chastity, which also defines an "ethical context." Thus, in contrast to those who root the evil of contraception in its being intentionally directed against the coming-to-be of a new human life and thus as intentionally analogous to homicide (as Grisez and his collaborators), I see the disorder in the very sexual and bodily behavior and thus as opposed to the requirements of the virtue of chastity.

"artificial" means or without them, for example, by means of coitus interruptus (*Humanae Vitae*, in fact, does not specifically condemn artificial contraception, but "every action which . . . intends . . . ," etc.), the moral problem inherent in contraception certainly does not consist in its "artificial" character. Rather, this disorder or moral evil is based in the twofold intention of having sexual relations with another person and of simultaneously depriving those relations of their possible procreative consequences, which in this case are obviously undesired.

Even when the reasons for which it is considered desirable to avoid a pregnancy are just and legitimate, contraception is not a behavior that respects the fundamental truth of man and woman as bodily-spiritual beings, and the truth of the mutual self-gift of the spouses. On the other hand, recourse to periodic continence would involve an essentially different type of behavior on the part of the spouses, assuming that the reason for avoiding a pregnancy is justified.[23]

It is not that continence *in itself* is by necessity morally good, meritorious, or better than sexual intercourse. Continence is morally called for, and therefore good, when it is necessary—among other things—to preserve in the spouses, through their self-dominion, the unity and mutual integration of spirit and body: in our case, the unity and mutual integration of responsibility and sexuality.

"Contraception," therefore, considered as an act proceeding from a free choice, and as such also morally qualifiable, is a way of acting that always refers to acts of sexual intercourse that are freely chosen, or at least consented to, by the agent. Contraception is objectively and essentially an integral part of one's own sexual behavior and of the free choices that pertain to it.

Distinguishing the Physical Level from the Moral Level

For such reasons, not every procedure, though "physically" inhibiting a possible conception, can be considered of the same moral species or kind as that disordered human act called "contraception" to which the moral

23. Cf. *Humanae Vitae*, no. 16; General Audience John Paul II, *Familiaris Consortio*, no. 32; *Discourse of August 22, 1984* (General Audience); *Discourse of January 10, 1992* (to the participants in a course of formation organized by the "Center for Studies and Research on the Natural Regulation of Fertility" of the Catholic University of the Sacred Heart), in *L'Osservatore Romano*, January 11, 1992, 5.

norm of *Humanae vitae* refers. Catholic moral theology has always distinguished between the "physical object" of an act and its "moral object," that is, the *genus naturae* from the *genus moris*.[24] *Morally,* an anovulatory procedure that is physically contraceptive is the evil of "contraception" only if the agent proposes (i.e., intends) with that procedure to avoid the necessity of abstaining from sexual intercourse that she fears could cause an unwanted pregnancy. In other words, the morally contraceptive act is an *alternative* to an act of continence. Such a reference to one's own freely consented sexual behavior enters therefore into the definition of the *object* of the act "contraception," considered as a moral act. With this, an *intentional* element enters into the definition of the object, referring to the fact that the act has been rationally *chosen* as a good to pursue, in a definite context and therefore as an object of practical reason.[25]

The specifically *moral* problem consists therefore in the intention to live—perhaps for reasons that in themselves are just and responsible—one's sexuality and the bodily dimension of conjugal love in such a way that one's own body and that of the spouse are treated, in their aspect of being the cause of human life, as a mere "instrument" or "object" of procreative responsibility; this is done rather than rendering their bodies, through acts of responsible continence, the *subject* of that loving responsibility. Such behavior is contrary to the requirement of the integration of one's sexual inclinations into the full personal truth of conjugal love.[26]

For this reason, an act that, considered *physically,* is anovulatory and physiologically contraceptive, does not fall necessarily under the moral

---

24. Cf. St. Thomas Aquinas, *Summa theologiae* I-II, q.1. a.3, ad 3; ibid., q.18, a.5, ad 3. See also M. Rhonheimer, *Natural Law and Practical Reason,* 475–83; and my *Die Perspektive der Moral,* 138–42, which is forthcoming as *The Perspective of Morality; Philosophical Foundations of Thomistic Virtue Ethics.* See also W. E. May, *Moral Absolutes, Catholic Tradition, Current Trends, and the Truth* (Milwaukee: Marquette University Press, 1989), 58–67.

25. Along these lines one can consider for example the definition of the object of the act "masturbation" in the *Catechism of the Catholic Church,* no. 2352: "By masturbation is to be understood the deliberate stimulation of the genital organs in order to derive sexual pleasure." The object therefore includes an intentional element, which indicates the "form" of the *"materia circa quam"*; so, the whole act is, in the light of reason, a practical good. The object is not only the material; at this level it could not be rationally chosen.

26. Cf. John Paul II, *Discourse of January 10, 1992;* see also *Familiaris Consortio,* no. 32. Cf. more thoroughly M. Rhonheimer, "Contraception, Sexual Behavior, and Natural Law: Philosophical Foundation of the Norm of *Humanae vitae,"* in *"Humanae vitae": 20 anni dopo. Atti del II Congresso Internazionale di Teologia Morale,* Rome, November 9–12, 1988

norm prohibiting contraception. An example would be to use anovulatory means to regulate a woman's rhythm or to suppress an athlete's menstruation on the day of an important race.

Furthermore, and in reference to the case under consideration, not even the use of a contraceptive with the primary and direct purpose of preventing a conception could be, as such, considered a contraceptive choice when such use is not part of a choice to carry out that sexual act from which a conception could be a possible and foreseeable consequence. To avoid or to prevent that the conception of a new life occurs is not, as such and per se, a moral disorder. Indeed, in some cases it may even be morally required.

The moral disorder resides, rather, in depriving one's freely chosen sexual acts of their quality of being a possible cause of procreation—and this precisely as an alternative to the act of abstaining from these potentially fertile sexual acts. In such a moral context, the matrimonial act could no longer be called an act "open to the transmission of life."[27] If, on the other hand, periodic continence is practiced for reasons of parental responsibility, in that case *both* acts of abstention and acts of intercourse during infertile periods bear a significance with respect to paternal and maternal responsibility; they retain their sense of being acts oriented to the transmission of life, a task in which the spouses cooperate responsibly precisely in the dimension of their sexual behavior—that is, in the bodily expression of their love.[28] In fact, even in acts of responsible continence the two inseparable meanings of conjugal love and human sexuality are realized and expressed, *both at the spiritual and at the bodily level*: the loving union of the spouses and their responsibility for the transmission of life.

When one speaks of "contraception," therefore, it is necessary to differentiate a merely technical use of the word "contraception"—as yet unqualified morally—from the moral use of the term, by which is specified a freely chosen type of human behavior. What at times causes confusion is the medical-technical use of the term "contraception" (at the

(Milan: Editions of the Italian Dominicans, 1989), 73–113; published also in *Linacre Quarterly* 56 no. 2 (1989): 20–57; and in an enlarged version as *Sexualität und Verantwortung. Empfängnisverhütung als ethisches Problem* (Vienna: IMABE, 1995). This is the version now available in English as the second and third chapters of the present book.

27. *Humanae Vitae*, no. 11.

28. Cf. also Anscombe, *Contraception and Chastity*, 22–23.

level that considers only the physical object of the act) in contexts where rather a judgment on the licitness of a specific human behavior as an object of a free choice is required—and vice versa.

For this reason, the encyclical *Veritatis Splendor* emphasizes that "[i]n order to be able to grasp the object of an act which specifies that act morally, it is therefore necessary to place oneself *in the perspective of the acting person*" (emphasis in the original), given that "the object of the act of willing is in fact a freely chosen kind of behavior"; every object is "the proximate end of a deliberate decision which determines the act of willing on the part of the acting person."[29] The teaching of *Veritatis Splendor* on intrinsically evil acts (no. 79) also operates on this level, as does the doctrine of the *Catechism of the Catholic Church*, cited in no. 78 of the encyclical, which states: "There are concrete acts that it is always wrong to choose, because their choice entails a disorder of the will, i.e., a moral evil."[30] This affirmation refers not only to "behaviors," or to the behavioral "form" or structure of certain acts, but to the *choice* of such acts. As the object of a *choice*, an "act" or a "behavior" is always more than a merely physical act or "occurrence." It is precisely a practical good, an object of reason, "a good apprehended and ordained by the reason" (*bonum apprehensum et ordinatum per rationem*).[31] And it is therefore at that level that moral norms are formulated.

The reason for the prohibition of contraception could not, therefore—nor in fact does it—consist in a violation of a natural, physiological order. At this level, a moral judgment on the use of a contraceptive means would not even be possible. The moral disorder of contraception, as with any moral disorder, does not consist in what occurs at the physiological or biological level, but in that which takes place at the level of the intentional and free behavior of the person: in this case, in the failure to fulfill the demands of the virtue of chastity.[32]

29. *Veritatis Splendor*, no. 78. Cf. M. Rhonheimer, "'Intrinsically Evil Acts' and the Moral Viewpoint: Clarifying a Central Teaching of *Veritatis splendor*," *Thomist* 58 no. 1 (1994): 1–39. This was reprinted in *Veritatis Splendor and the Renewal of Moral Theology*, 161–93, and as chapter 3 of *The Perspective of the Acting Person*.

30. *Catechism of the Catholic Church*, no. 1761 (this is the "in brief" text. In no. 1755, the principal text, which is identical, fornication is given as an example.)

31. Aquinas, *ST* I-II, q.20, a.1 ad 1. English Dominican translation (Westminster: Christian Classics, 1981).

32. Cf. Vatican Council II, *Pastoral Constitution Gaudium et Spes*, no. 51; *Humanae Vitae*, nos. 17 and 21; John Paul II, *Discourses of August 29 and September 5, 1984 (General Audiences)*.

Preventative Contraception under Threat of Rape:
A Choice of Self-Defense

Consequently, the use of contraceptive measures, such as an anovulatory pill or a device that impedes the penetration of sperm into the vagina, is not *per se* to be considered as a human act that falls under the moral norm prohibiting contraception. In fact, in the case of a preventative use in the face of the threat of rape, we are dealing with the use of a contraceptive measure (that is, one that prevents conception, in the physical sense) in an entirely different ethical context: not with the purpose of rendering infertile a freely desired and consented-to sexual act, thus eliminating the need for continence (given that pregnancy is undesired), but to defend oneself from the possible undesired and undesirable effects of an act imposed on oneself against one's will.

In such a situation, a woman is not only without any obligation to accept the possible procreative effect of such a forced copulation (we are obviously not speaking of abortion here). Instead, she has the right—and at times perhaps even a reasonable duty—to avoid a conception: out of respect for herself and her freedom to decide regarding her own life; out of respect and responsibility toward the new life, which has the right to proceed from an act of love; or in respect and fidelity toward her vocation, for example in the case of women religious.

It is clear that in this case we are not dealing with a *contraceptive choice or will*. Regarding the moral object, we are dealing with a legitimate *choice to defend oneself* from the undesirable and disadvantageous consequences of an assault on one's own body, a choice that is at the same time a choice to defend, to the extent possible, one's freedom in the face of a foreseen situation in which that freedom may be, in part, taken away by a violent aggressor. The fact that, in the case of rape, sexual intercourse is neither consented to nor freely carried out confers a completely different objective moral character on the act of preventing such an assault from resulting in the conception of a new life: precisely the character of an act of self-defense.

The Choice of Contraception Remains Intrinsically Evil

It cannot be said, therefore, that in this way an "exception" is established to the norm prohibiting contraception. At the same time, on this basis certain unfortunate and confusing statements given in the past can be avoided, such as "the prohibition of sterilization is not an absolute principle," or "direct sterilization is not necessarily an intrinsically perverse act," whenever a reason justifying it existed.[33] Such statements, in fact, find their explanation in the context of a legalistic, and therefore casuistic, logic, in which is also situated the proportionalist methodology; adherents of this methodology often make use of such statements.

If the Church's magisterium teaches that contraception (as well as sterilization) is an "intrinsically perverse" or "evil" action, it makes this judgment in reference to the act considered not at the level of its physical object (the physical act preventing conception), but at the level of its moral object. The statement, therefore, that "it is not clear that the use of the pharmaceuticals that we are discussing [i.e., contraceptive measures] is intrinsically evil,"[34] also seems irrelevant. Only an act considered as the object of the will of an agent who rationally chooses such a behavior can be intrinsically perverse. Such an act cannot be, however, *simply and exclusively* the physical procedure or "the use of a pharmaceutical that prevents conception." What is needed, rather, is that configuration of the act which, before practical reason, confers on the act its primary objective identity as a specific type of human act and of *bonum faciendum*. Therefore, the two cases we are considering are two objectively different human acts, which obviously do not fall under the same moral norm. "To impede, as an alternative to an act of continence, the procreative consequences of one's freely chosen sexual acts" is the act of contraception. "To prevent the possible procreative consequences of an assault on one's body and thus of an abuse of it" is an act of self-defense.

To repeat, the argumentation advanced here is essentially different from a proportionalist or consequentialist argument. It is true that these methods also aim to do nothing other than determine the *objective* significance of the act—proportionalism is in fact a method for determining the object of an act. It deals, however, with what it calls an "expanded object,"[35] that is an object in which all the circumstances and morally relevant intentions are included, and this as a result of a prior weigh-

33. Cf. the argumentation of F. Lambruschini, *Studi Cattolici*, 69–70.

34. Hürth, "Il premunirsi rientra," 67.

35. Cf. the above-cited article by R. A. McCormick, "Some Early Reactions to *Veritatis splendor*," 501, and my response, published shortly thereafter.

ing of ("pre-moral") goods and evils. Because this expanded object of proportionalism cannot be distinguished from the *ulterior* intentions, it is *indeed not an object*. In contrast, an understanding of "object" consistent with St. Thomas and *Veritatis Splendor,* nos. 78ff, does include a proximate or basic intention,[36] but this is clearly distinguished from those *ulterior* intentions *for which* such an object (a concrete human action) is chosen. According to the proportionalist methodology, every action could be redescribed or redefined, according to the circumstances and intentions regarding the foreseen consequences of the act. It would be impossible, then, to formulate a prohibitive norm that could not become inapplicable in a specific case.

As we have noted above, the proportionalist methodology derives from the casuistic tradition, and therefore from an ethics centered on norms, which treated the natural law as though it were a positive code. The methodology presented here, on the other hand, pertains to an ethic of virtue. Such an ethics analyzes human action and its objective meaning in specific ethical contexts, so as also to be able to distinguish the object of an act from *ulterior* intentions for which an act is chosen.[37] To arrive at a determination of the objective value of the action examined here, we have not had recourse to a weighing of goods or of "proportionate reasons." Our evaluation, rather, addressed the primary and fundamental content of the contraceptive choice as distinguished from the choice of an act of self-defense. Not all norms, therefore, as the proportionalists claim, are to be considered as the result of a prior weighing of various goods, a result that is always provisional. Some norms referring to concrete behaviors, precisely those that are prohibitive, express the "intrinsically"—*per se*—disordered character of such behaviors.[38]

36. For the notion of "basic intention" and "basic intentional action" see M. Rhonheimer, *The Perspective of Morality,* chapters 2, 3, and 5.

37. For a more detailed treatment, cf. M. Rhonheimer, "'Ethics of Norms' and the Lost Virtues: Searching the Roots of the Crisis of Ethical Reasoning," *Anthropotes* 9, no. 2 (1993): 231–43, reprinted in a slightly enlarged version as "Norm-Ethics, Moral Rationality, and the Virtues: What's Wrong with Consequentialism?" in chapter 2 of *The Perspective of the Acting Person.* See also the previously cited "'Intrinsically Evil Acts' and the Moral Viewpoint" and "Reply to Richard McCormick."

38. For this reason, the encyclical no. 77,1, states: "The weighing of the goods and evils foreseeable as the consequence of an action is not an adequate method for determining whether the choice of that concrete kind of behavior is 'according to its species,' or 'in itself,' morally good or bad, licit or illicit."

The methodology used here allows the formulation of negative norms regarding the choice of concrete behaviors *whose descriptions are unalterable*, norms that are valid *semper et pro semper*, provided that the description truly be that of a human act, that is, a description that includes those fundamental *intentional* elements that confer on the act its primary and fundamental moral identity, and with this its "objective" meaning.

PART II

Injustices Regarding
Human Life

Reproductive
Technology and Abortion

5

The Instrumentalization of Human Life
Ethical Considerations Concerning
Reproductive Technology

The Problem

In the following I will evaluate from an ethical point of view the technologies and modes of action associated with what is commonly called "artificial procreation."

When one speaks of "artificial procreation," "genetic engineering," and even of "artificial contraception," many believe they have already identified the core of the problem with the term "artificial"—even though many of these same people speak without moral reservations about "artificial nutrition," "organ transplants" (which in fact did create ethical concerns in the past), and other similar interventions. Indeed, "artificiality" is less likely to be judged negatively in a medical context, given that medicine, taken as a whole, is an art to which many people owe their lives. This positive reception would certainly be the case for those who can continue to be what they are "by nature"—living bodily-spiritual beings—due to surgical interventions using artificial technologies (such as bypass surgery).

And yet, the fulfillment of the desire to have children through in vitro fertilization, and the transfer of embryos, seem in some way to be "unnatural," and therefore suspect. Why is this?

Recourse to "human nature"—or to "nature" *tout court*—is a traditional argumentative strategy for the foundation of moral norms, claims, requirements, or prohibitions. If we follow the philosophical tradition, however, we cannot ignore the fact that, at least in the context of morality, the concept that is opposed to "natural" is *not* "artificial," but rather *irrational or opposed to reason*—precisely that which is opposed to man *as a rational being,* and therefore also opposed to his "nature." The rational element, in fact, is precisely that part of his "nature" which characterizes man as man.[1]

I have indicated with these comments the context in which I wish to situate my argument. In particular, I will propose an argumentative context upon which I hope to clarify why so-called artificial procreation is *morally evil*; it is so precisely because it is opposed to a basic component of human rationality, and *for this reason* it is also not in accordance with "human nature."

This argument will not be carried out at the level of questions such as: Will any "spare" (i.e., leftover or supernumerary) embryos be destroyed? What should be done in the case of the conception of twins? Are the risks and consequences involved foreseeable? How can abuses be avoided? These types of questions might pertain primarily to a practical political argument. My interest is rather in the fundamental ethical question: even if all these other questions were resolved, *is it licit to produce human life* in a test tube, so as to fulfill the desire for a child?[2]

The Inadequacy of Recourse to Nature

To begin our discussion of in vitro fertilization (IVF) as a primary form of contemporary reproductive technology, it is of no importance in the present context what type of technology we are considering. I will also essentially "put in parentheses" the question (which in practice is decisively important, but secondary here) of whether so-called spare embryos are destroyed, as well as whether we are dealing with ho-

1. Cf. on this R. Spaemann, *Das Natürliche und das Vernünftige, Aufsätze zur Anthropologie* (Munich-Zurich, 1987). See also my book *Natural Law and Practical Reason,* originally published in German as *Natur als Grundlage der Moral.*

2. I want to thank here Prof. Johannes Bonelli for posing valuable objections and corrections, as well as Prof. Josef Seifert, for his criticism and the debate that required me to make my argument more precise.

mologous or heterologous IVF (the case of a heterologous semen donor simply raises an *additional problem* with respect to homologous IVF). Also irrelevant for our discussion is the question of the transplanting of embryos, or that of surrogate motherhood; all of these are ulterior questions. I would also like to note that the following argumentation applies equally to artificial fertilization *in utero*. Leaving aside the previously mentioned ulterior problems, one cannot in fact identify any ethically relevant distinction between artificial fertilization *in utero* and IVF; the problem does not lie in the fact that conception takes place outside the body, that is, it is not a problem of the test tube itself.

This, then, is the basic question: is it morally licit, for whatever reason, to generate a human being outside of the "natural" act of sexual copulation, that is, *artificially*, by means of *technology*, and thus by means of a specific intervention that imitates nature and partially replaces it? To the extent that this is not accomplished by "magic" (which of course is impossible), "to intervene," "to make," and "artificiality" indicate here something along the lines of *to produce technically*, by means of the technologies that are commonly known.

We must proceed carefully, however. We must not allow the "technical" or "artificial" aspect of the procedure to indicate too quickly the direction of our argumentation. That which nature is unable to do inevitably cannot be produced but "artificially." On the question of whether this is morally permissible or not—and in not a few cases, if not most, it is—"artificiality" as such cannot give an answer, nor can moral reasoning condemn artificiality simply because it is "unnatural" (for example, Caesarian sections and the incubation of premature infants are not problematic morally, despite their "artificiality").

For this reason also it is insufficient to refer to the fact that human procreation is by nature linked to bodily sexual acts, a link that may be circumvented, dissolved, or substituted for through technology. To the extent that we want to avoid identifying "natural" with "given by nature," recourse to what is *given* by nature is not here an argument that such an intervention would go against what *conforms* to man's nature, that is, it does not regard *that which is good for man*. One could in effect object: what occurs is simply the fulfillment of a legitimate desire to have a child. Indeed this objection would argue that in this case a technical intervention would be entirely "in conformity with nature." In fact, a legitimate desire to have a child is "in conformity with nature," and that condition of being "unnaturally" incapable of procreation is rectified here through the use of reason, so as to realize by means of a human intervention what is, in itself, in conformity with nature.

To oppose this argument, recourse to "nature," that is, reference to the natural link between the sexual act and procreation, would be a vicious circle, inasmuch as such an argument would in effect presuppose what it needs to demonstrate. It would presuppose instead of demonstrate that the separation of "procreation" from "sexual act," or the substitution of the sexual act with technology—that is, the "technical" fulfillment of the desire for a child (a desire that seems entirely natural)—would go against what is good for man, and therefore in this *moral* sense would not be in conformity with his nature. Put otherwise, it would fail to demonstrate the *moral relevance* of the link, existing by nature, of procreation and the sexual act.

The argument in favor of the moral licitness of IVF, which implies the argument that this link can be circumvented, is in effect based on the following consideration. Taking for granted that the desire for a child as such is legitimate and good for persons x, y, z, then the fulfillment of this desire is likewise a good. Presupposing that the technical intervention in itself is not immoral for other reasons (e.g., spare embryos are not destroyed), the intervention itself is justified based on the end pursued. Consequently, the separation of procreation from the sexual act is as natural as other medical interventions, which in effect also pursue a human good in conformity with nature (i.e., health).

Against this, I will argue in the following manner: in the logic of such an action, the *coming into life* of a person that is technically "produced" rather than "generated" is recognized as a "good," not because it happens, but because it is desired by the parents. The "goodness" of the new human life is made dependent, *in the act of the decision for IVF and in the acts that effect the procedure,* on its "being desired," on the *recognition* or acceptance given by others (I want to emphasize here "in the act of the decision for IVF and in the acts that effect the procedure"; I will return below to the relevance of this specification). *I believe, however, that an act characterized by such an attitude toward human life is fundamentally immoral, because it is unjust.* With Robert Spaemann I would therefore affirm: "Regarding the baby conceived in a test tube, he is naturally, like every other baby, a creature in the image of God, and must be respected as a person. Nevertheless, the way in which he has been produced is unjust. It violates the fundamental equality of all people, which finds expression in the fact that every person—including the person's parents—owes his life to nature."[3]

The importance and validity of this thesis are certainly not immediately visible, and therefore we will explain it step-by-step in detail. The argument can nevertheless be found, if only in seminally, in the instruction *Donum Vitae*:

In his unique and unrepeatable origin, the child must be respected and recognized as equal in personal dignity to those who give him life. The human person must be accepted in his parents' act of union and love. . . . In reality, the origin of a human person is the result of an act of giving. The one conceived must be the fruit of his parents' love. He cannot be desired or conceived as the product of an intervention of medical or biological techniques.[4]

Donum Vitae, however, frames its entire argumentation based on the contraposition "conjugal love—technology," and it seems to me that a further justification of the moral relevance of this contraposition would be both fruitful and necessary. It is important to note that the following argument does not depart in the first place from the (technological) structure of the action of IVF, and from its implicit "control and dominion" over human life; rather it considers the *intentional relation* between the parents (or doctor) and the baby generated, a consideration that, it seems to me, is capable of fully clarifying the moral relevance (which is valid in this context) of the contraposition between "love" and "technology." In presenting the argument I will initially offer it in the form of a thesis, to then defend it against some serious objections while further specifying it, and end by drawing some conclusions.

3. R. Spaemann, "Kommentar zur Instruktion 'Donum vitae,'" in *Die Unantastbarkeit des menschlichen Lebens. Zu ethischen Fragen der Biomedizin. Instruktion der Kongregation für die Glaubenslehre. Mit einem Kommentar von R, Spaemann* (Freiburg: Herder Verlag, 1987), 92 s. Part II, section B, chapter 4c.

4. Ibid.

The desire "If only we had a child!" is in itself legitimate, because in principle it is a better condition for a married couple to have a child than to not have one. At least such an assumption seems to us completely legitimate, and it clearly underlies the decision to undertake IVF, and this, at least in principle, in exactly the same way as in the case of an act of natural procreation. The legitimacy of this desire, then, needs no further discussion.

Nevertheless, I would object, it is better to have *no* child rather than to "produce" a "child wanted at all cost." Why? Because the referred-to *legitimate* desire can ultimately only mean "If only we could *receive* a child." By this is expressed the fact that the goodness of the coming into being of a new baby is not measured by the fact that a *desire* of the parents is fulfilled, rather by the fact that the new human life has *come about* as the fruit of reciprocal love. According to the thesis proposed here, the desire for a child (even one felt deeply and ardently) is *legitimate* to the extent that it is reconcilable with:

(a) the readiness to also assent to the non-fulfillment of this desire, which implies an assent to the fact that human beings are not entitled to ordain the beginning and the ending of human life;

(b) the readiness also to accept, with the same assent and for the same fundamental reason, and at all times, that a child that was not explicitly desired, and even was "undesired," is a valuable human life. This in turn means: the legitimate desire to have a child can only be simply a *hope* for the coming about of a new human life, and not a desire in the sense of an "ordaining," in which the desire in effect brings about (so to speak) the fulfillment.[5]

In the case where these intentional conditions are *not* taken into consideration, the desire for a child leads to an instrumentalization or exploitation of the child for the end of fulfilling one's own desires. One would then consider the satisfaction of such a desire to be "good" not because a new life has begun and the parents have had a child, but precisely because now the desire to have a child has been fulfilled. A "wanted child" in *this* sense would amount to a degradation of human

---

5. I owe this last formulation to a suggestion by Johannes Bonelli.

life, because it implies an acceptance or recognition by the parents of this life that is *conditioned.* What makes being a "couple with children" to be a better state must not be the *fulfillment of a desire,* but the simple, and perhaps even unexpected, *existence of the child,* combined of course with the consequent enrichment for the spouses resulting from the absolute and loving acceptance of this existence.

In the case, however, where the *fulfillment of desire* is placed at the center, this amounts to saying, "It is good to have a child, because in this way my desire to have a child has been fulfilled." Indeed, one could say the same thing with respect to a car, or a vacation in the Canary Islands—these things are "good" for people precisely in the measure in which they are desired. For a person who gets nauseous traveling by car, a car is not something he would want. Conversely, if someone wants a car but "no one gives him one," he can simply go out and buy one. What matters in the end is simply that somehow he obtains the car to satisfy his desire. *The subjective evaluation of the goodness of the "existence" of the car is based exclusively on its "being desired"* (otherwise it would be felt to be "superfluous," "useless," "a bother"). Never, however, can human beings behave this way with respect to the existence of another human being.

Children, therefore—and about this everyone would agree—cannot be desired like an auto or a vacation in the Canary Islands. The subjective sense of the goodness of their birth and of their existence cannot consist in their being desired. *Children, as opposed to the case of a car or a vacation in the Canary Islands, must be desired as something that is good even if it were not desired*—even *if* in fact they are desired. But children must be desired as a good, even if they were not desired in the first place, and also if they are *different* from the way in which they were desired (one who wants a particular type of car, and unexpectedly wins a different model in a lottery, might sell it or give it away and buy the car he wants; and a vacation in the Canary Islands, if it ends up pouring rain, results in a frustrated desire for a vacation, even to the point where the vacationers might go home early).

Only with difficulty could one deny that such an instrumentalization of a baby at the service of the satisfaction of a desire for children involves a basic inhumanity. Similarly, it is difficult to deny the inhumanity of the implicit, merely conditional, acceptance of a human life generated in this way. It is a separate question, however, whether such an attitude is actually involved in IVF.

An Objection: IVF Does Not Necessarily Involve Instrumentalization

One could object: it *may be the case,* but not necessarily. And even natural procreation could come about only for the fulfillment of the desire for children. IVF, rather, could quite well be simply the "prosecution by other means" of an absolutely legitimate intentional relation with the new life. Indeed, the very low success rate of reproductive medical intervention could make it that a pregnancy and birth by such means would still be experienced as a "gift." And ultimately, it is a baby that arrives. The relationship with this (legitimately hoped for) arrival, which was the guiding idea of the spouses prior to the decision to undertake IVF, would be maintained in the decision for and implementation of IVF, in effect by simply simulating a natural process, effected by other means; the baby would nevertheless still be considered a "gift of nature." It would therefore be necessary to demonstrate why this simulation of the natural process employed as a means at the service of life is evil, because the intentionality implicit in the choice of this means and the intentionality that is the basis of natural procreation *could be* identical. This is an extremely important objection. If correct, the argument we have employed thus far would be effectively without object (even if there would still remain the possibility of objecting to IVF on the grounds, e.g., of the problematic relationship with spare embryos; but, as mentioned above, we want to argue the question at a more fundamental level, putting even this question in parentheses).

A Response Based on a Key Distinction:
Simple Wanting versus Intending

To overcome this objection, we must further specify two things. First, the difference between two forms of "wanting," that is, "to desire" and "to intend." Second, we must distinguish between how the will relates to the child—or more exactly, to the coming about of a human life—in the natural procreative act on the one hand, and in IVF on the other. The first case would be "to desire," and the second would be "to intend."

In the first place, returning essentially to Aristotle, we consider the *difference between* "to desire" and "to intend." *To desire* is a wish or a wanting directed toward what we ourselves cannot "do" with our own actions (because it is not in our "power"), that is, something that is not properly an *object* of our doing. A terminally sick person who is convinced that there is no possibility or means for him to be healed would certainly still want to be healthy—that is, he desires it. But he would do nothing else, unless perhaps to pray for a miracle. *To intend* on the other hand is a wanting that directs itself toward what we cannot do immediately, but that we believe we can do if we seek a means that will "translate" the intention to the level of concrete action; we look for a means, and concrete actions, to obtain that which has been intended, that is, to make it the object of our making and doing *by means of other actions* (the so-called means). An intention *leads* therefore to a search for means, and to action. The corresponding concrete actions (to visit a doctor, undergo an operation, take a medicine, etc.) would then be done with intention of becoming healthy. Intentions are therefore "practical" (they lead to concrete actions); desires, conversely, remain at the level of simply wanting something. One who, although only *desiring* health, nevertheless suddenly becomes well would consider this chance, luck, or a gift from heaven, but not the consequence of something he had done—that is, of a doing that possesses the character of a means for reaching an end.

The decisiveness of this distinction for our discussion is not immediately apparent. It becomes clearer, however, with the following thesis: a test-tube baby "is produced not only by the desire of his parents, but by the will to impose the fulfillment of this desire at all costs."[6] To clarify

---

6. Spaemann, *Kommentar*, 93. Cf. also M. Rassem, "Zur Revolution der Reproduktion," *Zeitschrift für Politik* N. F. 36 (1989): 347–57.

this thesis, it is now necessary to speak in second place of the sexual act or of the natural procreative act, which I call the *conjugal act*.[7]

The Relationship between the Conjugal Act
and the Desire for Children

To clarify the relationship between the conjugal act and the desire for children, I will first propose a brief thought experiment. A couple that as a last resort decides for IVF, carries out a series of actions whose purpose is manifestly to bring to fulfillment their desire for a child. If this desire didn't exist, or if after several attempts the couple concluded that reproductive medical intervention would not be successful, they would no longer carry out the actions involved in IVF (given that these actions, when the goal is seen as unreachable, would in effect lose their sense or purpose). A couple, on the other hand, that performs the conjugal act with the desire to have a child, even in the case where a lack of procreative results is certain, would nevertheless continue to perform such acts (in any case they would not abstain because of their infertility), because these acts of sexual union in no way lose their sense or purpose due to their lack of procreative results.

From this it follows that, distinct from the actions involved in IVF, the conjugal act (speaking in theoretical-practical terms) is not truly a "means" for reaching the goal of "a child." It could be such a means naturally, that is, at the level of the natural conjoining that occurs (which the spouses obviously must know, or they could not reasonably carry out such acts with the hope of having a child), if it were chosen as a "means" for the procreation of a child. Rather, what the spouses voluntarily do when they engage in intercourse (with or without an explicit desire for a child) can be described intentionally as a reciprocal self-gift, specifically in the totality of their being man and woman, which is under the impulse of the affective, emotional, and even instinctive dynamism, which manifests itself as integrated within the fully personal level of their being. The interior significance of the conjugal act as a personal act transcends the simply natural context of copulation and procreation. Certainly it is possible that a man and a woman could carry out the natural sexual act exclusively as a "means" toward the end of procreation (which means that they would no longer engage in intercourse, all other things

7. See chapter 3 on the object of the conjugal act.

being equal, if they foresaw that there would be no procreative result). This, however, would no longer correspond to the personalistic human meaning of this act as an act of *love* between two persons. "The generation of a child" is not therefore in every case an adequate description of what the spouses *do* when they have intercourse; at the most it can be the adequate description of that which (with the consciousness and desire of the spouses) *could occur* at the level of nature, and this *on the occasion of their union*. A case, however, where the conjugal act could be adequately described by "the procreation of a child" as a specific type of human *action*, would already be a perverted form of the conjugal act, precisely because it has been instrumentalized.[8]

Implications for the Moral Distinction between
IVF and Natural Procreation

From this results a first, provisional theoretical-practical result. The actions involved in IVF acquire their significance by means of and *only* by means of the end "generation of a child," and they are also performed only for this purpose (despite the fact that they could be carried out for other purposes as well, e.g., for research; this does not affect our conclusion). The conjugal act, on the other hand, is not carried out as a means for the generation of a child, even if (naturally) it is a means to this. Indeed it can be carried out in a reasonable manner, as the conjugal act, even when it is foreseen to be infertile.

This means that in the actions pertaining to IVF, the will to have a child is truly an *intention* ("the generation of a child") that seeks a means (the actions involved in IVF). At the base of such an intention is obviously the "desire to have a child"; this desire leads to the formulation of corresponding actions. *The component of desire* of this intention is in itself legitimate, and in principle is the same as in natural procreation. But the intention leads to actions whose sole significance consists in the *fulfillment* of the intention. Or rather, the actions pertaining to IVF are carried out with the intention of fulfilling the desire for a child. The act of procreation, *or better of "production," of the child is therefore a function of the fulfillment of the desire. It possesses no other significance,* which is precisely what we set out to demonstrate.

The case is different, however, with the natural act of procreation as

8. Cf. on this, in more detail, the third chapter of the present volume.

the conjugal act. Here an act is performed that is not chosen with the purpose (intention) of generating a child. Rather, the child is generated *on the occasion* of this act. Said otherwise, the child *arises from this act,* which is, in its personal structure, not an act or a means for the generation of a child, but an act of love, that is, an act in which two persons who love one another in their bodily-spiritual totality mutually give themselves, joining themselves the one to the other. *From this arises* a new human life. This is the case, as well, even when the act is not carried out with an explicit *desire* to generate a child. What specifies the conjugal act is that it consists in an action and a desire that do not have as their end the generation of a child, but rather an exchange of love between two persons; this is demonstrated by the fact that the act can be carried out in a meaningful way even when it is foreseen to be infertile. The consciousness of spouses who have intercourse, with a deep desire for a child, is precisely the recognition that from the deepest and most intense expression of their reciprocal love will come (or could come) a new life. And if they love one another rightly, and there are no serious reasons of procreative responsibility that dictate otherwise, they desire and hope that this would occur.

But the act is not performed solely to fulfill this desire. This means that it could also be reasonable, for reasons of procreative responsibility, to abstain from the act in fertile periods and carry it out only in foreseeably infertile periods. The more, however, the conjugal act is carried out solely with the *intention to generate a child* (something that would show itself in the tendency to *not engage* in the act if the desire for a child is not present), the more the natural procreative act becomes functionalized to the end of fulfilling this desire for children, which is to say the more it resembles IVF.

My thesis, then, is that this latter situation *could* occur in the case of the natural procreative act, and precisely as a consequence of its accidental deformation; but this, in the actions pertaining to IVF, occurs inevitably and necessarily, that is, these actions cannot be chosen and performed *reasonably* without the intention to generate a child.

An Objection and a Response: Recourse to IVF as a Last Resort

Here another objection might arise: spouses who as a last resort, and perhaps even reluctantly, decide for IVF, would do so only so as to realize their legitimate desire for a child, which had been there all along! They could therefore see a child conceived through IVF as a fruit, so to speak, of their sexual acts, which were infertile, but have been "made fertile" with the help of reproductive medicine. In this way, the couple pursues an entirely legitimate *end,* and the IVF act, which is *de facto* generative, becomes irrelevant in determining the will. One must therefore focus simply on the end in view and the legitimacy of the desire (and with these, there would be effectively no difference from the case of natural generation), and not on the intervention of reproductive medicine, which would be simply a phase in the entire process.

That the *end* which is ultimately pursued, and therefore also the *intention* in the actions involved in IVF are legitimate, is beyond discussion—nor have we tried to contest them here. But this is not the issue. My thesis consists precisely in this, that the will that pursues this end is erroneous and flawed in its manner of pursuing it, by the fact that the desired end actualizes in an intention whose actuation involves the choice of a means; that is, a concrete action is employed that has the character of a *means.* This same process could lead to an unacceptable attitude toward human life in other situations; the desire to die soon is without a doubt legitimate for a terminally ill person who is suffering gravely. But such a will is perverted as soon as a means is sought, and corresponding actions carried out, to realize this desire. A will animated by a desire that is, in itself, legitimate is perverted by willing an action by means of which this desire is *actuated.* The suffering person is therefore used (or uses himself) as a means for the fulfillment of the desire to "shorten his suffering." (Passive euthanasia, on the other hand, differs in the fact that one *renounces* the employment of further artificial means for the *prolongation* of life; this, from an intentional point of view, is exactly an opposite way of acting.)

The legitimate goal as such, or rather the legitimate *component of desire* for this goal, is not yet an argument in favor of IVF. What I want to make clear is that the will that is expressed in the actions pertaining to IVF is an erroneous will, perverted in its entirety, given that in each action human beings always possess only *one* will, even if this includes different "components" (choice of means, final intention, concomitant motives). The wickedness of *a single* component of an action perverts the *entire act,* the entire act of the will that in every action is precisely numerically *one*.[9] This will, then, could be described as the "instrumentalization of the generation of a human being so as to fulfill the desire for a child." The generation of new life in this case is not the consequence of a *doing* (*praxis*), but the object of a *producing, creation* (*poesis*). The natural means-end link between copulation and generation that, with respect to the performance of the *conjugal act,* is in no way decisive for or determinative of the act, becomes, in the *technical simulation* of this natural process, a rational productive action oriented toward a goal. "The generation of a person" in this way becomes an art (*ars imitat naturam*), and thus takes on an essentially different character than a natural act of generation.

The conjugal act, from which issues new life, is essentially a *doing,* a *praxis,* and not a *producing.* Indeed, human life is "made," or rather created, only by God—for this reason God alone is "Lord" over human life. The conjugal act of the parents gives "space" and occasion to this divine creative act; as such it is truly a "service of life," but not a "dominion over life." "Service of life," in relationships between human beings, can be understood—as opposed to "dominion over life"—only as *love,* as the instruction *Donum Vitae* explains: "The human person must be accepted in his parents' act of union and love; the generation of a child must therefore be the fruit of that mutual giving which is realized in the conjugal act wherein the spouses cooperate as servants and not as masters in the work of the Creator who is Love. . . . No one may subject the coming of a child into the world to conditions of technical efficiency which are to be evaluated according to standards of control and dominion."[10]

A Child as the Product of a Causative Will

Let us return, however, to our central thesis: the choice of IVF is a means for the fulfillment of the desire to have a child (as every means-end relationship is ordered to the fulfillment of some desire). This thesis is further clarified if we consider the perspective of a child generated in this way. Such a child, in relation to his parents, could say: "I exist because you *wanted* me, and only because of this." In effect, the existence

9. This corresponds to the well-known universal-ontological principle formulated by Pseudo-Dionysius the Areopagite: "Bonum ex integra causa, malum ex quocumque defectu."
10. *Donum Vitae,* 43, 44.

of this child would depend on the will of his parents—it is a function of this will (and at another level also a function of the will of the doctor; but we will ignore this aspect here). A child generated naturally, on the other hand, could never say: "I exist *because* you wanted me." In fact, in the generation of this child there was no causative will, only the *desire* for a child. Nor would it make sense to say: "I exist because you desired me." Desires do not refer to what is in our power to do, and therefore are not the cause of actions or events (desires are only "fathers of thoughts"), at least if one does not understand the statement to mean: "Nature, or God, has fulfilled your desire." Neither, however, in this case does the existence of the child depend on the will of the parents, but instead on the will of the one who fulfilled their desire. Different than with IVF, then, the existence of the child is not a *function of the will* of the parents; nor is it a *function of their desire* to have a child. The child's existence has simply "come about" as the consequence of the conjugal union, which contained within it the desire to generate a child, but without the desire itself in a proper sense generating the child; the child is rather the consequence of natural processes that unfolded independently of this desire. In cases where such a child knows that he was also *desired*, he would love his parents even more, and be grateful. But he would not be a *product of the willing and the producing of his parents; rather he would be conscious of being the fruit of his parents' reciprocal love,* and this is something fundamentally different. He could say: "I am, and only for this reason, that you love one another and have given each other the testimony of this love."[11]

This also means, then, viewing things according to our initial thesis and again from the perspective of a child conceived in vitro, that this latter child would experience his parents as persons who consider the goodness of his existence as a function of their will. "You exist because we wanted it so"; and "we wanted this because we thought it a good thing that you would exist"; he would very likely hear these kinds of statements from his parents. As such, the child would develop a relationship with his parents not of gratitude, but of an *existential obligation to give account of himself.* It is true that a child generated naturally would not

11. In Zeffirelli's film *The Champion* this is precisely the response of the father, who is separated from his wife, when asked by his son why his parents had given him life: "Because we loved each other" (and not "because we wanted a child").

exist without his parents, and as such he is a "debtor" toward them for the gift of life. A child *wanted by his parents* and generated in vitro, however, would have a measure of existential dependence with respect to his parents that contradicts both his fundamental *equality* as a person and his *freedom*. Only before God is such a dependence tenable, becoming, indeed, the *foundation* of one's freedom.

This is, to repeat, simply the expression of the fact (this time from the parents' perspective) that if a baby is "made," his actual creation, that is, his coming into life, would inevitably be considered as something good for the reason (and only for the reason) for which he was desired or *wanted,* and not simply because he has "come into being" or "arrived." Precisely for the reason that it corresponds to the nature of human life to be recognized as a "good" *independently* of our desires and of the acceptance or recognition of others, natural procreation can be seen as that which comes about, of course not independently of our will, but neither simply as a function of our desires.[12] Procreation according to nature recognizes the gift character of a new life (the correlate of "desire" is precisely "gift"), as well as the fact that human life has no need to be justified by being desired (which occurs when the life is the causal product of a will and of a "making" resulting from it). The opposite attitude would go against the most fundamental principle of *justice,* the "Golden Rule" ("that which you would not want done to you, don't do to others!"). It would therefore threaten the identity of the agent himself, given that every person wants to be recognized by others, not because his existence corresponds to the desire or pleasure of others (and much less because it implies "You exist because I wanted it and *only* because I wanted it"). Instead, he demands this acceptance or recognition on the pure and simple basis of his existence. One who considers the coming into existence of a child as "something good" *because* he has desired this existence[13] would lose an understanding of why it is a *good* for a human being to be alive, and why it is good to recognize the existence of others *unconditionally.*

At the outset we said that the goodness of a human life *in the act*

12. This latter occurs only when the desire actualizes in a causative productive will, without which the actions pertaining to IVF would not be done.

13. This necessarily corresponds to the intimate logic of IVF, inasmuch as in it the desire actualizes in a causative will.

of deciding for IVF and the actions involved in the procedure are made dependent on that life's "being desired," on its *acceptance* or recognition on the part of others. This claim must be further clarified, in brief, in response to another possible objection. I claim that this act of denying an unconditional acceptance shapes *the act of deciding for IVF, and the corresponding acts involved in implementing IVF.* It is nevertheless possible that, once the child is born, the parents will develop a "normal" relationship of unconditional acceptance toward the child. This could also happen in cases where, despite the practice of contraception, a child is born due to an "accident" or some other error. Very often the attitude changes once the child is born, especially on the part of the mother, who begins to accept and love the child. It is entirely possible that the relationship of parents to a baby that has been "produced" would develop bit by bit into a relationship similar to that toward a child who has "arrived." This implies, however, a *change* in the original attitude, a change that does not always occur. Even if it does occur, this does not alter the initial instrumentalization, and therefore the loss of dignity, of the child, nor can it justify the initial choice a posteriori. Moreover, if the baby does not develop properly, if it disappoints the parents' hopes in some way, if it becomes a burden or is even handicapped from birth, it could become an occasion of frustration. And where there has been no change in the initial attitude employed in pursuing IVF, that original attitude will develop in all of its inhumanity. In fact, this kind of child was not what the parents wanted. Without a *change* in the original attitude, it will be just a matter of time before a catastrophe develops (this type of situation is not limited to the case of IVF, but the fact that it occurs elsewhere is not an argument *in favor of* IVF).

Consequences: Moral Relevance of Link between the Sexual Act and Procreation

From the preceding analysis we can conclude that the dissolution of the link between the sexual act and procreation by means of a technique of production is "against nature," *not* because it violates a *fact of nature,* but because it contradicts the *unconditional* acceptance of a human life, and because *precisely this kind of unconditional acceptance is "according to nature" for man.* The procreative technologies we are discussing imply that the justification of the existence of a human life *depends* on our desires or on its desirability, because the baby becomes the product of a causative will (a necessary condition for something to "depend" on a desire, a condition that is fulfilled precisely in the case of IVF). This is fundamentally *unjust*; that is, this way of acting and the intentionality implicit in it contradict a fundamental judgment, carried out by practical reason, concerning what is "just": the golden rule.

IVF therefore makes the existence of others dependent on our desires and on our causative will, which in fact is the mirror image of abortion, despite the fact that the respective ends of IVF and abortion are completely different. The end, however, does not justify the means. Just as the undesirability of a child does not justify killing it, so the desire for a child does not justify its production, that is, its being wanted causatively. In fact, in each of the cases the value of a concrete life is made dependent on the desires, the will, and therefore on the power of others. In both cases one says: "You live *because and in the measure in which we want it.*" We must accept a human life *because and in the measure in which it is*; it cannot be that human life exists only because and in the measure in which it is accepted, desired, or willed. We would certainly not accept this attitude toward ourselves, and neither can we relate to others in this manner.[14]

Moreover, we cannot live together without difficulty with persons on whose desires and conditions, and indeed on whose causal will, our existence depends, because the humanity of human coexistence (with respect to what concerns *being human in its always concrete individuality*) presupposes the unconditional reciprocal recognition of the other as "equal to me." Similarly, we cannot expect that persons whose existence depends on our merely conditional acceptance—conscious of having been selected from among a number of embryos according to eugenic criteria, or proven healthy by prenatal diagnosis and *only because of this* alive—can live

14. This also demolishes the argument often used with respect to the supposed moral irrelevance of the killing of surplus or supernumerary embryos, i.e., that nature also "sacrifices" rather abundantly "extra" embryos in favor of life, and the doctor, in IVF, merely simulates this process of nature; according to this argument he therefore has no responsibility for the death of these surplus embryos. The argument fails because in IVF, ultimately, the death of the embryos is chosen as a means for the generation and birth of new life, in a way exactly similar to the way that the actions involved in IVF, taken together, have the character of a means for the generation of a person. Thus, the death of surplus embryos is in this case a consequence of human action, i.e., the effect of a causative will.

with us in a relationship of unconditional acceptance. And furthermore, conscious of being born only to fulfill my parents' desire for "a child"— "I" additionally am under constraint not to allow the initial fulfillment of this desire to become a frustration for my parents, like a vacation in the Canary Islands that started out well but was rained out.

It comes to mind how different the situation is in the case of *adoption,* where exactly the opposite occurs. The adopted baby experiences, so to speak (even if only when he knows himself to be adopted), a *second acceptance*: his existence and his acceptance do not depend in fact on the act of adoption, rather they are once again confirmed through his acceptance in *his individual* existence. Certainly an adopted child could also be "instrumentalized" for one's own desires, which is possible even with a child born naturally. But in both of these cases this is not *necessarily* the case, on the basis of the intentional structure of the concrete mode of action that has been chosen (the so-called object of the action); rather such instrumentalization would be based on motivations that are ulterior to what one concretely does. In both cases, in fact, *I am desired,* because and in the measure in which *I exist,* but I exist not because a child who was not me was desired, a child whom I became, that is, as the fulfillment of my parents' desire. Human beings always want to be desired and loved by others because they *are*; this is the fundamental law of *equality,* which is the basis of every concept of justice. Only in relation to God can we accept, and indeed rejoice in the fact, that we are because and in the measure in which he desires us, causally wills us, and loves us.

Only now can we recognize why the "coming about" of human life as a result of the sexual act is "natural": because children must "come" and must not be "made." The problem here is not artificiality, but the intentionality inevitably implied in IVF. Or rather, the problem is in the artificiality *in the measure in which* it is the expression of a merely conditional recognition of the value of the life of another, and therefore an expression of an *inequality* in virtue of the disposition of some over the lives of others. The link between procreation and sexual union is a necessary, even though insufficient, human condition for the transmission of life.[15] The human dignity of the generated life must be acknowledged

15. "Insufficient" because, as we have said, the act of natural generation can also be "used" simply for the generation of a "desired child"; i.e., this act as well could also include a merely conditional recognition of the goodness of the existence of the new life. Procreative

in a way that allows one to say to another: "It is a good thing that you exist, *because you exist*," and not "It is a good thing that you exist, and you in fact exist *because and in the measure in which I have considered it good that you exist,* that is, in the measure in which *I have wanted* your existence."

Often the tremendous suffering of parents over the inability to have children is cited as an important reason in favor of the justice of the use of reproductive medicine. That such suffering is natural and requires human attention is beyond discussion. It is worth asking, however, whether recourse to reproductive medicine so as to heal this suffering is not already a symptom of the unhealthy nature of such suffering. Indeed, the fact is that the large majority of sterile couples who suffer over this fact might find a new fulfillment of their reciprocal love in the choice for IVF. As such, it seems plausible that the hope of "healing" of this suffering by means of an intervention of reproductive medicine is not only an expression of an already unbalanced form of this suffering, but in general of a distorted relationship with the child. Indeed, here the generation of the child is instrumentalized even more clearly, that is, for therapeutic ends. The child would thereby obtain the "function" of healing the parents of their suffering over the lack of children. This argument, then, actually becomes an argument *against IVF.* Any medical therapy concerning suffering over the inability to have children, if it wants to remain human, must seek another solution.

Indeed, the proper response would be to counsel *adoption.* As we have already pointed out, in adoption the baby is not *necessarily* instrumentalized so as to fulfill a desire of the parents. Rather he receives, as a baby without parents or not wanted by his natural parents, a new acceptance and a new acknowledgment of his existence. Moreover, by choosing adoption a childless couple participates in a great task: to make a human existence possible for human beings who either have no parents or are unwanted. As such, the lack of children becomes a *new* challenge and task for conjugal love. By consciously *renouncing* certain things with re-

---

technologies are simply the technological actuation of this intentionality (and which prenatal diagnosis, in itself morally neutral, could also serve).

spect to human life and leaving their own desires unfulfilled, the couple would experience the fulfillment of a desire common to all of us: to live a happy, fulfilled life, precisely by adopting one of the many, many children who desire nothing more than to have parents. In doing good to such a child, the parents would experience a true happiness, and perhaps even understand more deeply the teaching of the Gospel (*cf.* Mt 25:34–40).

But one could object (though in fact only with respect to *homologous* IVF): parents want a child *of their own;* they want to reproduce genetically, having children of their own "flesh and blood." This desire is in itself legitimate. If it leads, however, to the decision to fulfill the desire by means of reproductive medicine, it shows—in a particularly clear way—the intentional structure of IVF: the instrumentalization of the child so as to fulfill the desires of the parents. In the face of the enormous need for adoptive parents, it is also difficult to ignore the selfishness of such a decision, a selfishness that does not auger well for the child brought to life through IVF. In any case the decision for the "production of one's own" brought about by IVF, *in place of* adoption, seems ethically even more difficult to justify.

So, whether by a decision to adopt a child, or by the assumption of other tasks (for example, assistance to other families, especially regarding their children), the understandable "suffering over being unable to have children" can be more effectively overcome through openness to others and solidarity with children and families who suffer for not having parents (which could also result from a continual absence of the parents due to work) or other difficulties than by recourse to reproductive medicine. Such an assumption of other tasks typical of parents could lead a childless couple to such fulfillment that their "being without children" may be much more easily accepted. And in this way, childless couples can become a blessing for others and for society in general.

The Decision for Procreation by Reproductive Medicine: An Intrinsic Contradiction

A final comment will demonstrate that the choice of artificial procreation contains within it an intrinsic contradiction. IVF is in fact a mode of action that brings about that one is no longer capable of understanding why it is a good thing to have a child, that is, to transmit human life, and indeed what is human life, and why it is a "good thing" as such. In fact, one desires a child because it is a "good." The presupposition of the argument in favor of IVF is in effect that the desire for a child is a good. Why, on the whole, is it good to desire a child? Certainly not because it is a good to have desires, and the generation of a child fulfills those desires! The good is not in the first place in the fulfillment of the desire, rather in the obtainment of that which was the *object* of the desire. In the same way, the good of joy does not consist primarily in the rejoicing, but in that *in which* one rejoices; and the good of pleasure is not in the pleasure itself, rather it is in the object of this experience, in what is enjoyed.[16] But why is it good to have a child? Certainly because a child is a good. But why is it a good? If one does not wish to degrade the child to a simple means of fulfilling the desires of other people, he can only say: it is good precisely because the existence of a person in a way absolutely independent of every desire is already *per se* a good, and according to the requirements of justice (the "golden rule"), it only *can* be desired as *such* a good. It is precisely this, however, which is negated with IVF, because it implies the acknowledgement of the birth of a new life as a "good" precisely in the measure in which it is an object of my causal will. Procreative technology is therefore a mode of action by which the person as the subject of action obscures, and even destroys, at least tendentially, the basis of his own freedom of self-determination to the good in general and to the just in particular. For this reason also, the separation of procreation and sexual union is not in conformity with man's nature, and precisely because it is opposed to reason, just as in order to gather wood, it is contrary to reason to saw off a branch on which one is sitting.

Ethical-Juridical and Juridical-Political Consequences

The same thing would be valid, it seems to me, for a juridical order and a society that legitimizes such modes of action. We can only speculate on the repercussions that this would have, but a corresponding change in the consciousness of an entire society *could* have an effect precisely in the way fundamental rights are understood. In fact fundamental rights are properly "rights," that is, demands whose legitimacy

16. This presupposes, for example, that the pleasures experienced by sadists and masochists are not in fact real goods, neither objectively nor for the one who experiences them.

does not depend on recognition on the part of others, rather the opposite: with basic rights, recognition *follows* from the understanding of their *unconditional legitimacy*. They are demands that, thanks to constitutional guarantees, are removed from the necessity of being legitimized on a *case-by-case basis* through a recognition on the part of the social community, and therefore are protected *generally*. To make, therefore, human life in its factual existence something that needs justification, and to make it dependent on the recognition of others, would be to give rise to the emptying of our concept of fundamental rights. As such, procreative technologies would contradict a demonstrated *public interest*.

The question of whether IVF should be prohibited by legislatures would require its own ethical-juridical and juridical-political evaluation, which it is not possible to undertake here. The positive juridical order is not the codification of the moral order in its entirety. Rather, legal policy is based on a fundamental affirmation formulated by Thomas Aquinas, according to which only those vicious actions should be prohibited whose prohibition is acceptable to the large mass of people, and without whose prohibition the life of the community would be made impossible.[17] To conclude that a general juridical prohibition of IVF follows on its moral objectionableness argued for here could only be shown by further *political-juridical* and *ethical-political* arguments.

Nevertheless, we can ask whether it couldn't be considered in the *public interest* that, in society, "human life" be recognized as a "good" not to the extent that it is desired, but rather always because "it is," and if such a public good shouldn't be protected juridically. I believe that it can be shown as plausible that such a public interest exists. In any case, democratic education of the will should include this principle. Indeed, a society in which this principle is lacking would perhaps be one in which there no longer existed any public interest, a society interested only in so-called personal freedom, which, frankly, the legislator could no longer guarantee, given that in this event personal freedom itself would be recognized as a public interest only to the extent that it was *desired*.

Other considerations, such as the protection of life (referring to the inevitable destruction of spare embryos), the unacceptability of inevitable "abusive" research on living embryos (including for the development of more advanced IVF methods), and the totally unforeseeable

17. Cf. Thomas Aquinas, *Summa theologiae* I–II, q.96, a.2.

consequences and risks involved in reproductive medicine, could perhaps much more easily be used to lead to an effective ban and juridical impediments to the practice of IVF.

Summary

I have attempted to demonstrate that in vitro fertilization, or rather reproductive technologies in general, and the actions that correspond to them, are opposed to two fundamental principles of justice. First, it opposes the principle of unconditional recognition (independently of our desires and criteria of "quality") of human life in its concrete individuality (therefore also human life that is handicapped, sick, "undesired," etc.). Second, it opposes the "golden rule," which prohibits us from denying others a recognition that we demand for ourselves as inalienable. This is a partial expression of what we call the "violation of the *sacredness* of human life."

Artificial procreation is in this sense *an unjust mode of action,* and not on the basis of its artificiality, but because it is an *abuse* of the medical arts, an abuse that indeed possesses a "Promethean" element. "Children are a gift from the Lord, the fruit of the womb, his reward" (Ps 127:3); gifts that have not been "received" cannot be "taken" from the owner without offense.

Moreover, I do not wish to claim that the argument presented here is the only one that can be offered against artificial procreation. It would also be worth considering an argument based on the problematic presence of a "third party," that is, the doctor or "procreative technician." Human life, in fact, must issue from the intimacy of conjugal love and from its fully human fulfillment in the act of intercourse. Is this origin of human life in the love of a man and a woman preserved in the case of reproductive medicine? Is it still clear in this case that the "dignity of human life" is linked to the fact that this life issues from an act of love that requires the intimacy *of two,* and that this dignity is attacked and even destroyed by the presence of a "third party"? Such an argument would deepen and complete the fundamental argument presented here. It would also show that the parents, with IVF, abuse themselves as well, making of themselves a simple means.[18]

18. Cf. R. Spaemann, *Kommentur,* 94.

The unconditional recognition of the existence of other human beings, independent of our subjective desires, and the "golden rule" are practical principles by which we form our actions in a way consistent with our identity as human persons. If we act against these principles, we pervert every mode of action employed, even if these appear "effective" from another point of view.

For this reason such practical principles, which are none other than ends of the moral virtues (in this case, "justice"), possess a priority and a governance with respect to all concrete decision-making processes and the logic involved in them. They do not derive, as with utilitarian rules, from the decision-making logic itself; rather, they form a moral parameter in themselves, one that cannot be circumvented, for concrete decision-making processes. For this reason it is possible to determine that some concrete decisions, apparently plausible and "effective" from other points of view, are in fact false, that is, they are opposed to a right will.

Such principles cannot be circumvented by the decision-making logic pertaining to specific matters; rather they form the direction and the limits for the rationality and moral legitimacy of such matters. *Within these limits,* however, it is thinkable for an ethics of virtue to have a variety of decision-making "logics," including an evaluation of the goods involved and a weighing of consequences. This latter depends, however, on the type of decision that is being made, or to what material it refers. The theme of "decision-making logic" is not per se an ethical theme, rather it pertains to various specialized areas (economics, social politics, education, scientific research, medicine, technology, etc.).[19] To understand ethics or morality itself as a type of "decision-making logic" is an enormous presumption with respect to such specialized competencies, or rather it tends to identify "morality" with *one* of these specialized logics, which results more or less in a dissolving of morality. Ethics arises, rather, from *global* questions, which have precedence over all specialized decision-making logics and which regard the compatibility of ev-

---

19. This despite the fact that these various competencies possess their own specific ethic, in the sense of a *Ethik der Kultursachbereiche,* "ethics of cultural environments" (Oswald von Nell-Breuning), in which they exert their influence on the decision-making logic specific to each area. For a good example of this cf. P. Koslowski, *Prinzipien der Ethischen Ökonomie. Grundlegung der Wirtschaftsethik und der auf die Ökonomie bezogenen Ethik* (Tübingen: Mohr Siebeck, 1988).

ery decision with the rightness of desire, that is, with its practical truth.

That conditions for the fundamental rightness of action exist, which are linked to basic structures of "right desiring" and "right willing," and which we rely on precisely as consistent with human nature, and that for this reason there are some concrete modes of action the *choice* of which always implies an erroneous will, is one of the most important fundamental claims of classic virtue ethics. That there are certain things that may never be done is not an invention of moral theologians thinking casuistically; rather, it was expressed by one of the first representatives of classical virtue ethics, Aristotle, in his Nicomachean Ethics: "But not every action nor every passion admits of a mean; for some have names that already imply badness, e.g., spite, shamelessness, envy, and in the case of actions adultery, theft, murder; for all of these and suchlike things imply by their names that they are themselves bad, and not the excesses or deficiencies of them. It is not possible, then, ever to be right with regard to them; one must always be wrong. Nor does goodness or badness with regard to such things depend on committing adultery with the right woman, at the right time, and in the right way, but simply to do any of them is to go wrong."[20]

20. Aristotle, *The Nicomachean Ethics*, trans. D. Ross, rev. J. L. Ackrill and J. O. Urmson (Oxford: Oxford University Press, 1998).

6

Human Fetuses, Persons, and
the Right to Abortion
Toward an Absolute Power of the Born?

Preliminary Comments

The Need for a Critical Discussion

In his book *Abortion in the Secular State: Arguments against §218* (hereafter *ASS*),[1] the German legal philosopher Norbert Hoerster develops in a compact and systematic manner an argument that, in its various versions, has been discussed in the English-speaking world for some time.[2] According to the argument, the traditional prohibition of the killing of unborn human beings cannot be based on rational arguments; rather, it is based on prejudices and taboos (especially religious taboos) that have developed over time. Moreover, a rational argument would clearly demonstrate the unsustainability in principle of such a prohibition.

Norbert Hoerster has developed this argument, one that

---

1. *Abtreibung im säkularen Staat. Argumente gegen den §218*, (Frankfurt am Main: Suhrkamp, 1991). Cited as AAS.

2. Cf., e.g., M. A. Warren, "On the Moral and Legal Status of Abortion," *Monist* 57 (1973), reprinted in *The Problem of Abortion*, 2nd ed., ed. J. Feinberg (Belmont, Calif.: Wadsworth Publishing, 1984), 102–19; M. Tooley, *Abortion and Infanticide* (Oxford: Oxford University Press, 1983); P. Singer, *Practical Ethics*, 2nd ed. (Cambridge: Cambridge University Press, 1993, 1999 reprint); B. Steinbock, *Life before Birth: The Moral and Legal Status of Embryos and Fetuses* (New York: Oxford University Press, 1992).

he believes to be convincing and evidently unassailable, in his book. Because Hoerster has taken the trouble to offer a clear presentation of arguments that are not in fact new, they merit discussion, rather than a simple rejection—an explanation for rejecting them, which is valid also for Peter Singer's position (see note 2), should at least be offered. I will limit myself here essentially to Hoerster's argument, along with the publications cited in the notes. Hoerster's argument differs somewhat in content from Singer's, and is formulated in a way both more detailed and less sensational. In my opinion, it is useful to limit an exemplary critical analysis to a version that is concrete and at the same time well stated and well known; for these reasons Hoerster's book is more appropriate for such analysis.

Another reason for discussing Hoerster's position is that it is based on this important presupposition: that contemporary arguments for a *limited* liberalization of abortion (i.e., "indicational" limitations based on medical diagnoses or "term" limitations based on trimesters), which maintain a fundamental right to life for the unborn, are unsustainable and (according to Hoerster) hypocritical. Indeed, departing from the fact that the unborn possess in principle a right to life, it *would* be impossible to nevertheless seek to morally legitimize abortion in certain cases. For example, it would then be impossible to legitimize abortion in situations of conflict, where the right to the woman's self-determination is at stake; it would also be impossible to hold that women who have an abortion should not be legally punished (with the exception of the classic case of a threat to the mother's life, in which case there is a right to life versus a right to life). If Singer and Hoerster are correct on this point (that it is not sustainable, without falling into a serious inconsistency, both to recognize the right to life of the unborn and to allow some abortions)—and I believe they are—one can assume that sooner or later the public discussion will inevitably tend in this direction, as well. This leads to the conclusion that those who want to legitimize abortions in *some* cases, must *on principle* and *altogether* deny the right to life of the unborn.

A Resulting Position

Hoerster's thesis—which is the only intrinsically consistent position, it seems to me—then, includes the following (to which we will return in more detail below): the human fetus (for simplicity's sake Hoerster uses the term "fetus" rather than "embryo") *is*—in accordance with current scientific knowledge—a member of the species *homo sapiens* (and therefore a "human individual"), but it is not a "man," that is a *person*. Because the fetus is not a person, neither does it possess a right to life that exceeds that of other non-human living beings. The same also holds both for newborn infants with certain grave forms of handicap or psychological illness, and for adults in a coma.

From this it can be deduced—according to Hoerster—that every fetus can be killed *for any reason whatsoever*; there is no fundamental need for any particular justification (expect of course a minimum of what is required for any sort of rational action; this, however, cannot be regulated by law). "Indications" (limitations based on medical diagnoses) as well as "terms" (i.e., trimesters) are superfluous, arbitrary, and unjustifiable. For Hoerster, every opinion according to which the fetus is already a man or a person possessing a corresponding right to life is not based on rational arguments; rather it is based on religion, deriving from the Christian idea of man created in the image of God. The secular state, however, being religiously neutral, cannot attribute juridical-political validity to any religious conception, and for precisely this reason an unlimited liberalization of abortion is acceptable. This position obviously also leads to the question of the lawfulness of the killing of babies, as well as of active euthanasia (especially eugenic euthanasia of newborns).

In what follows, I will limit myself to a critical analysis of Hoerster's argumentation, so as to present contrary arguments based on some of the intrinsic contradictions contained in his argument, with its at times absurd consequences. My analysis and counterargument will essentially follow Hoerster's argument. This seems to me the correct way to respond, although as a critic it is a disadvantage, as I will have to make my argument within the framework already established by Hoerster. My argumentation will demonstrate, however (and this is why I have chosen this strategy), that *on his own terms* Hoerster employs very weak weapons, simply argues poorly at times, makes a large number of logical errors, uses fallacious linguistic constructions, and presents arguments replete with vicious circles.

It can also be shown that Hoerster's argumentation contains strong metaphysical and anthropological presuppositions that, though not openly expressed, are nevertheless extremely controversial among philosophers.[3] Lastly, it can be shown that the entire argumentation depends on a specific ethical theory, which itself is open to discussion and not the least bit definitive. In any case, it is difficult to claim plausibility for a juridical-political position on such a delicate question when the position is based on premises that are as controversial and open to debate as those that found Hoerster's argument. In the end, it becomes evident that Hoerster's position is nowhere near as rational and unassailable as he would like to imply; it is indeed precisely by strongly rational arguments that doubt is cast on his thesis.

The errors and inconsistencies in Hoerster's argument, it seems to me, are sufficiently great as to nullify his role as a proponent of the renunciation of the recognition of a juridical-constitutional right to life of the unborn, and of an unlimited juridical-penal liberalization of abortion. Rather, a demonstration of these flaws offers strong reasons in favor of the *opposite* position, that is, one in favor of a right to life for the unborn.

An Ideology of Domination? A Suspicion
That Needs to Be Refuted

First, a comment on the title of this chapter: "An Absolute Power of the Born?" Absolute power is a power not limited by any right of anyone else. When unborn human beings possess no rights, not even the right to continue to live, then the dominion of the "already born" over them is absolute. Certainly, from the perspective of those who justify such a position by the argument that the unborn are not yet men, we would not be dealing with the dominion of men *over men*. If this latter position is doubtful, however, the title can shed light on what is at stake.

Laws currently in place and the still-dominant moral consciousness, in fact, consider the rights of the born to be *limited* by the rights of the unborn. Even claims of self-realization and freedom of choice are considered to be limited (something that is obvious with respect to men and women among whom we live), and this precisely to the extent that the rights and freedom of one person are violated by the freedom of an-

3. Cf. L. Honnefelder, "Der Streit um die Person in der Ethik," in *Philosophisches Jahrbuch* 100 (1993): 246–65.

other. All freedom extends to the point where the freedom of others is not violated. This is the basis of the ethos of law and freedom of a liberal constitutional state.

The practical relevance and the importance of this basic affirmation depends, in fact, on the old questions: Who is my neighbor? Am I limited in my rights? Do I have duties with respect to someone who is not of my nation? Of my race? And—with respect to an unborn human being?

Our rights are finite, and our freedom shows itself to be limited at the moment when we recognize that they collide with the rights and claims of others—and from this arises duties. If *in principle* we exclude a class of human individuals from this possibility, we discriminate against them.

If Hoerster's argument were correct—meaning that unborn individuals of the species *Homo sapiens* are, in fact, not persons and therefore not men, and as such do not have any right to survival—then his theory obviously would *not* be a theory of discrimination, but rather simply an "illumination," or rather the clearing up of a centuries-old prejudice whereby the range of freedom of the born was unjustly restricted. As with every theory that excludes a class of individuals of the human species from specific rights, this one at least falls under the suspicion that it is in fact a theory of discrimination. This suspicion needs to be refuted by those who would hold such a theory. This suspicion is reasonable, and rooted in responsibility and fairness. Indeed, to disagree that the suspicion is reasonable would render one suspect of having an interest in condemning the accused, like a judge who, having doubts, nevertheless condemns an accused.

Do in fact the interests of the already-born come into play here—interests converted into ideology? Without any doubt, these interests include, for example, those of every person who has been born, in his freedom, self-determination, and self-realization; otherwise there would be no reason for the debate. Hoerster's theory, then, falls under the suspicion of being an ideology, a suspicion that needs to be refuted. If this suspicion is not answered and laid to rest, it can then be presumed that his theory is an ideology of dominion, aimed at securing the absolute dominion of the born over the unborn, so as to impose the rights of former over the latter without hindrance. And, according to the logic of the argument, this would also amount to a securing of the dominion—the power to dispose—over newborns and those with grave handicaps. Even if one allows these to live, they are only *allowed* to live; no *right* to life is conceded to them.

Consequently, the question touches on the core of the liberal constitutional state. It is not a question of "private morality," but rather one of public juridical culture.

Critical Analysis of Hoerster's Argumentation

"Human Individual" versus "Man": "To Be a Man" as a Property

The Fetus as a "Human Individual"

Hoerster recognizes the achievements of modern genetics and embryology: the fetus or embryo is from the moment of its conception an individual of the species *Homo sapiens*.[4] "No different than a man already born, the fetus is unmistakably a human being, with a unique human trajectory. All of its physical and psychic properties[5] are already present in the fertilized ovum" (*ASS* 25). The process of development until birth is continuous—at no point is a leap in development or the beginning of a "new phase" discernable. If so, Hoerster says, it would be necessary to distinguish other developmental phases with corresponding consequences for differentiated degrees of protection, for example, from birth to school age, and from there to full maturity (*ASS* 49).

Nevertheless, Hoerster holds that "human individual" is not the same thing as "man." In the first place, a "man" would be a member of the human species; secondly, he would possess the rights that we concede to a man, first among these being the right to life (*ASS* 66). He would possess a right to life, however, only on the basis of precisely specified properties (i.e., precisely those properties that make an individual of the human species to be a man). These properties would be those of a *person*, and a

4. It is true that some researchers hold that the pre-embryo (*Frühembryo*, that is, the embryo prior to implantation) is not yet an individual of the human species; the genetic information necessary for that would be obtained by the embryo only after implantation. For practical questions concerning abortion, however, this question is less relevant, and in any case, Hoerster does not hold this idea.

5. Translation note: in the original German the author uses exclusively the word *Eigenschaft*, which in the following is translated consistently as "property," while "quality" was also a possible choice. Although it might be more stylistically appealing to translate it alternatively as "quality" or perhaps "characteristic," the consistent use of "property" gives more unity to the argument. The author prefers the English "property" to connote a neutral philosophical expression and a *logical* category, as opposed to what is substance, essence, or nature.

person would be one who possesses an *interest in survival.* We will need to return below to this conception of the basis of "personhood."

In the first place we must examine the claim that an individual of the human species becomes a "man" on the basis of specific properties. This idea is suspect, in that "to be a man" is reduced to one or more characteristic properties; being a man, however, cannot be a property, in exactly the same way that being a "person" cannot be a property. "Man" ("person") is a *subject* who possesses properties, and is not himself a property. This is already implied in the use of the word "property": a property is always a property *of* X (where X signifies a self-identical subject or the bearer of a property). To say that being a man is a characteristic property of men simply does not correspond to our linguistic practice. Furthermore, we are little inclined to make the statement that a man is an individual of the biological species *Homo sapiens* who possesses the property of being a "man."

The expression "property" is used here by Hoerster in a way contrary to its meaning. Properties are *not* things that are attributed to a subject X *in any way whatsoever.* Someone who wears a necklace is not for this reason considered to possess the property of a "necklace-wearer." Rather, properties are aspects of a being that we consider to be in some way *typical* of the being in question, and as such they express the being's nature. (This is true not only for *specific* properties pertaining to species, but also for properties of individuals: in saying "P is a necklace-wearer," we in effect are saying that P possesses the *individual* property of wearing necklaces, that is, it is typical of P to do so. In this way we say something about the type of person that the individual P is.)

If, however, "to be a man" were a *property* of an individual member of the species *Homo sapiens,* this would mean either that there are some individuals of this species who (for some more-or-less arbitrary reason) are men; being a man would be typical, however, only for these individuals, something that is clearly absurd. Or it would mean: it is typical in general for members of the species *Homo sapiens* (that is, it is in accordance with their nature) to be men, or to possess those characteristic properties (or the capacity to develop them) that makes them persons or men. In this latter case, however, one could not reasonably say that belonging to the species *Homo sapiens,* as a purely biological distinctive mark, has no further relevancy, considered in itself. Rather, one must conclude that precisely on the basis of this biological distinctive mark, we actually know with respect to these individuals at least that in the future they *will possess* those properties on the basis of which we consider them to be persons, and therefore men. We would then be dealing with a biological distinctive mark, which nevertheless would transcend the merely biological facts (as, for example, skin color).

Precisely for this reason, the notion that "to be a man" (that is, a human person) is a property must be rejected entirely. In fact, the "being a man" of a man *appears* in his properties (which develop gradually over time), but it does not *consist* in a property. To have human properties (or to be able to develop them), a subject must already *be* a man.[6] Only a man can develop the properties of man; only a person can develop the properties of persons.

The fetus does not develop until it becomes a man; rather it develops *as* a man.[7] And neither does it develop until it becomes a person, but *as* a person. It "becomes" what it "is." Being "a man" and "a person" must also be attributed to fetuses. Being a member of the species *Homo sapiens* implies also being a person and a man. We will return to this point later.

Hoerster's argument, on the other hand, presupposes the following four principles, which differ from what we have just asserted:

1. On the basis of the biological appellation "belonging to the species *Homo sapiens,*" one cannot attribute to the individual in question any property that would be constitutive of a "person" or a "man." In other words: belonging to the species is purely a "biological category" (similar to race, skin color, or sex).[8]

6. Cf. G. Pöltner, "Achtung der Würde und Schutz von Interessen," in *Der Mensch als Mitte und Maßstab der Medizin,* ed. J. Bonelli, vol. 1 of *Medizin und Ethik* (Vienna: Springer-Verlag, 1992), 3–32; 18.

7. Cf. *Urteil des Deutschen Bunderverfassungsgerichtes vom 28 Mai 1993* (Decision of the German Federal Constitutional Court from May 28, D. I a), in *Juristenzeitung,* special edition of June 7, 1993, 16–17.

8. Hoerster's expressions "biological characteristic," "biological category," and "biological property" are not entirely clear. The question with the term "biological"—in the present context—is on the one hand the aggregate of criteria of determination and subdivision that are generically zoological, or on the other hand properties that demonstrate that which is specifically human (personhood, spirit, freedom, etc.) For clarity, therefore, I will often use the term "biological-zoological."

2. Being a man and being a person are—though only in a later stage of development—*properties* of an individual that belongs to the species *Homo sapiens.*

3. The "being man" and the "personhood" of an individual are non-biological *characteristics* (or rather they are not "biological categories"). Neither therefore are they "biological properties" (such as race, skin color, and sex).

4. A "human fetus" and a "man" (a "human person") belong *to the same* species (where this belonging in turn has a purely biological significance).

As will be shown in the argumentation of this chapter, Hoerster gets himself in trouble by the fact that, according to these presupposed principles, the third principle is no longer tenable, namely, that to be a man or a person has a *non-biological* meaning and therefore also more than a purely biological-zoological meaning. At the same time, however, in order for his argument to remain valid, this third principle must necessarily be upheld; otherwise, as we shall see, his position would be the same as that of racists or sexists.

I will set aside this incoherence for the time being; as our analysis of his position deepens, its implications that lead to erroneous conclusions will become evident. At this point I want to focus simply on the fact that they are based on the erroneous idea, essential for Hoerster's argument, that individuals of the species *Homo sapiens* only gradually, based on certain properties that develop over time, *become* persons and therefore men with corresponding rights, or rather that individuals of the biological species "man" would only develop over time the property of being men (persons), and they could also lose this property and the rights associated with it, without for that ceasing to be living individuals of the human species.

Hoerster's Criticism of "Speciesism": Belonging to the Species "Man" as a Biological Characteristic

"Speciesism"

According to the well-known verdict of "speciesism," one cannot favor or restrict a class of individuals on the basis of purely *biological* characteristics or categories, such as belonging to the species *Homo sapiens.* Equally proscribed would be making such distinctions (and restrictions) based on the biological characteristics of "race" or "sex." To concede to the biological species *Homo sapiens* a special position relative to other species of the class "mammal," or to concede to *Homo sapiens* a similar privilege within the biological order of "primates," would be roughly equivalent to racial or sexual discrimination.

The comparison of "speciesism," as a vice that privileges one species over others, with racism and sexism must, however, be questioned at the outset, given that the latter vices refer to members *of the same* species, "man"; such vices would therefore follow from distinctions between members of the same species. We do not reject racism and sexism *only* because they are based on a purely biological characteristic, but because we are convinced that *within* the species "man," distinctions concerning race or sex are irrelevant and discriminatory with respect to the fundamental rights of man *as man*. The illegitimacy of such discrimination derives from the fact that members of other *human* races or sex are "men/women like us." It is precisely this that is missing with respect to members of other *species*; for this reason the fact that they are members of *other* species is relevant.

The rejection of racism or sexism in fact *presupposes* "speciesism," and in fact is based on it. For this reason Singer, Hoerster, and others do us a disservice with their argument, in undermining the rejection of these vices. Without the recognition of belonging to the human species as an "overriding fact," there is in fact no way of demonstrating why— and precisely *within* the species—biological differences such as race and sex are irrelevant. One who would reject belonging to the human species as an illegitimate biologism "saws off the branch on which he sits."

Also irrelevant, then, is the reference to the fact that human beings belong not only to the biological species *Homo sapiens,* but also to the more general biological class "mammals" (*ASS* 57). In fact, different than the species, the biological class (or logical genus) "mammal" is not determinative in any definitive way; it is a collective biological name for a class of species with particular identical characteristics. But "mammals," as such, do not appear in nature; rather, there are humans, dolphins, dogs, and cats.

In fact, technically, neither are there "dogs"; what would be apropos here is a further specification of subdivisions according to race, something with which—for dogs—we have no problem. Do we consider this necessary, however, with human beings? Is there insufficient meaning or differentiation to speak of "man," or to say, "X is a man"? Should we rather speak of Europeans, Asians, or Africans, or even of Pygmies, Chinese, Arabs, or Ethiopians, and stop using the expression "X is a man" to describe someone's fundamental identity, as opposed to, for example, "X is an Ethiopian"? And is "man" perhaps—similar to "wildcat"—only a collective name for a multiplicity of "types"?

It seems, rather, that the specific identity "man" is the decisive factor. The identity, based on the genus, of "belonging to the (logical) genus mammal" is irrelevant, also because the specific identity obviously always includes what is common to the genus. The fundamental identity of man is always precisely that of the species. This does not mean that we are therefore "speciesists." We are not favoring the "biological characteristics of the species"—rather, we are favoring *man*.

Thus it is also irrelevant for man that other species belong to the same genus as he does. Relevant, on the other hand, is the difference between a man and a cat, for example. And precisely this relevance is *not* applicable to the case of a "man with white skin" and a "man with black skin." The difference of both of these latter with respect to a cat is exactly the same, namely, that they are both men. Or perhaps one wants to claim, for instance, that a black man distinguishes himself from a black cat in a way essentially different than a white man does?

Relevance of Belonging to the Human Species

The question, then, that must be asked is this, and only this: on the basis of what characteristics of the species *Homo sapiens* is it legitimate to concede a *privileged* place with respect to other species of the genus "mammals"? Hoerster says (*ASS* 63): "The pure and simple characteristic of belonging to the human species—that is, belonging to the human species *as such*—is not a sufficient reason." This formulation is in the first place inconsistent; leaving this aside, in the second place it is trivial.

Inconsistent, because belonging to the human race cannot be a "property." Previously Hoerster had said simply that belonging to the human species was a biological "distinctive mark." Now this distinctive mark has surreptitiously changed into a "property," which, to complete the circle, is precisely a "biological property" (although it is not always clear what Hoerster intends by this expression).

Above all, however, it once more seems completely impossible to consider the belonging of an individual X to the human species as a *property* of X (analogously to "being human," which cannot be a *property* of X either). In fact, properties are *predicated of* subjects (X); they *are not* X, rather they are "something" *of* X. But X is a member of the human species. Consequently, this belonging cannot be a mere property or characteristic of X, because otherwise there would be no identifiable subject (no self-identical X) about which this property could be expressed; that is, X would not be X.

The claim is trivial, because in the final analysis it asserts no more than this: the simple fact that X is a member of the human species—the fact *as such*—is not a sufficient reason that X has more rights than a member of *another* species. This is enlightening, but nevertheless trivial. It is only in effect a simple statement that continues to ignore the question as to precisely why the human species should be privileged.

Nevertheless, Hoerster's triviality seems to confirm the idea that "speciesism" is equivalent to racism. This is due to the easily overlooked linguistic ambiguity of one of Hoerster's central statements: "Belonging to the species *Homo sapiens* is a purely biological distinctive mark" (or, as Hoerster says in other places, a purely biological "property"). "Distinctive mark" [*Merkma*] and "property" [*Eigenschaft*] certainly are not the same thing. Normally Hoerster speaks of "distinctive marks." ASS 63 speaks speciously, however, as cited above, of the "property of belonging to the human species." This is a significant source of confusion.

"Who Is a Human Individual" and
"What Is a Human Individual"?

The statement "Belonging to the species *Homo sapiens* is a purely biological distinctive mark" could mean two quite different things:

1. *A criterion of classification or of individuation for individuals:* In this case it would mean that the simple belonging to the (biological) species "man" would be decisive with respect to who is a man (for example, that the individual X is a man). According to this meaning, this statement would mean that one can decide merely on the basis of purely biological facts whether an individual X is a man or not.

2. *A statement concerning what an individual of the human species is:* The biological classification here becomes a content-laden determination concerning what a member of the human species *is* (and therefore a basis

for determination of all the "properties" attributable to him). The statement would in fact mean: "Belonging to the human species is a purely biological *property*," or in other words that the mere belonging of X to the human species tells us nothing about what extends beyond the purely "biological" (or "zoological") plane, and therefore also nothing more than, for example, what it means to belong to a race, to a people of a particular skin color, or to a sex.

An analogy might help clarify this. To discover *who* is the president of the United States, it is sufficient to find out who is the principal resident of the White House: a pure "distinctive mark according to residential sociology." It would clearly be false, however, to say the following so as to then vent all of one's indignation over the fact that X has so many rights and such power merely on the basis of the distinctive mark (clearly insignificant *politically*) of being the principal resident of the White House: "Since we can ascertain without a doubt that X is currently the principal resident in the White House, and since X *is* currently the president of the United States, *therefore the being president of the United States means nothing more than being the principal resident of the White House*; it means nothing more than a fact that is based purely on residential sociology." The absurdity is evident. But it is exactly the move Hoerster tries to make.

In fact, we normally consider the expression "belonging to the species *Homo sapiens* is a purely biological distinction" to be understood in the first sense given. However, in adopting this meaning, we do not mean that "being a man" or "belonging to the human species" are thus a purely biological fact, even less a purely biological *property,* in the sense of the second meaning given. On the basis of the fact that for X, belonging to the human species is a purely biological distinction—in the sense of the first thesis—we have not yet said anything concerning *what* X properly is. It is possible that the simple belonging to the human species means and involves *much more* than something purely "biological." Or put otherwise, that the simple fact of being an individual of the biological species *Homo sapiens* includes a whole range of other facts (dispositions, capacities, qualities) that far surpass purely biological-zoological categories; above all, it includes the decisive fact—which Hoerster seeks to set aside with every possible argumentative trick—that members of the human species are already exclusively for this reason *men* and *persons*.

Hoerster plays with the two meanings of the statement, and therefore he could surreptitiously suggest, based on a (purely biological) qualifying distinction, that belonging to the species *Homo sapiens* is simply a "biological property"; on the basis of this belonging, nothing would be established other than a biological fact. Put otherwise, belonging to the species *Homo sapiens* is distinguished on the basis of the belonging to this species *as such* only because of biological properties, which, similar to skin color, race, and sex, cannot be the basis for any particular right or privilege. With this, however, he has stealthily distorted the second meaning.

Even if, therefore, belonging to the human species is a purely biological *distinction,* one cannot deduce from this that the fact of this belonging is, as with skin color, only "biologically" relevant. Even if we could recognize *on the basis of biological distinctions* that X is a member of the species *Homo sapiens,* this in no way signifies that "being a member of the species *Homo sapiens*" is—analogous to the color of one's skin—simply a *biologically relevant fact.* Hoerster, following Peter Singer, presumes therefore that the "speciesistic" thesis is erroneous, because in his opinion it essentially means that the *pure and simple* belonging to the human species *as such* (the purely biological classification of X as a member of the human species) would be the basis of privilege, as though by this fact it were already decided—in the sense of our second thesis—*what* a man is, with a purely biological distinction being raised to a criteria of privilege.

Is Belonging to the Species Only Relevant Biologically?

The so-called speciesists, however, refer to the distinctive mark "member of the human species" because they believe that this membership is as a criterion decisive because individuals of the human species can be clearly identified as *men* precisely on the basis of this membership. And this also means: they can by this criterion be identified as *persons*—given that being a man implies being a person (that is, one who is not a person is also certainly not a man).

We must, however, pose the question that in truth decides everything: "What precisely does it mean to belong to the species *Homo sapiens*?" We can respond to this question only when we know what is a "man." And immediately we recognize that this has *profound* meaning.

If rather we pose the question: "What does it mean for X to belong to the race Y?" we respond that, considering the fact that X is a *man*, this latter fact means *very little* (or it *should* mean very little).

Similarly, we know what a dolphin fetus is (as a member of the biological species "dolphin") only if we know what a dolphin is. We could obviously limit the question to the dolphin *fetus*. ("What is a dolphin *fetus*, as opposed to an adult dolphin?") If, however, we don't already know what a "dolphin" is, we cannot in fact respond to this question, because we would not know what a *dolphin* fetus is. In the same way, we can have no idea of what an architecture student is unless we know what an architect is.

It seems, therefore, almost as if the fact of being a *fetus* is a purely biological property; and fetuses differ from adult individuals of the same species only in virtue of biological properties, which do not justify a segregation of fetuses with respect to adults of the same species. But even this is not entirely precise.

The fact of being a fetus is, however, for a member X of the human species, a (changeable) *property*. Precisely this leads us to the question: *What is* X? In fact it is not membership in the species *as such* that is relevant, but rather that which we call the *nature* of the species in question—the "nature of man"—entirely independent of changeable properties (including, e.g., the fact of being a fetus).

It is precisely this question that Hoerster succeeds in leaving aside. Or rather, he *asks the question too late*, only when he speaks of "persons." The at-a-first-glance astonishing plausibility of his idea that a member of the human species only later *becomes* a man ("person") derives from the confusion of the two meanings, mentioned above, of the expression: "Belonging to the human species is a purely biological distinctive mark." Because we can presuppose and depart from the fact that an individual adult X of the human species is precisely a "man," the idea that X *becomes* a man only over time is, on the grounds of Hoerster's confusion, purely a *petitio principii*, and as such, a vicious circle (because from the beginning he unreasonably presupposed that individuals belonging to the species *Homo sapiens* are *not yet* men). What would be needed, then, would be precisely to justify why a member of the human species, based on this very fact (not "property"), *is not already* a man.

Such a justification would be difficult if one begins from the idea that belonging to the human species is *not* a purely biological fact (even if, recall, membership in the human species can be *established* on the basis of purely biological distinctions). In exactly the same way as we can know how a human organism functions only based on *healthy* organs, we can know only based on adult, developed human individuals what it properly means to be a member of the human species, and thus *what* a member of the species *Homo sapiens* properly *is*. And these have always been the great questions of philosophical anthropology, which Hoerster passes over in silence, only to later brand responses to these questions as "religious prejudices."

Indeed, the entire remainder of Hoerster's argumentation is already decided at this point—what follows is merely consequence. Consequences drawn from mistaken presuppositions, however, cannot but include within them the errors and contradictions of the presuppositions, which we will now see.

The Foundation of the Person in Virtue of the Interest in Survival

Hoerster's Thesis: The Link between Interest in Survival, Personhood, and Right to Life

According to Hoerster: "[A] living being is manifestly violated in his interests by being killed when and only when he possesses an interest which can be violated precisely by being killed, i.e., when he possesses an *interest in survival*" (*ASS* 70).

This sentence contains some strong ethical-theoretical presuppositions, such as: only real interests of individual humans are ethically relevant; rights can be based only on interests; moral norms are always an expression of interests; and so on. I here want not to question the validity of such presuppositions, but rather to discuss Hoerster's views on the grounds of these very presuppositions.

A right to life, according to Hoerster, is possessed only by one who has a corresponding interest in his own survival. Such an interest presupposes a corresponding desire, which to be precise would not necessarily be a desire for *survival*. To have an interest in one's own survival, it is enough to have at least a desire "for the realization of which one's own survival is a necessary and adequate condition" (*ASS* 73).

Only one who "possesses consciousness of his identity over the course of time" (*ASS* 75) can have such an interest or corresponding desire: "The being who desires must therefore possess not only a momentary consciousness, but must possess a *consciousness of the I and of himself*—with the consequence that he can recognize himself as *the same* being over the course of time. Only a being with self-consciousness understood in this way can have desires regarding his future, and under this aspect an interest in survival."

A being who meets this criteria, then, would be called a "person," and only persons have an interest in survival and therefore also corresponding rights.

An Objection: Are Sleeping Humans Not Persons?

Frequently, in opposition to the basis of personhood just described, the objection has been raised that in this case men (adults) who sleep or who are unconscious would not be persons, because they cannot effectively have present desires to continue living.[9] Hoerster replies with the argument (which is sufficient in this context) that it is enough to have a *virtual* desire for survival or a corresponding desire with respect to which survival is a necessary condition. A desire once formulated effectively remains, even if the one who desires sleeps occasionally; moreover, this desire expressly extends to periods of sleep and to the time *following*. Even if one sleeps, he is a being who *has* this desire—as opposed to one who is unconscious, but has never had *any* desire because he is not (yet) capable of it (cf. *ASS* 76–79).

Up to this point, Hoerster seems to me to be correct. Yet, against this argument a further objection has been formulated, which says that this would be a criterion of personhood that—different from simple belonging to the species *Homo sapiens*—is in fact *unobservable*. How, then, could we ever know whether *any* physical body is a person?[10] At a minimum there would be a need for some linguistic expression on the basis of which we can conclude that this body possesses at least *a* desire that implies an interest in survival, which in turn would be recognizable as a "consciousness of his identity over the course of time."

And in fact this leads to various problems. In order to be recognized

9. Cf. a detailed treatment of this in S. Schwarz, *The Moral Question of Abortion* (Chicago: Loyola University Press, 1990).

10. Cf. A. Suarez, "Darf man dem Embryo den verfassungrechtlichen Schutz der Menschenwürde absprechen?" *Schweizerische Juristenzeitung* 86 (1990): 205–11.

as a person, everyone would have to demonstrate—by means of some linguistic expression or behavior—his being a person. There are, however, some adults unable to do this, yet we do not deny their personhood. Fetuses and newborns are also manifestly incapable of this; what allows us to deny their personhood, as well?

Personhood: A "Property" of Human Beings?

The following, however, seems to me to be more important: Hoerster again designates personhood, and therefore the capacity to have desires that imply an interest in survival, *as a property*. But a property "of whom"? Or "of what"? Clearly it is the property of a man or a person; more precisely the property of an individual of the species *Homo sapiens* in the state of development "man" ("person").

Why, we must immediately ask, has the individual X (belonging to the species *Homo sapiens,* for example, six years after his birth) developed this property of personhood? And why do all the members of this species *normally* develop this property? Clearly because they are capable of such a development, and this based on certain characteristics of the species *Homo sapiens.* Which means: members of the species *Homo sapiens* are beings who sooner or later develop personhood and therefore an interest in survival. This in turn implies that belonging to the species *Homo sapiens* is *more* than a merely *biological* category. At a minimum we can say that members of the human species are future persons.

I do not want to say more than this now; I have intentionally not spoken of "potential persons." And in my view, fetuses are not "future persons," or "potential persons," but simply persons.[11] The only thing that I want to point out here is that Hoerster's argument at *this* point contradicts his prior premise that belonging to the human species is a distinction that is relevant only biologically, that is, an exclusively biological category. This clearly cannot be true. It would be true only if such individuals X developed to the point of becoming persons *by chance, now and then, or based on contingent exterior conditions,* and so on. But in fact this development occurs normally, and we are also well justified in saying that it occurs *necessarily and predictably,* at least where no external circumstances or anomalies enter in which hinder it.

11. On this also see Schwarz, *Moral Question of Abortion,* esp. 86–103.

This is, consequently, relevant for the fact of being a member of the species *Homo sapiens*. This belonging to the species, *of itself*, clearly distinguishes man with respect to individuals of those species who normally *do not* develop to the point of becoming persons (the question of whether there are non-human persons being completely irrelevant to this argument).

The Actualization of Personhood as a Property

If, however, we must now make clear, a member of the species *Homo sapiens* is already by reason of this membership marked by a non-biological distinction (that of necessarily developing personhood under normal circumstances, or of becoming a person), then we must conclude that the (present) being a person, or (present) personhood, is not a *property* of an individual of this species. It is rather a *developed* property of a member of the species *Homo sapiens*.

More precisely, we must say that it is the *actualization* of a property that the simple member of the species *Homo sapiens* already possesses. I consider this an unfortunate linguistic expression, however. It seems better to say that present personhood is a property of a being who *has always been* a person, even if such a person does not have the property of possessing this "being a person" *actualized* at every stage of his development. This is precisely what is meant when we say: the fetus *is* a person.

My argument agrees exactly, it should be emphasized, with the description Hoerster gives of the *property* "actualized personhood." His error is not in this, but in missing the fact that only the *actualization* of being a person, or of the capacity to manifest this, is a "property"—but not being a person itself. "Being a person" is in fact attributed to the *subject* itself ("X is a person"). As G. Pöltner rightly points out, not every predicate of a sentence is a predicative expression,[12] and Hoerster clearly commits this *linguistic fallacy*. This principle is also valid for names: "X is John" does not mean that X has the property of being John, rather that he *is* John.

For this reason it is also not possible that the being-a-person of individuals who develop the property of actualized personhood be at the same time simply a property. Only a being that is already a person can

12. Pöltner, "Achtung der Würde," 19.

actualize its being a person. For this reason, individuals of the species *Homo sapiens are* persons.

The property of an actualized (developed) personhood with the desires and interest typical of personhood is therefore a property that only beings who *are* persons can develop and possess. Precisely for this reason one who sleeps continues to be a person, because he is a being who already *possesses* precisely this developed property of being a person. This does not mean, however, that beings who do not yet possess this property of actualized personhood are for this reason not persons; it means only that they are not yet persons who have actualized their being persons.

In other words, we can also establish that the being-a-person of the fetus is a *present fact,* and in no way merely potential. It is not the *being-a-person* that is potential, but personal behavior. Only a being who *is* already actually a person can demonstrate a potential for personal behavior, so as to eventually develop actual personal behavior.[13] Only persons can develop the properties of persons!

With this we have arrived at the fallacious concept of the fetus as a "potential person." What has been said thus far should be sufficient to show the problematic nature of the discussion concerning "potential persons." Hoerster, on the other hand, uses the concept starting from the subsequent section of his book. His introduction and discussion of the topic is consequently, to repeat, *too late* in the discussion. By the fact that he has already falsely insinuated to the reader that being a person is a *property* of X (that is, a property of a being of the human species), in the following step he continues to build on this presupposition, thus basing his position on an unfounded and moreover false premise: the fetus becomes for him, in a manner having the appearance of plausibility, a "potential person."

The Claim That Fetuses Are Not Persons
"Not a Person," or Rather "Persons Lacking the Property of Actualized Personhood"?

The question now is the following: "When in the course of his development, then, does the human individual begin to become a person?" (*ASS* 79). On the basis of what we have already said, the question itself

13. Schwarz, *Moral Question of Abortion,* chapter 7.

is erroneous. To answer this question is to already give a response that cannot possibly be right. In fact the human individual does not *become* a person (if he were not already a person, he would not in fact be a *human* individual), rather he is a human being (a human person) who gradually *actualizes* his being a person.

Undoubtedly, we can admit that the human individual in its status as a fetus certainly does not yet possess that which I would call the "property of actualized personhood" (in the sense of present personal behavior).[14] Hoerster states: "Newborns do not yet experience themselves as an identical subject over the course of time" (*ASS* 80)—they cannot yet have desires that imply an interest in survival. And what is true for newborns is true a fortiori for fetuses.

Clearly, from this can only be deduced that the fetus does not yet possess the property of actualized personhood. Hoerster, however, deduces: "The process of becoming a person is a process which clearly begins at a certain point *after* birth" (*ASS* 80).

Hoerster claims therefore that the fetus is certainly not a person, and for this reason, and from this perspective, neither can it claim any right to life; that it is unable to possess any interest in survival is explained later—again, too late for his argument, as we shall see.

Retrospective Identity of Persons, and Interest
in Survival of Fetuses

First, I want to put forward a counterargument that Hoerster mentions, but—not by chance—puts off until later in his argument. This counterargument would be: even if the fetus certainly does not yet bear within himself any indication of personhood (because he clearly does not yet possess the property of actualized personhood), an interest in survival must nevertheless be *attributed* to him, and therefore also a right to life. I will shortly express the argument more precisely; I want to emphasize, however, that Hoerster also addresses this argument, but *too late*. In fact, however, it must of necessity be treated here.

---

14. "Actualized personhood" is not the same as "currently possessing or presently existing personhood." In any case, I use the terms here in the following sense: the fetus is truly now a person (he therefore "currently possesses personhood"); at the same time, however, the fetus has not yet "actualized" his present being a person. "Actualized personhood" is therefore a property of persons, e.g., in specific stages of development.

All people who have been born and have an interest in survival know that they were once fetuses (they possess, so to speak, a "retrospective identity" of themselves as fetuses); they could look at an ultrasound image of themselves in the womb and say: "This is me." This results from the fact, conceded by Hoerster at the outset, that the fetus is a human individual with a continuous development, with no basis for any division of this development into phases. Even if the *fetus* cannot yet say: "This is me," the adult person *can* say this with respect to himself in the fetal state. Individuals are in fact identical.

Consequently, it would violate the *present* interest in survival and right to life of such persons *as* persons, if they had been killed *then* (as fetuses). At least this is how the counterargument could be understood. Or one could understand (retrospectively) one's own survival as a fetus to be "in one's own interest" (as an interest of myself as an actual person), and therefore "something good for me" even then (which also means: as a good for the person who "I" am *now*).[15]

As a consequence, there is no reason to deny a corresponding interest in life to other *present* fetuses; on the contrary, there is a grave reason for attributing such an interest to them. They are in the identical state to the "I" that I once was; they are, as individuals, now already identical with the person that they will one day become. I must therefore acknowledge that present fetuses are "equal to me" (in the same way that I acknowledge other adults to be "equal to me"). Thus, one arrives at the establishment of an *objective* interest in survival of the fetus, which can nevertheless not yet be presently realized as a will (because the fetus lacks the property of actualized personhood), but in fact "exists" (survival for a fetus is a "good"; it comes to be experienced as such precisely in virtue of the universal human experience of retrospective identity).

An "objective interest in survival" (and a corresponding "objective right") means an interest and a corresponding right that *demand* recognition, even if the fetus (subjectively) cannot yet request it. Nevertheless it is a "subjective right," because in effect the corresponding subject already exists (the existence of subjective rights is not in effect linked to the fact that one can also subjectively claim them).

15. In introducing the term "good," I am aware that this has no place in Hoerster's approach, oriented toward interest. This is a significant point, but does not need to be addressed in more detail here.

When such an objective interest in survival exists, then the "golden rule" takes effect, in virtue of which the killing of fetuses is shown to be a fundamentally unjust action. Hoerster also recognizes this, if it is true that he admits (further on, in *ASS* 97–98) that, if this argument were valid, it would be "manifestly unjust if we, the persons of today, did not admit for all other pre-personal beings that protection of life in which we ourselves are now interested, with respect to those pre-personal beings which we once were." For Hoerster also, whose moral sentiment here corresponds entirely to the universal sentiment, it would offend the golden rule.

Moreover, it must be said that this would be even more unjust than the killing of those who can understand and demand such an interest in life now, in virtue of their will, because the fetus is a true person, a man who is nevertheless unable to assert his interest or defend it, and therefore is all the more in need of protection. We feel similarly regarding one who is *incapable* of defending himself and is unjustly condemned, more so even than one who defends himself *poorly and ineffectively,* but in principle is capable of doing so.

As mentioned, Hoerster advances the argument of "retrospective identity" further on, seeking to discredit it; in fact his effort there is logically not valid, inasmuch as his argumentation presupposes that the argument he seeks to discredit *has not yet been adopted in the appropriate place,* which is precisely here, as we have just done.

What Is Meant by "Potential Person"?

On page 85 of his book, Hoerster seems to sense a difficulty the reader may have, and tries to prevent a possible "confusion": it could in effect seem that the "person" comes into the world from nothing. The "refutation" carried out by Hoerster of the idea that beings which develop the property of actualized personhood must in some way already *be* persons in order to be capable of such a development could, according to Hoerster, mislead the reader to the confused idea that the fetus is not yet a human being, rather a species of animal "which in some mysterious way suddenly transforms itself into a human person."

In Hoerster's view, however, things are not so: "This being is rather from the beginning a member of a quite specific biological species (the species *Homo sapiens*), which already bears in itself the possibility to develop [into] a human person. One can correctly call this being, the human fetus, a *potential* person—as opposed to an *actual* person—or also a *pre-personal* being."

Frankly, Hoerster here concedes—in a way that is fatal to the coherence of his argument—that to the species *Homo sapiens* pertains the possibility of development to the point of becoming a person, and therefore not by chance but *essentially*. We have already mentioned this, however, and precisely at the point where this mention was called for. We can draw two conclusions from this: in the first place, being a person is not a property; and secondly, belonging to the species *Homo sapiens* is from the beginning *more* than a distinctive mark relevant only in biological-zoological terms. Hoerster ignores these conclusions, putting them in parentheses, and merely states that being a person is a property. The rest of his argument is based on this premise, and therefore becomes simply a *petitio principii* and as such, a vicious circle.

The distinction made by Hoerster between "actual" person and "potential" person, however, is worth a closer examination. Hoerster's use of this distinction is in fact based on a confusion of two ways of saying "X is in reality[16] something."

We must—as we have already done—distinguish between (a) what X presently is (its "actual being") and (b) the later actualization of what X actually is.

For example: human gametes (an egg cell and a sperm cell) are, taken together and prior to fertilization, "potentially" an individual of the species *Homo sapiens*. They *are not* this in reality (i.e., *in actu*), however. An individual X of the species *Homo sapiens is* such an individual, but he has not yet actualized—in an absolute way—all that he actually, as X, is. The actuality in sense (a) refers to the *being* of X; the actuality in sense (b) refers rather to *properties* of this being (properties that are mutable in the process of development).

Both fetuses and adult persons are individuals of the species *Homo sapiens*. As such, they possess the same actual being (according to their nature). The unity of the species and its identity with itself are based on what the individuals belonging to it actually are, and not on their degree of actualization of that which they are.

16. Literally, *in actu*.

This means that, compared with an actual person, a potential person is a being of the same species who has not yet actualized much of what (on the basis of belonging to the same species) he is. The difference is not therefore in what the two individuals presently are (human persons), but in the degree of actualization of that which they are. The concept of "potential person," in the case of fetuses, cannot therefore be maintained if by "to become a person" one means only the actualization of that which the corresponding individual always was and is.

Otherwise one must admit (absurdly) that the human fetus and the human person belong *to two different* species. Or another alternative, that personhood also is merely a biological-zoological category (in which case neither would persons have a right to life, inasmuch as privileges based on purely biological distinctive marks are inadmissible). In effect, the concept of person would become obsolete.

Fetuses Are Not "Potential Persons"

It is better, therefore, not to use the term "potential person" at all, as it is too imprecise. A potential person is something that is not yet a person, but *in some way* can become one. A stone is not a potential person. Nor is a sperm cell or an egg cell, considered in themselves; *considered together,* however, they are a potential person (or rather: "they are potentially a person"). A fetus, on the other hand, is not a potential person, because it already is a person. It is, however, a person "in potential." Or rather, *on the basis of his actually being a person,* he possesses precisely that potentiality to develop personal properties (to "actualize" them), that is, those properties that can belong only to persons (even if they have not yet developed any of these properties). But even a ten-year-old child is still a "person in potential" in this sense, even if he has developed many, but precisely not all, of these properties. In fact, *every* person is always in some way a "person in potential," given that no one has developed all of the possibilities of a person.

"Potential" and "potentially" are in fact extremely ambiguous terms. At times they deal with a concept of *possibility* (including logical); at other times of a real *capacity* (a use that can be distinguished further, which distinction I will spare the reader). Human gametes are potential persons because, as distinct from other types of cells, it is *possible* that they, when fused, can become a person (the fusion itself is based on a contingent event, external to this possibility; neither of the gametes possesses entirely in itself the capacity to develop the properties of a person). A fetus, on the other hand, is a "person in potential" because a fetus is *capable* of developing to the point of becoming an adult person (and this is not only *possible,* but *certain,* on the basis of what a fetus is; only external contingent events can impede this development). In this latter sense, then, *every* person (including adults) is, in some respect, a "person in potential." So we can restate: only persons can develop over time the properties of persons (not the "property of being a person," but the properties of those beings that already *are* persons, as smiling, talking, being intelligent, or behaving reasonably).

Personality: A Biological Property?

The supposition was made above that Hoerster's argument necessarily leads to the conclusion that personhood is also purely a biological-zoological category and that, therefore, as said in the beginning, his third presupposed principle is inconsistent with the other three and cannot be upheld. Why? Hoerster states that belonging to the species "man" is *a purely biological* (i.e., zoological) category; on the basis of this category alone, one cannot therefore yet attribute to such an individual any property that exceeds the biological-zoological level.

This means, however, that a group of purely biological properties amounts to a *disposition* toward the non-biological property "personhood" (which Hoerster likewise affirms). The actualization of a purely biological property is, however, always itself also a purely biological property, that is, an "actualized biological property" (for example, of an adult female individual of the human species, the capacity to conceive and give birth to children, a property that this individual had only dispositively or potentially as a fetus).

Consequently, "personhood" would also be an (actualized) biological-zoological property. But how then could we distinguish and privilege beings possessing personhood without committing the same error as racists? Exactly at this point Hoerster's argument begins to break down: he wants to ground a right to life on personhood, claiming that such a right cannot be based on purely "biological properties"—yet now he is unable to show that "being a person" is something more than simply a more developed stage of a merely biological property!

If, however, personhood is not a biological property, then it is necessarily the actualization of a *non*-biological property, which nevertheless manifestly derives from and is implicit in membership in the human species. Nor is this membership, then, a purely biological category, and the comparison between racism and the "privileging" of an individual on the basis of their belonging to the human species ceases to hold. Hoerster's argument here continues to disintegrate.

Man as the Sum of His Properties

We have already seen how it is not possible to call "being a man" a *property*, and why this is so. Here I want to more deeply confirm this original statement. To do so, something else must be shown first, that is, that Hoerster's approach is based on a clearly dubious metaphysic or ontology. All of the arguments related to the questions we are dealing, including the arguments we are proposing in opposition to Hoerster, with are based on ontological presuppositions. Hoerster, however, does not expressly state the ontological presuppositions of his argument, something that makes it difficult to identify the equivocal nature of the argument.

One of Hoerster's fundamental assertions is that every being (thing, individual, etc.) is the sum of its properties, clearly referring in this to the British philosopher David Hume.[17] Hoerster expressly refers to Hume as the one who has demonstrated "with an argument which until now has not been refuted" that there is no "substance" in man transcending the contingent properties of individual humans, that is, a substance that would be independent of these properties (cf. *ASS* 120).

It is true that Hume's idea has not been refuted—but precisely because it is not refutable. Based on the presupposition that man is, like every other being, the sum of its properties, it is not possible to refute the idea that it would be impossible that, beyond these properties, there would be "something else"; this is a purely conceptual consequence of the premise that a being is nothing other than the sum, or an aggregate, of his properties. This premise, however, is simply nonsensical. It is not necessary to believe that there is such a substance, and that it be recog-

17. I will limit myself here to only one aspect of this question. For the ontological presuppositions of the concept of person that are the basis of an ethics of interest, cf. Honnenfelder, "Der Streit um die Person in der Ethik."

nizable (although even here the concept of substance one uses is crucial). The position of Kant, which I consider to be mistaken as well, is sufficient, however, to show at least that Hume's idea leads to contradictions. Kant deduced that reason requires that such a substance must be posed, at least at the foundation of thought—which nevertheless would only with difficulty protect the rights of the unborn, newborns, and those with chronic illnesses.

To claim that man is the sum of his properties (e.g., the property of being a member of the species *Homo sapiens* and the property of being a man, etc.) is also impossible for linguistic reasons (recall here our previous reflections on the meaning of the term "property"). Again, the being man of a man *appears* in his properties, but does not *consist* in a property. To have and develop human properties, a subject must already *be* a man (and likewise, to develop the properties of a person he must already be a person).

Precisely for this concrete reason Hoerster's argument tends necessarily to end by identifying being a man with "being a member of the species *Homo sapiens*," firmly understood in the sense of a purely biological-zoological definition of what a man is. And for this reason personhood also, as a "property" of this individual, becomes a purely biological property. As a result, man and his nature are defined in all their aspects exclusively on a biological level.

Hoerster certainly does not propose this *implicit biologism* explicitly. I believe that he simply does not see the extremely grave implications of his theory, and indeed would be horrified to accept them, given that a privileged right to life for adults of the human species, and therefore of persons, would in this case be no less opposable than racism, given that both would be based on purely biological criteria. "Persons" could therefore simply be individuals who are biologically higher! And if, vice versa, we were to nevertheless hold to such a privileging of certain persons (a sort of "personism"), we would no longer have any argument against racism. Indeed, such an argument would provide many reasons *in favor of* privileging those whom we believe to be biologically superior.

The Argument of the Preventing of an Interest in Survival

Under the title "The protection of future interests," Hoerster now addresses the counterargument I described in the previous section (*ASS* 97–102); there I claimed that Hoerster addresses this counterargument "too late." We must now show why, and with what consequences.

Hoerster admits that one can arrive at the counterargument that "I as a person" have an interest that "I as a fetus" had not been aborted. For this reason, according to the counterargument, "I" already as a fetus possessed an interest in survival and a corresponding right to life. On this basis, it would clearly be unjust not to concede a similar right to life to all other fetuses, who will one day all be persons with a present interest in not having been aborted as fetuses.

Hoerster believes that there are actions with respect to fetuses (for example, damage due to experimentation that harms the developed person) that violate the future rights of the person who develops. It seems, then, that one could say: if injuries to the body of a future bearer of rights should be prohibited, shouldn't killing him be prohibited all the more?

This—according to Hoerster—is undoubtedly correct, if the human being in question is already a person when he is killed. This however, he claims, is not the case. At this point it is necessary to be attentive: precisely *on the basis of the counterargument just expressed* (that of retrospective identity) and on the concept of "potential person," it was earlier shown that the fetus in fact must be considered to be a person; I also said that the point where I proposed the counterargument was its proper context. Hoerster, on the other hand, departs from the fact—for him certain—that the fetus is not a person, precisely because he has not taken the counterargument into consideration at the proper point in his argument. As such, it is a simple *petitio principii,* or begging the question. And with what results!

First, this leads to the conclusion that no interest in survival would be violated, because it does not yet exist; secondly (and this is the decisive point), "no interest in survival of a future person, developed from the fetus, would be violated! Rather, a being with an interest in survival would be *prevented* from developing from the fetus. And this is the difference: *the prevention of the development* of an interest in survival is something entirely different from the *violation* of an *existing* interest in survival, whether present or future" (*ASS* 100).

As I have said, the premises of this argument are false. In fact it can be shown at an earlier point in the argument that the fetus indeed possesses an interest in survival that must be acknowledged, and that is violated by killing him. It is therefore false to say that a development of an interest in survival is *prevented* by aborting the fetus. To repeat, the false premise is: "The fetus is not yet a person; it is a pre-personal being; it therefore does not yet have, *as* a fetus, that is, at the moment of its being killed, any interest in survival and therefore any right to life."

The counterargument that must be refuted, however, I already adopted when I was addressing precisely *this* false premise. In reality, the counterargument is an argument against the claim that the fetus *is not yet* a person, or that he would be a pre-personal being; *that* question provides the counterargument's proper context. Hoerster moves the counterargument to this point in his argument, however, and needs his claim that the fetus is not yet a person—in fact refuted by the counterargument—as justification for the claim that the fetus does not possess any (objective) interest in survival. The vicious circle in his reasoning is evident.

Moreover, it should be pointed out that Hoerster's argument is in reality not an argument that favors his position. Rather, because of its absurdity, his claim here gives a strong indication that his entire position is unsustainable. Another indicator would be his further claim that the non-generation of a human individual (through continence or contraception) would be *equivalent* to the killing of an already existing fetus; in both cases, he says, a person would be prevented from coming into existence. Conclusions such as these are so opposed to our well-founded basic moral convictions that they should serve as a warning bell, alerting us to the incongruity of Hoerster's argument.

Present and Future Interests

This becomes clear in a small footnote (n. 48, *ASS* 100–101): "For this reason, by the killing of a *person* his *future* rights are not violated. Rather, what are violated are his *present* interests in his future life!" This is a necessary consequence of Hoerster's argument, and it is honest of him to state it expressly.

But let us reflect on the significance of this claim using an example: I kill P, who is a scientist. P practices scientific research, exclusively with the *present* interest of earning enough money to have a stable retirement, so as to pursue his hobbies. He does not know now, however, that his research will lead to a spectacular discovery, for which he will win the Nobel Prize; all of a sudden, his retirement and his hobbies become irrelevant to him, because of his new position in the scientific community as a result of the discovery and new, fascinating duties that result. So—P is killed. Is the murderer merely responsible for the fact that after his retirement, P cannot dedicate himself to his hobbies?

Hoerster forgets that the future life of a person, every future, is *open* to indeterminate possibilities, which at the present are not *real* possibilities, to which therefore nor can there extend "*real*" interests. P's discovery is not the product of present desires, rather of a development over time, independent of desires. Nevertheless, such future interest can clearly be violated, or rather anyone who *prevents* their development must be held responsible for that. In reality, it is impossible for us to know, as in the above example, in what such future interests will consist. This does not mean, however, that we are not responsible for preventing them, only that we can in no way know exactly what we effect when we kill a person.

The above example is analogous to the case of a fetus; and in fact, we actually know something more. We know with certainty that a fetus will have the normal interests of a person, at a minimum the interest in survival. We cannot say that one who kills a fetus is not *responsible* for the violation of such a future interest; in fact, he is responsible precisely for the fact that he prevents it from coming into being.

Moreover, this is true not only with respect to killing the fetus. Let us again consider the case where fetuses are damaged bodily as a result of experiments. The fetus obviously at this point does not have a *present* interest in his *future* bodily health; he does not yet have *any* present interest in his future life. If, in the case of persons, only *present* interests can be violated, this is even more true for fetuses. There is a contradiction, however, at this point in Hoerster's argument. *Either* it is possible to violate future interests, which one does not yet have (an argument that Hoerster opposes), *or* it is permissible to damage the health of embryos and fetuses with experiments, because one cannot damage *future* interests.

Hoerster, to save his argument, would have to respond as follows: fetuses whose future health would predictably be damaged by experiments must be destroyed; in this way the development of a future interest in survival or in one's own health would be prevented. This "solution" brings us to the heart of the issue: Hoerster's position would lead to the conclusion that it is acceptable to do experiments on fetuses without hindrance; those that are damaged you simply do away with. The killing of the fetus would then become a *reason* why no injustice would result from such bodily damage! Fetuses damaged by experiment must therefore be killed—an utterly absurd conclusion—so that the present experiment does not become an immoral action through the future development of an interest in bodily integrity.

The Fetus as Potential Plaintiff

The following reflection also demonstrates how Hoerster's argumentation leads in other ways to absurd consequences, entirely contrary to intuition. Let us suppose that a doctor attempts to kill a fetus, but for some reason the attempt fails; the baby is born, and "develops to the point of becoming a person."[18] Can this person now sue the doctor for attempted homicide? In this case the development of an interest in survival has effectively not been prevented. Such an interest now exists that was previously violated, or at least an attempt was made to do so. Except for a possible prescription, there can be simply no argument against the justification of such an action. (Hoerster must be in agreement; but contradicting this—which he also says—is the fact that future interests *cannot* be violated, only present interests in one's future life.)

If this is true, however, then all aborted fetuses are also aborted *persons.* More exactly, they are potential, but *impeded,* plaintiffs against those who have aborted them. They cannot accuse only when and because the abortion is *successful.* This is not, however, a reason for which

18. A case has become well known of an attempted abortion via saline solution at the sixth month; thanks to the intervention of a nurse, the baby was injured but survived, and now lives a normal life.

this attempted killing is morally justified. The success of an action is never a reason for the possibility of being able to morally justify the action. This is precisely, however, the result of Hoerster's arguments.

The "Certainty" of the Impossibility of a Future Interest in Survival

It is precisely for this reason that a later formulation by Hoerster is astounding, in which he asserts that neither a future interest, nor a *possible* future interest in survival is violated by abortion, because it "brings about *with certainty* that there will be no particular interest in survival" (*ASS* 101).

This argument is rather weak, in my opinion. In fact, the impossibility of a future interest in survival, or the *certainty* with which it will not come about, are not in this case independent of the action and the will of the person who kills the fetus. Hoerster's argument could be debatable in one case only, where it is foreseen with certainty that the fetus would soon die *of itself*. The question in such case, however, is precisely the admissibility of the *act of killing* on the part of a man; in fact the admissibility of this action is what must be justified by Hoerster's argument, inasmuch as it is only the *action of killing* that ultimately brings about the referred-to certainty.

For this reason, one cannot consider this action to have merely "happened," so as to then conclude that the possibility of a future interest in survival no longer exists "with certainty." The question is rather whether the bringing about of this impossibility or certainty is morally admissible. The real possibility (and therefore the certainty) that such an interest in survival would one day exist *is a given*. And on *this* basis it must therefore be examined whether the action of killing violates *that* interest. Here Hoerster can only repeat: no such interest is violated, because the fetus does not have such an interest, and so on. With this, however, we are back at an earlier point in the argument, and the present point is shown to be simply without foundation.

Finally, Hoerster advances the claim that one who concedes a right to life to a fetus must also concede a "right to fertilization" to every egg cell (*ASS* 102). This, however, would be true only on the presupposition that the fetus (like the egg cell) is not a person (something that those who *do not* concede a right to fertilization to the egg cell do not have to accept; only Hoerster accepts this). The reasons justifying the fact that the fetus possesses a right to life are not in fact also a justification for the fact that an egg cell also possesses a right to fertilization. The egg cell is not, according to its actual being, a living being of the species *Homo sapiens* that has not yet actualized its present being a person. Nor is it, considered by itself and as such, a "potential person" or a "potential living being of the species *Homo sapiens*." Consequently, a "right to fertilization" of the egg cell does not result from the right to life of the fetus. With the non-fertilization of an egg cell the possibility of the development of a person is *prevented,* or rather the external event that actualizes the possibility does not occur, something that is entirely different than the case where a fetus already exists, given that the latter already *is* a person.

Some Consequences of Hoerster's Ethical Theory

Hoerster derives a number of problematic consequences from his application of an ethics of interest. These regard the concept of "human dignity," that of the "uniqueness of the person," the question of the killing of infants, the concept of law related to infanticide, and finally the question of discrimination against handicapped people. I will limit myself to these points, as Hoerster expressly treats them in his book.

The Concept of Human Dignity

According to Hoerster the concept of human dignity is a kind of "reformulation of the Christian concept according to which man would be the image of God"; from this it can also be claimed that unborn living beings also possess this dignity. This concept is therefore based simply on a religious outlook, which should no longer have any place in the juridical order of a secular state.

This assessment, however, is based on Hoerster's idea—which it seems to me has been shown to be untenable—that the fetus is not a person, or rather that it is only a "potential person" (a "pre-personal being"). If the fetus were not a person, it would indeed be unjustified to attribute "human dignity" to it. And indeed, in that case it would seem that one could plausibly show that a religious prejudice is at the basis of such an attribution.

Those who defend the human dignity of fetuses are not, however, of the idea that the fetus is a "potential person." They hold, rather, that the fetus *already is* a person, although he has not yet actualized his being a person—in the sense we defined earlier—and therefore nor has he yet manifested this "being a person."

On the basis of this vision of reality, the concept of "human dignity" acquires a possibility of meaning that is lost *completely* in Hoerster's argument. It in fact means that every person (including fetuses) always possesses, *entirely independent of his present properties* (or independently of the respective actualizations of what he actually is), that dignity which derives precisely from that which he already is: a human person; only for this reason can he then also possess the properties of a person, *even if* these latter only actualize, or develop, over time (or even if these properties *can no longer* be actualized over time). This meaning of "human dignity" falls entirely outside Hoerster's conception of things. Thus, for him the concept of "human dignity" is simply a "reformulation of the religiously based concept of the image of God."

Referral of man's "human dignity" to his being the "image of God" is not a *justification* of the fact that man possesses a "dignity"; rather it is another—and a much more profound—way of explaining that this is the case. Members of the human species possess human dignity in the first place because they are persons, and not because they are made in the image of God. Their being persons, however, can be represented and understood more deeply on the basis of their being a being made in God's image. Only in this way is human dignity based ultimately on being made in the image of God.

The concept of human dignity, therefore, ultimately shows itself to be another expression of the dignity of the *person*. The attribution of "human dignity" to a fetus is quite simply an expression of the fact that one considers fetuses to be persons.

Moreover, Hoerster's opinion (which follows Peter Singer) that the notion that unborn human beings already possess an inviolable human dignity is of religious (and specifically Christian) origin and therefore has no place in the juridical order of the secular state, seems to me to be not only incorrect as to content, but also historically inaccurate.

It is historically false, because at all times *there existed* the conception that it is unjust to kill unborn human beings; however, not everyone agreed (including during the Christian era) as to when the human life in the maternal womb began to be a human being. According to Roman law, abortion was permitted because the fetus was considered to be part of the viscera of the mother (a conception no longer scientifically sustainable, as Hoerster himself admits). In his *Politics,* Aristotle observes that the abortion of the fruit of the womb so as to limit the number of children is permitted only "before it possesses feeling and life . . . . Because what is here permissible and what is not permissible must be judged on the existence or not of sentiment and life."[19] The Hippocratic Oath can also obviously be cited in this context.

Similarly, the idea that man in general possesses a human dignity is not of Christian origin; it is a pre-Christian, Roman idea, deriving from Cicero. Our present concept of human dignity, on the other hand, was formulated only in the eighteenth century, too late to be called exclusively a "Christian inheritance."

Nor is the concept of man made in the image of God exclusively of Christian origin; we find it for example in Plato, and in Aristotle, his disciple. Key for both is the idea that the human spirit is "God in us," in virtue of which man possesses a likeness with God or with the gods. Only the *Christian* concept of the image of God is specifically Christian (which is as obvious as it is tautological). What is specifically *Christian* is a particular way of basing human dignity on likeness to God, and the subsequent expansion of this doctrine—but even here further specification is necessary.

In fact "likeness with God" is, even by Christian theologians, and in part with explicit reference to Cicero (e.g., in Thomas Aquinas), founded precisely *anthropologically,* based on man's spirituality, freedom, and rational self-determination. Based on these properties of the human person, it was claimed that *on the basis of these* man could be called the "image of God." Decisive, therefore, is not the concept of likeness to God, but rather the *content* that is associated with the concept. The content itself, however, is in large part of pre-Christian origin.[20]

19. Aristotle, *The Complete Works of Aristotle,* ed. J. Barnes (Princeton: Princeton University Press, 1984), VII, 16, 1335 b, 24–26. The suggestion to not raise deformed children, expressed in the same section, is not problematic in this context; it is merely the expression of the ancient pagan idea according to which a manifest deformity of the body would also justify the killing of a man. This conception is not, however, shared by Hoerster; paradoxically, he seems to be obliged rather to the Christian tradition.

20. Cf. the article *Würde* ["Dignity"] in O. Brunner, W. Conze, R. Kosellek, *Geschichtliche Grundbegriffe,* vol. 7, (Stuttgart: Klett-Cotta, 1992), 643–45.

That the concepts of human dignity and of man made in the image of God were articulated in an entirely Christian manner in the Christian era is an obvious fact of culture: this brings us to Hoerster's (and Singer's) second error. Even if certain ideas developed and became culturally effective only in a Christian context, this does not mean that they logically depend on specific contents of the Christian faith or *are based* on the claims of faith of this particular religion. It means only that evidently this religion formulated presuppositions particularly favorable for the effective establishment of these ideas. For example, immediately after the appearance of Constantine the Great, the branding of slaves on their faces was forbidden, on the basis that they also bore God's image in themselves, which cannot be damaged. It was not, then, that a religious dogma was incorporated into the juridical order; rather because of the Christian influence, an essential advancement for humanity was accomplished.

The same can be said for the fundamental assertion, recognized by Hoerster, regarding equal treatment for every man as a man. Neither the Greeks nor the Romans ever considered that slaves were *not* men; nevertheless, they were not treated equally with free men and were discriminated against in Roman law. The idea that every man as a man deserved equal treatment was affirmed only in the Christian period, and this principle became juridically effective only after centuries. Without Christian influence, therefore, the opening words of the American Declaration of Independence would be unthinkable; the idea of universal human rights in fact grew on Christian soil. Nevertheless, it is not necessary to claim that such rights are "Christian" in the sense that they logically derive from tenets of the Christian revelation and faith.

Consequently, it should be held firmly that members of the human species are men, and because men are persons, those who belong to the human species are by this very fact also persons, even if they are not yet (or are no longer) capable of manifesting their being persons. We cannot separate a man's being a person from the fact of his being a member of the human species. Otherwise, neither can we justify the fact that every human person possesses a dignity on the basis of what he is, and not on the basis of specific qualities, of developed capacities (for example, the capacity of being able to have conscious interests), or of his state of development or "decline." The subordination of being to the conscience, effected by an ethics of interest, precisely in the juridical-political context, is a threat to humanity too fundamental to be ignored.

Moreover, the Christian origin of what we consider to be humanly inalienable cannot be an argument against its enduring validity in a secular state. Even the idea of the "secular state" itself is of Christian origin. It is quite thinkable, and indeed probable, that without Christianity there would no longer be such a thing as the secularity of the state. In fact, the de-secularization of the state is not at all in the interest of the Christian Church but rather of the state, which desires power. Frankly, we are hardly in the habit of reflecting today on this kind of question.

Every political community has and lives its own history, without which that community and its political form would be unthinkable.[21] Even if so many things—such as, indeed, the idea of human dignity and of the fundamental equality of all men and women as creatures and children of God—have their origins, at the level of civilization, in Christianity, the renunciation of these historical origins would be tantamount to the renunciation of the ultimate roots of our ethos of human rights. What would become of the secularity of the state if this renunciation were to occur, no one can predict; in any event, secularity by itself is no guarantee of justice.

The "Uniqueness" of the Person

Alongside the discussion concerning the "dignity of man," is also that of the "uniqueness of the person." Reference to the "uniqueness" of every individual human would be for Hoerster, however, to refer merely to a "biological triviality." Individual cats are also "unique." They also, as members of their species, are genetically unrepeatable individuals (ASS 124).

Obviously, the validity of this argument would also depend on the presupposition that fetuses are *not* persons, or rather that belonging to the human species and belonging to another species of animals would be equivalent properties. As soon as we consider fetuses to be persons and depart from the fact that belonging to the human species means

---

21. Cf. also on this the reflections of the president of the German Episcopal Conference, Karl Lehmann, "Das Eintreten für das Lebensrecht des ungeborenen Kindes als christlicher und humaner Auftrag," in *Herausforderung Schwangersschaftsabbruch,* ed. J. Reiter and R. Keller (Freiburg: Herder Verlag, 1992), 34–60, esp. 53–56.

precisely to be a man, then the uniqueness of the individual human becomes more than a merely genetic fact; only according to Hoerster's argument does this become a "biological triviality." Does he not also run the risk that being a man will become a biological triviality, given that he, as we have seen, cannot *justify* why and in what sense "personhood" is a *non*-biological "property"?

This is even more clear with Peter Singer. For him, the qualitative difference between *personal* "properties" and purely *biological* "properties" is in fact not recognized, and remains confused. On questions regarding which limits—besides the "capacity for sensibility"—can be set on attention to the interests of others, Singer responds: "To mark this boundary by some characteristic like intelligence or rationality would be to mark it in an arbitrary way. Why not choose some other characteristic, like skin color?"[22] Thus, the "self-consciousness" of persons is facilely designated as "higher consciousness,"[23] whereas consciousness itself, in its turn, is not designated a characteristic proper to *persons.*

In this sort of purely quantifying ontology, there is indeed no longer any place for the distinction between "biological" and "non-biological." This would mean that racists are not so wrong after all; their only error would be that they have not employed their biologically based outlook with respect to *all* human properties.

Frankly, the critique raised by Singer and Hoerster against so-called speciesism ignores precisely the fact that the rejection of all racist and sexist definitions in a certain way *presupposes* "speciesism." The theoretical grounding of racist and sexist positions is undermined precisely on the basis of the conviction that the only decisive factor is that the particular being is a member of the human race, that is, that he possesses the dignity of a *person,* and that therefore all other distinctions *within* the species are insignificant. Otherwise, how could it be wrong to segregate a particular group of people on the basis of purely biological characteristics?

Singer and Hoerster can thus claim convincingly that segregation and privileges based on purely biological characteristics are invariably due only to the fact that they exploit a "conquest" of "speciesism," or that the only criteria for distinguishing who possesses human dignity

22. Singer, *Practical Ethics,* 58.
23. *Ibid.,* chapter 3.

are those who are "human beings." By the fact, then, that on the basis of their criticism of "speciesism" they tend to level the irreconcilable incommensurability between personal-spiritual properties and those that are purely vital-biological, eliminating the distinction, they destroy precisely the basis for the rejection of purely biological criteria of discrimination.

Indeed, Singer holds that an adult chimpanzee gives more indication of personhood than a newborn baby, and that it would seem "that killing, say, a chimpanzee is worse than the killing of a human being who, because of a congenital intellectual disability, is not and never can be a person."[24] As soon, however, as this "personhood" is only a more-developed form of biological properties ("higher consciousness") and becomes thus an empty shell of words, this means that an adult chimpanzee is biologically more advanced than a newborn baby and *for this reason* he also possesses more rights. This, frankly, would truly be a post-racist position, that is, a *pure* biologism.

Infanticide: Ideal Norm and Practical-Pragmatic Norm

What, then, is Hoerster's position regarding infanticide? According to the "ideal norm," he writes, the killing of *persons* would be prohibited; fetuses, on the other hand, could be killed for *any* reason whatsoever. From this it follows that in principle newborns could also be killed for *any* reason whatsoever; in fact these certainly are not persons. An individual human that has been born becomes a person only over time; exactly when, we don't know (*ASS* 128–43).

Because of this uncertainty, the following *pragmatic*-practical norm should be imposed: "The killing of an individual human that *has been born* is prohibited," so that those babies who are already human do not get killed by mistake. In fact we can never effectively know exactly when they begin to be persons; a limit of one month, for example, would not be correct. In the first place, it is not clear-cut, and secondly it is dangerous.

According to Hoerster, then, the killing of a newborn baby that is undesired for *whatever* reason is punishable, *even though* it is certainly not yet a person, and therefore possesses no right to life. The reason is a pragmatic one: not because the baby possesses a right to life, but so as

24. *Ibid.*, 117–18.

not to violate the right to life of those who are already persons without our knowing it.

In reality, however, it seems that a limit of one month would be clearer than at birth. If this were the case, it would relieve us of the irresolvable question of whether a baby can still be killed *during* birth, for example before the umbilical cord were cut, or only after. When does a human individual begin to be a "*born* individual"? But let me put aside such macabre questions.

Of more interest is the second reason that Hoerster offers in favor of the limit being birth: the setting of a limit of one month could be justified ethically and pragmatically only on the basis of the argument based on principles (the link between personhood, interest in survival, and right to life). But this justification "would require too much of the average citizen . . . intellectually and emotionally" (*ASS* 137). For this reason it would be better to establish the emotionally understandable criterion of birth. The "average citizen" and the "average observer" would relate emotionally in a different way to a born baby than to a fetus.

But even supposing that the citizen could overcome this block and would be ready to kill a baby (e.g., during the first month), even then the fixing of a limit of one month would not be advisable, because the "average citizen would have difficulty understanding the underlying reasoning" (the principal justification of the criteria of personhood) (*ASS* 139). He would also consider the killing of small children who are a bit bigger, and thus who are possibly already persons, to be open to debate; and this must be prohibited, on the basis of the protection of the right to life of *persons*.

I consider this argument to be extremely problematical, inasmuch as it is irrelevant for democratic societies in which laws are enacted on the basis of decisions of the majority of an elected parliament. The argument would be relevant only on the empirical condition—which is to be rejected for other reasons—of an expert-ocracy (of moral and legal philosophers?) with superior vision and advanced theoretical consciousness. If the average citizen were to overcome his emotional blocks and be emotionally ready to kill a baby, the corresponding laws would follow quickly, and this *precisely* in a democratic state.[25]

25. Precisely for this reason reference is often made in this context to the Nazi era. In fact the gradual breaking down of emotional blocks was decisive in producing an emotional

In the same way, it seems very problematic when Hoerster is inclined to refer, for example, the psychological problems of women after an abortion to the "external and internal pressure of specific philosophical traditions, indeed indoctrination" (*ASS* 149). In the place of such indoctrination Hoerster wants to impose a theory that he himself says the "average citizen" can understand only with difficulty, because it would require too much of him emotionally and intellectually. One who wants to base a public juridical order on such premises could in reality accomplish his goal *only* through indoctrination.

It is likely, however, that the emotional and intellectual disposition of the "average citizen," which even today is still spontaneously inclined to see in the unborn living human being a person and a baby, is superior to Hoerster's—precisely because the existence of such an "average" disposition requires *no* indoctrination!

Two Kinds of "Rights"?

It should be evident that Hoerster's argument bears within it a decisive turn in legal thinking. According to his position there are in fact two types of "right to life": "persons" *possess* a right to life (on the basis of their being persons), that is, on the basis of the "ideal norm." Newborns, on the other hand, do not *possess* a right to life, rather it is *conceded* to them, and precisely for pragmatic reasons. This means that there is a right to life that is (pragmatically) conceded, so as to not violate the "true" or "principle" right of persons.

This leads to considerable confusion with regard to what properly a "right" or a "human right" is. This confusion is increased by the fact that Hoerster—correctly—formulates his argument based on the fact that for the average citizen, not only the justification of the principle norm, but also the distinction between ideal norms and pragmatic norms is intellectually very difficult to understand. For the average citizen, human rights (fortunately) are still something that you "possess," and not something that one "obtains by attribution" or that are "conceded" to someone (for pragmatic motives). One must not *underestimate* the intellectual capacities of "average citizens."

---

disposition toward increasingly wide practices of killing. Cf. on this K. Dörner, *Tödliches Mitleid* (Gütersloh: Jakob van Hoddis Verlag, 1988); T. Bastian, ed., *Denken—Schreiben—Töten. Zur neuen "Euthanasie"—Diskussion*, (Stuttgart: Hirzel, 1990).

From this, two things are conceivable. Either the "average citizen" (who, according to Hoerster, is unable to understand the entire argument) would understand all the rights attributed pragmatically to be "ideal norms." He would thus be expected to be convinced that the birth of a human being is that change in human life that *founds* a right to life *in principle* (in the sense of an ideal norm). One who thinks such an expectation is acceptable in the long term definitely *underestimates* the intellectual capacities of the average citizen.

Or the other, more likely possibility is this: all norms would come to be seen over time as pragmatic norms, and the concept of human rights as rights *in principle* would be emptied. Those would possess "rights" whose rights could be founded *pragmatically*.

For this reason the following claim seems to me particularly insidious (*ASS* 67–68): "That gypsies are 'men' has no need in today's society—at least publicly—of any explicit justification. Conversely, that fetuses are "men," in the context of the present debate on abortion, can be held to be true only *after* one has given the individual arguments in favor of the fact that a right to life is to be conceded to fetuses." To this one must reply decisively: that gypsies are "men" should not need to be demonstrated in *any* society; the burden of proof would rather be on those who would claim they are *not* men. With this I mean that we consider gypsies to be men is not due to the fact that today we have luckily reached the conclusion that they actually *are* men. Whoever denies gypsies and blacks to be men does not do so because he has not yet found valid arguments in favor of their being men, but rather because he does not recognize their belonging to the human species as decisive, that is, because he discriminates against them. To deny legitimately the members of a class of living things to be men is only possible by showing precisely that they are *not* members of the species *Homo sapiens*. Consequently, we consider gypsies, whites, blacks, and so on as "men," because we are speciesists! Only if—in Hoerster's way—we were not speciesists, would we need "explicit arguments" in order to convince ourselves of their being men. Thank God that today we have not yet arrived at a point in which such proofs are necessary!

All of this should show how important it is for our juridical culture to determine the right to life solely and exclusively on the basis of the criterion of whether or not an individual is a member of the species

Homo sapiens. Otherwise we would get bogged down in the mire of the "pragmatic attribution or negation" of rights—of *human* rights!

No Discrimination against the Handicapped?

An objection raised against Singer and Hoerster's thesis is that the handicapped would be considered people that should be aborted. Hoerster attempts to respond to this objection with the following reflection: the fact that someone can be aborted as a fetus has no influence on his future rights and on his status as a person. This is valid also for those who are not handicapped: every person, "even my non-handicapped neighbor," effectively could have been aborted as a fetus *for any reason whatsoever*. From this point of view, then, the handicapped are not discriminated against (*ASS* 157).

Against this, however, the following could be raised: in the case of my neighbor who is healthy, the potential having-been-aborted is a purely hypothetical possibility. He currently bears no external indication that one day, for *any* reason, he could have been aborted. With the handicapped, however, things are different: he bears the "mark" of being handicapped. He is therefore one who, according to the judgment of many (and perhaps one day of the majority), could reasonably have been aborted, or indeed *should* have been aborted. (Hoerster in fact says on p. 158 that a woman "who aborts a 'handicapped' fetus and *in place of this* gives birth to a healthy fetus—later to be a healthy person—deserves for this more praise than blame"). Concerning my healthy neighbor I can only say: clearly he *was* desired. With the handicapped, I must say: how is it that he was not aborted? There in fact would have been *clear* reasons for this. Did the mother not have access to prenatal diagnosis? Or did she irresponsibly neglect to have such diagnosis done? As opposed to the existence of my healthy neighbor, the existence of a handicapped person—and even of his parents' decision—is obliged to justify itself. And finally: he would perhaps come to be accepted because he is in fact a person; but *not* in his being handicapped, and therefore as this concrete, real human being. Certainly he would be helped, but only because his mother neglected to "laudably" abort him.

This is obviously not true only for the handicapped. They are, however, a socially clear group, even publicly identifiable. Frankly, Hoerster's argument at this point remains purely abstract, mere normative theory.

As such, the handicapped and those who advocate for them consider this argument to be the abstract, cold reasoning of a brains behind the scenes.[26]

When Hoerster stresses that this has nothing to do with considering the life of a handicapped person to be "without value," even admitting that the life of one who is handicapped could have, because of his handicap, an even *greater* value than if he were not so, he falls into an obvious contradiction with his prior claim that a woman is praiseworthy if she gives life to a healthy baby in the place of a handicapped child that she had aborted. In fact if what *we* have just said is true, the mother cannot and therefore must not decide which life would be better. If she does, she disposes over the future life of a person, and moreover implicitly reduces the value of life according to eugenic criteria. Is she praiseworthy also for this?

Hoerster notes that his solution is not a selective discrimination. In this he might be right. Contrary to those who advocate a solution based on the so-called eugenic indication, he is not in favor of the injustice of conceding a general right to life of unborn living human beings, and to then deny this right to unhealthy fetuses, thus *discriminating against them*. He does not, therefore, favor a *selective* discrimination against the unborn. Presupposed, however, that unborn living human beings *possess* a right to life, he *is* in favor of a *general* discrimination toward the unborn, and *moreover* of selective discrimination against those who have been born concerning whom there *clearly* would have been a socially recognized reason for aborting them. Thus, the baby is literally thrown out with the bathwater, according to the dictum: to eliminate sicknesses, eliminate the sick.[27]

Conclusion

It is unlikely, then, that Hoerster can cast off the suspicion that his theory is a justification of the absolute dominion of the born over the unborn—and of the healthy over the sick. Such discrimination against

26. Translation note: the German original uses the word *Schreibtischtäter,* which is the person who is intellectually responsible for crimes that he did not directly plan, want, or foresee, but for which he created the preconditions.

27. Cf. on this also R. Baumann-Hölzle, "Ethische Probleme der prenatalen Diagnostik," in *Neue Zürcher Zeitung* 10/11, no. 83 (April 1993): 9.

a "life without value" is not characteristic of Hoerster's (and Singer's) argument exclusively (also a legislation allowing for the eugenic indication is discriminatory). They, however, *accept* such discrimination with all of its consequences, and indeed attempt to articulate it in juridical-political terms. If, however, unborn human beings possess a right to life that we consider to be a legal good worthy of protection, Hoerster's position is shown to be an ideology of dominion, justifying the imposition of the interests and rights of one group of people at the cost of the interests and rights of another group.

Some Concluding Observations Concerning the Ethics of Interest

To this point I have not addressed the theoretical and meta-ethical presuppositions of the ethics of interest, which are inherently more broad. My reflections have perhaps shown the kinds of difficulties that result if we trace the rights of persons to particular actualized properties of these persons, in particular the property of being able to have desires that imply an interest in one's own survival.

It is difficult to understand, in fact, why the interests of others should be taken into consideration, or rather why such interests imply *rights*. Peter Singer approvingly cites Michael Tooley on this theme, for whom "to violate an individual's right to something is to frustrate the corresponding desire."[28] The less intense a desire there is for something, therefore, the less a right to that thing exists; if there is no (actual or virtual) desire, then no right exists at all.

This is not how we normally speak of rights. Indeed, at times we have rights that we don't even know exist. If someone is arrested, the first thing that is done is his rights are explained to him. Did he not possess these rights before they were explained? Wouldn't it be easier, then, to simply not explain anything?

For this reason it is much more reasonable to hold that the individual human has rights before he becomes conscious of them, or can have corresponding desires. This conception of rights, in reality, cannot be justified on the basis of a utilitarian ethics of interest or preferences.

28. Singer, *Practical Ethics*, 96.

Even subjective rights, in fact, are not based on a subjective fact—for example desires—but on *objective* relationships (for example, the fact of being a human being). The right of the heir to the throne of England to one day become the king of England is not based on his desire to become king, but rather on the fact that he is the oldest descendent of the reigning monarch. And he possesses this right before he is conscious of it, and even before he is *capable* of being conscious of it and of formulating corresponding desires. He even possesses this right when he has the explicit desire *not* to become the king of England.

This example is derived from Peter Singer, who says: "Prince Charles is a potential king of England, but he does not now have the rights of a king."[29] This is enlightening. Neither does the fetus, as a potential citizen, have the rights of a citizen (e.g., active and passive electoral rights). Prince Charles, however, as "potential king" already has now the right to *become* king one day. If Singer then asks, based on this example: "Why should a potential person have the rights of a person?" one should at least analogously respond: this "potential person"—allowing for the sake of argument that a person can be only potential—has at least the right to *become* a person one day; or, to put it more simply: he has the right to be born and to develop as what he is: a man, a human person. Singer does not see that the characteristic of Prince Charles being the heir to the throne of England ("potential king") consists precisely in a right that is *independent* of his desires.[30]

This means that "potential persons" can also have rights. Otherwise, Prince Charles would not have the right to one day become the king of England. In that case, however, he would not be the heir to the throne, nor even the "potential king of England." A potential person from whom you take away the right to become an "actual person" is therefore not a

29. Ibid., 153.
30. Even B. Steinbock, *Life before Birth*, 59, who typically argues with extreme precision, at this point falls into the same error. No one would want to claim that fetuses have the same rights as born persons or even as adults. When Steinbock writes: "It is a logical error to think that potential personhood implies possession of the rights of actual persons," one must bear in mind not only the ambiguity of the expression "potential personhood," but also that one must distinguish between the "rights of an adult person" and the "right to become an adult person," or the right to not be prevented from becoming one. Regardless of the concept of person used, the fetus is precisely an individual who possesses the right to become an individual born human, with all of the ulterior rights that such a born individual human in turn possesses.

potential person at all. According to Singer and Hoerster, however, he must at least be *this* absolutely.

We have already shown that and why the expression "potential person" must be avoided. Here we are addressing only the fact that we cannot reasonably speak of rights if we render such rights dependent on the knowledge and desires of the subjects to which rights must be attributed.

And this means that rights, and in particular human rights and in a completely unique way the most fundamental right, the right to life, are based on objective relationships. To be able to evaluate them, therefore, we need a theory that makes possible a *valuation* of such relationships. And it is precisely this that *is not* possible in an ethics oriented toward interests. In fact "the idea of a gradation of value of the various living beings" is held by Singer to be fundamentally mistaken.[31]

As external observers—writes Singer—we give precedence to a human life with respect to that of a mouse. But we cannot know this with certainty, because in effect we are men and therefore we have *human* interests. Moreover, Singer tends toward the opinion that "every life from the point of view of the respectively diverse beings has equal value. . . . The joys of a mouse's life are all those of a mouse, and it is to be supposed that such joys mean as much for a mouse as the joys in the life of a person mean for this person. We cannot say that one thing would be more or less precious than the other."[32]

If the value of human life is this unclear, so also will be the corresponding rights. One must always be aware of this foundation of the ethics of interest. In any case, Singer's notion contrasts even with the idea, expressed by John Stuart Mill, that the satisfaction of desires is not the only value; everything depends on the *quality* of the desires.

Beings that, even if only potentially, have qualitatively higher desires, that is, spiritual desires, are to be considered as superior to beings that possess lower desires, even if they experience these desires presently. Mills concedes even more: "It is better to be an unsatisfied human being than a satisfied pig; an unsatisfied Socrates is better than a satisfied idiot. And if the idiot or the pig are of another opinion, this is because they have *their* view of things."[33]

31. Ibid., 122.   32. Ibid., 123.
33. J. S. Mill, "Utilitarianism," chap. 2 in *Utilitarianism, On Liberty, and Considerations on Representative Government* (London: Everyman, 1972), 9.

This statement implies a doctrine of values that contrasts with every ethics of interest. It leads to the conclusion, irreconcilable with Singer's position, that, for a person, his *unsatisfied* life as a person must mean more than the "joys of a mouse's life" for a *satisfied* mouse (leaving aside the question of whether for a mouse *anything* can "have meaning"). For Mill himself, who essentially argues according to an ethics of interest, his statement implies an irresolvable paradox—yet he at least accepts it as a fact. Frankly, according to his method he would never be able to explain what is meant by the term "better." This term, the comparative of "good," is in fact not part of the vocabulary of an ethics of interest. Rather, it derives from another type of doctrine of values, which alone can explain what a "right" is.

7

The Legal Defense of Prenatal Life in
Constitutional Democracies

Introduction: The Defense of Life and the
Challenges of a "Culture of Death"

The defense of human life in its physical integrity is, unquestionably, a traditional duty of the state. This duty, however, is currently being contested in two specific areas: the beginning and the end of life. The encyclical *Evangelium Vitae* (1995) denounces the inhumanity of what it calls a "culture of death": a culture within which killing becomes an ordinary means to resolve conflict and end suffering, at times grievous and tragic, and caused to a great extent by a remarkable irresponsibility within the area of sexual behavior. The encyclical also appeals to the responsibility of the state, the legislator, democratic institutions, and the people, so that they continually guarantee a more effective safeguard of life, above all the life of the weakest, including the unborn, the elderly, the handicapped, and the terminally ill.[1]

In the following pages, I would like to show how the chap-

1. *Evangelium Vitae*, no. 90. Numerical references for *Evangelium Vitae* and the other encyclicals cited within are to the paragraph(s) of the encyclical. Quotations from *Evangelium Vitae* are from the Vatican translation (St. Paul, Minn.: Leaflet Missal Company, n.d.). The present chapter was originally published as "Fundamental Rights, Moral Law, and the Legal Defense of Life in a Constitutional Democracy: A Constitutionalist Approach to the Encyclical *Evangelium Vitae*," *American Journal of Jurisprudence* 43 (1998): 135–83.

ter in *Evangelium Vitae* that discusses the relationship between moral and civil law adopts a line of reasoning that could be called "constitutionalist." It follows closely the reasoning already propounded in the document *Donum Vitae* (1987) and in the encyclical *Centesimus Annus* (1991), which in its fifth chapter proposes a conception founded on the basic principles of modern constitutionalism: the idea of the supremacy of law over power; the separation of powers; and the protection of individual freedom based on fundamental rights. These are the constitutional presuppositions of a democracy that seeks to avoid degenerating into a tyranny of the majority.

I shall pay particular attention to the problems involving the legal protection of prenatal human life; the principles developed there are only partly applicable to the problem of euthanasia. Starting from the conviction that mere moral argument is insufficient, this essay intends to propose a line of reasoning that can insert the doctrine of *Evangelium Vitae* into the real legal-political context of today. So I shall begin with a short yet necessary reflection on the difference between a strictly moral dimension and a legal-political one. Later we shall see whether and to what extent such a distinction seems justified against the setting of traditional Christian thought. Then we shall proceed to an exposition of the doctrinal core of *Evangelium Vitae* on this subject, and to a comparative and critical analysis of the constitutional jurisprudence of the Federal Republic of Germany and of the United States of America; this analysis will yield criteria and categories for dealing appropriately with the chosen subject. In the next section, I will point out the main propositions in opposition to the legal defense of the unborn, propositions that intend to "neutralize" and render irrelevant the fundamental truths that the unborn child is a human person and that with respect to human dignity, he or she is equal to any other living person. Finally, starting from the teaching of *Evangelium Vitae* on the subject, I shall propose two arguments to show the fundamental nexus between the legal-political order and the moral law within the area of my chosen subject, the legal defense of human life.

Distinguishing between the Legal-Political and the Moral Plane

To focus effectively on the question of the defense of life through legislative action and perhaps even social assistance by the state, we must recognize two well-differentiated planes: the moral and the legal-political. *Evangelium Vitae* deals not only with ethical but also with complex legal-political themes. Addressing the relationship between the civil and the moral law, it affirms that "the purpose of civil law is different and more limited in scope than that of the moral law."[2] Not only are there *limits* regarding civil law, but the civil and the moral law have different tasks. The moral and the civil law are not subject to the same practical logic. Civil law is saturated with a *specific* ethical-practical rationality within a *specific* ambit.

Moral law—as "natural law"[3]—is nothing other than the light of the intellect or of practical reason, which orders the actions of individual human beings toward happiness, the end of human life. The moral law simply distinguishes what is good from evil within human actions. It comprises those principles that steer free and responsible human actions toward moral virtue and toward the good that perfects the agent. It ensures that a person perfects himself through his life and actions and becomes a just person with well-ordered sentiments: self-controlled, strong, courageous, and patient.

Legal-political logic is not alien to moral law or practical moral rationality, nor is it opposed to it. Nevertheless, what we could call its "formal objective" is different: it tends to make it possible for people to live in community. It tends, therefore, toward peace, freedom, and justice, which principally means "equality in freedom." The main precondition for reaching such goals is the security (conferred by the state) of being able to survive without becoming the easy prey of the stronger or the more cunning. That is why citizens grant to state authority a "monopoly of legitimate violence" (in the words of Max Weber). Only the state may legitimately use physical force or delegate such a right to specific persons or institutions. Backed by coercive authority of the modern state, civil law guarantees above all the survival and physical security of every person. This is the first element of the common good, a necessary presupposition for any other good that falls within the legislative competence of the state.

In summary, the moral law regulates the actions of the individual,

2. *Evangelium Vitae*, no.71.
3. See John Paul II, *Veritatis Splendor*, nos. 40–44.

aiming at the *goodness of one's own actions*; civil law (positive constitutional, civil, and penal law) instead regulates the relationship between individuals, aiming at the *common good*. This does not mean that moral law and the individual actions it regulates are not directed toward the good of others. Quite the contrary. The just relationship with others (which is not the "common good," but rather the "good of others") is an integral part of the goodness expressed by the actions of each individual person. The moral law dictates the corresponding behavior through its requirement that "my actions"—the actions carried out by each person— be good, so that "I may be or become just or good." Civil law, instead, seeks to regulate the *relationship between persons* so that they may live together in peace, security, and freedom, and so that among them may be established that justice which guarantees equal freedom, both political and economic. Accordingly, civil law does not aim at making men good, even if public legislative action certainly has great responsibility to promote and favor the conditions and environment where it may be possible to lead a life that is good, virtuous, and worthy of man.

Such diversity in task and logic between moral and civil law may correspond to a different logic on the basis of which the two laws may prohibit an action, such as induced abortion, or the suppression of the embryo or fetus in the womb of the mother. The moral law—that is, the moral reason that distinguishes good from evil—forbids such an action as evil and unjust. It is a sin, an act contrary to virtue, a crime against the love of one's neighbor. The person who carries it out acts in an immoral way, thus becoming a morally bad person. The moral law imposes duties so as to make good every single moral agent.

For example, the moral law prohibits all types of lies as actions contrary to the virtue of justice. Civil law, instead, will forbid lying only insofar as it is an action that harms the relationship among persons to the point of threatening the social order and their living together in peace and security. Hence, at the legal level, only lies and fraud in commercial relations (and so forth) are forbidden and punished. This prohibition means that such an action has a particular moral seriousness: an action that harms not only the good of others but also the common good (the good of order, peace, and security, as well as the existing trust among men) is morally more negative.

What is forbidden by civil law is in a moral sense very important, but the converse is not necessarily true. What may appear morally relevant and grave need not be regulated solely for that reason by civil law; in other words, it does not fall within the province of civil law to sanction moral order with the coercive power of the state. The state is not the "executor of the moral law": "to the unconditional duty to abstain in every case from directly and intentionally killing an innocent person—that is, to the absolute moral prohibition, without exception, of abortion—does not correspond an identical unconditional duty of the state to prevent all killings."[4]

If civil law were to prohibit and even punish an action such as abortion, it would do so not simply to impede an immoral act with the aim of leading men through state authority to practice virtue, to become good, and to attain happiness. It does so merely to protect the life of the one who, through such an act, would be threatened by death and deprived of his or her right to live. In addition, it would do so to protect an expectant woman from possible pressure from her environment, for instance, from the father of the baby, if he wanted to avoid the duty of paying child support. So the reasons that will lead a legislator to take legislative measures will pertain to the intrinsic nature of state authority: it would be for political reasons, in the most inclusive and noble sense of the word (in a sense, however, not contrary to "moral").[5] Safeguarding human life—that is, positive right—through civil law is a political task. The argument for justifying legislative intervention in this field must necessarily be a political or legal-political argument, which, however, *will imply* a whole series of premises: biological, anthropological, and ethical.

4. R. Spaemann, preface to the German edition of Stephen D. Schwarz, *Die verratene Menschenwürde. Abtreibung als philosophisches Problem* (Köln: Communio Verlagsgesellschaft, 1992). This was originally published as *The Moral Question of Abortion* (Chicago: Loyola University Press, 1990). With these words, Spaemann corrects the position of Schwarz, which is insufficiently developed on this point.

5. That is, in the sense of a specific "political ethics," which is "ethics," though not ethics *tout court,* but rather that specific part of ethics that refers to human actions, whose object is the common political good. The acts of institutions and public agents (e.g., legislators) are also included. On this, see Martin Rhonheimer, "Perchè una filosofia politica? Elementi storici per una risposta," *Acta philosophica* 1 (1992) 233–63. This does not mean that two different norms exist, one "moral" and the other "political," for the same act. This essay is forthcoming in English as "Why Is Political Philosophy Necessary? Historical Considerations and a Response," in a volume of my essays edited by William F. Murphy Jr., and tentatively entitled *The Common Good of Constitutional Democracy: Essays in Political Philosophy and on Catholic Social Teaching.*

From Aristotle to the Patristic Tradition

The distinction between the moral level and the legal-political level presupposes abandoning an "Aristotelian" vision of the function of the *polis* and of civil law. To Aristotle, man finds his fulfillment in the state— not the modern state, but the ancient *polis*, a community of life and law, of culture and religion. For this Greek philosopher, the task of law is to lead men to virtue. Aristotle believes that the purpose of the laws of the *polis*—conceived, still in the Platonic tradition, as an educational enterprise—is to compel corrupt men to behave according to virtue under the threat of punishment: "It is difficult to have a correct education in virtue from one's youth if one is not reared under such laws."[6]

Law is needed for everything, "even, in general, for life as a whole; as a matter of fact, more people obey out of necessity than reason, and more for punishment than for propriety."[7] The law, then, with "coercive power . . . prescribes what is morally suitable."[8] Thus, we can understand why Aristotle's *Politics* constitutes the very crown of his *Ethics*.[9]

So begins a whole tradition that understands the education of people in moral virtue to be the function par excellence of civil law. This tradition is still present in the thought of St. Thomas Aquinas, in whom, however, it is possible to identify another trend of thought, which preexisted in patristics, for instance in St. Irenaeus, but above all in St. Augustine. It was precisely Christianity, with its typical dualism, that rendered impossible the unitary conception of the Aristotelian ethics of the *polis*.

Saint Irenaeus asserts that the task of the state is nothing other than to provide security under the threat of punishment: to prevent the big fish from eating the small ones.[10] The image of the fish is not too far from Hobbes's wolves. It is, however, St. Augustine who finally includes the tempo-

---

6. Aristotle, *Nicomachean Ethics*, X, 9 1179 b 33–34.

7. Ibid., 1180 a 5–6.   8. Ibid., 1180 a 20 e25.

9. See Rhonheimer, "Perchè una filosofia politica?" For the link between Aristotelian ethics and politics, see Martin Rhonheimer, *Praktische Vernunft und Vernünftigkeit der Praxis. Handlungstheorie bei Thomas von Aquin in ihrer Entstehung aus dem Problem-kontext der aristotelischen Ethik* (Berlin: Akademie Verlag, 1994), 391 et seq. See also Martin Rhonheimer, *La prospettiva della morale. Fondamenti dell'etica filosofica* (Rome: Armando, 1994), 184 ff; this is forthcoming in English as *The Perspective of Morality: Philosophical Foundations of Thomistic Virtue Ethics* (Washington, D.C.: The Catholic University of America Press).

10. Saint Irenaeus of Lyon, *Adversus haereses*, V, 24.

ral order in the level of "fallen" reality, and who reserves to the Church the task of guiding men to salvation and moral integrity, while entrusting to the state the task of taking care of temporal goods, the foremost being peace among men. The *civitas caelestis,* or the community of believers in Christ, is not concerned with "quidquid in moribus, legibus, institutisque diversum est, quibus pax terrena vel conquiritur vel tenetur." Let the state, then, take care of *pax terrena* and it will do so legitimately "si religionem qua unus summus et verus Deus colendus docetur, non impedit."[11]

This relative indifference toward the legislative system of the state is quite distant from what will develop later as "political Augustinianism"—a program for integrating state power in an attempt to create a *res publica christiana,* in which temporal power is in the service of the salvation of the soul.[12]

St. Thomas Aquinas

St. Thomas is totally immune from this last trend, which culminates in the hierocratic theories of some curial canonists of the thirteenth century.[13] In St. Thomas we encounter both the patristic and the Aristotelian traditions, but also the very important tradition of Roman law, as well as canon law, with its propensity to limit law to the external realm.[14] In a formula that is clearly Augustinian, St. Thomas asserts that "the end of human law is temporal peacefulness in society, an end for which it is sufficient that the law prevent those evils that may disturb the peaceful conditions of society. It is instead the concern of divine law to lead men to eternal happiness."[15]

11. Saint Augustine, *De civitate Dei,* XIX, 17. See also Augustine's *De libero arbitrio,* I, 5, 39: "Ea enim [positive human law] vindicanda sibi haec adsumit, quae satis sint conciliandae paci hominibus imperitis et quanta possunt per hominem regi."

12. See H. X. Arquilliere, *L'Augustinisme politique. Essai sur la formation des théories politiques du Moyen Age,* 2nd ed. (Paris: J. Vrin, 1955); J. J. Chevalier, *Storia del pensiero politico,* vol. 1, 2nd ed. (Bologna: Il Mulino, 1989), 256–80; R. W. Carlyle and A. J. Carlyle, *A History of Mediaeval Political Theory in the West,* 6 vols. (Edinburgh-London: William Blackwood, 1903–36, 1970 reprint).

13. M. Grabmann, *Studien über den Einfluss der aristotelischen Philosophie auf die mittelalterlichen Theorien über das Verhältnis von Kirche und Staat* (Sitzungsberichte der Bayerischen Akademie der Wissenschaften, Philosophisch-historische Abteilung, 1934, Heft 2), (Munich: Verlag der Bayer. Akad. d. Wiss./ C. H. Beck, 1934), 41–60; Carlyle and Carlyle, *History of Mediaeval Political Theory,* vol. 2,

14. See Thomas Gilby, *Principality and Polity: Aquinas and the Rise of State Theory in the West* (London: Longmans, Green,1958), xxiii.

15. "Legis enim humanae finis est temporalis tranquillitas civitatis ad quem finem per

St. Thomas is aware that not everything that is regulated by divine law can also be regulated by human law. This asymmetry, however, is not necessarily a defect; it belongs instead to the order anticipated by eternal law.[16] Nevertheless, human law must never approve what divine law forbids.[17] "Not regulating" and "not prohibiting" is not the equivalent of "approving" or even commanding. From the moral viewpoint, imperfection—a deficient character—belongs to the very nature of human law. What is morally "imperfect" may be optimal, and (more or less) perfect from a legal-political point of view (therefore, also from the standpoint of political ethics).

This is how St. Thomas gives his celebrated formula according to which civil law does not intend to suppress all human vices: "but only the most serious ones, from which even the majority of men are able to abstain, and above all those that harm others, *without the prohibition of which the preservation of society would not be possible*—just as human law forbids murder, theft, and similar things."[18]

It seems evident that such an assertion is very far from the Aristotelian spirit. St. Thomas certainly does not deny that even civil law must create an environment favorable to human virtue. But these conditions are above all conditions of justice, of human interrelations, which constitute the cornerstones for living a good life. St. Thomas already distinguishes *peccatum* from *crimen*;[19] not everything that in conscience is sin can be the subject of human legislation. That subject matter is limited to what may be ordered for the common good of civil society

---

venit lex cohibendo exteriores actus, quantum ad illa mala quae possunt perturbare pacificum statum civitatis. Finis autem legis divinae est perducere hominem ad finem felicitatis aeternae." *Summa theologiae* I-II, q.98, a.1.

16. See ibid., I-II, q.93, a.3, ad 3: "Unde hoc ipsum quod lex humana non se intromittat de his quae dirigere non potest, ex ordine legis aeternae provenit."

17. Ibid.: "Secus autem esset si approbaret ea quae lex aeterna reprobat."

18. Ibid.: "sed solum graviora, a quibus possibile est maiorem partem multitudinis abstinere; et praecipue quae sunt in nocumentum aliorum, *sine quorum prohibitione societas humana conservari non potest,* sicut lege humana prohibentur homicidia et furta et huiusmodi" (I-II, q.96, a.2). See also II-II, q.69, a.2, ad 1: "multum secundum leges humanas impunita relinquuntur quae secundum divinum iudicium sunt peccata, sicut patet in simplici fornicatione"; ibid. q.77, a.1, ad 1: "lex humana non potuit prohibere quidquid est contra virtutem, sed ei sufficit ut prohibeat ea quae destruunt hominum convictum."

19. Gilby, *Principality and Polity,* 175–87. Beginning with Thomas Hobbes, this distinction will become crucial for criminal law.

either in an immediate manner, as when something is established directly for the common good, or in a mediated manner, that is, when something is established by the legislator insofar as it is part of the good discipline characteristic of citizens so that the common good of justice and peace is preserved.[20]

The phrase "good discipline" refers to external behavior between persons, a characteristic of the limitations and specificity of human law that does not address simply the province of the goodness of men or of citizens, but rather the conservation of peace and justice in the social order, the *common good* of men living in society.

We must add, however, that neither the patristic-Augustinian tradition nor the thought of St. Thomas corresponds to a theoretically elaborated differentiation in principle between an area of virtuous perfection of the person and a more properly legal-political area. For St. Augustine, the limited character of the duty of any temporal authority is due to the transient character of any reality of this world. Salvation and moral perfection are the prerogative of the spiritual power of the Church: one becomes good and saintly as a member of the *civitas caelestis*. According to St. Thomas, also, it is not the specific duty of human law to make men good, despite the fact that for him social reality and state authority are "natural" and not a consequence of original sin as they are for St. Augustine. In the end, it is a typically Christian reservation, echoing the principle of giving to Caesar what is Caesar's and to God what is God's.

The Modern Conception of the State and Civil Law

The principle and the reservation just mentioned undergo a radicalization and transformation in modern thought. Against the background of the bloody ideological-religious conflicts of early modernity, an answer is sought to the question of the rational basis for the sovereign power of the state. The state is no longer conceived as a fact; rather, its existence requires a logical, well-constructed justification that must simultaneously clarify the duty and function of both the state and its legislative power.

---

20. "sed solum de illis qui sunt ordinabiles ad bonum commune, vel immediate, sicut cum aliqua directe propter bonum commune fiunt; vel mediate, sicut cum aliqua ordinantur a legislatore pertinentia ad bonam disciplinam, per quem cives informantur, ut commune bonum iustitiae et pacis conservent" (*Summa theologiae* I-II, q.96, a.3).

The first answer, whose unquestionable proponent is Thomas Hobbes, bases the legitimacy of the state on its ability to ensure the survival of the individual: his right to live and prosper is guaranteed only if he can live in security, if his neighbor is not an insidious wolf but a person with whom he can live in trust. It is therefore necessary to transfer the right to self-defense and recourse to violence to a sovereign above everyone. Thus, peace, the first condition for a dignified and prosperous life assured by freedom, is established through a pact of mutual and spontaneous renunciation of self-defense, with the consequent submission to a sovereign authorized to defend everyone's life and enforce the laws.[21]

In its fundamental traits, even though it is only a part of the truth, the utilitarian logic of a pact for the mutual and spontaneous renunciation of self-defense, as delineated by Hobbes, is still valid today. An essential part of the civil behavior of a normal citizen can be explained only on the basis of his willingness to submit to a civil power in exchange for a guarantee of certain vital goods. He has renounced protecting them by himself for the purpose of reaching in this way a more advantageous state in the long run. Perhaps we do not realize that as citizens we have already internalized such a logic, accustomed as we are to this renunciation of self-defense and to the functioning of the institutions guaranteeing our security.

History soon provided evidence of the need to guarantee security not only from the wolves that are other men, but also from the only remaining wolf: the state with its institutions. Thus we come to the birth of a more nuanced thought, represented by Locke and Montesquieu in line with the Anglo-Saxon tradition of the rule of law. Rights of liberty—fundamental rights directed to limiting the power of the state—are discovered, positively guaranteed, and made capable of being claimed before a judge. It is the birth of modern constitutionalism.

It is within this context that we must place today the question of the legal defense of life, especially prenatal life. It is insufficient simply to underline the immoral character of procured abortion, or of what is called "active euthanasia," in order to establish the need for a corresponding legislative, even penal, rule. We could then ask why the state

21. In addition to many other studies on the philosopher from Malmesbury, I take the liberty of referring to my analysis: Martin Rhonheimer, *La filosofia politica di Thomas Hobbes: coerenza e contraddizioni di un paradigma* (Rome: Armando, 1997).

must protect the life of the unborn, when its abstention from taking any measure in that regard would not constitute any threat to peaceful coexistence among men.

It is clear that according to basic principles, Thomistic as well as Hobbesian, the law must repress and criminalize those sins that would be harmful to peace among men. The logic of the modern, contractarian tradition is decidedly utilitarian, and in this sense limited. It does not work in those cases where we discriminate against a group of human beings—not yet born or of a particular race or color—among whom, by definition, the discriminators cannot ever be included.

It seems obvious that within the context of the principles stated, an argument favorable to the legislative regulation of abortion takes on a particular difficulty. In what sense is a human legislator competent to prohibit an act that is undoubtedly sinful but that seems to disturb only minimally the peaceful coexistence among men living in tranquility, order, and justice? We shall come back to this crucial problem later.

Civil Law and the Defense of the Unborn before the Contemporary Age

It seems that within the pre-modern tradition, one can find scarce help in addressing the problem just mentioned, since only two criteria were then prevailing. One determines what was to be forbidden by civil law, that is, those vices that make it impossible for men to live together. The other criterion identifies iniquity, the intrinsic injustice of a law, the fact that the law *may command* something contrary to natural or divine law, or that it *may impose excessively onerous obligations or burdens* on citizens. Such a "law" would be a form of violence rather than a law, and would give rise to an obligation to disobey.[22] These criteria do not, in principle, anticipate the case of a possible legislative tolerance toward the practice of abortion. Yet we cannot derive from the practice of abortion a legislator's duty to repress it by law and to impose punishment for it. At least this is not evident and requires a broader treatment of the question.[23]

22. See *Summa theologiae* I-II, q.96, a.4. We should also interpret I–II, q.93, ad 2, in this way.

23. Let us not forget that the idea of a state as the comprehensive ordering power, obligated to safeguard the goods of the citizens and, moreover, with the possibility of unjust *legislative omissions*, presupposes the concept and modern reality of the state.

A second problem follows. Even if the moral verdict of Christian tradition with respect to abortion was clear, usually it did not satisfactorily distinguish between abortion and contraception. Under the influence of St. Augustine, both contraception and the killing of the fetus were considered sins against one of the goods of marriage, the *bonum prolis*.[24] The legal defense of the unborn through punishment by temporal authority was almost never considered. In twelfth-century England, abortion cases seem to have been delegated to ecclesiastical courts for trial.[25] The first great European penal code to provide for a penalization of abortion was the Constitutio criminalis Carolina of 1532. It was difficult, however, to prosecute abortion in court because of the lack of proof. One finds convictions for infanticide, but rarely for procured abortion.[26] Even in English common law, under the influence of the theory of later quickening, abortion as simple *misprision* (infraction or crime) was distinguished from actual *homicide*. Only in the seventeenth century, with new scientific discoveries, does awareness increase of the beginning of human life with conception.[27] This scientific progress is reflected in the first codifications of law infused by an Enlightenment spirit. Thus, the Preussische Allgemeine Landrecht of 1794 (I, 1, 10) decrees that "the universal rights of humanity are applicable also to children not yet born, from the moment of their conception." The Austrian Allgemeine Bürgerliche Gesetzbuch of 1811 (para. 22), still in force today, and the

24. Moreover, under the influence of St. Augustine and the later decretal *Si Aliquis*, medieval penitential practice treated as "murderers" both he who procured an abortion of a "formed" fetus (i.e., animated with human life, after the fortieth day) and those who practiced contraception because of lust, whereas it was considered less serious to procure the abortion of a "non-formed" fetus (i.e., before the fortieth day from conception). Saint Augustine's decisive text is *De nuptiis et concupiscentiis*, I, c. 15, n. 17 (CSEL: vol. 42, p. 230), taken up again in the *Sententiae* by Peter Lombard, lib. iv, Dist. XXXI, cap. 3, and then commented on throughout the Scholastic age. For the decretal *Si Aliquis*, see Noonan, *Contraception*, 168–69; 176–77.

25. See John Keown, *Abortion, Doctors, and the Law: Some Aspects of the Legal Regulation of Abortion in England from 1803 to 1982* (New York: Cambridge University Press, 1988), 5; D. J. Horan and T. J. Balch, "*Roe v. Wade*: No Basis in Law, Logic, or History," in *The Abortion Controversy. 25 Years after Roe v. Wade: A Reader,* ed. Louis P. Pojman and Francis Beckwith Seconde Edition (Belmont Calif.: Wadsworth Publishing Company, 1998), 74–94, esp. 76–84.

26. See R. Jütte, ed., *Geschichte der Abtreibung, Von der Antike bis zur Gegenwart* (Munich: C. H. Beck, 1993), 85.

27. A brief summary of the development of concepts regarding the beginning of human life can be found in Norman M. Ford, *When Did I Begin? Conception of the Human Individual in History, Philosophy, and Science* (New York: Cambridge University Press, 1988), 19–51.

Bavarian Penal Code of 1813 followed in the same spirit. In 1803, the first statute against abortion was issued in England, narrowing further the equivalence between abortion and homicide of the "quick fetus" (a fetus that already moves). This represents a noteworthy change relative to the common law; all subsequent legislation is subject to the influence of new medical knowledge.[28]

Without going into the particulars of a very complex history, we can see that the problem of the state's defense of unborn life is a relatively modern theme. The problem became more urgent with progress in science and health. As Robert Spaemann has written, in the past abortion was a drama performed in the penumbras of society.[29] That is no longer true today. Abortion has become readily accessible in an easy, safe manner. The great problem of the "liberalization" of abortion, which has been made into an ordinary service in medical institutions and is even financed by health insurance, is that society and the state, with full responsibility, officially plan the killing of unborn human beings. It is no longer a question of tolerating what is notoriously an evil, but rather of making it easily accessible to anyone, with the backing of the state. Causing directly the death of innocent beings thus becomes an ordinary means protected by law for resolving conflicts as old as human sexuality.

The problem of the "culture of death" is not, therefore, that of a "moral collapse" of society, but rather the effect of the acquisition of a new power over life, made accessible by modern science. This is also true in a special way for the problem of euthanasia, made more acute by the fact that within the framework and ethos of modern medicine it no longer seems justifiable to take every action capable of prolonging life. By contrast, the modern state is the first in history that possesses the means to guarantee an effective defense of prenatal life; the modern state may nevertheless become an accomplice in the planned killing of unwanted human lives, or life that has become burdensome for the welfare system.[30]

28. See Keown, *Abortion, Doctors, and the Law*.
29. R. Spaemann, "Sind alle Menschen Personen?" in *Bioethik*, ed. R. Löw, *Philosophisch-theologische Beiträge zu einem brisanten Thema* (Cologne: Communio, 1990), 48–58; here: 56.
30. Interesting impressions of this problem in Holland are reported by O. Tolmien, *Wann ist der Mensch ein Mensch? Ethik auf Abwegen* (München: Hanser, 1993), 77–96. See also Dörner, *Tödliches Mitleid*; Bastian, *Denken-Schreiben-Töten*.

It is just this social context that has stimulated the magisterium of the Church to intervene against the increasingly widespread trend to "justify certain crimes against life in the name of the rights of individual freedom," demanding "not only exemption from punishment but even authorization by the State, so that these things can be done with total freedom and indeed with the free assistance of health care systems."[31]

So, according to *Evangelium Vitae*, it is not simply a question of asking the state not to interfere in a "private sphere," but instead of claiming "abortion rights," such as the right to be able to dispose of the life of the unborn, even with the support and help of public health systems and coverage by health insurance. It is within the context of the call for a "legal legitimation" of an alleged "right to kill" that the magisterium reminds us of certain principles regarding the relationship between moral and civil law.[32]

According to *Evangelium Vitae*, the problem is twofold. It is first a problem of democracy, in which on the basis of the vote of the majority any law may be sanctioned. Second, however, it is also a problem of constitutional law, which as such rises above democratic and legislative mechanisms.

The encyclical maintains that "objective moral law which, as the 'natural law' written in the human heart, is the obligatory point of reference for civil law itself,"[33] will always be the measure of the legitimacy of any vote in a democracy. The democratic process cannot be "reduced to a mere mechanism for regulating different and opposing interests on a purely empirical basis."[34] To assert that at times it is necessary to accept such a reductive role, for lack of a better way to assure social peace, certainly contains "some element of truth"; but in that case, the encyclical adds, "without an objective moral grounding not even democracy is capable of ensuring a stable peace."[35]

In this way, *Evangelium Vitae* confirms the central doctrine of the encyclical *Centesimus Annus*,[36] that an absolute truth about man, not a relativist philosophy, is the foundation of democracy. When reading

---

31. *Evangelium Vitae*, no. 4; cf. ibid., no. 11.
32. Cf. *Evangelium Vitae*, no. 68.
34. Ibid.
36. See nos. 44–47.

33. Ibid., no. 70.
35. Ibid.

Evangelium Vitae, one should not forget that the innovation of *Centesimus Annus* was the affirmation of a fundamental congruence between this truth about the human person and the modern culture of human rights, which is clearly seen in the principle of *the submission of democracy to law and human rights,*[37] that is, according to the tradition of the rule of law and the corresponding separation of powers.[38]

Obviously, in the absence of such an institutional-juridical perspective, referring to "objective moral law" or to the existence of "essential and innate human and moral values which flow from the very truth of the human being and . . . safeguard the dignity of the person" would remain a sterile and ineffective appeal. Hence "no individual, no majority and no State can ever create, modify, or destroy" such values, but instead they "must only acknowledge, respect, and promote" them.[39] At this point, we are much closer to the language of modern constitutionalism than to that of tradition.

In my judgment, *Evangelium Vitae* does not intend to cast any doubt on the legitimacy of democratic majoritarian mechanisms. It does not even suggest that a law not in full consonance with the moral law is *ipso facto* illegitimate. The encyclical does not establish an opposition between democracy and a culture of human rights on the one hand and the moral law on the other. It declares, instead, that *civil law—meaning, primarily, constitutions with fundamental personal rights—includes a morally relevant dimension: the expression of that truth about man which in the end is also the measure of the legitimacy of any decision made by a democratic majority.*

We can thus assert that the argument of *Evangelium Vitae* is strictly constitutionalist. It situates itself at the legal-political level, but with the peculiarity of integrating that level (following its own "political" logic) and the ethical sphere, that is, the source of all human rights inasmuch as they are a secularized product of an ethos formed within the Judeo-Christian tradition with the support of Greek philosophy.

Here it is useful to cite the central passage of *Evangelium Vitae* (no. 71) on the subject:

---

37. *Centesimus Annus,* no. 47.   38. Ibid., no. 44.
39. *Evangelium Vitae,* no. 71.

Certainly *the purpose of civil law* is different and more limited in scope than that of the moral law. . . .[It] is that of ensuring the common good of people through the recognition and defense of their fundamental rights, and the promotion of peace and of public morality. The real purpose of civil law is to guarantee an ordered social existence in true justice. . . . Precisely for this reason, civil law must ensure that all members of society enjoy respect for certain fundamental rights which innately belong to the person, rights which every positive law must acknowledge and guarantee.

The constitutionalist imprint of these formulations is easily perceived: the power of the state is subordinated to the acknowledgment and guarantee of individual rights. The words just quoted, however, recall the essentially *ethical* or moral status of these rights. Thus, the mediation between moral exigencies and the legal-political order is carried out through constitutional law insofar as it includes fundamental rights. The encyclical does not deny the "diverse" and "limited" character of civil law and its specific ends (peace, orderly social coexistence, justice, public morality); at the same time, however, it teaches that such functions have their roots in that truth which came to be known as "human rights."

Admittedly, there are other interpretations that ignore fundamental rights understood as an expression of a truth and view them as a sort of least common denominator in a pluralistic society that forgoes any formulation of a "common good" in terms of substantive values. Without discussing the problem at this point, let us continue with the text of the encyclical, which now goes a step further:

First and fundamental among these [rights] is the inviolable right to life of every innocent human being. While public authority can sometimes choose not to put a stop to something which—were it prohibited—would cause more serious harm, it can never presume to legitimize as a right of individuals— even if they are the majority of the members of society—an offense against other persons caused by the disregard of so fundamental a right as the right to life. (No. 71)

Finally, here is the passage that includes perhaps the decisive argument from a practical-legal viewpoint:

The legal toleration of abortion or of euthanasia can in no way claim to be based on respect of the conscience of others, precisely because society has the right and duty to protect itself against the abuses which can occur in the name of conscience and under the pretext of freedom. (No. 71)

So the encyclical proposes a three-part thesis:

1. The unborn (individuals belonging to the species *homo sapiens* in embryo and fetal form) possess a right to life. The question therefore is placed within the scope of fundamental rights.

2. It follows that such unborn individuals are human persons appropriately entitled to such rights.

3. The state has the duty not only to respect fundamental rights of liberty, but also to have them respected against interference by others; in the case of abortion, this means interference by the mother (perhaps under pressure by others) and by the doctor.

This last point is the decisive one, because it clearly implies affirmations 1 and 2. There are those who deny point 3. There are also those, however, such as Ronald Dworkin, who deny that this question is pertinent to "individual rights." Finally, there is the most extreme theory, but very influential because it is internally coherent, which does not deny that 1 is relevant, *provided that the unborn is truly a person,* the acknowledgment of which is, however, denied both to the unborn and to the baby after birth at least up to a certain stage (the view of Mary Anne Warren, Michael Tooley, Peter Singer, Helga Kuhse, and Norbert Hoerster). We will discuss this later.

The doctrine of the encyclical truly opens an avenue for an argument regarding fundamental rights and freedoms in a constitutional state.[40] Let us see now how the question presents itself in two concrete cases: the Federal Republic of Germany and the United States of America. The ethical-political discussion, if it hopes to be practical and truly relevant, must necessarily face the real problem within the juridical order of the state.

The Protection of Life in Constitutional States: The Federal Republic of Germany and the United States of America

The constitutional state that recognizes fundamental individual rights, more than any other type of state, is compelled by its own inner

40. I omit the first paragraph of no. 72 because I consider it unimportant: the doctrine of the law that is unjust because it goes against natural law is applicable only in those cases in which civil law *commands* or *orders* something to be done that is immoral. In the case of

legal-political logic to provide an effective defense of life, including the lives of the unborn. A thorough analysis of the differences between Germany and the United States will give us sufficient grounds for judgment. What interests us in both cases is the jurisprudence of the supreme constitutional courts. Their approaches take on a paradigmatic value insofar as they are antithetical.[41]

To a certain extent it is possible for the constitutional state not to recognize and protect the right to life of the unborn. It depends on the political will. My argument, therefore, is a judgment not of political facts—which, in my view, do not correspond to what legal logic requires—but of the legal-political ethics that animate democratic constitutionalism. What I am concerned to highlight is that such a will can never be based on law; rather, it is precisely the legal-political logic that points the way toward an effective legal defense of prenatal life.

The Jurisprudence of the German Constitutional Court and Its Implications

In Germany, the recognition of fundamental rights began in the 1960s to evolve from their interpretation as simple individual "freedoms" claimed in order to protect the individual from the state to a more "institutional" understanding of them. Fundamental rights not

---

abortion, this is not the fundamental problem. No one defends the right of the legislator to order the carrying out of abortions. In the extreme case of the state's total abstention from protecting the life of the unborn, there is no unjust law for the simple reason that there is no law.

41. See also Mary Ann Glendon, *Abortion and Divorce in Western Law* (Cambridge, Mass.: Harvard University Press, 1987), 24 ff; H. Kaup, *Der Schwangerschaftsabbruch aus verfassungsrechtlicher Sicht. Eine rechtvergleichende Untersuchung anhand des deutschen und des amerikanischen Rechts* (Frankfurt: Peter Lang, 1991); H. Reis, *Das Lebensrecht des ungeborenen Kindes als Verfassungsproblem* (Tübingen: J. C. B. Mohr Paul Siebeck, 1984). For information on legislation and related problems in different countries, see United Nations (Department of Economic and Social Development), *Abortion Policies: A Global Review,* 3 vols. (New York: UN, 1992); P. Sachdev, ed., *International Handbook on Abortion* (New York: Greenwood Press, 1988); A. Eser and H. G. Koch, eds., *Schwanger-schaftsabbruch im internationalen Vergleich. Rechtliche Regelungen—Soziale Rahmenbedin-gungen—Empirische Grundlagen* (Teil 1: Europa; Teil 2: Aussereuropa) (Baden-Baden: Nomos Verlagsgesellschaft, 1987 and 1989); E. Ketting and Ph. von Pragg, *Schwanger-schaftsabbruch. Gesetz und Praxis im internationalen Vergleich* (Tubingen: Reihe DGVT, 1985); S. J. Frankowski and G. F. Cole, *Abortion and Protection of the Human Fetus: Legal Problems in a Cross-Cultural Perspective* (Dordrecht: Martinus Nijhoff, 1987); E. von Hippel, "Der Schwangerschaftsabbruch in rechtsvergleichender Sicht," in *Chancen für das ungeborene Leben,* ed. H. von Voss et al. (Cologne: Cologne University Verlag, 1988), 69–94.

only represent the freedoms of the individual in relation to the state but also express an order of values to be realized by the political community; they constitute the aims that define state functions and tasks.[42]

From the standpoint of the theory of fundamental rights, a decision of the Federal Constitutional Court on 25 February 1975[43] regarding an attempt by the Bundestag to liberalize abortion,[44] was a decisive turning point. It was a turning point in understanding that fundamental rights (in particular the right to life) not only guarantee immunity from interference or threats by the state (the liberal idea of the *status negativus,* of law that protects *against* the state), but also confer on the individual, through state action, the right to protection from similar interference by others, as is the case of the unborn with respect to the mother or doctors.[45]

The decision of the Federal Constitutional Court thus includes two fundamental affirmations. First of all, the *nasciturus* (literally, "one who is to be born") is not a being "not yet human," but is in the course of de-

---

42. See H. P. Bull, *Die Staatsaufgaben nach dem Grundgesetz* (Kronberg: Athenäum Verlag, 1977), esp. 155 ff; P. Häberle, *Die Wesensgehaltgarantie des Art. 19 Abs. 1 Grundgesetz. Zugleich ein Beitrag zum institutionellen Verständnis der Grundrechte und zur Lehre vom Gesetzesvorbehalt,* 3rd expanded ed. (Heidelberg: C. F. Müller, 1983), partially translated into Italian under the title: *Le libertà fondamentali nello Stato costituzionale,* ed. P. Ridola (Rome: La Nuova Italia Scientifica, 1992); K. Löw, *Die Grundrechte. Verständnis und Wirklichkeit in beiden Teilen Deutschlands* (Munich: UTB/Verlag Dokumentation, 1977).

43. The most important passages from the judgment are found in the excellent book by H. Thomas and W. Kluth, eds., *Das zumutbare Kind. Die zweite Bonner Fristenregelung vor dem Bundesverfassungsgericht* (Herford: Busse-Seewald, 1993). The original version of Häberle's important study, mentioned in the preceding footnote, goes back to 1962, and it therefore does not include this pivotal decision of the *Bundesverfassungsgericht.* In the expanded edition of 1983 the decision is mentioned briefly (at 289) in a manner that shows how this judgment establishes that the *nasciturus*'s right to life unconditionally prevails over competing interests.

44. For the history of the debate, see M. Gante, §218 in *der Diskussion. Meinungs- und Willensbildung 1954–1976,* Forschungen und Quellen zur Zeitgeschichte vol. 21 (Düsseldorf: Droste Verlag, 1991).

45. Fundamental in this respect: J. Isensee, *Das Grundrecht auf Sicherheit. Zu den Schutzpflichten des freiheitlichen Verfassungsstaates* (Schriften der Juristischen Gesellschaft e.V. Berlin, Heft 79) (Berlin-New York: Walter de Gruyter, 1983); E. Klein, "Grundrechtliche Schutzpflicht des Staates," *Neue Juristische Wochenschrift* 42 (1989): 1633–40; H. Tröndle, "Der Schutz des ungeborenen Lebens in unserer Zeit," *Zeitschrift für Rechtspolitik* 22 (1989): 54–61; D. Lorenz, "Recht auf Leben und körperliche Unversehrt-heit," in *Handbuch des Staatsrecht der Bundesrepublik Deutschland,* vol. 6, ed. J. Isensee and P. Kirchhof (Heidelberg: C. F. Müller, 1989), 3–39. See also W. Kluth, "Verfassungauftrag Lebensschutz. Vorgeburtlicher Lebensschutz zwischen staalicher Anmassung und verfassungsrechtlicher Pflicht," 93–117, and W. Höfling, "Die Abtreibungsproblematik und das Grundrecht auf Leben," 119–144, in Thomas and Kluth, *Das zumutbare Kind.*

veloping its humanity; it is a human being that is developing at all time *as a human being* (a process that obviously continues for many years after birth). On the basis of that premise, the court equates the right to life of the unborn with that of any other human life, explicitly declaring that in the phrase "everyone possesses the right to life" (in article 2, section 2 of the *Grundgesetz*), the word "everyone" refers to each living human individual, including therefore the unborn human being. It follows that his or her right to life prevails at any time over the mother's right to self-determination.[46]

The second affirmation recognizes that the right to life of the unborn requires the state not only to abstain from any interference with the life of the unborn, but also to protect that life if threatened by others. Since the right to life is the fundamental good, the source for any other right or legal entitlement of the individual, any legally recognized interference that would contradict it cannot be tolerated in principle, with the exception of a case relating to the application of the principle of proportionality (for instance, when the life of the unborn child seriously threatens the mother's life).[47]

A dissenting opinion in this case asserted that fundamental rights should have the function only of protecting the individual from interference by the state; a right to life would exist only to safeguard oneself from the state's threats to life. This theory—which I shall henceforth refer to as a "proto-liberal" view—assumes that conferring a duty on the state to restrict the freedom and ostensibly private choices of its citizens perverts the essential meaning of the aforementioned rights.[48] Precise-

46. According to article 1, section 1, of the *Grundgesetz,* the state has a duty to respect and protect human dignity. In the abortion decision by the German Constitutional Court in 1993, the court stated that the Human Dignity Clause of article 1 is the basis of the state's duty to protect the right to life, which is affirmed in article 2, section 2.

47. This position has been confirmed by the second judgment of the German Constitutional Court, in 1993; the whole text can be found in *Juristen Zeitung* (special edition) of June 7, 1993. On the law voted by the *Bundestag* in 1992 that brought about this judgment, see the study, stemming from an expert's report requested by the Bavarian government, by M. Kriele, *Die nicht-therapeutische Abtreibung vor dem Grundgesetz* (Berlin: Dunker and Humblot, 1992). The report commissioned to Professor Albin Eser by the Bundestag instead reached a conclusion favorable to the law that was finally declared unconstitutional by the Constitutional Court; cf. A. Eser, *Schwangerschaftsabbruch: Auf dem verfassungsrechtlichen Prüfstand. Rechtsgutachen im Normenkontrollverfahren zum Schwangeren- und Familienhilfegesetz von 1992* (Baden-Baden: Nomos Verlagsgesellschaft, 1994).

48. This argument has remained without decisive influence on legal doctrine: see P. Preu,

ly this theory, however—underlying the decision of the U.S. Supreme Court in *Roe v. Wade*—is rejected by the German Federal Constitutional Court with the double affirmation that the unborn child possesses a fundamental right to life, just as any other living human being does, and that the state is obliged to intervene to protect it from aggression by third parties.

Such a stand in favor of state intervention is based on a Hobbesian argument: the coercive power of the state is legitimized precisely by its function of establishing security, order, and peaceful coexistence among men.[49] For this purpose, the citizens delegate to the state a monopoly of legitimate violence, renouncing the right to defend themselves or to take the law into their own hands, thus establishing a mutual linkage of subordination and protection. This development, however, clearly implies that the state also has the duty of guaranteeing the security and protection of the individual, who has freely deprived himself of the possibility of self-protection. The "liberal" notion of freedoms *in opposition* to the state, to protect *against* the state's interference, is established only later in history. As Professor Isensee stresses, the liberal and constitutionalist idea of freedoms asserted against the state already presupposes the state's protective function. Liberty has two sides: security *by means of* the state and security *in relation to* the state. These are the two sides of civil liberty.[50]

Especially in the case of the unborn, the mere *status negativus* (freedom and security from the state) is obviously insufficient. For the unborn, the greatest threat is not the state, but the mother. So if the state does not confer protection, the right to life would serve no purpose for the unborn (the same is true for babies already born but still small and totally defenseless). It seems logical, then, that the only means for the

Freiheitsgefährdung durch die Lehre von den grundrechtlichen Schutzpflichten, *Juristen Zeitung* 46 (1991): 265–71, esp. 266; and R. Wahl and J. Masing, "Schutz durch Eingriff?" *Juristen Zeitung* 45 (1990): 553–63. The notion "protoliberal" refers to the first of two historical phases of liberalism. The first phase is characterized by the establishment of individual rights against the state (e.g., the absolutist state). The second phase adheres to the view that individual rights are to protect persons not only from the sovereign state but also from one another (that is, from other persons). In this second historical phase, it is widely understood that a political society is shaped by persons living together in mutual respect of rights.

49. See Isensee, *Das Grundrecht auf Sicherheit*; and also Klein, *Grundrechtliche Schutzpflicht des Staates*, 1635–37.

50. Isensee, *Das Grundrecht auf Sicherheit*, 6; 21–26.

unborn to enjoy an effective right to life is through the state's guarantee to protect that life from private interference, from whoever may be interested in eliminating it.

As we have already mentioned, however, the problem is that the implicit calculation in a self-renunciation of private defense, even if it turns out to be particularly suitable as the basis for the duty of the state to safeguard life against threats from third parties, does not seem to work in the case of the unborn. Even if protecting prenatal life now appears to be an incontestable duty of the state, it is not clear how it can be sufficiently motivated by a purely contractarian logic. Once the right to life of the unborn is granted, we cannot see how to deduce in a cogent manner the duty of the state to protect prenatal life on the basis of a merely utilitarian conception, whether of the Hobbesian or Lockean type. It seems that the state protects only the interests of the *born,* that is, those who represent the parties to the social contract. This appears to be implied, at least hypothetically, in the image of mutual self-renunciation and subordination to state power.

The dilemma is evident also in the question of the measures with which the state must carry out its protective role. These must be proportional, reasonable, and not excessive. For instance, it would be contrary to those principles to expect that the state place under the surveillance of a policeman every expectant mother until birth, to prevent a possible abortion. The protection of the unborn must nevertheless be effective. Discussions mainly concern the question of whether the most appropriate means is the penal code or some other measure(s). In 1975, the Federal Constitutional Court established that whenever other measures for the defense of the life of the unborn prove to be ineffective, the state is obliged to intervene with the criminal law.[51]

Abortion undoubtedly remains an *unlawful act* (*rechtswidrig*). So it

51. According to the 1993 judgment and the subsequent law adopted in 1995, the legislator can, without violating the Constitution, largely renounce the use of the criminal law, resorting to preventive and compulsory counseling in order to encourage the expectant mothers to accept the baby. By renouncing the resort to the criminal law, appealing to the woman's sense of responsibility, and stressing the availability of social assistance, the court's decision was meant to ensure that this counseling gave more effective protection to the unborn. That objective, however, seems to have been undermined by the 1995 law, which declares that the counseling must be "open to any outcome," in the sense of precluding any attempt to influence the women's decision. In most instances, this effectively limits the counselor to providing information about the availability of abortion and issuing the required certificate, which,

is out of the question that it could be regulated as an ordinary service, provided by the health care system. It cannot be financed by insurance, because the state would thus be favoring, indirectly, an illegal act. We can also affirm that the state is obliged to promote measures capable of preventing situations of serious conflict, creating a climate of respect for life (and therefore rejecting any pro-abortion propaganda by public means). Furthermore, it is the task of public authorities to organize or stimulate specific private initiatives, to promote a social net capable of guaranteeing the survival of babies born but rejected by their mothers, thereby encouraging expectant mothers to give birth to their babies. In a culture of life, not death, completion of the pregnancy would be made attractive to the women even in cases of true conflict. The alternative, the planned elimination of these human beings,[52] implies the assassination of a woman's conscience, to use Mother Teresa's strong expression.

Reality shows, however, how such measures are still inadequate. The need for the criminal law appears inevitable. It provides protection for the woman herself, often exposed to pressure from others, such as the father of the baby or the surrounding family or social environment. It is almost impossible for a woman facing such pressures to resist choosing a procedure that is legal and therefore presented as an ordinary medical service financed by health insurance. In this respect, it is precisely the criminal law that provides legitimate help to the woman and often represents a last appeal. This does not automatically imply the need to inflict the expected penalty upon the woman, since criminal law applies upon recognition of the guilt of the incriminated person. Criminal law is very flexible, and it would be just for abortion doctors, especially those who make a business of abortion, to be the ones punished.[53] Finally, to

---

de facto, is a "license to abort." As of August, 1999, the Constitutional Court has not had occasion to determine the constitutionality of the 1995 law.

52. W. Geiger, "Rechtliche Beurteilung des Schwangerschaftsabbruchs," in von Voss, *Chancen für das ungeborene Leben*, 55.

53. Fundamental rights rest with the holder of the right and therefore cannot be made relative. Criminal law, instead, allows a differentiation according to the culpability of the accused for injury to the fundamental rights of others. Such differentiation, however, cannot ever attenuate the duty of safeguarding the fundamental right; see Daniel Rhonheimer, "Das Recht des hilflosen Lebens: Zum Zusammenhang von Menschenrechten, Existenzrecht, Rechtsfähigkeit und Rechtsstaat," in *Begründung der Menschenrechte*, ed. P. P. Müller–Schmid, *Archiv für Rechts—und Sozialphilosophie*, Supplement 26 (Stuttgart: Franz Steiner Verlag, 1986), 45–127, esp. 47.

maintain in society and in individual conscience an awareness of the injustice and violation of the law implied by a given behavior, its criminalization will usually prove to be indispensable.[54] The fact that this criminal law cannot be enforced systematically is analogous to the case of rape within marriage. Though difficult to apply, this penal measure is being promoted by some who justify it because of the grave wrongfulness of raping one's spouse.

Even though I consider the intervention of criminal law to be inevitable, its legitimacy must be based on a specific and well-articulated reasoning. The German Federal Constitutional Court clearly affirms that the question of a possible intervention through the criminal law is not equivalent to the question of whether the state is obliged to punish particular actions because they are immoral. To provide an answer, the Constitutional Court affirms that one must consider not only the importance of the good involved (in this case life), but also the limits beyond which its injury may become *harmful to society*. The real effectiveness and applicability of penal sanctions must be evaluated as well.

While it remains a morally unjustifiable act, a valid argument cannot be found to punish an abortion carried out in the event of a diagnosed danger to the life of the mother. In that case—a well-chosen example of the difference between moral and legal-political logic—the superiority of the right to life of the unborn would not be even defensible, according to the common view of pro-life jurists. The state, in fact, cannot force a woman to sacrifice her life to save the life of the unborn. Two *equal* goods are involved here. Furthermore, it is difficult to show the harm to society and human coexistence caused by such behavior. This type of abortion, then, should not even be considered illegal (with respect to the *Grundgesetz*), but justified.[55]

The case of what is known as the "embryo-pathological diagnosis" appears to be different from the preceding. (At present, under the German legislation of 1995, this diagnosis is now likened to a life-threatening pregnancy, giving rise to more problems.) Contrary to a widespread mis-

---

54. *Evangelium Vitae* asserts this in no. 90. Cf. also Kriele, *Die nicht-therapeutische Abtreibung vor dem Grundgesetz*; Gante, §218 in *der Diskussion*, 218.

55. The problem, pointed out by some authors, consists in the intention initially to favor the mother's life, but "later the same criterion has been used to protect the mother's health, then her psychological health, then for social reasons"; cf. E. Sgreccia, *Manuale di Bioetica*, 1, 2nd ed. (Milan: Vita e pensiero, 1994), 399.

understanding, this diagnosis is not based strictly on "eugenic" grounds, in the sense of intending to decriminalize or even declare legal the killing of an unborn human who is handicapped or subnormal or disabled, because its future life is considered unworthy of being lived. That is to say, this diagnosis is intended to legalize the killing of a fetus not "in his own interest" (as Peter Singer and others would say), but in the interests of the mother. It is not considered possible to demand that the mother give birth and take care of a baby with such disabilities. Thus, the embryo-pathological diagnosis is based on a weighing of the good of the "unborn life" and an ill-defined right of the mother, which might be called the "right to a healthy baby."

We can immediately perceive the inhumanity inherent in the proclamation of a right of this sort. It is incoherent inasmuch as the German legal system had previously equated the constitutional protection of the life of the unborn with the protection of the life of any other individual who is already born. The embryo-pathological argument must also in principle justify infanticide for analogous reasons (it would even seem more logical since prenatal tests have a margin of error, so it appears much more sensible to wait for the birth of the unborn child and then proceed to infanticide).

The implicit reasons for such a procedure are revealed in the general attitude toward the physically and mentally disabled. It is also evident that the practice of such behavior will deeply change the conditions of the handicapped within our society, precisely together with the growth of knowledge of the embryo and the fetus as a result of scientific progress. The value of mutual respect for life will weaken and become corroded. This clearly applies also to other diagnoses, such as the "psychosocial" one, which ultimately renders the embryo-pathological one superfluous since it declares legal any abortion carried out whenever the unborn may constitute a potential threat to the psychological stability or the social or professional prospects of the woman (or possibly of the couple).[56]

56. I am not speaking here of the case of verified criminality (that is, rape). Not because I believe it to be licit, but because here again the problem is different, in the sense that the pregnancy cannot be imputed to the mother; it is not the effect of a free act. For the legislator, it can then be a case in which he does not have to intervene, at least not necessarily, out of motives of *Zumutbarkeit* (reasonableness), for instance. Supposing, however, that even in this case the unborn has a right to life, it will be difficult to establish the basis for the *lawfulness* of such an abortion.

What is certain in all these cases is that the legal-political argumentation adopted by the German Federal Constitutional Court does not appear disposed to tolerate a generalized "right to self-determination" of the woman that would prevail even for a limited time over the right to life of the unborn. But this appears to have been exactly what the Supreme Court of the United States has granted in *Roe v. Wade,* the decision that declared unconstitutional a Texas law of 1857 that prohibited abortion except in the case of a diagnosed danger to the life of the mother.

The United States of America: The Right to Abortion as a Liberty Protected by the Constitution

The Constitution of the United States of America, unlike that of the Basic Law of the Federal Republic of Germany, does not explicitly recognize a "right to life." The American Constitution did not even originally include any separate list or "bill" of fundamental rights. The Bill of Rights was added only in 1791, and other specifications concerning civil rights were inserted subsequently, according to the requirements of the historical situation.[57]

An example of such an addition is the Fourteenth Amendment, ratified in 1868. The Due Process Clause of this amendment, analogous to the Fifth Amendment of 1791, affirms the constitutional right of every person to lawful judicial proceedings, and the Equal Protection Clause mandates that persons be treated equally before the law. The relevant part of the text reads as follows: "nor shall any State deprive any person of life, liberty, or property, without due process of law; nor deny to any person within its jurisdiction the equal protection of the laws."

At least two previous decisions (*Griswold v. Connecticut*[58] in 1965 and *Eisenstadt v. Baird*[59] in 1972) had interpreted these clauses as admitting the existence of a constitutional right to privacy. In declaring invalid a Massachusetts law that prohibited the sale or distribution of contraceptives to unmarried persons, *Eisenstadt* applied this right to what some scholars have called "procreative autonomy." In *Roe v. Wade* this right was extended to abortion.[60]

---

57. The Fifth Amendment, ratified in 1791, protects the "life" of a "person" against deprivation by the national government without "due process of law."

58. *Griswold v. Connecticut,* 381 U.S. 479 (1965).

59. *Eisenstadt v. Baird,* 405 U.S. 438 (1972).   60. *Roe v. Wade,* 410 U.S. 113 (1973).

The majority opinion in *Roe*, written by Justice Harry A. Blackmun, justifies the decision in the following terms: a law, or any other intervention by the state that would prohibit a woman from freely disposing of her unborn child, would be a violation of her constitutional right to privacy. Blackmun writes that "we feel" that the Fourteenth Amendment encompasses the right of the woman to decide "whether or not to terminate her pregnancy."[61] The opinion also maintains that such a right is not absolute. It is said to find its limit when reaching certain matters that are of interest to the state, such as the woman's health, the quality of the health care system, and finally *prenatal life,* beginning from the moment the fetus is viable (that is, capable of living independently from the mother, in case of premature birth).[62]

These elements immediately distinguish it from the German constitutional situation: on the basis of the German *Grundgesetz,* a law that forbids abortion has the juridical meaning of protecting a fundamental right of the unborn, provided for in the constitution. In the United States, by contrast, the same law is deemed an intrusion on the woman's freedom to decide whether or not to go forward with a pregnancy. The difference reflects the development of German juridical doctrine, which sees in fundamental rights an order of values to be realized by political society, whereas the United States' conception remains at a protoliberal, individualistic level, relating to the freedoms to be set "against the state."[63]

From this point arises the question whether it is possible to include the unborn also within the "persons" mentioned in the Fourteenth Amendment. For Blackmun, however, it is fundamental that the unborn

61. Ibid., 153.

62. Ibid., 153–55; 161–66. Note that in *Doe v. Bolton,* 410 U.S. 179 (1973), the companion case to *Roe v. Wade,* maternal health was defined in extremely broad terms. It was said to comprise all factors ("physical, emotional, psychological, familial, and the woman's age") relevant to the patient's well-being (*Doe v. Bolton,* at 192). When read in conjunction with the concluding paragraphs of *Roe v. Wade,* this broad understanding of maternal health suggests that the pregnant woman is at liberty to have an abortion even after viability so long as "in appropriate medical judgment" it is necessary for the "health" of the mother (*Roe v. Wade,* at 165).

63. See Glendon, *Abortion and Divorce in Western Law,* 33–39. An important contrary position, in defense of *Roe,* is taken by Ronald Dworkin, *Life's Dominion: An Argument about Abortion and Euthanasia* (London: Harper Collins, 1993). For an interesting, resolute criticism of Blackmun, see Hadley Arkes, *First Things: An Inquiry into the First Principles of Morals and Justice* (Princeton: Princeton University Press, 1986), chapters 15, 16, and 17. (The author nevertheless seems to me to be exaggerating in denying the existence of a private sphere, immune from the interference of civil law.)

child cannot be a "constitutional person"; he submits that the use of the word "person" in the Constitution has only postnatal applications.[64] Furthermore, according to Blackmun, the allegedly higher level of tolerance toward abortion in the nineteenth century is evidence that the word "person" used in the Fourteenth Amendment does not include the unborn.[65] There is no precedent that recognizes the unborn child as a person within the meaning of this amendment, says Blackmun.[66]

It may seem correct, then, to affirm that on the basis of conventional legal sources (constitutional text, case law, and nineteenth-century statutes) it is not possible to bestow any right on the unborn. Nevertheless, the simple deduction of procreative autonomy deriving from the text and precedent implies other presuppositions, and here begin the "mysteries" of *Roe v. Wade*. We may ask:

1. In a legal question concerning the life of the unborn, why did the Court limit itself to the text of the Fourteenth Amendment, which does not address the question of (possible) rights of the unborn?

2. Why suppose that the right to privacy might not be limited by another possible right, such as the right to life of the unborn?

Let us look at the second question first. We may recall that the German Federal Constitutional Court did not encounter any difficulty in affirming that the word "everyone" in article 2, section 2, of the *Grundgesetz* ("everyone possesses the right to life") includes every "living human being, and therefore also the one not yet born." The German Constitutional Court assumed that the decisive basis for an entitlement to be treated equally to others plainly consists in being a (living) human, that is, a living being belonging to the biological species *homo sapiens*. *Roe v. Wade* is distinguishable in that the German court did not dwell on an alleged meaning of "the text," but acknowledged the reality of the new existence of a human being, a reality sufficiently known on the basis of the evidence furnished by modern science.[67]

---

64. *Roe v. Wade*, 410 U.S. 113, 156–57.   65. Ibid., 158.
66. Ibid., 157–58.

67. It is important to note that such evidence is not denied today even by the most relentless advocates of freedom of abortion, such as the followers of the theories of Michael Tooley, Peter Singer, Norbert Hoerster; they merely deny that an individual of the human species is already a *person* with the corresponding right to life. We shall speak briefly about them later.

Even if for Justice Blackmun the right to privacy is "not absolute," but limited where the "interests of the state" are implicated in relation to prenatal life, this obviously does not confer any indefeasible right on the carrier of that life. Consequently, the decisive point does not seem to consist in the existence or nonexistence of a right to privacy—a question that in this context seems irrelevant—but rather whether the unborn, in the embryonic stage or in the fetal stage, is or is not a human being with a corresponding right to life capable of restricting the "right to privacy," as well as any other freedom or right of the mother.

The question of whether the unborn is a person in the constitutional sense does not depend so much on the different passages where the Constitution speaks of "persons," not even those of the Fourteenth Amendment, but rather from the answer *tout court* to the question of whether the unborn is a person or not. The fact that the unborn is not a person in one or more specific legal contexts, such as the Fourteenth Amendment, does not necessarily mean that it is not to be considered a person. Nor does it mean that it is undeserving of those protections and entitlements that every person enjoys precisely insofar as he or she is a human being. This, rather than the putative right to privacy, is the decisive point here. And the very exclusion of this question is the foundation of *Roe v. Wade*.[68]

Furthermore, Blackmun did not show that the legal analysis could proceed without philosophic analysis. As Mary Ann Glendon has written, Justice Blackmun "has diligently avoided describing the fetus either as human or as alive."[69] In this regard, Blackmun wrote: "We need not resolve the difficult question of when life begins."[70]

For Blackmun, it is a question on which there are as many opinions as there are religions, philosophies, and scientific theories. He therefore concentrates on the issue of "viability."[71] In his view, only the right to life of the fetus already able to survive independently from the mother would be defensible, from both "logical and biological" standpoints.[72]

---

68. Blackmun admits that if the unborn were a "constitutional person," the entire argument against the Texas law would collapse. The same is affirmed by Dworkin, *Life's Dominion*, 116.

69. Glendon, *Abortion and Divorce in Western Law*, 34.

70. *Roe v. Wade*, 410 U.S. 113, 159.

71. For a criticism of the concept of viability, see Arkes, *First Things*, 376–79.

72. *Roe v. Wade*, 410 U.S. 113, 163.

In defending Blackmun more than twenty years later, Ronald Dworkin writes that an idea of some antiabortionists, according to which the unborn is a constitutional person, derives from the theological-religious conviction that "God, at the moment of conception provides the human fetus with a rational soul and that a rational soul possesses the moral right to live."[73] Yet Dworkin's account is mistaken because the "person" is not "the soul," and we cannot affirm that the human fetus is a person because it has a rational soul. Rather, it is maintained that the living fetus has a soul *because it is a human person and that it is a person precisely because and inasmuch as he or she is a living individual of the species homo sapiens.* The latter point is a matter of scientific fact, not "religion." Both Blackmun and Dworkin err in refusing to recognize the fundamental relevance of an individual belonging to the human species—the truth that it is just such belonging that *implies* being a person with an equal right to life.[74]

Denying the status of the unborn as a person, Blackmun referred to tradition of the common law, with the words: "the unborn have never been recognized in the law as persons in the whole sense."[75] What, however, does "a person in the whole sense" mean? Does it mean, perhaps, that in the common law the unborn is considered a sort of half-person? A person in some lesser sense? A person, but somewhat less than a born one? This is impossible. Half-persons, or three-quarter persons, do not exist. Instead, there exist individual humans who are true and authentic persons, but who have not yet developed all of the properties typical of persons (for example, certain physical attributes; a certain level of intelligence and formation; and the capacity to act freely and responsibly).

---

73. Dworkin, *Life's Dominion,* 110.

74. On this matter, see A. Suarez, "Ist der menschliche Embryo geistig beseelt?" *Annales Theologici* 4 (1990) 69–107, esp. 93. A certain inability to understand the position of the magisterium of the Catholic Church on the fundamental identity between "human person" and "human individual" has become almost universal. Even authors engaged in refuting the so-called Catholic position seem to err on this point, thinking that "person" is the individual soul, and not the human individual, a substantial unity of body and soul. This error, which invalidates the whole argumentation by such authors, can be found in A. Leist, *Eine Frage des Lebens. Ethik der Abtreibung und künstlichen Befruchtung* (Frankfurt: Campus, 1990), 110, where surprisingly he links himself to N. M. Ford, *When Did I Begin?* whose exposition on this point (61–101) is clearly correct. According to Ford, the person is not "the human soul," but the individual of a human nature.

75. *Roe v. Wade,* 410 U.S. 113, 162.

These properties may develop in such individuals precisely because they *are* persons.[76]

The fact that the law does not extend all of the rights of persons to the unborn—because the unborn, for example, lack the present capacity to exercise or to benefit from those rights—does not mean that they would not benefit from a right to life. Clearly, they would. Distinctions before the law do not mean, for example, that a legal adult is "more of a person" with an "elevated right to life" than, say, a minor. The right to life obviously plays a special role. Every other right, even if still not accorded to the unborn, may be granted to them at a later time, according to suitability and maturity; other rights may even be revoked from a mature person and later restored. This is not the case with respect to the right to life, which therefore occupies a singular place. The necessity of recognizing it is not based on the development of specific properties typical of persons, but on the fact of being an individual who will develop such properties—in other words, on the basis of "being a person."

It does not appear to be a problem that the Constitution confers certain rights only to those who satisfy certain conditions—such as age—as long as the principles of equality before the law are protected. As we

76. Effectively, Anglo-Saxon common law has recognized the so-called Born Alive Rule since the thirteenth century, according to which the killing of a fetus prior to birth, although considered to be misprision (i.e., wrongdoing), was not a homicide according to the law. Bonnie Steinbock, *Life before Birth: The Moral and Legal Status of Embryos and Fetuses* (New York: Oxford University Press, 1992), 105–7 (a book that defends the judgment in *Roe v. Wade* as well as the idea that the unborn cannot be the holder of a right to life), makes an attempt—referring to Edward Coke, Chief Justice and the famous author of the Petition of Right in the 1600s—to read the Born Alive Rule as reflecting, first, the fact that at the time the fetus was considered to be a part of the mother and not to have a separate existence (an opinion that we can now say is obsolete), and second, the belief that "a fetus is not yet a fully developed human being, a person like the rest of us" (106). Even if this were the opinion of Edward Coke (and later of Blackstone), on the basis of the still dominant influence of the Aristotelian-scholastic theory of the later "animation" of the fetus, it is certainly possible to correct the venerable jurisprudential tradition of the common law on the basis of more current and modern scientific knowledge. It seems, however, that Blackstone was thinking instead about the question of a judicial ascertainment of the existence of a human being at the time of an indictment for homicide: in order for someone to be condemned for homicide there must be clear and visible proof—*in rerum natura*, as it was said—of the prior existence of the victim, not just of the incriminating act. See also Keown, *Abortion, Doctors, and the Law*, 3–12; Clarke D. Forsythe, "Homicide of the Unborn Child: The Born Alive Rule and Other Anachronisms," *Valparaiso University Law Review* 21 (1987): 563; Joseph W. Dellapenna, "The History of Abortion: Technology, Morality, and Law," *University of Pittsburgh Law Review* 40 (1979): 359; Horan and Balch, "*Roe v. Wade*," 93.

shall see later in the chapter, however, granting such rights *assumes* that the individual in question is a person, with a right to live; otherwise, it would not be plausible to confer on him or her *any* civil right. No civil norm is legitimately capable of conferring on or withholding from a person the right to life. The civil law is for human persons, but it cannot (without arbitrary and therefore unjust discrimination) make the question of *who* counts as a human person a matter of intrasystemic legal analysis. Or it does so, as did the *Roe* Court, at the risk of catastrophic moral error.

Possessing the right to life cannot depend on the law, but instead depends on a fact antecedent to the law. The legislator is therefore obliged simply to ascertain whether the individual is or is not, in truth, a human person, with a corresponding right to live. The fact that the law does not define who is a "human person" does not change anything. Accordingly, the Supreme Court of the United States should have been obliged to decide what it expressly refused to discuss: when human life begins.

Given that the unborn is a human person with all of the rights connected with "being man," we must conclude that *Roe v. Wade* is simply based on an error. In the text of the American Constitution there is no basis for establishing whether the right of privacy does or does not include a woman's right to decide whether the unborn will live or die before reaching viability.

The Court could have declared that it was not qualified to decide the question, leaving it to the legislative competence of the several states.[77] I nevertheless think that, instead of declaring itself unqualified, the Court in 1973 could have appealed to sources of law not explicitly contemplated in the text of the Constitution. The Court's decision to limit itself to the express provisions of the Constitution could be justified only on the basis of a "positivist" or "originalist" interpretation of the Constitution.[78]

---

77. This was the argument of the famous article of John Hart Ely, "The Wages of Crying Wolf: A Comment on *Roe v. Wade*," *Yale Law Journal* 82 (1973): 920. Criticisms of the judgment in *Roe v. Wade* on the part of eminent specialists in constitutional law—many of whom favored abortion—were numerous; see the discussion in Glendon, *Abortion and Divorce in Western Law*, 44–50; 171–72 (bibliography at note 175). A more extensive and recent bibliography can be found in Maureen Muldoon, *The Abortion Debate in the United States and Canada: A Sourcebook* (New York: Garland, 1991).

78. A notable representative of this line of thought is Robert H. Bork, *The Tempting of America: The Political Seduction of the Law* (New York: Simon and Schuster, 1989). See also Bork's article, "Natural Law and the Constitution," *First Things*, March 1992, 16–20, and the

This is not, however, the position of those who currently defend the decision in *Roe v. Wade*, such as Ronald Dworkin.[79]

A non-positivist approach could offer the possibility of having recourse to sources of law outside of the text of the Constitution, which in its Ninth Amendment states that "The enumeration in the Constitution, of certain rights, shall not be construed to deny or disparage others retained by the people." According to this amendment, which was adopted in 1791, there is an explicit guarantee of rights unmentioned in the written text of the Constitution. One of the reasons for this was to calm the concerns of those who were initially opposed to the inclusion of a bill of rights in the Constitution, for fear that it could imply an abrogation of rights that existed but were not enumerated in the written text.[80]

Whatever its precise meaning, the Ninth Amendment is a legal text that affirms the existence of sources of law antecedent to and outside of the text of the Constitution. We should not forget that prior to the creation of the federal United States, individual states already had their own bills of rights. The most famous codification of rights was that of Virginia, in 1776, which states in its first paragraph, as a "right of the people":

That all men are by nature equally free and independent and have certain inherent rights, of which, when they enter into a state of society, they cannot by any compact deprive or divest their posterity; namely the enjoyment of life and liberty, with the means of acquiring and possessing property and pursuing and obtaining happiness and safety.[81]

This text does not speak of the procedural rights of citizens, but instead of "rights naturally inherent in man." It is the language of the modern tradition of human rights, based on the fundamental idea that

---

critical responses to it in the May issue from the same year. More systematically: Russell Hittinger, "Natural Law in the Positive Laws: A Legislative or Adjudicative Issue?" *Review of Politics* 55 (1993) 5–34. Also useful for understanding the problem is Michael J. Perry, *Morality, Politics, and Law* (New York: Oxford University Press, 1988), chapter six.

79. Dworkin, *Life's Dominion*. See also Dworkin's *Taking Rights Seriously*, 2nd expanded ed. (London: Duckworth, 1977), 131–44.

80. See Alexander Hamilton's polemic in *Federalist* No. 84 against the idea of including a bill of rights in the Constitution; cf. Hadley Arkes, *Beyond the Constitution* (Princeton: Princeton University Press, 1990), chapter 4.

81. The constitution of Massachusetts speaks of "certain natural, essential and inalienable rights," and the Declaration of Independence of 1776 asserts as "self-evident truths" that all men "are endowed by their Creator with certain inalienable rights," among which is also the right to life.

humans possess certain rights *because they are human* and not because the rights have been conferred on them by society, and that the most fundamental of these rights is the right to life. As we have already seen, in the Prussian Allgemeine Landrecht, following the progress of embryological knowledge toward the end of the eighteenth century and under the influence of Enlightenment ideas, "the universal rights of humanity" were extended even to "children not yet born, beginning from the time of conception."

I do not mean to assert that the constitutional texts of the several states are to be considered binding on the case law of the Supreme Court of the United States; they are valid, of course, within the jurisdictional sphere of the respective states. Nevertheless, they could be sources of a law that has until now remained partially circumscribed in the United States for specific historical reasons. As Martin Kriele has observed,[82] an important reason for not having introduced the "rights of *man*" into the 1791 Constitution, let alone the concept of "human dignity," was the acquiescence in the interests of the slave states. Not even the Virginia language "that *all men*" had any legal effect. In Massachusetts, instead, the declaration on the liberty and equality of all men led in 1783 to the abolition of slavery. Certainly, the slave owners could not accept the inclusion of any similar language in the Constitution. This explains why the idea of an equality of rights founded solely on "being man" or "human dignity" remained absent from U.S. constitutionalism. Here, in addition, is the logical premise of the famous *Dred Scott v. Sandford* decision in 1857, which denied the status of citizenship to slaves.

In light of the preceding, we can now see that the Court's legal options were open. The Court could have chosen to rely on the Ninth Amendment as justification for answering the pressing philosophic question, When does life begin?[83]

As we have observed, at key junctures in *Roe v. Wade* the Court adopted a rigidly positivist attitude to the rights of the unborn. Curiously,

82. *Einführung in die Staatslehre. Die geschichtlichen Legitimätsgrundlagen des demokratischen Verfassungsstaates,* 4th ed. (Opladen: Westdt Verlag, 1990), 160–62.
83. We should not forget that Blackmun contends, with respect to the argument of the District Court of the State of Texas, that the woman's right to decide whether to terminate her pregnancy might also be derived from the Ninth Amendment (*Roe v. Wade,* 410 U.S. 113, 153). If that is possible, it also opens the door to asserting the unborn's right to life, as long as it is recognized to have the status of human.

however, the Court also accepted the expansive account of the unenumerated right to privacy offered by the plaintiffs, and without serious analysis of legal materials such as text, precedent, and statutory practice. This discrepancy seems to have been the basis for the remark in Justice White's dissent that the Court's decision was "an exercise of raw judicial power."[84]

A later effort to have *Roe v. Wade* overruled in the 1992 case *Planned Parenthood v. Casey* was unsuccessful.[85] The latter decision partly modified the former without overruling it, inasmuch as it declared constitutional certain statutory provisions in Pennsylvania, which imposed restrictions on the freedom to abort. Based on the principle of *stare decisis*, the joint opinion in *Planned Parenthood v. Casey* argued that it is not possible simply to declare as erroneous a judgment that for over twenty years has stamped the politics of abortion and the public conscience of the nation. Moreover, according to the joint opinion, even if the result in *Roe v. Wade* was mistaken, overruling it would be the equivalent of unnecessarily weakening the legitimacy of the Court and the fidelity of the whole nation to the rule of law. In a dissenting opinion, Justice Scalia asserted instead that, supposing that there is a near-unanimous conviction on the part of specialists that the arguments in *Roe v. Wade* were inconsistent and erroneous, one could arrive at a conclusion that the principle of *stare decisis* should not be applied to this case. In sum: the *fact* that there exists a precedent, and that it was applied, does not dispense with the need to ask whether that precedent was mistaken.

Strategies against the Legislative Defense of Life

Our discussion of the abortion decisions of the German Constitutional Court and the U.S. Supreme Court allows us to identify a few decisive points in our attempts to justify an effective protection of prenatal life in a constitutional democracy. We have seen that a coherent legal argument in defense of the unborn depends on the recognition of the un-

---

84. *Doe v. Bolton*, 410 U.S. 179, 222. Justice White's dissent in this case was joined by Justice Rehnquist, and a note indicates that White's dissent in *Doe v. Bolton* also applies to the Court's decision in *Roe v. Wade*. See *Doe v. Bolton* at 221.
85. *Planned Parenthood of Southeastern Pennsylvania v. Casey*, 505 U.S. 833 (1992).

born as a human person who is therefore endowed with a corresponding right to life. *Evangelium Vitae* also takes up this line of thought.

There are, however, strategies favoring a broad legalization of abortion that are founded on the attempt to abolish the recognition of the unborn as a *person*. The first strategy consists in distinguishing between "human individual" and "human person." The second is that of declaring irrelevant, legally as well as politically, the question of the "personhood" of the unborn. The third is to avoid such discussions by appealing solely to a woman's right to self-determination.

The Problem of Democracy

Allow me to digress briefly. The text of *Evangelium Vitae* could give rise to the impression that abortion is a question arising exclusively in democracies. In some sections, especially 67 and 70, the encyclical seems ultimately to be identifying the problem of abortion with the power of democracies to decide anything arbitrarily, based on the will of the majority. The truths included in these passages seem to be taken for granted. They cannot, however, be interpreted to mean that democratic mechanisms favor the legalization and promotion of abortion. Even if this were the correct interpretation of these sections, this opinion would be difficult to defend empirically, because communist dictatorships were among the first nations to liberalize abortion, providing for its support with the assistance of the state.

In the United States, abortion was liberalized by a decision of a court—with more of an aristocratic, rather than democratic, character—that *opposed* an antiabortion law passed by a democratically elected legislature. The decision in *Roe v. Wade* did not represent the outcome of a majoritarian vote, but instead gave into the claims of what was at the time only a minority in American society. Furthermore, even the parliaments that have liberalized abortion in other countries are *representative* institutions, and their democratic legitimacy is not always clear. In this respect, the case of Switzerland is significant, where in the 1970s the people voted on a proposal to liberalize abortion in the first three months of pregnancy, and a majority rejected it. (An attempt to insert a definition of the beginning of human life in the Swiss constitution was, however, unsuccessful.) Such a definition was included in the

Irish constitution, by a majority vote. In Poland, democratization meant also a revocation of the liberalized abortion that existed under the communist regime. Thus, it is not clear on what empirical facts one could maintain that democracy, in a special way, favors the introduction of legal abortion. Given certain cultural presuppositions, a democracy is capable of introducing and permitting abortion, as is every other form of government. (It would be more difficult to have abortion on demand if there were a "Catholic" dictatorship or monarchy, but is that form of government really desirable?)

At present, we are clearly facing a widening of the "culture of death," which is advancing at the same pace as the diffusion of democracy. This, however, is not the point, and we would be blind to maintain it in the face of the real problems of society, culture, people, and public opinion.

More than democracy, the real problem seems to be that represented by the institutions of the mass media, which are biased in this area. Even if their freedom is one of the great values of a democracy and represents a significant victory of democracy, they do not present themselves as subordinated to democratic control. This is, nevertheless, the price one must pay for the existence of an authentic and free public opinion, formed only in a climate of liberty. If a dictatorship were to permit the formation and articulation of public opinion (which normally would not occur), once it is subject to the pressure of the latter, the dictatorship would give in—much more easily than a democracy—to the temptation to liberalize abortion. Yet dictatorships are also prone to call for plebiscites (when they consider them convenient), premised on a majoritarian, but not democratic, logic (because they exclude a free process for the formation of public opinion and, in addition, offer no alternative in the vote itself). It is therefore not democracy that constitutes the problem, but the mechanisms and persons that form public opinion. It is not a question of democratic institutions as such, but of human and cultural formation. In sum, the problem of the "culture of death" is not caused by political institutions, but reflects a problem of the society, and only indirectly becomes also a problem having to do with the institutions of the state and democracy. This is certainly one of the most important messages of *Evangelium Vitae*.

As we have seen, a fundamental premise for the legal defense of the life of the unborn in a constitutional democracy is recognizing that the unborn, in an embryonic as well as fetal state (and, by analogy, the physically or mentally impaired, no less than the person in an irreversible coma) must be considered human beings before the law, as much as any other human who is already born. This principle is one of the explicit premises of the German constitutional case law; by contrast, in *Roe v. Wade* the principle was supposedly "bracketed" by Blackmun, but its denial constituted the main premise of the decision. Given the present-day scientific knowledge of genetics and embryology, no one today can reasonably deny that an individual formed by the fusion of gametes coming from individuals of the species *homo sapiens* is also of the species *homo sapiens*—an individual who needs nothing else to be defined as "human."

The first strategy for rendering this fact innocuous or irrelevant is the theory according to which the human fetus—and *a fortiori* the embryo—may be an individual belonging to the species *homo sapiens* but is not yet a *person*. According to this strategy, a "person" can be defined only as a being endowed with a sufficiently developed self-awareness to have the desire and/or interest to survive, and therefore a corresponding *right* to life. This theory is thus based on the idea that every right corresponds to a subjective interest, one that is consciously formed by the holder of that right. The concept of a "person" is profoundly altered: "being a person" is reduced to a *property* of an individual of the human species that appears to begin only at a certain interval after birth and that can be lost during the course of life.[86]

This is evidently an idea imbued with strong anthropological-philosophical implications.[87] It can thus also be refuted with relative

86. As discussed in chapter 6, some of the most notable representatives of this view are Peter Singer, *Practical Ethics* (Cambridge: Cambridge University Press, 1979); Mary Anne Warren, "On the Moral and Legal Status of Abortion," *Monist* 57 (1973): 43; Michael Tooley, *Abortion and Infanticide* (Oxford: Clarendon Press, 1983); Hoerster, *Abtreibung im säkularen Staat*. See also Steinbock, *Life before Birth*.

87. See R. Spaemann, "Sind alle Menschen Personen? Über neue philosophische Rechtfertigungen der Lebensvernichtung," in J. P. Stüssel, *Tüchtig oder tot. Die Entsorgung des Leidens* (Freiburg/Br.: Herder, 1991), 133–47 (this article is also found, slightly revised, in the

ease.[88] The theory nonetheless has the advantage of a certain intuitive plausibility based on the imprecise character of expressions such as "the fetus is not a person in the full sense," or "it is *potentially* a person" or "a potential person." We have already seen that this lack of precision was present in Justice Blackmun's opinion. In fact, there are no such things as "potential persons," just as there are no individuals who are "potential birds" (but there are gametes that potentially can become human persons, although the gametes themselves do not constitute an individual of the human species). The fetus is not a potential person but an *actual* human person, with potentialities not yet developed. The fact of having such potentialities, which later will be actualized, shows precisely that it is not a question of development "toward being a human" but development "of a human being."

Therefore, the distinction between "being human" and "being a person" implies that being considered a human or a human person, with corresponding rights, depends on factors other than the mere fact of belonging to the species *homo sapiens* (to affirm the latter would be "speciesism"), such as self-awareness and the capacity to have permanent and future-oriented desires. This means that a human being who has not yet reached this stage (or who has lapsed from it in a manner presumed to be definitive) can be killed for any reason, without any justification before the law.

Another Strategy for Denying the Right to Life: Separating It from the Intrinsic and Specific Value of Human Life

A second strategy that tries to immunize against recognition of the fact that the unborn is a human person consists in an affirmation of the necessity of distinguishing the question of the status of the unborn (and thus possible right to life) from the question of the intrinsic value or "sacredness" of life. This is Ronald Dworkin's central thesis.[89] Dworkin

---

volume edited by Thomas and Kluth, cited above in note 43); L. Honnefelder, "Der Streit um die Person in der Ethik," *Philosophisches Jahrbuch* 100 (1993): 246–45.

88. I refer to Pöltner, "Achtung der Würde und Schutz von Interessen," 3–32; Schwarz, *The Moral Question of Abortion*. See also chapter 6 of this book, which was originally published as my *Absolute Herrschaft der Geborenen? Anatomie und Kritik der Argumentation von Norbert Hoersters Abtreibung im säkularen Staat*, IMABE-Studie No. 5 (Vienna: IMABE, 1995).

89. Dworkin, *Life's Dominion*.

argues that one can be opposed to abortion and require the pro-life in-tervention of the state for two reasons: either for a "derivative" reason—that is, because one thinks that the unborn child is a human person with a right to life, from which is *derived* the responsibility (including that of the state) to protect the fetus—or for a "detached" reason, not otherwise derived, but simply founded on the conviction that human life, as such, possesses an intrinsic and sacred, even if intangible, value from which springs an obligation—to be assumed by the state—to pro-tect that life.[90]

Dworkin asserts that in reality the question of the personhood of the fetus and the related right to life do not and could not represent the core of the question, even within the scope of the Catholic tradition.[91] Thus, according to him, it is not crucial to determine when the existence of a human begins. Dworkin denies that the unborn can be considered a "constitutional person," and thus defends the decision in *Roe v. Wade*. He nonetheless submits that the real reason why some show a propensity either for or against abortion comes from a different evaluation of the intrinsic value, or "sacredness," of human life. This evaluation depends on premises that are ideological, religious, and theological, concerning which there exist a plurality of opinions—very subjective ones, more-over—that in a pluralistic society are not susceptible to regulation in a uniform manner for all. It would be unjust, writes Dworkin, to impose on all citizens the opinions of the majority regarding the intrinsic value of human life. We may be able to arrive nevertheless at a peaceful com-promise, *precisely because it is possible to bracket, as irrelevant, the question of whether the unborn is, or is not, a person endowed with a corresponding right to life.* Proposing with admirable ability an interpretation of the jurisprudence of the Supreme Court founded on "freezing" the question of the status of the unborn, Dworkin succeeds in conferring juridical logic on a legal situation that is, in reality, profoundly contra-dictory.

90. Ibid., 11.
91. Ibid., 39–50. Obviously, this assertion is not wrong, but it is banal, since the fram-ing of the issue in terms of "rights" is specifically modern. It is, however, quite typical of the "Catholic position" on the subject to identify an essential connection between the intrinsic value—sacredness—of human life and the right to life of every living human. *Evangelium Vitae* affirms this from the beginning, in no. 2.

Nevertheless, this position has two implications that are unacceptable:

1. To deny the right to life (and the corresponding legal protection) of certain living beings *it is not important to know whether they are persons or not, and thus also whether they are the holders of a right to life.* Dworkin's position is in any event incompatible with that of Warren, Singer, Tooley, and Hoerster, which are based on a certainty that the unborn is not a person and consequently lacks any right to life. *For Dworkin, instead, it is enough that it not be considered a person under positive law.*

2. In Dworkin's theory, enjoying a right to life, on the one hand, and admitting the "sacredness of life" to be a good that is indispensable for man, on the other, appear to be two different realities, lacking any relationship between them. Here, then, is the crux. On the basis of that premise, *the legal recognition of the person* (that is, whomever the law and the constitution recognize as such) *has no foundation other than the same recognition on the part of positive law* and also, therefore, on the part of the majority vote that sanctioned its enactment.

The "right to life" of whoever is a "human person" according to an explicit legal or constitutional recognition would not, in accordance with the implication in point 1, depend therefore on some fact that transcends the law itself, but precisely and only on the fact that the law established it. It is thus a question of a complete separation of the two types of morality: a "pre-legal," pre-political, and private morality (to be politically bracketed) and a legal, political, and public morality (independent of the first). In accordance with the implication in point 2, such a right would not depend on any property *intrinsic* to human life, either, but again only on positive law to the extent that the latter establishes what is relevant and normative for "public morality."

In the case of Dworkin, who in principle does not want to be, and is not in any real sense, a representative of legal positivism,[92] such an extreme positivist attitude is surprising. I do not believe that Dworkin, a jurist, followed the logic of his argument. Otherwise, he would certainly

92. See Dworkin, *Taking Rights Seriously*, especially chapters 1–3. Clearly, neither Dworkin's opposition to so-called originalist theories nor his choice to see the Constitution not as a collection of detailed rules so much as moral principles to be constantly reinterpreted, seem positivist; see *Life's Dominion*, 119–25.

have realized that his fundamental legal-political formula, the demand for "equal concern and respect," requires a foundation able to demonstrate *why concern and respect are due to the human person.* In truth, the argument that establishes the value to which equality refers must precede the argument in favor of equality. Equality is always a value relative to a substantive value such as life or liberty.[93]

It is not possible that the foundation of the value of respect is the same law that is supposed to guarantee its equality; in that case, it would not be a foundation at all. It is thus not possible that there is no relationship at all between being the holder of an equal right to life on the one hand, and the intrinsic value of human life, on the other. In this way, a large part of Dworkin's argument fails.

A Third Strategy for Denying the Right to Life: Appealing to a Woman's Self-Determination

The third strategy, which is linked to certain strands of contemporary feminism, is perhaps the most widespread, and it consists in deference to a woman's right to self-determination. It would be a morally as well as legally reasonable position if the unborn is not a human person with a right to live. Even Singer and Hoerster explicitly admit that if the contrary were true, an appeal to women's self-determination could not claim any legal validity.[94] Note, however, that this claim is not usually based on an explicit assertion that the fetus is not a person with a right to live,[95] but it simply—and thus in a very emotional way—claims the woman's right to self-determination, *without regard to a possible right of one who has no voice, who is not visible, and who cannot defend himself or herself.*

Even if there are really cases of grave and even tragic conflict[96]— which should be resolved with love and solidarity, without leaving the pregnant woman alone—the demand for the woman's self-determination has a different justification. It is intrinsically united with a lifestyle that

93. Agnes Heller, *Beyond Justice* (Oxford: Basil Blackwell, 1987), 120–27; 154.

94. The arguments of N. Hoerster in *Abtreibung im säkularen Staat*, 26–54, based on the conviction that the fetus has a right to life, conclude that only a diagnosis of danger to the life of the mother would be justified on those premises. Only later does he abandon this premise, inasmuch as it is based on "speciesism." I think that the position of Hoerster (a jurist) and others is really the only coherent position contrary to the "Catholic" one.

95. It is a matter of what A. Leist defines as an *Umgehungsstrategie* (a strategy of avoidance); see Leist, *Eine Frage des Lebens*, 32.

96. Cf. *Evangelium Vitae*, no. 58.

interprets sexuality as lacking any relationship to the purpose of transmitting human life and thus to the corresponding responsibilities of parenthood. But every pregnancy is the fruit of a sexual act, ordinarily freely chosen or consented to. In this context, the existence of a new life, a pregnancy with the consequent expectation of the birth of a child, is considered to be a threat to one's own liberty (this also arises, analogously, when faced with relatives who may be old, suffering, and in need of intensive care). Its growing cultural predominance, based on a claim of "self-determination" together with a profound crisis in female identity, constitutes a radical threat to society.[97]

Politically, this position finds support in a "protoliberal" attitude, which is incapable of identifying in fundamental rights anything other than rights of liberty to be asserted against the state and the risks arising from an abuse of state power. We have seen how German constitutional jurisprudence some time ago overcame this imperfect concept in its first decision relating to a proposal to liberalize abortion. There, rightly, the protection of the life of the unborn when threatened by third parties—exactly what the "protoliberal" insists is an illegitimate intervention of the state—was confirmed as a duty of the state.

We come across a strange coalition, therefore, which invokes an account of the woman's right to self-determination, an account that is protoliberal in its understanding of fundamental rights and that has been superseded by the development of the institutions of the liberal tradition. Such an argument is founded on two premises, both of which are incorrect—one from a jurisprudential point of view, and the other for biological-anthropological reasons provided by modern science.

The Argument in Favor of the Legal Defense of Life: The Connection between Civil Law and Moral Law

The Argument of *Evangelium Vitae*

If these three strategies—partly incompatible with one another—turned out to be true, or if they could really be included in constitutional law, our culture of human rights would undergo a profound, if not actually perverse, transformation.

97. Cf. *Evangelium Vitae,* no. 13. On the nexus between procreative irresponsibility, the contraceptive mentality, and abortion, see chapters 1 and 2 of the present volume, which were

This is just what *Evangelium Vitae* seems to want to demonstrate in one of its fundamental passages. The encyclical gives two reasons that show the incompatibility between a legal-political culture based on respect for human rights and one founded on a general consent to abortion, as well as real euthanasia (identifiable on the basis of acts or omissions based on an intention to cut short, in the patient's interest, a life no longer considered worthy of being lived). The first turns on the idea of equality before the law: "laws which legitimize the direct killing of innocent human beings . . . are in complete opposition to the inviolable right to life proper to every individual; they thus deny the equality of everyone before the law."[98]

The second reason springs from what we might call the "non-disposability" of life, a principle that is also harmed through the legalization of the suicide-homicide of euthanasia (understood here as procuring death with the assistance of a doctor; it is another question whether suicide as such should be punished or given support). The reason is clear: "In this way the State contributes to lessening respect for life and opens the door to ways of acting which are destructive of trust in relations between people."[99]

Finally, the encyclical explains that the political reason that makes this question important is not merely the good of the individual (inasmuch as that is not necessarily enough to prompt the intervention of the state):

Laws which authorize and promote abortion and euthanasia are therefore radically opposed not only to the good of the individual but also to the common good; as such they are completely lacking in authentic juridical validity. Disregard for the right to life, precisely because it leads to the killing of the person whom society exists to serve, is what most directly conflicts with the possibility of achieving the common good. Consequently, a civil law authorizing abortion or euthanasia ceases by that very fact to be a true, morally binding civil law.[100]

---

published in earlier forms as *Sexualität und Verantwortung. Empfängnisverhütung als ethisches Problem,* IMABE Studie No. 3 (Vienna: IMABE, 1995), especially 115–23., and "Contraception, Sexual Behavior, and Natural Law: Philosophical Foundation of the Norm of *Humanae Vitae,*" *Linacre Quarterly* 56 (1989): 20–57.

98. *Evangelium Vitae,* no. 72.   99. Ibid.

100. Ibid.

In the final paragraph of the main text, before the "Conclusion," the encyclical even says:

Only respect for life can be the foundation and guarantee of the most precious and essential goods of society, such as democracy and peace. There can be no true democracy without a recognition of every person's dignity and without respect for his or her rights. Nor can there be true peace unless *life is defended and promoted.*[101]

These texts show, above all, how the magisterium has adhered to, and even appropriated for its own, a legal-political type of argument. The encyclical confirms the incongruence, with respect to the common good, of legislation favoring abortion and euthanasia, a contradiction that reveals itself in the specific and peculiar reason that such legislation originates in a society (including political society) that is oriented toward "the service of the person" and that, consequently, cannot contemplate a legal norm declaring it legal to kill an innocent person (or one that does not condemn it by a legitimate judge and a punishable crime under positive law).

Moreover, the encyclical mentions, among the fundamental goods of social life threatened by a culture of death, equality of all before the law, respect for life, and trust in relations between people. Finally, *Evangelium Vitae* affirms that authentic democracy and peace are impossible where life is not respected.

To be sure, the text needs further specification in some places. In particular, it is not at all clear what it means to assert, in this context, that a law instituting abortion is not "morally binding," since such a law does not command that anything be done, but rather permits and decriminalizes certain actions. The assertion could be understood to mean that such a law is contrary to the morality that citizens in legislative and judicial institutions are bound to follow insofar as they are the authors of acts of public relevance (e.g., legislative acts), that is, which are of interest to the civil society as a whole. Moreover, in this context it is important to clarify the difference between the "decriminalization" ("de-penalization") of certain acts (*Tatbestandsausschluss*) and their "legalization" or "justification" (*Rechtfertigung*). To fail to intervene with the criminal law is not obviously the equivalent, in certain cases,

101. Ibid., 101.

of declaring specific acts to be "legal" (*rechtmässig*) or legally justifying them, especially because, in the latter case, it will also be possible to have recourse to public support through the health system and the supporting community that maintains health insurance financing for such acts. It could even be possible to impose on health personnel an obligation to offer the corresponding services.[102] It is also important to emphasize, however, the large social and psychological difference between abrogating an existing penalty on the one hand, and not introducing a penalty that never before existed, on the other.

The only justifiable case foreseeable by juridical logic in which abortion could be declared *legal,* that is, in accordance with the law, is an interference with the right to life of the unborn in order to save the life of the mother. In fact, here there are two juridical goods at stake, which in constitutional terms are equivalent and thus offer the possibility of juridically justifying such an interference.[103]

It remains to consider why the legal advancement of abortion and euthanasia entails the steady abolition of equality before the law, trust in relations between people, and, ultimately, democracy and peace. At this level, we encounter the connection between civil law and moral law: the "culture of death" is contrary to the moral premises of the social order and of the legal-political culture of the constitutional democratic state.

Civil Law and Moral Law: The Moral Premises of Democratic Constitutionalism

In the course of our inquiry we have asked ourselves, more than once, how to justify the protection of prenatal life within a political culture based on a more or less Hobbesian-type utilitarian calculation.

102. Even if it can be imagined, it is highly problematic to declare an act illegal without arranging for a corresponding sanction provided by criminal law. This is what the German Constitutional Court proposed in its second judgment of 1993, and the proposal would mean that an action is illegal and permitted at the same time. See W. Kluth, "Der rechtswidrige Schwangerschaftsabbruch als erlaubte Handlung," *Zeitschrift für das gesamte Familien-recht* 1993 (Heft 12): 1382–90.

103. We should not forget that all fundamental rights are valid with reservations determined by the existence of a law that may restrict them (*Gesetzesvorbehalt*). Thus even article 2, section 2, of the *Grundgesetz* provides that it is only possible to interfere with the right to life on the basis of a law. At the same time, however, article 19, section 2, provides that no fundamental right can be impaired in its "essential content" (*Wesensgehalt*); homicide would be such an example. Juridically, however, one could choose to balance it against the life of the mother—a path that is not practicable from a strictly moral point of view—given that it is not

Within that sphere, those who submit to the coercive power of a state renounce part of their liberty in order to gain thereby a civil liberty, which includes security, peace, and the possibility of prosperity. We have seen how fundamental this logic is in the search for a guarantee of civil liberty; it is needed to justify the state's juridical duty to protect basic rights threatened by third parties and thus to show that such rights are a defense not only against the state. What is more, such rights serve to guarantee certain basic values, the protection of which defines the elementary task of state authority: protecting everyone's life and guaranteeing their security.

It is evident that this is a powerful argument on which to base any state law that prohibits homicide and punishes the guilty man for the killing of another. Without such a law, human coexistence would be impossible. The state could no longer fulfill its most elementary functions. The link between protection and obedience would be broken. But how would the unborn fall within this? Even a law that establishes a right to kill embryos and fetuses does not yet represent any threat to citizens. Thus, Peter Singer, not without a measure of cynicism, quotes Bentham's noted remark, according to which "infanticide is not capable of stealing tranquillity even from the most fearful soul," adding that "once we are old enough to understand this policy we are already too big to feel threatened by it."[104]

The logical structure of the "strategies" outlined above nonetheless demonstrates that legislative demands in favor of abortion and euthanasia contradict the foundations of a democratic culture and of a state engaged in guaranteeing security and peace to its citizens.

Moral Premises of the Culture of Death

We need to bear in mind that the proposals of a culture of death are ruinous not just because of what they propose. They are destructive also because their acceptance excludes alternatives, which can even be erased from memory. The culture of death is an alternative to that of

---

the state's role to oblige men to behave with moral rectitude, but instead to protect human life according to the principle of equality before the law. Obviously, no public authority, on the basis of such a balancing, can be permitted to force anyone to abort.

104. Singer, *Practical Ethics,* chapter six, 170; cited according to the German edition (Stuttgart: Reclam, 1984).

solidarity, of *unconditional* respect for life, of the permanent willingness of those who are living and strong and endowed with greater capacity for achievement to renounce certain advantages and rights in favor of others who are defenseless, weak, and needy. As the encyclical declares, such a "culture which denies solidarity"[105] is based on a *"notion of freedom* which exalts the isolated individual in an absolute way, and gives no place to solidarity, to openness to others and service to them."[106]

The "culture of death" represents the alternative not only to a civilization of love, but also to a civilization of profound respect for one's neighbor based on the simple affirmation that one finds oneself before another human being. We have confirmation of this when the handicapped are insulted and even physically assaulted by other citizens who reprimand them for being public burdens, or when parents of a handicapped child are seemingly disliked because it is thought that they have—irresponsibly—committed the error of not having chosen abortion at the appropriate time. The ethic of the value of life strongly contrasts with that promoted by the supporters of infanticide as a form of "mercy killing,"[107] who assert that "life is not a good in itself, but a means to something else—for example, to reach pleasant states of consciousness."[108]

This places in doubt what we commonly define as "human dignity" and the dignity of human life in general, given that human life—and thus the existence of the individual person—becomes a mere means for values *connected* to life, reducing life to an instrument to attain those goods. Here it is unnecessary to take up a discussion of this central point; it is sufficient to show that in the end the aforementioned strategies are oriented toward eliminating from our culture and our most deeply rooted convictions the truth expressed by Kant in a crucial moment of modern history: that a human being has no price, but dignity; and that he can never be treated as a mere means, but always also as an end. This truth is the heritage of a civilization, which originated in Christianity.

---

105. *Evangelium Vitae*, no. 12.

106. Ibid., no. 19.

107. H. Kuhse and P. Singer, *Should the Baby Live? The Problem of Handicapped Infants* (Oxford: Oxford University Press, 1985).

108. H. Kuhse, *The Sanctity-of-Life Doctrine in Medicine: A Critique* (Oxford: Clarendon Press, 1987), 213.

Furthermore, according to the strategies outlined above, our legal system ought to recognize a series of principles such as the following (not necessarily all of them together, however, given that they are in part logically incompatible):

1. Being considered a human, or a human person, with corresponding rights, depends on factors other than the mere fact of belonging to the species *Homo sapiens*. That is, it depends on specific properties and capacities that an individual human may or may not possess, and that may be lost even during an individual's life. It is the task of society (that is, philosophers, biologists, jurists, and others) to determine what properties are capable of providing a foundation for the right to life and, accordingly, of defining who is a person. Obviously, it is not possible to be certain that this process will remain immune from the influence of the specific interests of those who affect such a determination;

2. The intrinsic value of human life, its dignity and sacredness, has no relation at all with those possible "rights" that ought to be connected with that life (from this principle the next one follows);

3. It is the role of the positive law alone to determine who, by law, may be considered a "person," and therefore who is the object of equal treatment before the law; that is to say, independently of biological and anthropological facts, which are generally considered to be morally irrelevant. In contrast to the first principle, this third one would allow only politicians, legislators, and judges to determine who can be recognized as a person with a right to equal treatment on the part of the law (in practice, however, it has an identical effect);

4. Any possible limit to the self-determination of a subject (for example, a pregnant woman) justifies the elimination of the cause of that limit, assuming that that cause is not, in turn, already a subject with a present capacity for self-determination (something not possible for the unborn, or persons in an irreversible coma, or even the elderly in need of intensive care without hope of recovery).

No one would desire, in my opinion, a society and a legal system based on such principles. On the contrary, we take pride precisely in having overcome, in our legal-political culture, a similar danger. Nevertheless, perhaps this aversion survives only at an intuitive level. I shall now propose two basic arguments to make these intuitions, which are correct, more rationally explicit. Both of the arguments are based on the premise that the unborn is, as is every human, an individual belonging to the species *Homo sapiens,* and is thus a human person (since the existence of such individuals, except insofar as they are persons, is not possible).

The Pre-political Character of the Right to Life:
The Contrary Logic of Discrimination

Even remaining within Hobbesian logic, we must realize that the fundamental right on which the entire subsequent edifice is built is the right to life. For Hobbes, the primary and fundamental *bonum* is identified precisely with life, survival, and self-preservation. The *summum malum,* in contrast, is represented by violent and painful death, unnatural and undesired, in frustration of one's self-interest.[109]

The critical point is that this right is not, even in Hobbesian thinking, founded in a utilitarian way. On the contrary, the entire utilitarian calculus that leads to the institution of state authority is placed in the service of "the value of life." The right to live, for any man, is a presupposition for the legitimacy of any legal and civil order. Hobbes, in a radical way, understands a threat to one's own life to be the sole but decisive reason for not being obliged to submit to the sovereign, given that it is precisely the sovereign who has been authorized to protect life.

The advantage of Hobbesian thought, in this context, is that it provides a theory that formulates the minimum requirements for demonstrating a common heritage of Western culture: the right to live is not conferred by political power or by law. It is prior to them. Political society and the state are always in the service of the life of every individual, acknowledging the human dignity even of subjects who do not participate in the hypothetical social contract, inasmuch as they are too weak to represent any threat to the peaceful coexistence and prosperity of men (and who, moreover, make no contribution whatsoever to others but instead constitute a burden on them, a limitation on their liberty). If this is true, no utilitarian calculus can justify respect for life. Here is where the principle of "human dignity" comes into play, as a foundation

---

109. Hobbes, *De Homine,* XI, 6.

for the unconditional respect for the other, respect based simply on *being human.*[110]

It follows from this that one who is "human" but excluded from such protection and security is *discriminated against,* because for whatever reason he is not capable of consciously assuming the contractual bond holding together the political community, or because his exclusion is sanctioned by a majority. The first case applies to the unborn, and also concerns newborns and children; the second, for example, is the case of blacks in the United States until the latter half of the nineteenth century. It is a question of discrimination because a "non-species" criterion of exclusion is applied, that is, a criterion that differs from one that takes into account membership in the species *Homo sapiens.*

The important result of these reflections is that the utilitarianism of the Hobbesian calculus—and *a fortiori* of the Lockean and similar ones—cannot relativize the right to life of every individual human; it is rather presupposed as a pre-political right. Thus, this reasoning coincides with the idea that there exists a level of "value"—that of life and security—that must be respected by the legislator. As we have already discussed in connection with *Roe v. Wade,* no legislator has ever *conferred* such a right on a human; on the contrary, the legitimacy of legislative power—which is the core of Hobbesian thought—depends on the effectiveness of the protection of the life of the individual person. The only limitation that can even be *contemplated* would be to restrict this to the *innocent* person, that is, one who is not guilty of a crime that by law carries with it capital punishment. Nevertheless, even in this case it was not the state that conferred the right to live to anyone; it simply *revoked* it, but does so *ad personam* and assumes a judgment for a crime for which the accused is found guilty. It is not revoked, therefore, on the basis of a discriminatory law, but on the basis of an individual judgment constitutive of guilt.

Certainly, the Hobbesian formulation is minimal, poor, and not free of ambiguity, insofar as it reduces everything to mere survival. But in

110. This is the argument in Kriele, *Die nicht-therapeutische Abtreibung vor dem Grundgesetz,* 95–100. The category of "human dignity" obviously goes beyond Hobbesian political theory. Nevertheless, in the Lockean version of contractualism, found in the Declaration of Independence of the United States of 1776, we can find the formulation: "that all men are created equal, that they are endowed by their Creator with certain inalienable Rights, that among these are Life, Liberty and the pursuit of Happiness. That to secure these rights, Governments are instituted among men"(cf. Locke, *Second Treatise of Government,* §§ 87, 94).

the present context it is more than sufficient to show that the respect for life has priority and is immune from every utilitarian calculus, *even in so utilitarian a thinker as Hobbes.* Now we can also understand why, according to Hobbes, the science of these terms of peace, or the precepts of reason that lead to conditions of peace among men, represent in his opinion "the true and only moral philosophy"; this is why Hobbes defines them as "natural laws."[111] Preserving and protecting human life because it is the life of a man and "my life" is the fundamental point of convergence between moral law and civil law.

With respect to the protection of legally enforceable rights, to allow a criterion different from that of belonging to the species *Homo sapiens* means legitimizing discriminatory laws elsewhere as well. People are apt to discriminate in this way, so long as it corresponds to the interest of an "exclusive" majority—a majority able to protect itself in such a way as to ensure that none of its members ever risks being counted among the members of the class discriminated against. The unborn are surely the prime candidates for such discrimination.

While racial, ethnic, religious, or social discrimination tends to become attenuated and is gradually overcome (since those discriminated against become historical actors who vindicate their rights), this is impossible in the case of those who are not yet born. They find themselves in a situation of total dependence on the born. Consequently, the initiative for respecting their right to life is the duty only of those who potentially discriminate against them. Thus we arrive at the second argument.

The Golden Rule and the Sense of Justice

Granting that the unborn is a human person with a right to life, legalizing abortion means favoring—with the support of state authority and the entire society of the living—a weakening of the sense of justice. We shall be required to become accustomed to violating the good of others—the same good that, if it were our own, we would instead want respected by others—as not contrary to the most elementary sense of justice, *only because we have nothing to fear from that other person: neither he nor any other member of the "class" of the as yet unborn will ever be able to make us pay for this injustice of ours.*

111. Hobbes, *Leviathan,* chapter XV.

Hobbes maintained that his theory of natural laws—which are the terms of peace that lead to the agreement instituting the sovereign power of the state—would be nothing more than a new formulation or a "succinct formula" of the "law of the gospel," and in particular of the golden rule contained therein: "do not do to others what you would not wish done to you."[112] It is here that Hobbes's theory seems insufficient, inasmuch as it does not correspond at all to the logic of the golden rule but rather to what Gregory Kavka has called the "copper rule" (which is less perfect and bright): the principle "Do unto others as they do unto you."[113]

The golden rule, however, which commands us (not) to do unto others what we would (not) want others to do unto us, is not based on the expectation of an effective reciprocal behavior on the part of others—impossible in the case of the unborn and in many other cases—but only on the *desirability* of that behavior toward us. It is a question of a way of behaving that—and here lies the essence of the principle of "justice"—becomes "for me" a norm of behavior "with respect to the other" and "in the interests of the other."[114]

None of us, at present, would wish to have been aborted while in a fetal state. Or better yet, no one would consider someone a benefactor who decided at that time to terminate our nascent life. No one would even make the following concession: "I cannot take issue with the behavior of that person, given that at the time, I, not then being a person, did not have interests and desires." On the contrary, if we were to find out about someone who, at that time, attempted to perpetrate a similar act but failed, we would be inclined to accuse him of attempted homicide before a court. (This demonstrates that every aborted fetus, while not a "potential person" but already a person in fact, is a potential *actor*. But being an actor in a court is a property that the fetus only potentially possesses, which seems to constitute a further reason for assigning to the state a duty to take up the protection of the unborn.)[115]

---

112. Hobbes, *Leviathan*, chapter XV. I refer, for this, to my book: *La Filosofia politica di Thomas Hobbes*, 6.2 and 6.5.

113. Gregory S. Kavka, *Hobbesian Moral and Political Theory* (Princeton: Princeton University Press, 1986), 347.

114. Rhonheimer, *La prospettiva della morale* 243–48.

115. See M. Rhonheimer, *Absolute Herrschaft der Geborenen?* 46 ff. A very similar argument is that of H. J. Gensler, "The Golden Rule Argument against Abortion," in Pojman and Beckwith, *The Abortion Controversy*, 305–19.

As emphasized, with reference to an argument by Richard M. Hare that is equally founded on the golden rule,[116] every application of this fundamental rule of justice assumes an identity between the unborn (embryo or fetus) and the person after birth.[117] It is true that various theories exist, in the tradition of Locke's concept of "person," that attempt to contest that identity, on the basis of the previously noted distinction between "person" and "human individual."[118] Nevertheless, we have no reason to think that a fetus—say, this author at eight and a half months in my mother's womb, visible in an ultrasound image—is not "me," or that the photograph that my father took of an already smiling two-year-old is not my image, even if there are some philosophers who would assert the opposite simply because, they say, we cannot *remember* those "fetal" moments. It would follow that that fetus was an individual other than the one I am now.

Each one of us would perceive it as intrinsically unjust to imagine our own abortion committed on the basis of the argument that this human individual did not yet enjoy that right to life which is now ascribed to him, having been born and thus having acquired the rights of a citizen; or that he unfortunately was an obstacle to the self-determination of his mother and her projects (or simply that he was the "unwanted" fruit of a sexual act with a defective contraceptive); or that ultimately it was not so important whether he was a person at the time since the law did not consider him a "constitutional person" and since, in general, the state cannot impose on all citizens the majority's notion of the value of life.

In sum, if we are disposed to cultivate the consciousness of having all been, at one time, embryos and fetuses—clearly not aborted—perhaps we will be in a position to recall that a state that does not consider itself bound to protect those not yet born, and the society that absolves it of that duty, are both founded on a grave injustice incompatible with the essence of law. In a society where something that is manifestly a crime and where a primordial violation of justice is converted into a "right" supported, planned, and administered by the state,[119] interpersonal rela-

116. R. M. Hare, "Abortion and the Golden Rule," *Philosophy and Public Affairs* 4 (1975): 201–22.

117. Leist, *Eine Frage des Lebens*, 103–4.

118. See Spaemann, *Sind alle Menschen Personen?* and Honnefelder, *Der Streit um die Person.*

119. Cf. *Evangelium Vitae*, no. 11.

tions must inevitably suffer serious damage, given that living together in society, a common good par excellence, is based precisely on justice.

In order to qualify not only as the claims of persons but also as a genuine legal order, law presumes that people act not only in light of their individual good but also for the good of others *because it is the good of the other,* seeking such a good not so much because it foreseeably results in the long term in my own good, but because it is good for the other person. This basic solidarity in seeking not just the "good for me" but also the good of the other, *because it is good for the other,* reflects the profundity of the golden rule, which is founded on the recognition that the other is a human being as much as I am. This is what we could define as "willful self-transcendence of the subject with respect to the other," which is just what Hobbesian philosophy ends up denying.[120] All of social life is based on this self-transcendence of the person with respect to the other. The logic of "collective advantage," in compensation for the mutual exchange of renunciations of "natural" liberty, is insufficient. The reason for conferring the monopoly of legitimate violence on a sovereign power does not, therefore, contain the whole truth.[121] It can be the basis for the logic of security, but not at the same time for that of living together in society, of interpersonal community, or of mutual trust. If it could be attributed only to *propter retributionem,* it would correspond to "economic," rather than genuinely moral, behavior.[122]

In short, the Hobbesian calculus—and any contractualism of a utilitarian type—is able to provide the basis for only the state's obligation to protect my life, but not my obligation to respect and protect also the *life of others,* except insofar as I can foreseeably benefit from it. Thus Hobbes is not capable of providing a basis for solidarity, but only for a calculus directed toward one's own benefit (in the long term).

The mere logic of mutual benefit or "collective advantage" is always open to excluding and discriminating against entire groups from its cal-

120. "[T]he necessity of nature leads men to will and desire the bonum sibi, that which is good for themselves": Hobbes, *Elements of Law Natural and Political,* I, chap. 14, 6. The search for the good (and right) of others enters into Hobbesian philosophy only as a result of a utilitarian calculus.

121. This is admitted, without offering a solution to the problem, by O. Höffe in *Politische Gerechtigkeit. Grundlegung einer kritischen Philosophie von Recht und Staat* (Frankfurt: Suhrkamp, 1989), 427.

122. See David L. Norton, *Democracy and Moral Development: A Politics of Virtue* (Berkeley and Los Angeles, Calif.: University of California Press, 1991), 25–31.

culations. It is insufficient for founding an unconditional respect for the other as my equal—unconditioned, that is, by factors such as "not being born," "mentally infirm," "object of heavy treatments that force others to make serious sacrifices." It cannot be denied, however, that true peace and the values of democracy take root at just this level, where moral law and civil law interpenetrate in a fundamental way. I have argued from the outset that the immoral character of a certain way of acting does not constitute a sufficient reason for it being prohibited and suppressed on the part of the civil law and the coercive power of public authority. Nevertheless, once we make clear the connection between the immorality (or, more accurately, the injustice) of the action in question and the common good, understood in terms of specific political ethics, the way is opened for a legal-political argument able to provide the basis for a corresponding intervention of the state and the legislator. This is what we have done in these pages, demonstrating that it is a line of argument akin to the one in *Evangelium Vitae.*

Conclusion

State authority and the law are not capable of creating society. They are, however, capable of protecting—or of destroying by means of an irresponsible passivity and tolerance—those premises that are essential for life in society, such as that of the respect for the life of every living individual who belongs to the human species. We are at present in a very peculiar situation. Compared to other eras, we *know* more and we can also *do* much more. We can kill better, in simpler and more painless ways. We also know much more about prenatal life. We are aware that the life of an individual human being—concretely, this or that person—already began even before the mother realized that she was pregnant. Furthermore, we have a knowledge of prenatal life and associated techniques that allow us to do what must not be done, and what is—at least up to now—against the law to do after birth. The weight of our responsibility has increased, sometimes in a way that makes it almost unbearable to resist the corresponding temptations. Nevertheless, modern man has a responsibility for life that is much more extensive with respect to that of every preceding generation. We must learn to assume that responsibility in accordance with our human dignity.

In *Evangelium Vitae,* John Paul II speaks of a "cultural change," in which what he calls a "new feminism," founded on a new sensitivity with respect to the "experience of motherhood," will have a preeminent role. In particular, the encyclical affirms that which seems to be almost a synthesis of what has been said up to this point, namely, that motherhood is a sort of "school of humanity":

A mother welcomes and carries in herself another human being, enabling it to grow inside her, giving it room, respecting it in its otherness. Women first learn and then teach others that human relations are authentic if they are open to accepting the other person: a person who is recognized and loved because of the dignity which comes from being a person and not from other considerations, such as usefulness, strength, intelligence, beauty, or health. This is the fundamental contribution which the Church and humanity expect from women. And it is the indispensable prerequisite for an authentic cultural change.[123]

We would be blind if we did not see that here is the core of the problem. A new feminism, however, need not reproduce a simple return to forms of disrespect toward women that are typical of a society saturated in a one-sided way with masculine values. The drama of abortion is a drama caused in large part by men. In this sense, also, the cultural change concerns everyone, engages everyone, and depends on everyone.

123. *Evangelium Vitae, 99.*

Appendix

An Initial Response to Todd A. Salzman and Michael G. Lawler

My argument in support of *Humanae Vitae,* as it was exposed in the original and shorter 1989 article in the *Linacre Quarterly* and in *Natural Law and Practical Reason,* has been challenged by Todd A. Salzman and Michael G. Lawler in their *The Sexual Person: Toward a Renewed Catholic Anthropology* (Washington, D.C.: Georgetown University Press, 2008), 75–84. The criticism of these authors, however, who try to set forth a clearly revisionist sexual anthropology and morality, fails because, though they discuss at some length what they call my "admirable" argument against contraception, they do not even mention—in their critical reflection on my approach to contraception—its core, and therefore seriously misconstrue it. This is hard to understand because their preceding discussion of my approach to natural law recognizes crucial elements of it that they then neglect when criticizing my approach to contraception (i.e., the body-soul unity of the person, the grounding of natural law in the body—although natural law pertains properly to reason—and the grounding of virtue in the body). Although my analysis recognizes that intentionality is crucial (though not sufficient) for an adequate definition/description of the relevant human acts—whether contraceptive acts or acts of periodic abstinence—my argument for the immorality of contraceptive acts is *not*

based, as Salzman and Lawler suggest, on a purely intentional difference between contraception and periodic abstinence. This is the key reason why their criticism of my view, while sophisticated in some respects, is far off the mark. More specifically, they argue—against my approach—that since both contraception and periodic abstinence involve an "intentionality" to prevent conception, they are morally indistinguishable. This argument, however, relies upon a reading into my analysis of their own broad—and highly inadequate—understanding of "intentionality." Whereas my understanding follows Aquinas in holding that intentions depend on reason (which truthfully grasps the relevant matter and circumstances of the action) and are measured by reason, their broad notion of "intentionality" is something different, corresponding to the subjective preferences of the agent.

In their critical remarks, the authors fail to mention that the core of my argument is about the *embodiment* of procreative responsibility in the concrete sexual behavior; that it is, thus, an argument centered in the "language of the body," in the moral requirement, anthropologically founded, that the body and bodily sexual behavior are to act as subject, and not only an object, of procreative responsibility. By this I mean that the body, with its procreative power, is not to be seen as an object to be manipulated (i.e., via anovulant pills) but as part of an acting subject who is a unity of body and soul. This recognition of the body as integral subject of procreative responsibility is central to a proper construal of the nexus between the virtue of chastity and sexual acts. According to my argument, this nexus is not simply an intentional relation, as Salzman and Lawler make me say (by forcing my thought under their broad notion of "intentionality"), but a relation based on the insight that the virtue of chastity, part of temperance, requires the body to participate as subject and active principle in procreative responsibility (which itself is shown to be a constitutive part of marital chastity). So, everything that Salzman and Lawler induce against my argument is based precisely on the omission of mentioning its core rationale.

When this core rationale is thus neglected, quotations from my article (to which they do not even give a complete bibliographical reference) are thus taken out of context, and their meaning is thereby changed. What in my text is often already a conclusion of the argument is presented as the argument itself and then easily shown as not demonstrating the conclusion. By omitting that, for me, part of the intentionality included in contraception is precisely to render superfluous the modification of *bodily sexual behavior,* they ask: "If, however, the intentionality of periodic abstinence is not to procreate, why cannot artificial contraception, which has the same intentionality, be considered a marital act as well?" (82). Everything in this question is wrong. Salzman and Lawler are able to formulate it plausibly because they treat periodic abstinence as a kind of (non-artificial) contraception, while I precisely showed why this is a crucial mistake. Their fundamental misunderstanding of my argument is manifest in their claim that my position is close to that of Germain Grisez; they mistakenly think that he "argues similarly" to me in holding that "a contraceptive act is distinct from any sexual act" (ibid.). Yet, it is clear that I precisely reject the idea that contraception can be described, in a way that is adequate for moral evaluation, without including its relation to sexual acts! My argument is actually based on showing how this relation is constitutive for the very definition of the contraceptive choice and its moral evaluation; these essential aspects of my argument, however, are completely absent from the theory misleadingly criticized as mine by Salzman and Lawler.

They further add confusion by constantly using the term "artificial contraception," suggesting that my argument is one against *artificial* contraception. One of my central points, however, was precisely to show how the talk of *artificial* contraception is misleading. My argument against contraception is an argument against *contraception* as such, that is, the willing preventing of freely consented sexual acts from being fertile. Although the book can be commended for its civil tone, and for what seems to be a serious attempt to become familiar with aspects of my work, it remains deficient in advancing the hoped-for dialogue mentioned in its prologue because—as the above remarks should be sufficient to show—it ends up badly misrepresenting the argument of at least one of those it intends to engage in dialogue with.

This is not the place to refute the general approach of Salzman and Lawler's book, which unfortunately includes an apology not only for contraception, but also for extramarital sex, homosexual sex, and artificial reproductive technologies. One point of their general approach, however, I should mention because it also directly affects a central aspect of my argument against contraception. It is their claim that with

Gaudium et Spes, the Second Vatican Council has brought, as they say on page 3 of the prologue of their book, "a radical evolution in Catholic sexual teaching and, by implication, the sexual anthropology reflected in this teaching, *by eliminating the language of the hierarchy of the ends of marriage*" (emphasis added). The traditional "hierarchical language of the two ends of marriage is rejected and 'the nature of the human person and his acts' is posited as the foundational principle of harmonizing the ends of marriage."

Many readers do not know perhaps that what Salzman and Lawler call the "foundational principle" of their new approach to sexuality is in reality the most well-known and traditional commonplace of post-conciliar revisionist moral theology. While at the beginning of this revisionist moral theology it was normally said only that *Gaudium et Spes* "did not anymore speak" about the ends of marriage, but only of the person, and this silence was thought to be extremely significant and conveniently interpreted as a major doctrinal change, Salzman and Lawler now know even more: they inform us that the council in reality has "eliminated" and "rejected" the idea of a hierarchy of ends of marriage. What is new in their approach is not their rejection of the traditional view about the "ends of marriage," but the assertion that it was the Second Vatican Council that eliminated and rejected this doctrine.

However, Salzman and Lawler's interpretation of *Gaudium et Spes* and, therefore, their foundational principle, is based on the very confusion I have tried to explain in the course of my argument against contraception. Throughout their book, they confound the concept of *ends* (or "functions") of marriage (which was traditionally thought to be transmission of life and mutual assistance of the spouses) with the concept of *meanings* of marital sexual intercourse; or else they think, as on page 125, that the expression of love through the marital act is a "role and function" of human sexuality, confounding again "function" and "meaning"! Here they see the "radical evolution" effected by the council. In particular, whereas traditional sexual morality restricted sexuality to the two ends (or "functions") of marriage (the first of which was procreation), Salzman and Lawler claim that the new teaching of the council "eliminat[es]" this prior teaching such that sexuality is now seen as serving the "function" (but the text says "meaning") of expressing love and mutual self-giving. Procreation, according to the council, is no longer part of what defines the essence of human sexuality. This is the whole point of Salzman and Lawler's book.

But as far as this book claims to be an exegesis of the Second Vatican Council, it relies upon a misreading of the quoted passage of *Gaudium et Spes*. In reality, if this passage does not speak about hierarchically ordered *ends of marriage* this is not because it intends to reject the traditional teaching about the ends of marriage but simply because this passage does not speak about *marriage*. It instead speaks about marital sexuality and, concretely, the *marital act*. Considering the question of contraception, which the council did not want to tackle, *Gaudium et Spes* simply states that this question has to be resolved by considering "the nature of the human person and his acts"—which was, of course magisterially done by Paul VI 1968 in his encyclical *Humanae Vitae*.

So, Salzman and Lawler's "foundational principle" actually rests on the traditional and well-known revisionist misreading of this famous passage of *Gaudium et Spes* and, moreover, on their proper confusion between the concepts of "ends of marriage" (or "functions" of marriage) and "meanings of the marital act." The confusion is rather obvious because, if "ends of marriage" (procreation and mutual assistance) and "significations of the marital act" (procreation and union) were conceptually convertible, this would imply that according to the traditional teaching regarding the ends of marriage (which is allegedly "rejected" by the Second Vatican Council), marital sexual intercourse (union) would have been—rather absurdly—equated with the mutual assistance of the spouses! Instead, the traditional and still valid doctrine about the two ends of marriage was a doctrine not about marital sexual acts, but about the *natural institution of marriage*. And this means: the teaching about marital sexuality in the context of "the nature of the human person and his acts" does not in the least "eliminate," but *presupposes* the teaching about the double ends or functions of the natural institution of marriage, this teaching being precisely *part* of a true conception of the "human person and his acts." This is how the real "radical evolution" of the postconciliar Magisterium's teaching of sexual morality has to be seen and appreciated: it complements the traditional doctrine about the ends of marriage *with a doctrine about the meaning of marital sexuality* and the *marital* act. It is proper to this teaching not to focus solely on the procreative meaning of the marital act—which is obviously grounding the procreative end or function of marriage—but to see also, as essentially and inseparably united to this procreative meaning, the unitive meaning of expressing love and mutual self-giving. It's the inseparability of these two meanings that is the originality and newness of this conciliar and post-conciliar doctrine of the Magisterium. Exactly this originality and newness is clearly rejected by Salzman and Lawler and eliminated from their approach, which pursues one main argumentative goal: to separate sexuality from its intrinsically and essentially procreative meaning, and egregiously but indefensibly, to attribute such a "radical evolution" to the Magisterium of the Second Vatican Council.

This is why I think that, as far as its main thesis and outlook is concerned, Salzman and Lawler's book does not really teach us anything new. It is simply a very well presented form of an old argument that, in my conviction, has been proved to be one of the most pernicious to modern civilization: the separation between sexuality and procreation.

Bibliography

Abbà, Giuseppe. *Lex et virtus: Studi sull'evoluzione della dottrina morale di San Tommaso d'Aquino.* Rome: LAS, 1983.

Anscombe, G. E. M. (Gertrude Elizabeth Margaret). *Intention.* 2nd ed. Oxford: Basil Blackwell, 1963.

———. *Contraception and Chastity.* London: Catholic Truth Society, 1975.

———. "You Can Have Sex without Children: Christianity and the New Offer." In *The Collected Philosophical Papers of G. E. M. Anscombe.* Vol. 3: *Ethics, Religion and Politics,* 82–96. Oxford: Basil Blackwell, 1981.

Aznar Gil, Federico R. Derecho. *Matriomonial Canónico.* Vol. 1: *Cánones 1055–1094.* Salamanca: Publicaciones Universidad Pontificia Salamanca, 2001.

Aquinas, Thomas. *De Malo. Quaestiones disputatae de malo.* Leonine edition, vol. 23. Sancti Thomae de Aquino opera omnia. Rome, 1882–.

———. *De Veritate. Quaestiones disputatae de veritate.* Leonine edition, vol. 22. Sancti Thomae de Aquino opera omnia. Rome, 1882–.

———. *In duo praecepta caritatis et in decem legis praecepta exposition.* Opuscula Theologica, vol. 2. Turin: Marietti, 1975.

———. *Summa contra Gentiles: Book Three, Providence,* Part II. Translated by Vernon J. Bourke. Notre Dame: University of Notre Dame Press, 1956, paperback 1975.

———. *Summa theologiae.* Translated by the English Dominicans. Westminster: Christian Classics, 1981.

———. *On Evil.* Translated by John A. and Jean T. Oesterle. Notre Dame: University of Notre Dame Press, 2001.

Aristotle. *The Complete Works of Aristotle.* Edited by J. Barnes. Princeton: Princeton University Press, 1984.

————. *The Nicomachean Ethics.* Translated by David Ross. Revised by J. L. Ackrill and J. O. Urmson. Oxford: Oxford University Press, 1998.

Arquilliere, Henri-Xavier. *L'Augustinisme politique. Essai sur la formation des théories politiques du Moyen Age.* 2nd ed. Paris: J. Vrin, 1955.

Auer, Alfons. "Die Autonomie des Sittlichen nach Thomas von Aquin." In *Christlich glauben und handeln,* edited by Klaus Demmer and Bruno Schüller. Düsseldorf: Patmos Verlag, 1977.

Bajda, Jerzy "Verantwortete Elternschaft und Antikonzeption." In *Elternschaft und Menschenwürde,* edited by Ernst Wenisch, 243–60. Vallendar: Patris Verlag, 1984.

Bastian, Till, ed. *Denken—Schreiben—Töten. Zur neuen "Euthanasie"—Diskussion.* Stuttgart: Hirzel, 1990.

Baumann-Hölzle, Ruth. "Ethische Probleme der prenatalen Diagnostik." *Neue Zürcher Zeitung* 10/11, no. 83 (April 1993): 9–10.

Belmans, Theo G. *Le sens objectif de l'agir humain. Pour relire la morale conjugale de Saint Thomas.* Vatican City: Libreria Editrice Vaticana, 1980. German edition: *Der objektive Sinn menschlichen Handelns: Die authentische Ehemoral des heiligen Thomas von Aquin.* Vallendar: Patris Verlag, 1984.

Bertsch, Ludwig. "Akzente der kirchlichen Ehelehre von Pius XI bis Johannes Paul II. Überlegungen aus der Sicht eines Pastoraltheologen." In *Der umstrittene Naturbegriff,* edited by Franz Böckle, 128–29. Düsseldorf: Patmos Verlag, 1987.

Böckle, Franz "*Humanae vitae* und die philosophische Anthropologie Karol Wojtylas. Zur päpstlichen Lehrposition zur künstlichen Befrüchtung und ihrer Begründung." *Herder Korrespondenz* 43 no. 8 (Freiburg: Herder, 1989): 376.

Boyle, Joseph M. "Human Action, Natural Rhythms and Contraception: A Response to Noonan." *American Journal of Jurisprudence* 26 (1981): 32–46.

Brock, Stephen L. "*Veritatis splendor* §78, St. Thomas, and (Not Merely) Physical Objects of Moral Acts." *Nova et Vetera* (English ed). 6, no. 1 (2008): 1–62.

Brunner, Otto, Werner Conze, and Reinhart Kosellek. *Geschichtliche Grundbegriffe.* Vol. 7. Stuttgart: Klett-Cotta, 1992.

Brunelli, L. "La pillola Congolese." *Il Sabato* (March 13, 1993): 32–33.

Carlyle, Robert Warrand, and Alexander James Carlyle. *A History of Mediaeval Political Theory in the West.* 6 vols. Edinburgh-London: William Blackwood, 1903–36, 1970 reprint.

Chevalier, Jean-Jacques. *Storia del pensiero politico.* Vol. 1. 2nd ed. Bologna: Il Mulino, 1989,

Curran, Charles E. "Natural Law and Contemporary Moral Theology." In *Contraception: Authority and Dissent,* edited by C. E. Curran. New York: Herder and Herder, 1969.

Doms, Herbert. *Vom Sinn und Zweck der Ehe*. Breslau: Ostdeutsche Verlag, 1935.

———. *The Meaning of Marriage*. Translated by George Sayer. London: Sheed and Ward, 1939.

Dörner, Klaus. *Tödliches Mitleid*. Gütersloh: Jakob van Hoddis Verlag, 1988.

De Finance, Joseph. "Autonomie et Théonomie." In *L'Agire Morale*, edited by M. Zalba, 239–60. Atti del Congresso Internazionale (Roma-Napoli, 17–24 April 1974). *Tomasso d'Aquino nel suo settimo centenario*. Vol. 5. Napoli: Edizioni Domenicane Italiane, 1974.

Faggioni, Maurizio Pietro. "AIDS. Questioni Disputate in Ambito Coniugale." *Antonianum* 72, no. 3 (July–September 1997): 447–67.

Finnis, John. "*Humanae Vitae*: Its Background and Aftermath." *International Review of Natural Family Planning* 4 (1980): 141–53.

———. "Personal Integrity, Sexual Morality and Responsible Parenthood." *Anthropos* (now *Anthropotes*) 1 (1985): 43–55.

Fucek, Ivan. Interviewed by L. Brunelli. "La pillola congolese." *Il Sabato*, March 13, 1993, 32–33.

Fuchs, Josef. *Lex Naturae. Zur Theologie des Naturrechts*. Düsseldorf: Patmos, 1955.

———. "Biologie und Ehemoral." *Gregorianum* 2 (1962): 225–53.

———. "Der Absolutheitscharakter sittlicher Handlungsnormen." In *Testimonium veritatis: Philosophische und theologische Studien zu kirchlichen Fragen der Gegenwart*, edited by Hans Wolter. Frankfurter theologische Studien, vol. 7. Frankfurt: Josef Knecht, 1971.

———. "Das Problem Todsünde." *Stimmen der Zeit* 119 (1994): 7–86.

Ginters, Rudolf. Die Ausdruckshandlung: Eine Untersuchung ihrer sittlichen Bedeutsamkeit. Düsseldorf: Patmos-Verlag, 1976.

Glendon, Mary Ann. *Rights Talk: The Impoverishment of Political Discourse*. New York: Free Press, 1991.

Grisez, Germain. "A New Formulation of a Natural-Law Argument against Contraception." *Thomist* 30, no. 4 (1966): 343–44.

———. "Dualism and the New Morality." In *L'Agire Morale* (*Atti del Congresso Internazionale: Tommaso d'Aquino nel suo settimo centenario*, vol. 5), edited by M. Zalba, 323–30. Naples: Editions of the Italian Dominicans, 1974.

———. *The Way of the Lord Jesus*. Vol. 1: *Christian Moral Principles*. Chicago: Franciscan Herald Press, 1983.

———. *The Way of the Lord Jesus*. Vol. 2: *Living a Christian Life*. Quincy: Franciscan Press, 1993.

Grisez, Germain, Joseph Boyle, and John Finnis. "Practical Principles, Moral Truth, and Ultimate Ends." *American Journal of Jurisprudence* 32 (1987): 99–151.

Grisez, Germain, et al. "'Every Marital Act Ought to Be Open to New Life':

Toward a Clearer Understanding." *Thomist* 52, no. 3 (1988). In Italian: *Anthropotes* 4, no. 1 (1988).

Häring, Bernard. "The Inseparability of the Unitive-Procreative Functions of the Marital Act." In *Contraception: Authority and Dissent,* edited by C. Curran. New York: Herder and Herder, 1969.

———. *Lexikon für Theologie und Kirche,* 2nd ed., vol. 14 (supplementary vol. 3), 423–46. Freiburg: Herder Verlag, 1986.

Hittinger, Russell. *The First Grace: Rediscovering the Natural Law in a Post-Christian World.* Wilmington, Del.: ISI Books, 2003.

Hoerster, Norbert. *Abtreibung im säkularen Staat. Argumente gegen den §218.* Frankfurt am Main: Suhrkamp, 1991.

Honnefelder, Ludger. "Der Streit um die Person in der Ethik." *Philosophisches Jahrbuch* 100 (1993): 246–65.

Hürth, P. Franz. "Il premunirsi rientra nel diritto all legittima difesa." *Studi Cattolici* 27 (1961): 65.

John Paul II. *Lubliner Vorlesungen.* Stuttgart: Seewald Verlag, 1980.

———. Discourse of January 10, 1992, to the participants in a course organized by the Center for Studies and Research on the Natural Regulation of Fertility of the Catholic University of the Sacred Heart. *L'Osservatore Romano,* January 11, 1992, 5.

———. *Man and Woman He Created Them: A Theology of the Body.* Boston: Pauline Books and Media, 2006.

Kluxen, Wolfgang. "Menschliche Natur und Ethos." *Münchener Theologische Zeitschrift* 23 (1972): 17.

———. "Anima separata und Personsein bei Thomas von Aquin." In *Thomas von Aquino: Interpretation und Rezeption,* edited by Willehad Paul Eckert. Mainz: Matthias-Grünewald, 1974.

Knauer, Peter. "La détermination du bien et du mal moral par le principe du double effet." *Nouvelle revue théologique* 87 (1965): 356–76. In English: "The Hermeneutic Function of the Principle of Double Effect." In *Readings in Moral Theology,* no. 1, edited by Charles E. Curran and Richard A. McCormick, 1–39. New York: Paulist, 1979.

Koslowski, Peter. *Prinzipien der Ethischen Ökonomie. Grundlegung der Wirtschaftsethik und der auf die Ökonomie bezogenen Ethik.* Tübingen: Mohr Siebeck, 1988.

Lehmann, Karl. "Das Eintreten für das Lebensrecht des ungeborenen Kindes als christlicher und humaner Auftrag." In *Herausforderung Schwangersschaftsabbruch,* edited by J. Reiter and R. Keller, 34–60. Freiburg: Herder Verlag, 1992.

Lehu, Léonard. *La raison, règle de la moralità d'après Saint Thomas.* Paris: J. Gabalda et Fils, 1930.

Levering, Matthew. "Natural Law and Natural Inclinations: Rhonheimer, Pinckaers, McAleer." *Thomist* 70 (April 2006): 155–201.

————. *Biblical Natural Law: A Theocentric and Teleological Approach.* Oxford: Oxford University Press, 2008.

Martelet, Gustave. "Morale conjugale et vie chrétienne." *Nouvelle revue théologique* 87 (1965): 245–66.

May, William E. "The Meaning and Nature of the Natural Law in Thomas Aquinas." *American Journal of Jurisprudence* 22 (1977): 168–89.

————. *Moral Absolutes, Catholic Tradition, Current Trends, and the Truth.* Milwaukee: Marquette University Press, 1989.

McCormick, Richard. "Some Early Reactions to *Veritatis Splendor.*" *Theological Studies* 55 (1994): 481–506.

McInerny, Ralph. "*Humanae vitae* and the Principle of Totality." In *Why Humanae Vitae Was Right: A Reader,* edited by Janet Smith. San Francisco: Ignatius Press, 1993.

Mill, John Stuart. "Utilitarianism." In *Utilitarianism, On Liberty, and Considerations on Representative Government.* London: Everyman, 1972.

Navarrete, Urbanus. "De Notione et Effectus Consummationis Matrimonii." *Periodica der re Morali, Canonica, Liturgica* 59 (1970): 619–60.

Noldin, Hieronymus. *Summa theologiae moralis.* Vol. 3, edition 31. Edited by G. Heinzel. Oeniponte: F. Rauch, 1955.

Noonan, John T. *Contraception: A History of Its Treatment by the Catholic Theologians and Canonists.* Cambridge, Mass.: Harvard University Press, 1965; 2nd ed., 1986.

Oeing-Hanhoff, Ludger. "Der Mensch: Natur oder Geschichte." In *Naturgesetz und christliche Ethik. Zur wissenschaftlichen Diskussion nach Humanae vitae,* edited by F. Henrich. Munich: Kosel Verlag, 1970.

Palazzini, Pietro, Francesco Hürth, and Ferdinando Lambruschini. "Una donna domanda: come negarsi alla violenza? Morale esemplificata. Un dibattito." *Studi Cattolici* 27 (1961): 62–72.

Perico, Giacomo. "Stupro, aborto e anticoncezionali." *La Civiltà Cattolica* 3 (1993): 37–46.

Pinckaers, Servais. *Le renouveau de la morale.* Tournai: Casterman, 1964.

Pöltner, Günther. "Achtung der Würde und Schutz von Interessen." In *Der Mensch als Mitte und Maßstab der Medizin,* edited by Johannes Bonelli, 3–32. Vol. 1 of *Medizin und Ethik.* Vienna: Springer Verlag, 1992.

Rahner, Karl. "Das 'Gebot' der Liebe unter den anderen Geboten." In *Schriften zur Theologie,* vol. 5. Ensiedeln-Zürich-Cologne: Benziger, 1962.

Rassem, Mohammed. "Zur Revolution der Reproduktion." *Zeitschrift für Politik,* N. F. 36 (1989): 347–57.

Rhomberg, McCaffrey, Riehle and Wiliken. At the 1988 "World Conference on Love, Life and Family." *"Arbeitsgemeinschaft Artikel 1 Grundgesetz": Dokumente zur Abtreibung-Embryohandel-Gentechnik-Euthanasie,* no. 6, 1988. Part 1, edited by Rudolf Ehmann.

Rhonheimer, Martin. *Familie und Selbstverwirklichung. Alternativen zur*

Emanzipation. Cologne: Verlag Wissenschaft und Politik, 1979.

———. "Sozialphilosophie und Familie. Gedanken zur humanen Grundfunktion der Familie." In *Familie—Herausforderung der Zukunft* (Familiensymposium der Universität Freiburg/Schweiz, November 1981), edited by B. Schnyder, 113–40. Freiburg: Freiburg University Press, 1982.

———. "Die Konstituierung des Naturgesetzes und sittlich-normativer Objektivität durch die praktische Vernunft." In *Persona, Verità e Morale. Atti del Congresso Internazionale di Teologia Morale* (Rome, April 7–12, 1986), 859–84. Rome: Città Nuova, 1987.

———. *Natur als Grundlage der Moral. Die personale Struktur des Naturgesetzes bei Thomas von Aquin: Eine Auseinandersetzung mit autonomer und teleologischer Ethik.* Innsbruck-Vienna: Tyrolia Verlag, 1987.

———. "Gut und böse oder richtig und falsch—was unterscheidet das Sittliche?" In *Ethik der Leistung* (Lindenthal-Colloquium 1987), edited by Hans Thomas, 47–75. Herford: Busse-Seewald, 1988.

———. "Contraception, Sexual Behavior, and Natural Law: Philosophical Foundation of the Norm of *Humanae vitae.*" In *"Humanae vitae": 20 anni dopo. Atti del II Congresso Internazionale di Teologia Morale,* 73–113. Rome, November 9–12, 1988. Milan: Editions of the Italian Dominicans, 1989. Also in *Linacre Quarterly* 56, no. 2 (1989): 20–57; and expanded in *Sexualität und Verantwortung. Empfängnisverhütung als ethisches Problem.* Vienna: IMABE, 1995. Available in Italian as *Etica Della Procreazione.* Rome: Pontifical Lateran University/MURSIA, 2000. The second and third chapters of the present book begin with the above-cited English text, which is stylistically revised and combined with a translation of the expanded text.

———. "Menschliches Handeln und seine Moralität. Zur Begründung sittlicher Normen." In *Ethos und Menschenbild: Zur Überwindung der Krise der Moral,* by M. Rhonheimer, et al. *Sinn und Sendung,* vol. 2, 45–114. St. Ottilien: EOS Verlag, 1989.

———. "Ethik—Handeln—Sittlichkeit. Zur sittlichen Dimension menschlichen Tuns." In *Der Mensch als Mitte und Maßstab der Medizin* (*Medizin und Ethik,* vol. 1), edited by Johannes Bonelli, 137–74. Vienna: Springer Verlag, 1992.

———. "Perché una filosofia politica? Elementi storici per una risposta." *Acta philosophica* 1, no. 2 (1992): 233–63. This is forthcoming in my *The Common Good of Constitutional Democracy: Essays in Political Philosophy and on Catholic Social Teaching,* edited by William F. Murphy Jr., as "Why Is Political Philosophy Necessary? Historical Considerations and a Response."

———. "Zur Begründung sittlicher Normen aus der Natur. Grundsätzliche Erwägungen und Exemplifizierung am Beispiel der I.v.F." In *Der Mensch als Mitte und Maßstab der Medizin* (*Medizin und Ethik,* vol. 1), edited by Johannes Bonelli, 49–94. Vienna: Springer Verlag, 1992; or a more detailed version: "Die Instrumentalisierung des menschlichen Lebens. Ethische

Erwägungen zur In-Vitro-Fertilisierung." In *Fortpflanzungsmedizin und Lebensschutz,* edited by Franz Bydlinski and Theo Mayer-Maly. Pubblicazioni del Centro di Ricerca Internazionale per le Questioni di fondo delle Scienze, Salzburg, Nuova Collana, vol. 55. Innsbruck-Vienna: Tyrolia Verlag, 1992.

———. "'Ethics of Norms' and the Lost Virtues: Searching the Roots of the Crisis of Ethical Reasoning." *Anthropotes* 9, no. 2 (1993): 231–43. A revised version of this essay is reprinted in *The Perspective of the Acting Person: Essays in the Renewal of Thomistic Moral Philosophy,* edited by William F. Murphy Jr. Washington: The Catholic University of America Press, 2008.

———. "'Intrinsically Evil Acts' and the Moral Viewpoint: Clarifying a Central Teaching of *Veritatis splendor.*" *Thomist* 58, no. 1 (1994): 1–39. Reprinted in *Veritatis splendor and the Renewal of Moral Theology,* edited by Joseph Augustine DiNoia and Romanus Cessario, 161–193. Princeton: Scepter Publishers; Huntington: Our Sunday Visitor; Chicago: Midwest Theological Forum, 1999. Also reprinted in *The Perspective of the Acting Person: Essays in the Renewal of Thomistic Moral Philosophy,* edited by William F. Murphy Jr. Washington, D.C.: The Catholic University of America Press, 2008.

———. *Praktische Vernunft und Vernünftigkeit der Praxis: Handlungstheorie bei Thomas von Aquin in ihrer Entstehung aus dem Problemkontext der aristotelischen Ethik.* Berlin: Akademie Verlag, 1994.

———. "Diritti fondamentali, legge morale e difesa legale della vita nello Stato costituzionale democratico. L'approccio costituzionalistico all'enciclica 'Evangelium vitae.'" *Annales Theologici* 9 (1995): 271–334.

———. "Intentional Actions and the Meaning of Object: A Reply to Richard McCormick." *Thomist* 59, no. 2 (1995): 279–311. Reprinted in *Veritatis Splendor and the Renewal of Moral Theology,* edited by J. A. DiNoia and Romanus Cessario, 241–68. Princeton: Scepter Publishers; Huntington: Our Sunday Visitor; Chicago: Midwest Theological Forum, 1999. Also reprinted in *The Perspective of the Acting Person: Essays in the Renewal of Thomistic Moral Philosophy,* edited by William F. Murphy Jr. Washington, D.C.: The Catholic University of America Press, 2008.

———. "Contraccezione, mentalità contraccettiva e cultura dell'aborto: valutazioni e connessioni." In Pontifical Academy for Life, *Commento Interdisciplinare alla "Evanglium vitae,"* edited by Ramon Lucas Lucas and Elio Sgreccia, 435–52. Vatican City: Libreria Editrice Vaticana, 1997.

———. "Lo stato costituzionale democratico e il bene commune." *Contratto, Rivista di filosofia tomista e contemporanea* 7 (1997): 57–122.

———. "Sulla fondazione di norme morali a partire dalla natura." *Rivista di filosofia Neo-Scolastica* 89 (1997): 515–35.

———. "Fundamental Rights, Moral Law, and the Legal Defense of Life in a Constitutional Democracy: A Constitutionalist Approach to the Encyclical Evangelium Vitae." *American Journal of Jurisprudence* 43 (1998): 135–83.

———. *Natural Law and Practical Reason: A Thomist View of Moral Autonomy.* Translated by Gerald Malsbary. New York: Fordham University Press, 2000.

———. *Die Perspektive der Moral. Philosophische Grundlagen der Tugendethik.* Berlin: Akademie Verlag, 2001.

———. "Sins against Justice (IIa IIae, qq. 59–78)." In *The Ethics of Aquinas,* edited by Stephen J. Pope, 287–303. Washington D.C.: Georgetown University Press, 2002.

———. *Abtreibung und Lebensschutz. Tötungsverbot und Recht auf Leben in der politischen und medizinischen Ethik.* Paderborn: Schöningh, 2003.

———. "The Moral Significance of Pre-Rational Nature in Aquinas: A Reply to Jean Porter (and Stanley Hauerwas)." *American Journal of Jurisprudence* 48 (2003): 253–80.

———. "The Perspective of the Acting Person and the Nature of Practical Reason: The 'Object of the Human Act' in Thomistic Anthropology of Action." *Nova et Vetera* (English ed.) 2, no. 2 (2004): 461–516. Also reprinted in *The Perspective of the Acting Person: Essays in the Renewal of Thomistic Moral Philosophy,* edited by William F. Murphy Jr. Washington, D.C.: The Catholic University of America Press, 2008.

———. *La prospettiva della morale. Fondamenti dell'etica filosofica.* 2nd ed. Rome: Armando, 2006.

———. "The Use of Contraceptives under Threat of Rape: An Exception?" in *Josephinum Journal of Theology* 14, no. 2 (August 2007): 168–81. Originally published as "Minaccia di stupro e prevenzione: un'eccezione?" *La Scuola Cattolica* 123 (1995) 75–90; also reprinted in *Etica Della Procreazione.*

———. *The Perspective of the Acting Person: Essays in the Renewal of Thomistic Moral Philosophy.* Edited by William F. Murphy Jr. Washington, D.C.: The Catholic University of America Press, 2008.

———. *Vital Conflicts in Medical Ethics: A Virtue Approach to Craniotomy and Tubal Pregnancies,* edited by William F. Murphy Jr. Washington, D.C.: The Catholic University of America Press, 2009.

———. *The Common Good of Constitutional Democracy: Essays in Political Philosophy and on Catholic Social Teaching* (forthcoming).

———. *The Perspective of Morality: Philosophical Foundations of Thomistic Virtue Ethics.* Washington, D.C.: The Catholic University of America Press (forthcoming).

Rotter, Hans. "Tendenzen in der heutigen Moraltheologie." *Stimmen der Zeit* 4 (1970).

Schelsky, Helmut. *Soziologie der Sexualität. Über die Beziehung zwischen Geschlecht, Moral und Gesellschaft.* Hamburg: Rowohlt, 1955.

Schwarz, Stephen. *The Moral Question of Abortion.* Chicago: Loyola University Press, 1990.

Seifert, Josef. "Der sittliche Unterschied zwischen natürlicher Empfägnisregelung und künstlicher Empfägnisverhutüng." In *Elternschaft und Menschenwürde*, edited by Ernst Wenisch. Vallendar: Patris-Verlag, 1984.

Singer, Peter. *Practical Ethics*. 2nd ed. Cambridge: Cambridge University Press, 1993; reprint 1999.

Smith, Janet. "The Morality of Condom Use by HIV-Infected Spouses." *Thomist* 70, no. 1 (2006): 27–69.

Spaemann, Robert. "Wovon handelt die Moraltheologie? Bemerkungen eines Philosophen." *Internationale Katholische Zeitschrift* 6 (1977): 307–8.

———. *Das Natürliche und das Vernünftige, Aufsätze zur Anthropologie*. Munich-Zürich, 1987.

———. "Kommentar zur Instruktion *Donum vitae*." In *Die Unantastbarkeit des menschlichen Lebens. Zu ethischen Fragen der Biomedizin. Instruktion der Kongregation für die Glaubenslehre. Mit einem Kommentar von R. Spaemann*. Freiburg: Herder Verlag, 1987.

———. *Personen—Versuche über den Unterschied zwischen "etwas" und "jemand."* Stuttgart: Klett-Cotta, 1996. In English as *Person: The Difference between Someone and Something*. Oxford: Oxford University Press, 2006.

Steinbock, Bonnie. *Life before Birth: The Moral and Legal Status of Embryos and Fetuses*. New York: Oxford University Press, 1992.

Suarez, Antoine. "Darf man dem Embryo den verfassungrechtlichen Schutz der Menschenwürde absprechen?" *Schweizerische Juristenzeitung* 86 (1990): 205–11.

Teichmann, Jenny. "Intention and Sex." In *Intention and Intentionality: Essays in Honour of G. E. M. Anscombe*, edited by Cora J. Diamond and Jenny Teichmann, 147–61. Brighton: Harvester Press, 1979.

Tooley, Michael. *Abortion and Infanticide*. Oxford: Oxford University Press, 1983.

Valente, Giuseppe. "La pillola e la leggitima difesa." *30 Giorni* 7/8 (July–August 1993): 12–17.

Warren, Mary Anne. "On the Moral and Legal Status of Abortion." *Monist* 57 (1973). Reprinted in *The Problem of Abortion*, 2nd ed., edited by Joel Feinberg, 102–19. Belmont, Calif.: Wadsworth Publishing, 1984.

Weber, Leonhard M. "Excurs über *Humanae vitae*." In *Lexikon für Theologie und Kirche*, vol. 14 (added vol. 3). Freiburg-Basel-Vienna: Herder Verlag, 1968; reprint, 1986.

Wojtyla, Karol. *Love and Responsibility*. Translated by H. T. Willetts. Rev. ed. San Francisco: Ignatius Press, 1993.

Zalba, Marcellino. *L'Agire Morale, Acts of the International Congress of April 12–17 1974: Tommaso d'Aquino nel suo settimo centenario*. Vol. 5. Naples: Editions of the Italian Dominicans, 1975.

Zagrebelsky, Gustavo. "Le false risposte del diritto naturale." *La Repubblica* 80, no. 4 (2007): 1–23.

Index

biologistic, 43, 52–53, 87, 137. *See also* naturalistic, physicalistic

birth control, 33, 121. *See also* artificial, contraception

Blackmun, Harry A., U. S. Supreme Court justice, 254–57, 261n83, 265–66

Böckle, F., 43n7, 47n13, 72n2, 100n41, 107n48

Bonelli, J. xv-n4, 126n65, 154n2, 158n5, 186n6

Boyle, J. M., 61n28, 63n32, 78n12, 99

Brock, S. L., 17n28

Brunelli, L., 138n15

Brunner, O., 214n20

Bull, H. P., 246n42

Carlyle, A. J., 234nn12–13

Carlyle, R.W., 234nn12–13

Carozza, Paulo, vii, xxi

Casti Connubii, 47n12, 142

Catechism of the Catholic Church, xv-n3, 133n2, 144n25, 146

categories: biological (zoological), 186–87, 191, 196, 203-5; intentional (moral), 22n36, 42

Centesimus Annus, 229, 241–42

Cessario, R., 140n17

chastity: conjugal (marital), xv, 9, 33, 36, 38, 104, 286; contraception and, xiii, 12, 15n22, 34, 38, 48, 63–64, 123n62, 146; procreative responsibility as a form of, xv, 48, 90–95, 99, 106, 125, 128, 286; virtue of, xiii, 12, 34, 36–37, 48, 64, 91–94, 96, 99, 106, 108, 124–25, 142n22, 146, 286

Chevalier, J. J., 234n12

choice, 15n22, 18, 21, 29, 73, 80n16, 81, 84, 95, 140, 146, 178, 182, 247; contraceptive 15n22, 35–37, 50–51, 59, 61, 64, 65–69, 95, 100–101, 103, 105, 119–21, 122n59, 123n62, 133, 139, 141–43, 145–50, 287; of in vitro fertilization, 160, 165–66, 169, 172–74; of periodic continence, 56, 105; preferential, 123n62; of self-defense, 147

Church: Catholic, xiii, 2, 20–22, 39–40, 47n14, 52, 78n13, 105n45, 131–34, 136, 139, 141, 146, 234, 236, 284; Christian, 216. *See also* magisterium

Cole, G. F., 245n41

commandments, xiii, 24; of the natural law, 16, 23, 28, 30, 130; negative, 19. *See also* Decalogue

common good, xvii, 230–31, 232n5, 235–36, 243, 271–72, 282–83

Congregation for the Doctrine of the Faith (CDF), 20n35, 26n39, 28, xiii

conjugal act: as an act of love, 35, 43, 44–45, 78n12, 80, 84, 88n29, 96, 137, 164; contraceptive, 37, 115, 129, 136, 287–89; and desire for children, 162–3; as a doing and not a producing, 166; "functions," 49, 52n18, 76–81, 83, 84n23, 88–89, 288–90; in *Humanae Vitae*, 35, 41–46, 48, 68, 78n12, 79, 80, 142; object of, 81–88, 117; requirement of openness to life, 12, 34, 38, 42–45, 78, 80, 83–84, 95, 98–99, 103, 116–17, 137, 142, 145. *See also* intercourse, marital act, meanings of human sexuality, sex

conjugal unity, 37, 98

conscience, xx, 40–41, 57, 59, 91, 108, 131–32, 215, 235, 243, 250–51; collective, 38, 262

consequentialism, xvi, 111n49, 125, 140, 148. *See also* goods

continence, 91, 94, 97, 100, 103, 107, 117, 124, 143, 147–48, 208. *See also* periodic continence

contraception: as alternative to acts of continence, 36, 38, 99–105, 108–9, 130, 144, 148, 287; arguments about, 12, 15n22, 45–48, 51–65, 78n12, 138–39; as defined in *Humanae vitae* no. 14, 35; general acceptance of, xviii, 38, 120; relation to abortion, xiii–xiv, xviii–xix, 66, 103, 118–24, 270n97; as violation of natural law, 39–44, 47–48, 127–32; as violation of the Inseparability Principle, 37, 44–45, 47, 69–70, 81, 90, 116; and virtue, 33-38. *See also* artificial, birth control

contraceptive mentality, 50, 98, 119–20, 122–23, 270n97

contraceptives, 122, 253; artificiality, 46n11; use under threat of rape, ix, xv, 67, 133–50

contralife-will argument, 61–64, 121, 122n61. *See also* contraception

Katva, Gregory S., 280
Kaup, H., 245n41
Keller, R., 216n21
Keown, John, 239n25, 240n28, 258n76
Ketting, E., 245n41
killing: abortion as, xii, xvi, xix, 66, 121–23, 179, 239–40; in capital punishment, 19, 22, 24; contraception as potential, xix, 62–63; direct, 20–21, 232, 240, 271; as homicide or murder, 18, 20–21, 24; indirect, 22; legal sanction of, 241, 252, 258n76, 266, 271–72, 274, 283; as means to resolve conflict, 228; prohibition of, xiii, 20–30, 148–49, 274; in war, 19, 21, 24, 144. *See also* embryo; Hoerster; infanticide; innocent; self-defense
Kirchoff, P., 246n45
Klein, E., 246n45, 248n49
Kluth, W., 246n43, 246n45, 265n87, 273n102
Knauer, P., 136n10
Koch, H. G., 245n41
Korff, W., 72
Kosellek, R., 214n20
Koslowski, P., 177n19
Kriele, M., 247n47, 251n54, 261, 278n110
Kuhse, Helga, xvi, 244, 275n107–8

Lambruschini, F., 134n3, 135–36, 148n33
Lawler, Michael G., 285–90
Laws: biological, 40–41, 43, 75; civil (criminal, positive), xvii, xx, 23–24, 82, 181–83, 212, 219, 229–32, 233–46, 247n47, 248–51, 253–55, 256n68, 257–63, 265, 268–69, 270–83; constitutional, 241, 243, 259n77, 270; eternal (divine), 4–6, 16, 127, 234–35, 238; moral, xiii, xvii (n8), 41, 136, 229–32, 242–43, 270–83; of nature, 5, 12, 39, 41–42, 73n3, 81n17, 128. *See also* natural law
Lehman, Karl, 216n21
Léhu, Leonard, 10–11, 13, 17n29, 18n30
Leist, A., 257n74, 269n95, 281n117
Lenshek, Damian, x, xxi
Leo XIII, Pope. *See* pope.
Levering, Matthew, 8n12
Libertas Praestantissium, 1, 5
Life (human): culture of, xx, 38, 250; defense (protection) of, xi–xxi, 175, 201,

219, 224, 228–84; produced as opposed to generated, xiv, xvi, 154–58, 161, 169; sacredness of, 20–21, 23, 176, 266–68; 276; threats to, xi–xxi; transmission of, xiv, xvii, 9, 12, 33–34, 36, 38, 44–45, 49, 68–69, 77, 78n13, 80, 84n24, 85-86, 88n29, 89, 100, 104, 109, 115, 117, 125, 141–42, 145, 171, 288
Locke, John, 237, 249, 278, 281
Lombard, Peter, 239n24
Lorenz, D., 246n45
Lottin, Odon, 10
love: bodily, xiv, 74, 76–77, 87, 98–99, 114, 145; civilization of, 38, 275; of God, creative, 55-58, 61, 84, 130, 141, 166; marital (conjugal), 33–38, 42–45, 48–49, 51, 55–56, 58, 60–61, 69, 74, 76, 78n12, 79–81, 83–88, 92, 94, 97–98, 100–102, 104, 106, 107–24, 130, 141, 144–45, 157, 164, 166, 172, 176, 288, 290; of neighbor, 231; personal, 9, 15, 36–37, 73, 77, 86, 91, 102, 110–11, 113–15, 117, 125, 129; spiritual, 73–77, 111, 114–15, 129. *See also* conjugal act; meanings of human sexuality
Löw, R., 240n29
Löw, K., 246n42
lying, 18–19, 231

magisterium, xiii, 9, 22, 44, 132, 134, 140, 148, 241, 257, 272, 289–90; of John Paul II, 1, 29
manuals, 18
marital act, object of, 71–90. *See also* conjugal act
marriage, procreative task of. *See* procreative
Martelet, G., 54n25, 88n29
Masing, J., 247n48
materially (*materialiter*), 127n67
May, W. E., 61n28, 81n18, 90n32, 126n64, 127n66, 144n24
McCormick, Richard, S.J., 136n10, 140n17, 148n35, 149n37
meanings (unitive and procreative) of human sexuality, twofold, inseparable, xiv, 35–38, 44–45, 48–49, 51, 55–60, 65, 69–70, 71–90, 97–98, 100–102, 110, 112, 114–18, 123–25, 145, 162–64, 288–90. *See also* Inseparability Principle

meaning of the conjugal (marital) act, twofold. *See* meanings of human sexuality

means: conception and life as (for fulfilling parents' desire for a child), xvi, 86, 158–59, 162, 166, 173–74, 176; in moral sense (as human acts ordered to ends), xix, 21–22, 24, 29, 35, 46, 62n29, 68, 103, 122–24, 136, 138, 142, 161, 165–66, 170; in technical sense, 29, 36, 38, 44-45, 46n11, 51, 58, 60, 62, 66, 74, 91, 98, 105n45, 107, 110, 112, 114, 121–22, 130, 138–39, 143, 145–46, 155, 160–65, 170n14, 228, 240, 275

medicine: reproductive, xviii, 73n3, 165, 172–74, 176

metaphysics of creation argument, 55-61. *See also* contraception

method: and regulation of birth, 13, 15n22, 34, 36, 41n3, 45–46, 52, 65, 68, 70, 96, 100, 103, 107

Mill, J. S., 226–27

Montesquieu, 237

moral (ethical) perspective, 28, 38, 90, 107. *See also* perspective

moral object, 11n16, 28–30, 147; as a *forma a ratione concepta*, 17, 81-82; versus physical object, 81–83, 135–36, 144, 146, 148

moral order, 41–42, 53, 91, 175

moral species (*genus moris*). *See* species

Müller-Schmid, P. P., 250n53

murder, xi, xviii, 19–21, 63, 123n62, 178, 209, 235, 239n24

Murphy, William F. Jr., x, xvii-n9, xx, 2n1, 140n17, 232n5

natural family planning, 70. *See also* periodic continence, procreative

naturalistic: approach to natural law, 33, 40; argument against contraception, 51–53, 55, 81n19, 102, 104, 137. *See also* biologistic, perverted faculty argument, physicalistic

natural law: according to Thomas Aquinas, 1–30, 127; basis in natural inclinations, 4, 127, 130, 285; as basis of moral action and norms, 1–2, 20–29; as distinguished from divine law; in *Humanae Vitae*,

39-48; as a law of reason, 3–20, 30, 39, 127–28, 130, 230, 285; naturalistic understanding of, 15n22, 33, 40–42, 67; as a participation in eternal law, 5-6, 16-17, 91, 93; as part of human nature, 4–5, 10, 39, 108, 128; precepts of, 4, 19, 130; in relation to objective natural order or laws of nature (in a Stoic sense), 3, 12, 81n17, 128; in *Veritatis Splendor*, 3–20; why contraception violates, 38–44, 47–48, 67, 70, 124–30. *See also* norms, reason

nature, human, 7–10, 12–15, 74, 128, 154, 178, 157n74, 193; biological structures of, 12, 14–15, 40–41, 48, 89, 91, 105; not dualistic, 9, 37, 75, 94, 114n54; recourse to in ethical argumentation, 13–16, 154–57. *See also* natural law, person

neo-thomistic, 10, 12

Noonan, John T., 43n8, 46, 47n12, 52n17, 78n12, 87n28, 99, 239n24

norms: basis in reason, 6–8, 10–12, 14–15; of behavior, 73, 280; civil, 259, 268, 272; in *Humanae Vitae*, 35, 46, 68–69, 79, 81, 99, 105n45, 126–27, 136n9, 141–42, 144–45, 147–48; "ideal," 218–21; moral, 2, 7–9, 12–15, 21, 26, 35, 69n36, 73, 78n12, 81, 99, 108, 118, 132, 134–35, 139–41, 146, 149, 154, 194, 232n5; of the natural law, 2, 5–6, 8; negative (prohibitive), 134, 149–50; "practical-pragmatic," 218–21

Norton, David L., 282n122

object, moral. *See* moral object

Oeing-Hanhoff, L., 41n3, 81n17

omission (as conscious choice regarding an act), 28–29, 96, 271

ontological: versus epistemological, 4, 8n12; foundation of personhood, 26–27; presuppositions of Norbert Hoerster, 205; presuppositions of Peter Singer, 217; status of human sexuality, 111n50

openness to procreation (per se orientated to or *per se destinatus*), 95, 99, 117; intentional, 12, 34, 42–45, 80, 83–84, 98

Palazzini, Pietro, 134n3, 135–36

Papa, Joseph T., vii, x, xxi

periodic continence, 15, 35–36, 45–46, 49–51, 56–57, 64–67, 70, 81, 89, 94,

95–99, 101, 103, 106–9, 115–19, 124, 125, 137, 143–45. *See also* continence
Perico, G., 134, 136–40
Perry, Michael J., 259n78
person(s): as distinguished from an individual of the human species (*homo sapiens*), xvi, 26, 28, 181, 183–87, 190–94, 195–202, 218, 221–22, 244, 255n67, 257–59, 263, 265–66, 276–79, 281, 283; good of, 34, 40, 52n18, 54, 59, 70, 75, 108, 200, 271, 238n23; as image of God, 1, 4–5, 12, 21, 30, 130, 157, 181, 212–15; innocent, 20–21, 23, 34, 232, 272, 278; manipulation of, 36, 73n3, 107; marriage as loving communion of two, 9, 36, 54, 59, 74, 76, 83, 85–87, 100, 114, 125, 129, 141, 164; as a property versus nature, 27, 185–87, 189–90, 196–99, 202, 204–6, 217–18, 265; potential, 27, 196, 198, 201–4, 207–12, 225–26, 266, 280; recognition of fetuses as, xvi, 25–27, 207, 212–13, 229, 244, 255–57, 258n76, 262–63; 266–69, 276–77, 279; substantial body-soul (body-spirit) unity of, xv, 7–9, 14–15, 37, 71–75, 77–78, 80, 83, 88, 92–93, 101, 105–6, 108, 111, 114n54, 117–18, 124–26, 129, 143, 257n74, 285–86. *See also* embryo, equality, personhood
personhood, 41, 87, 108, 115, 117, 219, 263, 267; actualized, 197–204, 212–13, 224; versus the possession of properties, 185, 186n8, 187, 194–201, 203–6, 217–18; potential, 225n30
perspective (viewpoint, point of view), of the acting person, ix-x, 17, 19, 146. *See also* moral perspective
perverted faculty (naturalistic) argument, 51-53, 54n25, 59-60, 65. *See also* naturalistic.
petitio principii (begging the question), 45, 54, 58, 65, 90, 193, 202, 207
physical: acts, 28–29, 34, 41, 42n5, 43, 62-63, 66, 68-69, 83, 102, 135, 138–39, 143–46, 148; object, 144, 146, 148
physical species. *See* species.
physicalistic, 52. *See also* biologistic, naturalistic
Pius XII, Pope. *See* pope
plane: legal-political, 229; moral, 229

Pöltner, G., 186n6, 197, 266n88
Pojman, Louis P., 239n25, 280n115
pope: John Paul II (Karol Wojtyla), xiii-n1, xvi, xix, 1–4, 7, 9–12, 14, 15n22, 16, 20, 24, 29, 35, 106–7, 113n53, 129n68, 143n23, 144n26, 146n32, 230n3, 284; Leo XIII, 1, 5-6; Pius XII, 47n12, 142
practical reason: x, 8n12, 11, 16, 23, 28, 63n32, 82n21, 94, 127–28, 144, 148, 170, 230, 285; principles of, 19. *See also* reason
praeter intentionem (outside the intention, unintentional), 24
pregnancy: and abortion, 122, 123n62, 254; intention to avoid, 58, 65, 88–89, 96, 103, 105, 118, 120, 133, 138, 143; difficulties deriving from, 25, 49, 123n62, 251; marital act during, as open to life, 78n13; resulting from IVF, 160; resulting from rape, 252n56; in Swiss law; as a threat to a woman's freedom, 269–70; unwanted, 144; in U.S. law, 254, 261n83
Preu, P., 247n48
principle(s): of human acts, 30, 93-94, 100–101, 106, 177–78; of double effect, 136; foundational, of Salzman and Lawler 288–89; of human dignity, 277; of modern constitutionalism, 229; of the practical intellect, 4, 11, 14, 16, 19; of proportionality, 247; of *stare decisis*, 262; of the submission of democracy to law and human rights, 242. *See also* equality, Inseparability Principle, justice, Totality Principle
Prince Charles, 225
procreation, human, xiv, 35, 52n18, 66, 90–92, 102–3, 128, 145, 155–56, 158, 160, 162–63, 169–74; in the context of love, 33, 38, 74–78, 82, 82–84, 104; as cooperation with the Creator, 55, 58, 60, 84; as disjoined from sexuality, 38, 156, 290; as an "end" of marriage, 87–88, 116, 288–89; ethics of, ix, xv; exclusion from marriage, 49, 61, 137; natural (versus IVF), 158, 160, 162–64, 168; norm regarding, in *Humanae vitae* no. 14, 35, 46–47, 68, 142. *See also* artificial, meanings of human sexuality, openness to procreation

procreative: autonomy, 253, 255; "function," versus meaning, 76–81, 83, 84n23, 86, 110–12, 288-90; responsibility, xiv–xv, 15, 36–37, 48, 51, 58, 60–61, 69–70, 88–101, 103, 105–6, 109–10, 120, 123–25, 128, 130, 137, 144, 164, 270n97, 286; task (dimension, function) of marriage and sexuality, 38, 41, 45, 48–49, 74, 77–81, 83, 87, 100, 103, 115, 119, 135. *See also* meanings of human sexuality, technology

prohibition of killing. *See* killing

proportionalism, 125, 134, 136–37, 139–41, 148–49. *See also* goods

public interest, 175

punishment: capital, 24, 34, 278; of crimes (including abortion) by law, 233, 238–39, 241. *See also* killing

Rahner, Karl, 8n12, 36, 72, 73n3, 75n8-9

rape: use of contraceptives under threat of, ix, xv, 67–68, 133–50

reason: capacity of to distinguish good and evil, 3–6, 9, 16, 39, 128, 231; good or goods of, 9, 14, 16–17, 19, 21, 25, 30, 91, 94, 110, 127–28, 144, 146; light of, 3–4, 6, 9, 15–17, 30, 39, 144n25, 230; as normative, 6–8, 10–12, 14–15; practical, x, 8n12, 11, 16, 19, 23, 28, 63n32, 82n21, 94, 127–28, 144, 148, 170, 230; Wojtyla on reason as rule of morality, 10–12. *See also* natural law

Reis, H., 245n41

Reiter, J., 216n21

responsibility. *See* procreative, responsible parenthood, sexuality.

responsible parenthood, 15, 34, 40–41, 48–51, 57, 60–61, 91–92, 109, 129n68, 131, 137, 142, 145. *See also* procreative

Rhonheimer, Daniel, 250n53

Ridola, P., 246n42

right(s): to abortion, xvi, 179–227, 241, 253–62, 281; to avoid conception from rape, 147; bills of, 253, 260; civil, 22, 253, 259; of God as Creator, 55, 58, 60–61; to fertilization, 211–12; fundamental human, 22, 174–75, 188, 215–16, 220–22, 226, 229, 237, 239, 242–47, 250n53, 253–54, 260–61, 270–71, 273n103,

274, 276, 278n110; individual, xx, 241, 243–44, 247n48; to life, xiv, xvi, 22–23, 25, 28, 38, 56–58, 180–82, 184, 194–95, 199–200, 203–4, 206–8, 211–12, 218–21, 223–24, 225n30, 226, 232, 237, 243–49, 251, 252n56, 253, 255–59, 260n81, 261, 263, 265–71, 273, 276–79, 281; limited by rights of others, 182–83; mutual, of spouses, to sexual relations, 142; to privacy, 253–56, 259, 262; related to desires (ethics of interest), 224–26, 265; to self-defense, 237, 248; woman's, to self-determination, 180, 247, 253, 263, 269–70

Rotter, H., 72n2, 73n3

rhythm (biological rhythms, natural rhythms, rhythm method), 15n22, 42, 59, 78n12, 96, 99, 105, 107, 145

Sachdev, P., 245n41

Salzman, Todd A., 285–90

Schelsky, H., 112n51, 118n56

Schüller, B., 72n2

Schwarz, S., 195n9, 196n11, 198n13, 232n4, 266n88

Seifert, J., 56n26, 154n2

self-defense, legitimate, 19, 22, 68, 134–36, 138–39, 147–49, 237. *See also* killing

sex: contracepted, xiv, 35–38, 46, 49, 64, 69, 89, 94-110, 112, 114, 118-124, 129-30, 135, 142-45, 148, 287. *See also* conjugal act, intercourse, marital act, meanings of human sexuality, sexuality.

sexuality, xiv, 15, 35–38, 45, 52, 54n25, 69, 80, 94, 99, 129, 131, 240, 288–89; disintegration of, 107–125; and responsibility, xv, 93, 95, 101, 143–44, 270; matrimonial (spousal) meaning of, 84–85, 88, 98, 124, 289. *See also* meanings of human sexuality, responsibility.

Sgreccia, E., xiii–n1, 251n55

sin (or vice) against nature (*peccare contra naturam*), 53

Singer, Peter, xvi, 179n2, 180, 188, 192, 213, 215, 217–18, 222, 224–27, 244, 252, 255n67, 265n86, 268–69, 274, 275n107

sodomy, 19, 102

Spaemann, R., xvi–n6, xviii–n10, 114n55,

154n1, 156, 157n3, 161n6, 176n18, 232n4, 240, 265n87, 281n118

species: of acts, 17, 84, 101; moral (*genus moris*), 17, 81n19, 136, 143–44, 149n38; natural or physical (*genus naturae*), 135, 144

species, human: belonging to (member of), 28, 181, 183–98, 201–6, 213, 215–17, 221, 244, 255, 257, 265–66, 276–79, 283; preservation of, 9, 86, 110

speciesism, 187–90, 192, 217–18, 221, 266, 269n94

state (modern), xi, 105n45, 183, 212, 216, 219, 233, 236–38, 273; authority and (coercive) power of, 230, 232, 236–37, 238n23, 243, 246, 248–49, 251, 270, 274, 279–80, 283; authorization of abortion by, 241; duty to uphold moral values, 242, 244, 247n46, 273n103, 274; and protection of human life (including unborn), xii, xvi–xvii, 179, 181, 184, 213, 228–29, 232, 237–38, 240, 244–63, 267, 270, 277–78, 280-83. *See also* laws

Steinbock, Bonnie, xvi, 179n2, 225n30, 258n76, 265n86

sterilization, 66, 99–100, 135–36, 141, 148

Stüssel, J. P., 265n87

Suarez, A., 195n10, 257n74

suicide, 271

Summa theologiae (Aquinas), 5n7, 6n9, 10n15, 15n21, 16n23, 18n30, 19n34, 22n37, 72n1, 75n9, 91n33, 93n35-36, 131n69, 144n24, 175n17, 234n15, 236n20, 238n22

survival, interest in, 185, 194–96, 199–201, 207–12, 219, 224

technology: medical, xix, 153; reproductive (procreative), xv–xvi, 76, 153–78, 287

teleological ethics, 125. *See also* consequentialism, proportionalism

temperance, 36, 92–95, 99, 130, 286

theft, 19, 82, 178, 235

theonomy, participated (autonomy), 6, 7n11

Thomas, H., 126n65, 246n43, 246n45, 265n87

tolerance: of contraception, xviii, 120; legal, of abortion, 38, 238, 243, 255, 271; as recognition of anti-life practices, xii, xviii, 283

Tolmien, O., 240n30

Tooley, M., xvi, 179n2, 224, 244, 255n67, 265n86, 268

Totality Principle (*Ganzheitsprinzip*), 45, 48, 58, 89, 136

tube (test), xii, xiv, xviii, 154–56, 161

unitive: psychologically, 37. *See also* meanings of human sexuality

Valente, G., 134n4, 136n9

Veritatis splendor: The Splendor of the Truth, ix, xvn3, 1, 3, 12, 14, 15n22, 17, 39, 131–32, 133–34, 135n5, 140n17, 146, 149, 230n3

virtue, moral, xx, 11, 13, 30, 33–38, 54n25, 90, 94–95, 107–8, 117, 127–28, 130, 177, 230–33, 235, 285; procreative responsibility as, xv, 48, 69, 89, 90–95, 97, 123, 125; in *Veritatis Splendor*, 15n22. *See also* chastity, justice, temperance

von Hippel, E., 245n41

von Pragg, Ph., 245n41

von Voss, H., 245n41, 250n52

Wahl, R., 247n48

Warren, Mary Anne, xvi, 179n2, 244, 265n86, 268

Wolter, H., 140n17

Ethics of Procreation and the Defense of Human Life:
Contraception, Artificial Fertilization, and Abortion was
designed and typeset in Minion with Myriad display type by
Kachergis Book Design of Pittsboro, North Carolina. It was
printed on 60-pound A-50 Natural, and bound by
Versa Press of East Peoria, Illinios.